Frommer's®

Amsterdam

16th Edition

by George McDonald

A John Wiley and Sons, Ltd, Publication

Published by:

WILEY PUBLISHING, INC.

Copyright © 2011 John Wiley & Sons Ltd, The Atrium, Southern Gate, Chichester,
West Sussex PO19 8SQ, UK

Telephone (+44) 1243 779777

Email (for orders and customer service enquiries): cs-books@wiley.co.uk. Visit our Home Page on
www.wiley.com

UK Publisher: Sally Smith
Project Manager: Daniel Mersey
Commissioning Editor: Jill Emeny
Development Editor: Caroline Sieg
Content Editor: Erica Peters
Cartography: Elizabeth Puhl
Photo Editor: Jill Emeny
Front cover photo: Credit © ImageShop/Corbis. Description: Building facade, Amsterdam.
Back cover photo: Credit © Photos to Go. Description: Tulips are a common sight in Amsterdam's
flower market.

Wiley also publishes its books in a variety of electronic formats. Some content that appears in print may
not be available in electronic books.

For information on our other products and services or to obtain technical support, please contact our
Customer Care Department within the U.S. at 877/762-2974, outside the U.S. at 317/572-3993 or fax
317/572-4002.

British Library Cataloguing in Publication Data

A catalogue record for this book is available from the British Library

ISBN: 978-0-470-97129-1 (pbk), ISBN 978-0-470-97951-8 (ebk), 978-1-119-99444-2 (epub),
978-1-119-99462-6 (emobi)

Typeset by Wiley Indianapolis Composition Services

Printed and bound in the United States of America

5 4 3 2 1

WILEY

CONTENTS

LIST OF MAPS

ABOUT THE AUTHOR

George McDonald has lived and worked in Amsterdam, as deputy editor of KLM's inflight magazine, *Holland Herald*. Now as a freelance journalist and travel writer, he has written extensively about Amsterdam and the Netherlands for a variety of magazines and travel books.

DEDICATION

This edition of Frommer's Amsterdam is dedicated to the memory of Dutch photographer Dirk Buwalda (1947–2009). His travels took him from the unappreciated wonders at the end of the street to the marvels at the ends of the earth, and finally to a tranquil churchyard in Edam.

HOW TO CONTACT US

In researching this book, we discovered many wonderful places—hotels, restaurants, shops, and more. We're sure you'll find others. Please tell us about them, so we can share the information with your fellow travelers in upcoming editions. If you were disappointed with a recommendation, we'd love to know that, too. Please write to:

Frommer's Amsterdam, 16th Edition
Wiley Publishing, Inc. • 111 River St. • Hoboken, NJ 07030-5774

AN ADDITIONAL NOTE

Please be advised that travel information is subject to change at any time—and this is especially true of prices. We therefore suggest that you write or call ahead for confirmation when making your travel plans. The authors, editors, and publisher cannot be held responsible for the experiences of readers while traveling. Your safety is important to us, however, so we encourage you to stay alert and be aware of your surroundings. Keep a close eye on cameras, purses, and wallets, all favorite targets of thieves and pickpockets.

FROMMER'S STAR RATINGS, ICONS & ABBREVIATIONS

Every hotel, restaurant, and attraction listing in this guide has been ranked for quality, value, service, amenities, and special features using a **star-rating system.** In country, state, and regional guides, we also rate towns and regions to help you narrow down your choices and budget your time accordingly. Hotels and restaurants are rated on a scale of zero (recommended) to three stars (exceptional). Attractions, shopping, nightlife, towns, and regions are rated according to the following scale: zero stars (recommended), one star (highly recommended), two stars (very highly recommended), and three stars (must-see).

In addition to the star-rating system, we also use **seven feature icons** that point you to the great deals, in-the-know advice, and unique experiences that separate travelers from tourists. Throughout the book, look for:

special finds—those places only insiders know about

fun facts—details that make travelers more informed and their trips more fun

kids—best bets for kids and advice for the whole family

special moments—those experiences that memories are made of

overrated—places or experiences not worth your time or money

insider tips—great ways to save time and money

great values—where to get the best deals

The following **abbreviations** are used for credit cards:

AE	American Express	DISC	Discover	V	Visa
DC	Diners Club	MC	MasterCard		

TRAVEL RESOURCES AT FROMMERS.COM

Frommer's travel resources don't end with this guide. Frommer's website, **www.frommers. com,** has travel information on more than 4,000 destinations. We update features regularly, giving you access to the most current trip-planning information and the best airfare, lodging, and car-rental bargains. You can also listen to podcasts, connect with other Frommers. com members through our active-reader forums, share your travel photos, read blogs from guidebook editors and fellow travellers, and much more.

THE BEST OF AMSTERDAM

Amsterdam is a city built on a human scale. Few tall buildings mar the sky's clarity, and most of the populace walks or rides bicycles. The oldest part of town recalls the city's 17th-century *Gouden Eeuw* (Golden Age), a period when it was the hub of a vast trading network and colonial empire. It was then that wealthy merchants constructed gabled residences along neatly laid canals.

A delicious irony is that these placid old structures now host brothels, smoke shops, and some extravagant nightlife. The city's inhabitants, proud of their pragmatic, live-and-let-live attitude, have decided to control what they cannot effectively outlaw. They permit licensed prostitution in the Red Light District—as much a tourist attraction as the Rijksmuseum or the Van Gogh Museum—and the sale of hashish and marijuana in designated "coffeeshops."

But don't think most Amsterdammers drift around town trailing clouds of marijuana smoke. They're too busy zipping around on bikes, in-line skating through Vondelpark, sunning on their porches, browsing arrays of ethnic dishes, or watching the parade of street life from a sidewalk cafe. A new generation of entrepreneurs has revitalized old neighborhoods like the Jordaan, turning some of its distinctive houses into offbeat stores, bustling cafes, hotels, and restaurants. Along the waterfront, old harbor installations have either been put to bold new uses, or swept away entirely in favor of cutting-edge architecture.

The city will quickly capture you in its spell. At night, many of the more than 1,200 bridges spanning 160 canals are lined with tiny lights, giving them a fairy-tale appearance. Some mornings, the cityscape emerges from a slowly dispersing mist to reveal its enchanting form. Amsterdam doesn't merely have style; it has substance too (and not merely substance abuse). Besides the many canals and bridges, antiquarian bookstores, brown cafes (the Dutch equivalent of neighborhood bars), gin-sampling houses, and chic cafes and nightclubs, it offers up treasures such as the Jewish Historical Museum, the Rembrandt House Museum, and the modern-art Stedelijk Museum. Perhaps its greatest asset, though, is its inhabitants. Many speak English fluently and virtually all are friendly to visitors. Plop yourself down amid the nicotine-stained walls of a brown cafe to enjoy a beer or a *jenever* (Dutch gin), and you'll quickly find yourself chatting with an amiable local.

Much of Amsterdam's pleasure arises from just being in it, so toss out any "miles and miles to go before I sleep" mindset. Between dips into artistic and historic treasures, take time to simply absorb the freewheeling spirit of this vibrant city.

THE most unforgettable
TRAVEL EXPERIENCES

- **Cruising the Canals:** Hop aboard a glass-topped tour boat for a cruise on Amsterdam's storied canals. From this vantage point, you get the best possible view of all those gabled Golden Age merchants' houses. Ignore anyone who tells you it's a tourist trap—it *is* a tourist trap, but it got that way by being justifiably popular. See p. 172.

- **Biking the City:** To pass for an authentic Amsterdammer, pick up a bicycle so ancient, rusted, and worn that no self-respecting thief would waste a second of his time trying to steal it (ah, but he will, so make sure you have an adequate lock). Then charge into the ruckus of trams, cars, buses, and other bikes. Better yet, rent a bicycle that's in decent condition—and go carefully. See p. 173.

- **Riding a Canal Bike:** Lifelong Amsterdammers—and even expats who ought to know better but aim to pass as natives—scoff long and loud at this. Let them. Pedal yourself through the water for an hour or two on your own private *pedalo*. Go at your own speed to view the canals in style (not much style, I'll admit). See p. 172.

- **Skating the Canals:** When the canals freeze in winter (sadly, it's happening less and less) you'll find few locals who'll argue against the proposition that God is a Dutchman. Giving Amsterdammers the chance to go around on ice is one of the few ways to pry them off their bicycles. Strap on a pair of long-bladed *Noren* skates (long-distance/long-bladed skates) and join in. See p. 176.

- **Walking on the Wild Side:** Stroll through the district know as *De Wallen* (The Walls) to examine the quaint 16th- and 17th-century canal architecture, peruse second-hand bookstores, and observe inhabitants as they walk their dogs, ride their bikes to the shops, and take the kids to school. Oh, and since this is the Red Light District, you're bound to see certain minimally attired women watching the world go by through red-tinted windows. See p. 157.

- **Hunting for Antiques:** Five hundred and more years of Amsterdam history, including a guaranteed piece of the city's 17th-century Golden Age, is on offer in the Spiegelgracht antiques quarter. And all you need to acquire it is a fistful of euros or some flexible plastic. See chapter 9.

- **Shopping for a Steal at a Street Market:** You'll have to get up pretty early and be pretty slick to hoodwink a Dutch street trader and score a genuine kill at the Waterlooplein flea market or the Albert Cuyp street market. But bargains do occasionally appear at both, and glimpsing local color is guaranteed. See chapter 9.

- **Whiffing a "Coffeeshop":** It's true—smoking marijuana is officially tolerated in Amsterdam's "marijuana smoking coffeeshops." These aren't your neighborhood cafes, and they're not for everyone, but they're an established part of Amsterdam's alternative tradition. You'll be able to buy and smoke marijuana inside, and no law-enforcement agency will hassle you. See chapter 10.

Amsterdam Orientation

North Sea

↑Alkmaar

Hoorn ↖ ○Edam

A9

Alkmaarder-meer A7

PURMEREND ○Volendam

BEVERWIJK

E22

○Zaanse Schans

Monnickendam Marken ○

IJssel meer

IJMUIDEN

Noordzee Kanaal

ZAANSTAD

Broek in Waterland N247

Nationaal Park Zuid-Kennemerland

A8

Zaandam

Uitdam

Bloemendaal aan Zee

A9

A10

A10

Zandvoort

E22

Durgerdam

IJsselmeer

HAARLEM A200

N200

AMSTERDAM

Almere-Stad

E35

A9

Diemen Muiden

Almere-Haven

Badhoevedorp ○

A1

E231

A6

N201

Schiphol Airport

AMSTELVEEN

AMSTERDAM-ZUIDOOST

N208

✈

Vogelenzang Hoofddorp ○

Ouderkerk aan de Amstel

Naarden ○

Amsterdamse Bos

BUSSUM

←Lisse (Keukenhof)

A4

○Aalsmeer

Amstel

Ankeveense Plassen

E19

Westeinder-plassen

A2

E35

A44

Vinkeveense Plassen

Wijde Blik N201

Kager-plassen

Brassemer-meer

N201

Amsterdam-Rijnkanaal

HILVERSUM

Loosdrechtse Plassen

A4

E19

Alphen aan den Rijn ○

Breukelen ○

Maarsseveense Plassen

←Leiden

Nieuwkoopse Plassen

N230 A27

N11

UTRECHT

A12 E25 E30

↖The Hague

Reeuwijkse Plassen

A2
E25

A12 E30

E25

GOUDA

NETHERLANDS

A20

IJssel

Area of detail

←Delft

Hollandse

Amsterdam ✸

Rotterdam

Lek

✈ Airport
🌷 Bulb fields

0   5 mi
0   5 km

0   50 mi
0   50 km

ROTTERDAM

THE best SPLURGE HOTELS

o **Eden Amsterdam American,** Leidsekade 97 (✆ **020/556-3000**): This hotel boasts the best location in town—it's on Leidseplein, Amsterdam's liveliest square, and is close to theaters, cinemas, and a casino. Location aside, this is a fine hotel, and its Art Deco-style **Café Americain** is a city institution. See p. 90.

o **Hotel de l'Europe,** Nieuwe Doelenstraat 2–8 (✆ **020/531-1777**): Modernization has brought the once slightly tired-looking *Belle Époque* grande dame on the Amstel River bang up to date, thereby affording the visitors who patronize the rival InterContinental Amstel Amsterdam Hotel an alternative drop-off point for their moneybags. See p. 76.

o **Pulitzer,** Prinsengracht 315–331 (✆ **020/523-5235**): No fewer than 25 old canal houses on Prinsengracht were converted to create this hotel, which would ordinarily be considered a serious loss, except that the Pulitzer is a real prizewinner. See p. 86.

o **Sofitel Amsterdam The Grand,** Oudezijds Voorburgwal 197 (✆ **020/555-3111**): The Grand really is rather grand, both inside and out; it once served as the seat of the Amsterdam Admiralty and the city council, among other official municipal functions since the 15th century. Now it guards its virtue along a tranquil canal edging the Red Light District. See p. 77.

THE best MODERATELY PRICED HOTELS

o **Agora,** Singel 462 (✆ **020/627-2200**): Those canal-house hotels that don't hit you over the head with opulence more than make up for it with the personal touch. This paragon of the type feels like a canalside home. See p. 87.

o **Ambassade,** Herengracht 341 (✆ **020/555-0222**): Here, in 10 neighboring canal houses just off the Golden Bend (for centuries the city's most fashionable district), you'll feel like you're in the home of a rich 17th-century merchant. Most of the spacious, individually styled rooms have large windows overlooking the canal. See p. 87.

o **Arena,** 's-Gravesandestraat 51 (✆ **020/850-2410**): What this unusual place has, in spades, is an action-oriented and informal temperament that's typical of Amsterdam—the kind of shared outlook that attracts many to this city in the first place. Arena combines this unpretentious bustle with genuine style and a judicious level of comfort. See p. 99.

o **De Filosoof,** Anna van den Vondelstraat 6 (✆ **020/683-3013**): Few—if any—hotels have an operating philosophy as distinctive as this one, which takes its inspiration from the great thinkers of the past. And this is no shameless sophistry disguising a grim underlying truth. In this case, idealism has produced a more-than-acceptable reality. See p. 94.

o **Seven Bridges,** Reguliersgracht 31 (✆ **020/623-1329**): In some hotels, you realize the owners aren't just running a business, but doing what they love. This is that kind of place. It's obvious that all the furniture, fixtures, and fittings have been selected with loving care, and guests receive the same conscientious attention. See p. 88.

THE most unforgettable
DINING EXPERIENCES

- **Pop a Herring:** Amsterdam folk like their herring fresh and raw from a neighborhood fish stall. The best in a fishy business is **Stubbe's Haring,** Haarlemmersluis, at Singel (𝄢 **020/623-3212**). Eat your fish in the approved Dutch manner—whole, holding the fish by its tail, with your face to that wide Holland sky. Amsterdammers prefer theirs chopped, on a bed of raw onions and pickles/gherkins. See p. 116.
- **Eat on the Water:** I can't say you'll never eat better than on a Dinner Cruise. But you'll have the music, the candlelight, the canals, and, if you're lucky, the moon over the water. Variations on this theme are cooked up by most of the canal tour-boat lines. See p. 132.
- **Feast in the Park:** Tucked away behind the trees of Vondelpark, **Vertigo,** Vondelpark 3 (𝄢 **020/612-3021**) lends a touch of the country to a convivial venue that's backed up by some fine food. See p. 131.
- **Try a *Rijsttafel*:** Dutch settlers in the East Indies created the banquet-style "rice table." Comprising from 10 to 30 little dishes, some as fiery as rocket propellant, *rijsttafel* is a great introduction to Indonesian cuisine. See p. 104.
- **Live the Americain Dream:** Join Amsterdammers for coffee and *gâteau* in the stunning Art Nouveau and Art Deco ambience of the Eden Amsterdam American Hotel's **Café Americain,** Leidsekade 97 (𝄢 **020/556-3000**). You'll be pleased to learn that the service has improved in the half century since a Dutch writer described the waiters as "unemployed knife throwers." See p. 122.
- **Get Thee to the Waterfont:** Amsterdam is rediscovering its old harbor zone along the IJ channel. Experience lively harbor views and fine Continental cuisine at **Wilhelmina-Dok,** Nordwal 1 (𝄢 **020/632-3701**). So on the waterfront is this breezy eatery that a wayward canal barge once plowed right into it—how's that for local color! See p. 115.

THE best FREE (OR ALMOST FREE) THINGS TO DO

- **Sail the IJ Ferry:** The short free ferryboat ride across the IJ channel between Centraal Station and Amsterdam-Noord (North) is a great micro-cruise that affords fine harbor views. See p. 43.
- **View Golden Age Paintings:** Usually it costs a bundle to see paintings from the Old Masters period of Dutch art. A free exception is the multiple images of Civic Guards (Militia) companies hanging in the **Schuttersgalerij** of the Amsterdams Historisch Museum. See p. 143.
- **Visit the Begijnhof:** Even though admission is free, there's a price to pay for stepping into the cloistered community that for centuries has been a residence for women of "sound character." You need to be tolerably quiet and comport yourself with dignity—or you'll get tossed out by the guards. See p. 152.
- **Visit the Flower Market:** The vast array of flowers and potted plants in their "floating" home on the Singel canal comprises the city's largest and most colorful plant assortment. However, purchasing the flowers is not free. See p. 227.

- **Take in a Lunchtime Rehearsal Concert:** If you can live with the occasional duff note and a program that doesn't always follow the script, treat your ears to classical music from 12:30 to 1pm at the Muziektheater (Tues) and the Concertgebouw (Wed), every week from October to June. See p. 235.
- **Stroll through Vondelpark:** Its 48 hectares (120 acres) of trees, ponds, flower beds, and picnic grounds comprise the city's green lung—even if the fresh air is often spiked with marijuana smoke. In summer, concerts and all kinds of open-air activities take place. See p. 167.

THE best OUTDOOR ACTIVITIES

- **Cross Bridges over Untroubled Waters:** Amsterdam has more bridges, and more canals, than Venice—a city Italians have proudly dubbed "the Amsterdam of the South." Find out what humbles Italians, by crossing as many of Amsterdam's 1,200-plus bridges as you can; the views are unparalleled. See chapter 7.
- **Tiptoe through the Tulips:** Join 4 centuries of Dutch tradition by going overboard for a flower of Persian and Turkish origin that's become synonymous with Holland. In spring, you'll find them everywhere. Sharp promotion (and a seed of truth) says the best place to pick up a bunch is at the Flower Market on Singel. See p. 168 and 227.
- **Beach about Zandvoort:** Come rain, hail, or shine (and often enough, all three on the same day), Amsterdammers ride the rails for a short hop out to its brassy—but not classy—coastal resort. The bracing North Sea air serves to blow away all that marijuana smoke. See p. 259.

THE best MUSEUMS

- **Anne Frankhuis:** The clear and haunting words of a young Jewish girl trying to survive and grow in unimaginable circumstances have moved millions since her diary was first published in the aftermath of World War II. It's a melancholy but unforgettable experience to spend a reflective moment in Anne Frank's stark hideout from Nazi terror. See p. 138.
- **Rijksmuseum:** The State Museum houses some of Holland's most important artworks: Rembrandt's world-famous *The Night Watch,* four of Vermeer's miniatures, and numerous pieces by Frans Hals. In all, this is one of the world's most impressive Old Masters collections. See p. 139.
- **Van Gogh Museum:** The world's largest collection of Vincent's works is housed here—some 200 paintings and 500 drawings—ranging from *Sunflowers* to earless self-portraits. Here, you can trace this great, tragic painter's artistic development and psychological decline. See p. 140.

THE most INTRIGUING NEIGHBORHOODS

- **De Wallen:** Just below the low-life sin section of "The Walls"—that is, the Red Light District—is a contrast: This delightful southern district of Old Amsterdam encompasses tranquil canals lined with handsome 16th-century houses and the University of Amsterdam's bustling campus. See p. 157.
- **Het IJ:** Day by day, Amsterdam's future unfolds before your eyes along the narrow channel on which the city's old port zone east and west of Centraal Station stood. A whirl of gargantuan redevelopment projects and modern architecture is transforming the waterway. See p. 160.
- **Jordaan:** Bounded by Brouwersgracht, Singelgracht, Prinsengracht, and Leidsestraat, this former artisan neighborhood has become gentrified. With its own small canals, street markets, and an array of minor attractions, it's a great place for random wandering. See p. 157.

AMSTERDAM IN DEPTH

Prosperity, in the shape of everything from crass commercialism to genteel gentrification, has settled like a North Sea mist around Amsterdam's graceful cityscape of 17th-century canals and canalside houses. Yet "free thinking" and "anything goes" still maintain their place: They're the catchphrases by which Amsterdam lives its collective life. And all this free living is fueled by a robust Dutch economy, not by the combustion of semi-legal exotic plants.

City government has worked hard to transform Amsterdam from a hippie haven to a cosmopolitan business and cultural center—and it seems to be succeeding.

A side effect of the city's concern with economics and image is that youthful backpackers who don't wash much, stay in cheap hostels, and think smoking hash is the high point of the city's cultural life aren't as welcome as they once were. But when they come back with a paycheck that allows them to stay at an upscale hotel, buy tickets for the Concertgebouw and the Muziektheater, eat in a Japanese restaurant, and splash out on a diamond or two, well, that's another story. Still, all is far from lost for the bohemian souls: If they want, they can smoke hash all the livelong day. And anyone can partake in Amsterdam's culture, history, and scenic cityscape, without stretching credit card limits.

So step aboard for a cruise through highlights from 800 years of history in this city of canals; a working knowledge of Amsterdam's history will add dimension to your visit. Then, go below the surface to fathom why the Dutch capital's lifestyle provokes heated debate in other countries, and to permit some of the impassioned artists and architects who helped to make Amsterdam worth visiting to take a bow from their places in the corridors of time.

AMSTERDAM TODAY

Amsterdam is the capital and major city of the Netherlands. Today, this sophisticated international city has a multicultural population of over 760,000 (and 600,000 bicycles), a busy harbor, multistory apartment communities, and elevated highways—all hallmarks of a modern urban center. The modernization process has had its pluses and minuses: Much tranquillity has been lost along the way, but has been replaced with an increased vibrancy. Despite it all, Amsterdam remains a kind of big village, retaining a human scale that at least affords the illusion of simplicity.

More and more people from Holland, Europe, and farther afield are making tracks toward the city. Footloose young Hollanders seem to have no other ambition than to live here—and who can blame them when you consider the "excitement" of growing up in a squeaky-clean Dutch village? Young Americans and Europeans still see Amsterdam as a kind of mecca of youth rebellion to which a pilgrimage must be made.

Immigrants find social support systems and a relative absence of the discrimination they face in many other European cities, though some immigrant-heavy districts, like Zeeburg, Amsterdam-Nieuw West (New West), and the Bijlmermeer housing project in Amsterdam-Zuidoost (Southeast), are experiencing growing social problems. Amsterdammers continue to mix tolerably well in their multiracial melting pot, despite growing signs of discontent with continued immigration, and a dialing back of multicultural policies in favor of securing civic integration among poorly assimilated immigrants.

Although flowers gleam in window boxes on gabled houses, shopkeepers keep their portals tidy, and a few homemakers still wash their steps each morning, graffiti, grime, and other problems of city life inhabit Amsterdam as much as any other urban center. (The ubiquitous mounds of dog poop on the sidewalks have become something of a symbol of the city.)

> ### Impressions
>
> *Amsterdam will at least give one's regular habits of thought the stimulus of a little confusion.*
>
> —Henry James,
> *Transatlantic Sketches*, 1875

But maybe you just want to know what to expect from the person in the street and behind the shop counter. Amsterdammers can be rude or cordial (it may depend on the weather), domineering or ready to please (it may depend on you). In a shop, they may get annoyed with you if you don't accept what they have, or get mad at themselves if they don't have what you want.

Fortunately, it's easy to overlook all these shortcomings. The city's historic heart is still there to beguile you with its tree-lined canals, gabled houses, and graceful bridges. The Bureau of Monuments and Archaeology has exercised great foresight in working to preserve the 17th-century feel along the canals. You'll have no problem finding the legacy of the city's Golden Age, 400 years ago, in the new Amsterdam. Fuming traffic, power drills, payphones, bicycles, tour boats, and souvenir stores have dulled some of the luster, yes, but a moment always arrives when a window in time opens and Amsterdam's radiant heritage peeks out.

When in Amsterdam . . .

"The Dutch Disease" is what a conservative U.S. columnist once called Holland's social liberalism. But not many of the hookers in Amsterdam's Red Light District are Dutch, and relatively few denizens of the smoking coffeeshops are Dutch. If Amsterdam's a latter-day Sodom and Gomorrah, it's one for foreigners mainly. A stable history in a small, densely populated land has led the Dutch to seek social consensus rather than confrontation whenever possible.

For centuries, Amsterdam has been a magnet for the oppressed and persecuted, particularly in the 17th century, when it became a haven for Jews and Protestant Huguenots driven from France and other Catholic countries (though, for a time, Catholics in Holland were not allowed to practice their faith openly). That tradition of tolerance has continued into the 21st century, though signs suggest it may be beginning to fray around the edges. In 2006, a law was proposed to outlaw any other language than Dutch in public. The idea never flew but seemed to be a sign of the times.

The liberalist tradition impacts areas of personal and social morality that in other countries are still controversial issues. Such topics are researched and debated, and perceived solutions implemented, with a surprising lack of partisan passion—indeed often without passion of any kind. In 2001, the world's first same-sex marriage with legal status identical to heterosexual matrimony took place in Amsterdam, and the Dutch parliament legalized regulated euthanasia ("mercy killing"), making the Netherlands the world's first country to do so. And then there's the easygoing approach to prostitution and drug use.

Authorities aren't duty-bound to prosecute criminal acts, which leaves a loophole for experimentation in areas that technically are illegal. It's been said the Netherlands has one of the lowest crime rates in Europe because whenever something becomes a criminal problem, the Dutch make it legal, thereby reducing crime with a stroke.

Thin Red Line

Prostitution is legal in Holland, and prostitutes in Amsterdam's Red Light District work in clean premises, pay taxes, receive regular medical checks, are eligible for welfare, and even have their own trade union.

Don't laugh, at least not in Holland. The Dutch will take aim at anyone, on any issue, outside their borders. Just so long as it's understood that everything *inside* has arrived at that hallowed state of perfection. Run through any list of America's international misdemeanors and the Dutch will nod sagely and open-mindedly in agreement. Laugh to your heart's content about the soap-opera antics of Britain's House of Windsor, and they'll laugh right along with you. But refer, however obliquely, to negative aspects of the Dutch Way, and watch the air turn cool. Go so far as to openly criticize the country, or to joke about Queen Beatrix, and you'll quickly find that you have touched the natives where they are tender.

Drug Haze

Popular misconceptions notwithstanding, narcotic drugs are illegal in the Netherlands. But the Dutch treat drug use mainly as a medical problem rather than purely a crime, and there's no Dutch "war on drugs." Treatment—not arrest—of addicts is the Dutch way. Authorities distinguish between soft drugs like cannabis, considered unlikely to cause addiction or pose a serious health risk, and hard drugs like heroin and cocaine, which are addictive and significantly deleterious to the users' health. Both types are illegal, but the law is tougher on hard drugs. Dealers who import and export drugs face 4 years in jail for soft drugs and 12 years for hard drugs.

Amsterdam's casual acceptance of pot-smoking and pot-smokers makes some dissidents crazy enough to make you wonder what *they* are smoking. In recent years, the Netherlands has bowed to pressure from surrounding countries regarding its drug policy and has tightened the rules for "coffeeshops"—establishments in which hashish and

Impressions

To understand the Dutch, you've got to start out with the word gedogen. *It basically means to permit, to live with, to be able to tolerate. A lot of what you see in terms of legislation has been subject to* gedogen *for years. By the time it's written into law, it almost doesn't make a difference.*

—K. Terry Dornbush, former U.S. ambassador to the Netherlands, 2001

marijuana are sold. You used to be allowed to buy and retain 30 grams (1 oz.) of soft drugs for personal use; now, you can buy only 5 grams (⅓ oz.) at a time, though you're still allowed to possess 30 grams (1 oz). Coffeeshops aren't allowed to sell hard drugs, to advertise, or to sell to minors. If they create a public nuisance, the local *burgemeester* (mayor) can shut them down. Yet despite these new, stricter rules, Amsterdam remains a mecca for marijuana smokers and seems likely to remain that way.

Supplying free heroin to addicts, with medical support, has helped prevent the spread of HIV and slashed the drug's street price so that addicts commit fewer crimes to feed their habit, and so that healthcare and law-enforcement costs have gone down. The Netherlands has significantly lower rates of drug use, drug-related deaths, and heroin addiction than Britain, France, Germany, and other western European countries that criticize Holland so fiercely on this issue.

LOOKING BACK AT AMSTERDAM
Amsterdam's Origins

Amsterdam was founded at the place where two fishermen and a seasick dog jumped ashore from a small boat to escape a storm in the Zuiderzee (Southern Sea). The dog threw up, thereby marking the spot. Sound like a shaggy-dog story? Well, the city's original coat of arms backs up the tale. In some ways, it's an appropriate metaphor for a city with a lifestyle that has about as many boosters and detractors as did Sodom and Gomorrah. Some first-time visitors want to throw up everything and live this way forever; others just want to throw up.

At any rate, fishermen, with or without a seasick dog, did play the decisive role in founding Amsterdam. Around 1200, they realized that the area at the mouth of the Amstel River allowed their wooden cog boats easy access to rich fishing on the Zuiderzee beyond. They built their huts on raised mounds of earth called *terpen.*

The low-lying marshy terrain left these early settlers at the mercy of tides and storms, and many must have perished or lost their homes as a result of flooding. In an effort to control periodic flooding, the populace dammed the Amstel (they'd likely been damning it from the beginning) at the point where today's square called the Dam stands. This is the source of the city's original name, Aemstelledamme.

Archaeological finds show that by 1204, local big wheels were moving in on what the ordinary folks had created. Count Gijsbrecht II of Aemstel made the first power play, building a castle at the settlement and lording over the locals. In the 1990s, archaeologists uncovered the castle's foundations under Nieuwezijds Kolk, a side street off Nieuwendijk—and brought to light the earliest known clog shoe, made from alder wood and dating from the early 13th century.

BELOW sea level

Amsterdam lies up to 5.5m (18 ft.) below mean sea level. The city's solid, timeless buildings stand, and its 760,000 inhabitants live, where waves should by all rights be lapping. If the sea-dikes should ever go down, most of the city would vanish beneath the waves. Vondelpark would become a lake, the Metro would be truly drowned, and the trams would float away. If you happened to be standing on top of Oude Kerk's tower, however, you wouldn't even get your feet wet.

Don't get too worried. The dikes are built to repel almost everything the North Sea can throw at them. Only a 1-in-10,000-years super storm could take them down (famous last words?). And because of climate-change concerns, the government plans to raise that safety margin to 1 in 100,000 years.

There are few records of Aemstelledamme (or Amestelledame, or Amstellodame, as it was also known in an age without spelling bees) before 1275, when Count Floris V of Holland granted village locals the right to trade anywhere in the Holland and Zeeland counties without having to pay tolls along the way. This is the settlement's first official documentary record, and the year that's now celebrated as Amsterdam's foundation date.

Trading Center

Amsterdam began its rise to commercial prosperity in 1323, when Count Floris VI established the city as a toll point for beer imports. Later, Amsterdam was granted toll rights on exported ale. Beer thus became a major component of the city's prosperity, and remains important to this day, as anyone who visits a traditional *bruine kroeg* (brown cafe) will see.

Always skillful merchants, Amsterdammers began to establish strong craftsman guilds and to put ships to sea to catch North Sea herring. They expanded into trading salted Baltic herring; amber; Norwegian salted or dried cod and cod-liver oil; German beer and salt; bales of linen and woolen cloth from the Low Countries and England; coal from England; Russian furs and candle wax; Polish grain and flour; Swedish timber, pitch, and iron. They opened up lucrative trade by both doing business with and competing against the trading towns of the powerful Baltic-based Hanseatic League.

The city's merchants, growing rich on the contents of the warehouses they built along the canals, trampled over the Hanseatic League in the competition for wealth, and by the 1600s had come out head and shoulders in front.

Wars of Religion

During the Middle Ages, the Netherlands was a bastion of Catholicism, with powerful bishops in the cities of Utrecht and Maastricht, and a holy shrine in Aemstelledamme that attracted pilgrims. No one is sure when Amsterdam became an independent parish, but it's thought to have been around 1334, when the Oude Kerk (Old Church) is first mentioned in the city's records—though a small timber chapel on the spot dated from around 1300.

As the town grew in prosperity, churches, monasteries, convents, and cloisters called *begijnhofen* sprang up. Eventually, there were 18 *begijnhofen*, which functioned as social welfare agencies, providing care to the sick, orphaned, and poor, and hospitality to travelers and pilgrims. You can visit the main Begijnhof (see p. 152).

Protestantism emerged at the same time as the Low Countries came under the rule of Charles V, the intensely Catholic Habsburg emperor and king of Spain. Holland, and Amsterdam in particular, became a fulcrum for the shifting political scene the Reformation brought about everywhere in Europe. John Calvin's rigorous doctrines and his firm belief in separating church and state began to take root in Amsterdam.

In 1555, Philip II, son of Charles V and great-grandson of Emperor Maximilian I, became Spain's king and the ruler of the Low Countries. An ardent Catholic, he was determined to defeat the Reformation. The Dutch resented Philip's intrusion into their affairs and began a resistance movement. Within 10 years, William of Orange, Count of Holland (known as William the Silent), formed a League of Protestant Nobles. Philip's response, in 1567, was to send the ruthless Duke of Alba, Fernando Álvarez de Toledo, to the Low Countries with an army of 9,000 men (accompanied by 2,000 courtesans) to enforce the death-to-heretics policy.

The Dutch nobles fought back, though they had no army and no money. William of Orange and his brother, John of Nassau, managed to wage war on Spain despite all this, their only ally a ragtag "navy" of Protestant privateers called the *Geuzen* (Sea Beggars). When Spain levied a new tax on the Dutch, the action was so unpopular that it rallied the majority of Dutch—Protestant and Catholic alike—to the anti-Spanish cause.

Amsterdam's Calvinist merchants expelled the Catholic city council in a 1578 revolution called the *Alteratie* (Changeover). As the Protestant Reformation took hold, the city's many Catholics were forbidden to hold public office or to worship openly, a situation that continued for more than a century.

The Golden Age

Over the first 75 years of the 17th century, the legendary Dutch entrepreneurial gift would come into its own. These years have since become known as the Golden Age. It seemed every business venture the Dutch initiated during this time turned a profit, and each of their many expeditions to the world's unknown places resulted in a new jewel in the Dutch trading empire. Colonies and brisk trade were established to provide the luxury-hungry merchants at home with new delights, such as fresh ginger from Java; jewels, spices, and silks from the Orient; foxtails from America; fine porcelain from China; and flower bulbs from Ottoman Turkey that produced big, bright, waxy flowers and grew quite readily in Holland's sandy soil—tulips. Holland was rich and Amsterdam was booming.

In 1589, Amsterdam's greatest commercial rival, Antwerp, fell to the Spanish, prompting its many industrious Protestant and Jewish merchants and craftspeople to flock to Amsterdam. Of the Jewish influx, the jurist Hugo Grotius wrote in 1614: "Plainly God desires them to live somewhere. Why not here rather than elsewhere?"

These migrants brought with them their merchant skills and industries—including diamond dealerships—establishing what is still a famous part of Amsterdam commerce.

Amsterdam grew into one of the world's great cities; its population reached 50,000 by the end of the 16th century. In 1602, Dutch traders set up the Vereenigde Oostindische Compagnie (V.O.C.), the United East India Company. It was the world's first limited-liability joint-stock corporation, which was granted a monopoly on trade in the East.

It was a runaway success—in 1611, the V.O.C. paid its shareholders a dividend of 162%—and established the Dutch presence in the Spice Islands (Indonesia), centered on their colony at Batavia (Jakarta), which was run by a company-appointed governor-general. The big V.O.C. merchant vessels could hold twice as much cargo as their English rivals. A full-size replica of one of these sailing ships, the *Amsterdam*, is tied to a wharf at the city's Science Center NEMO (p. 163).

Great wealth flowed back to Amsterdam, and the merchants used it to build the canals and the impressive 17th-century architecture along Herengracht's Golden Bend. The merchant owners of canalside mansions liked to put up a good facade, but canal frontage was expensive, so the houses behind those elegant gables were built long and narrow. Their upper floors were storerooms bulging with their owners' wares, hoisted up with loft-mounted ropes and pulleys.

In 1613, work began on the three concentric waterways of the *Grachtengordel* (Canal Belt)—Herengracht, Keizersgracht, and Prinsengracht. City planners designed a system for smaller transverse canals to connect the large canals, making travel by water more convenient throughout Amsterdam. They decided the wealthy would live facing the major canals, while the connecting canals were set aside for middle and lower classes. Thus began the popular comparison with Venice—though Amsterdam has more canals than the Italian city.

Golden Age Amsterdam can be compared to Renaissance Florence and Periclean Athens for the great flowering that transformed its society. Of Amsterdam's Golden Age, historian Simon Schama wrote, "There is perhaps no other example of a complete and highly original civilization springing up in so short a time in so small a territory." Artists like Rembrandt worked overtime, cranking out paintings for newly affluent merchants obsessed with portraying themselves and filling their homes with beautiful images (see "Art & Architecture," later in this chapter).

> ## Impressions
>
> *You lose no time, of course, in drawing the inevitable parallel between Amsterdam and Venice, and it is well worth drawing, as an illustration of the uses to which the same materials may be put by different minds.*
>
> —Henry James,
> *Transatlantic Sketches*, 1875

Decline & Fall

A long period of decline set in during the 18th century. At the Museum Willet-Holthuysen (p. 146) and the Museum Van Loon (p. 146), you get an idea of the decadent, French-influenced style in which wealthy Amsterdam families lived during the Golden Age's fading afterglow, rich with Italian majolica and Nuremberg porcelain.

> ### 💬 Flower Power
>
> With the profits from global trade flooding in, Amsterdam's merchants needed a visible sign of their vast disposable income to flaunt in the faces of friends and rivals. These strait-laced, parsimonious Calvinists went astonishingly overboard for tulips. Bulb prices skyrocketed from virtually zero in 1620. By 1630, single bulbs were going for 1,000 florins ($200,000 in today's U.S. dollars) and the price finally topped out at 30,000 florins ($6 million in today's U.S. dollars) for three bulbs in 1637. To give that context, that was also the going rate for the most prestigious houses along Amsterdam's canals, with the garden and coach house thrown in. When the Tulip Mania bubble burst soon afterward, more than a few fortunes vaporized with it.

By the second half of the century, revolution was in the air. The "Patriots," pro-French, anti-royalist democrats, seized control of the city on April 27, 1787. Prussian troops rescued the House of Orange, tramping into the city to put down the rebellion. In 1799, the United East India Company was liquidated, a key indicator of the nation's steep commercial decline.

Revolutionary France invaded Holland in 1794, capturing Amsterdam and establishing the Batavian Republic the following year, headed by the Patriots. Napoleon brought the republic to an end in 1806 by setting up his brother, Louis Napoleon, as king of Holland, and installing him in the town hall on the Dam in Amsterdam, which was converted into a palace. In 1810, Napoleon deposed his brother and brought Holland formally into the empire.

The French reign was short-lived, but the taste of royalty proved sweet. When the Dutch in 1814 recalled the House of Orange from exile in England, it was to fill the role of king in a constitutional monarchy.

For 2 centuries after Amsterdam's Golden Age, the city's population remained at a quarter of a million. Between 1850 and 1900, however, it jumped to half a million. As did most major cities during the Industrial Revolution, Amsterdam began to face overpopulation issues. Housing was in short supply, and the canals were increasingly befouled with sewage.

Holland was neutral during World War I, but the city suffered from acute food shortages. During the 1930s, widespread unemployment brought on by the Great Depression convinced the government to use the army to control the populace.

Amsterdam was just beginning to recover from the Depression when, on May 10, 1940, the Germans invaded. The overmatched Dutch army resisted for a time, but with Rotterdam blitzed into ruins, the end came quickly.

Hitler managed to gain a following in Amsterdam. However, Amsterdammers mostly opposed the way Nazis treated Jews, Gypsies, and homosexuals. In February 1941, city workers organized a strike to protest the deportation of 400 members of the city's Jewish community. Today, in the old Jewish Quarter, stands *The Dockworker*, a statue in tribute to the February Strike. Unfortunately, the strike did little good; by 1942, the Nazis had forced all Dutch Jews to move to three isolated ghettos in Amsterdam. Between July 1942 and September 1943, most of Amsterdam's Jews were sent to death camps. Of Amsterdam's 80,000 Jews, only 16,000 survived.

Among the murdered was a girl who has come to symbolize the Holocaust's many victims: Anne Frank (1929–45). Anne is famous the world over for her diary, a moving record of a teenager's struggle to cope with coming of age amid the horrific realities of war and the Nazi occupation. When the Germans began deporting Jews, Anne and her family hid in an Amsterdam canal house, now the Anne Frankhuis (p. 138). Cut off from other outlets for her energies, she began to keep a journal telling of her thoughts, feelings, and experiences. Sadly on August 4, 1944, Anne and her family were discovered by the German Security Police following an anonymous tip-off.

On May 5, 1945, the grim ordeal came to an end when German forces in the Netherlands capitulated. Canadian troops reached Amsterdam first, on May 7.

Hippie Haven

In the 1960s, the city was a hotbed of political and cultural radicalism. Hippies trailing clouds of marijuana smoke took over the Dam and camped out in Vondelpark and in front of Centraal Station. Radical political activity, which began with "happenings" staged by the small group known as the Provos—from *provocatie* (provocation)—continued and intensified in the 1980s. In 1966, the Provos were behind the protests that disrupted the wedding of Princess Beatrix to German Claus von Amsberg in the Westerkerk; they threw smoke bombs and fighting broke out between protesters and police.

Some radicals joined neighborhood groups to protest specific local government plans. The scheme that provoked the greatest ire was a plan to build a Metro (subway/underground) through the Nieuwmarkt area. In 1975, demonstrations aimed to defend the housing that had been condemned for the subway. The most dramatic confrontation between the police and the human barricades happened on Blue Monday, March 24. Thirty people were wounded and 47 arrested in a battle of teargas and water cannons against paint cans and powder bombs. Despite the protests, the Metro opened in 1980.

Protests similar to those against the Metro were launched against proposals to build a new Stadhuis (Town Hall) and Opera (Muziektheater) side by side on Waterlooplein, a complex that became known as the Stopera. Despite an energetic and at times violent campaign to "Stop the Stopera," both buildings were completed in 1986, and the Muziektheater (p. 236) is now a star in the city's cultural firmament.

Though the turbulent events of the 1970s and 1980s seem distant today, the independent spirit and social conscience that fueled them remain—*Make Sex Not Guns,* reads a typical retro piece of graffiti—and Amsterdam is still one of Europe's most socially advanced cities.

New priorities have emerged, however, with the general aim of boosting Amsterdam's position as a global business center and the location of choice for foreign multinationals' European headquarters. The city aims to consolidate its role as one of Europe's most important transportation and distribution hubs. These goals are aided by an ongoing effort to change the city's hippie-paradise image to one more in tune with the needs of commerce.

ART & ARCHITECTURE

Dutch art came into its own during the 17th-century Golden Age. Artists were blessed with wealthy patrons whose support allowed them to give free reign to their talents. The primary art patrons were Protestant merchants who commissioned pictures depicting their world: Portraits, landscapes, seascapes, domestic scenes, and still lifes—not the kind of religious works commissioned by the Church in Catholic countries.

Art held a cherished place in the hearts of average Dutch citizens too, and few were the houses not adorned with paintings, as the Englishman Peter Mundy, who traveled to Amsterdam in 1640, observed: "Many times blacksmiths and cobblers will have some picture or other by their forge and in their stall."

Early-17th-century Utrecht artist **Gerard van Honthorst** (1590–1656), who studied in Rome with Caravaggio, brought the new "realism of light and dark," or *chiaroscuro,* technique to Holland, where he influenced Dutch artists like the young Rembrandt. Honthorst often used multiple hidden light sources to heighten the dramatic contrast of lights and darks, an effect that can be seen in his painting *The Merry Fiddler* (1623; Rijksmuseum, Amsterdam).

Art, Anyone?

An estimated 20 million paintings were produced in Amsterdam during the Golden Age.

Among this period's great landscape artists, **Jacob van Ruisdael** (1628–82) stands out. His *Windmill at Wijk bij Duurstede* (ca. 1665; Rijksmuseum, Amsterdam) combines characteristic elements of his style: The windmill stands in a somber landscape, containing a few small human figures, a cloud-laden sky, and a foreground of agitated water and reeds.

Antwerp-born **Frans Hals** (ca. 1580–1666), the Haarlem school's undisputed leader (schools differed from city to city), was a great portrait painter whose relaxed, informal, and naturalistic portraits contrast strikingly with the traditional formal masks typical of Renaissance portraits. His light brushstrokes help convey immediacy and intimacy, lending his works a perceptive psychological quality. Hals had a genius for comic characters, showing men and women as they are and a little less than they are. It's worth taking a day trip to Haarlem just to visit the Frans Hals Museum (p. 258) and view such works as his *A Banquet of the Officers of the St. George Civic Guard* (ca. 1627) and *Officers and Sergeants of the St. Hadrian Civic Guard* (ca. 1633).

The period's great genius was **Rembrandt Harmenszoon van Rijn** (1606–69), one of few artists of any period to be known simply by his first name. This painter, whose works hang in places of honor in the world's great museums, may be *the* most famous Amsterdammer. But he was born in Leiden. He earned acclaim in Amsterdam as a portraitist. Later, as he refused to compromise his artistic ideas, he began to lose popularity. One of his most famous paintings, *The Night Watch,* was refused by those who had commissioned it. In 1656, Rembrandt declared bankruptcy, a financial state from which he would never recover.

Rembrandt pushed *chiaroscuro* to unprecedented heights, blending together light and dark gradually and softly—which may have diffused some of *chiaroscuro*'s inherent drama, but helped his works achieve a more truthful appearance. The etching *Self-Portrait with Saskia* (1636; Rijksmuseum, Amsterdam) shows him with his wife at a prosperous time when he was being commissioned to do portraits of many wealthy merchants. Later self-portraits are more psychologically complex, often depicting a careworn old man whose gaze is nevertheless sharp, compassionate, and wise.

In group portraits like *The Night Watch* (1642) and *The Syndics of the Cloth Guild* (1662), both in the Rijksmuseum, it's clear that each individual portrait was done with care. The unrivaled harmony of light, color, and movement in these works is a marvel. Compare, too, these robust, masculine works with the tender *The Jewish Bride* (ca. 1665), also in the Rijksmuseum.

Jan Vermeer (1632–75) of Delft is perhaps the best known of the "little Dutch masters" who specialized in one genre of painting (Vermeer focused on portraiture). Although they confined their artistry within a narrow scope, these painters rendered subjects with exquisite care and faithfulness to actual appearance.

Vermeer's work centers on domestic life's simple pleasures—a woman pouring milk or reading a letter, for example—and all of his simple figures positively glow with color and light. A master at lighting interior scenes and rendering true colors, Vermeer was able to create an illusion of three-dimensionality in works such as *The Love Letter* (ca. 1670), in Amsterdam's Rijksmuseum. As light—usually afternoon sunshine pouring in from an open window—moves across the picture plane, it caresses and modifies all the colors.

Jan Steen (ca. 1626–79), born in Leiden, painted marvelous interior scenes, often satirical and didactic in their intent. The allusions on which much of the satire depends may escape most of us today, but any viewer can appreciate the fine drawing, subtle color shading, and warm light pervading such paintings as *Woman at Her Toilet* (1663) and *The Feast of St. Nicholas* (ca. 1665), both in the Rijksmuseum. Many of his pictures revel in bawdy tavern scenes fueled by drunken overindulgence—being an innkeeper afforded him plenty of opportunity for research. Then there are his sly *double-entendres,* like the ostensibly innocent *Girl Eating Oysters* (ca. 1660), in The Hague's Mauritshuis—oysters were considered to be an aphrodisiac, and the girl's Mona Lisa smile could easily be interpreted as a come-on.

Architecture

Hendrick de Keyser (1565–1621), an architect who worked in Amsterdam at the height of the Renaissance, is known for using decorative, playful elements in a way that was practical to the structure. For instance, he combined hard yellow or white sandstone decorative features (like volutes, keystones, and masks) with soft red brick, creating a visually stimulating multicolored facade, while utilizing the sandstone as

BEHIND THE gables

You might think all Amsterdam canal houses look similar. Many do, so far as basic shape goes. Look closer, though, and you'll notice a wonderful mix of architectural detail ranging from classical to Renaissance to modern.

Most of Amsterdam's 6,800 landmark buildings have gables. These hide the pitched roofs and demonstrate the architect's vertical showmanship in a city where hefty property taxes and expensive canal-facing land encouraged pencil-thin buildings. If you can pick out Amsterdam's various gable styles without developing Sistine Chapel neck syndrome, you can date the buildings fairly accurately.

Of the earliest, triangular wood gables (1250–1550), only two remain, at no. 34 in the Begijnhof and at Zeedijk 1. Later developments in stone on this theme (1600–50) were the pointy spout gable and the stepped gable, which, as the name suggests, looks like a series of steps. The graceful neck gable (1640–1790) looks like a headless neck with curlicues on the shoulders; look for the first one at Herengracht 168. These were complemented by the less elaborate bell gable, which looks like a church bell's cross section.

Daniel Marot, a French architect who lived in Amsterdam from 1705 to 1717, introduced the Louis styles, common to 18th-century buildings. The heavy baroque Louis XIV style suited neck gables; the asymmetrical, rococo Louis XV was better for bell gables.

Among the most lavish gables is one with tritons blowing horns at Herengracht 508. And next door at no. 510, a pair of stone sea gods ride leaping dolphins.

Around 600 old *gevelstenen* (gable stones)—ornamental tiles, sculptures, or reliefs that often play on the original owner's name or profession—still exist (they even have a society of admirers). Walls in the Begijnhof and on Sint-Luciënsteeg at the Amsterdam Historical Museum have interesting gable stones, including the oldest known, from 1603, showing a milkmaid balancing her buckets.

Incidentally, the *hijsbalk*—the hook you see on many gables—might look to be ideal for a hanging (the kids maybe), but is actually used with rope and pulley for hauling large, heavy items in and out of homes that have steep, narrow staircases.

Stepped gable (Herengracht 81, ±1625)　　　*Neck gable (Rokin 45)*

A New School

Between 1900 and 1940, various Amsterdam architects purveyed many different styles of architecture. One of these styles stands out above the others: The Amsterdam School, with **Eduard Cuypers** (nephew to P. J. H. Cuypers) at the helm, and **P. L. Kramer, M. de Klerk,** and **J. M. van der Mey,** all employed by Cuypers, as contributors. These architects succeeded in creating forms of brickwork that had existed only in earlier architects' fantasies. Their buildings are massive yet fluid, and feature decorations like stained glass, wrought iron, and corner towers.

protection from rain erosion. **Philips and Justus Vingboons** were architects and brothers who worked in the Renaissance style; while walking along Herengracht, Keizersgracht, and Prinsengracht, you'll see many of their buildings. With them, the medieval stepped gable gave way to a more ornate one with scrolled sides, decorative finials, and other features.

Many other 17th-century buildings have typically classical elements, such as pilasters, entablatures, and pediments. These details give a sense of order and balance and move away from de Keyser's playful Renaissance style. The classical pediment, often used as a protective element against the rain, was typically used to shield windows and to cap gable ends. During this time, a harder brown brick also replaced the red brick used in the 16th century.

Because classical elements tend to have straight lines and don't flow like the Renaissance elements did, facades shifted to a more boxed-in, central look that eventually grew into the raised-neck gable (a tall, narrow, rectangular gable). Fruits and flowers were used as ornamentation in the scrolls. Soon, the raised-neck gable gave way to the neck gable (which looks relatively similar, only shorter) with human and animal figures carved into the scrolls. **Jacob van Campen** (1595–1657), who built the elaborate **Town Hall** at the Dam, now the Royal Palace, was probably the single most important architect of Amsterdam architecture's classical period.

Around 1665, **Adriaan Dortsman** (1625–82), best known for his classic restrained Dutch style, began building homes with balconies and attics, leaving off the pilasters and festoons that adorned earlier facades. The emphasis had once again shifted, this time from decorated ornamentation to space utility and harmonization with structure.

AMSTERDAM IN POPULAR CULTURE: BOOKS, FILM & MUSIC

Books

FICTION

The Booker Prize-winning short novel *Amsterdam* plays with themes of love and friendship, death and mortality, and on Amsterdam's status as a city where euthanasia laws are relatively liberal, but most of it actually takes place in England. In that sense the city is more of a city of the mind than a real place. Amsterdam is actually quite familiar with playing the role of a screen on which outsiders project both their fantasies and their fears. Far more sense of place is provided by Nicolas Freeling's *Love in Amsterdam*, the first in his series of Inspector Piet van der Valk detective novels, and even though it's the Amsterdam of almost a half century ago, the city is easily recognizable, and something of a co-protagonist. Much the same could be said of Alistair MacLean's thriller *Puppet on a Chain*, though written at a time when the author had descended into faintly ridiculous, formulaic tales.

HISTORY

Simon Schama's **The Embarrassment of Riches: An Interpretation of Dutch Culture in the Golden Age** lets you inside Amsterdam's greatest period. Schama, adeptly, is simultaneously lighthearted and scholarly—a chapter headed "The Pretzel and the Puppy Dog" refers to a portrait by Jacob Cuyp. Most of the 700 pages feature works of art, which are explained in the text. Though Schama modestly describes his essays as "more eccentric than persuasive," he succeeds in his intention "to map out the moral geography of the Dutch mind, adrift between the fear of deluge and the hope of moral salvage."

If a single individual personifies the Holocaust, that person must be Anne Frank. Her diary, compiled as a series of letters addressed "Dear Kitty," and kept for more than 2 years until her arrest on August 4, 1944, has come to symbolize the plight of millions of Jews during Nazi terror. **The Diary of a Young Girl** includes photos of Anne and the people she hid with, plus a map of the secret annex in the house on Prinsengracht. Her candid descriptions of living as a teenage girl in tragically restricted conditions, of her thoughts and dreams, hopes and fears, boredom and anguish, provide an unusually moving account of a life cut far too short.

Anne Frank is the best known but was not Amsterdam's only notable wartime Jewish diarist. Lawyer and poet Abel Herzberg, a survivor of the same concentration camp where Anne was held, kept a secret diary during his incarceration, which he later published as **Between Two Streams: A Diary from Bergen-Belsen.**

Roving through 800 years in 300-some pages, Geert Mak's **Amsterdam, A Brief Life of the City,** lays bare the city's soul, linking tales about ordinary folk with historical fact. Amsterdam's journey from boggy 12th-century fish-and-farm settlement to modern metropolis is populated with princes and painters, Calvinists and Catholics, Provos and rebels; in this book, it's enlivened with black-and-white illustrations. Mak's journalistic skill and historical insight amply fulfill his ambition to write an historical work readable enough that you can read it in your hotel room before going to bed.

ART

Painters of Amsterdam: Four Centuries of Cityscapes is the kind of book that makes you wonder why nobody thought of putting out something like it before. Spread by spread, the large-format book unfolds a veritable gallery of paintings depicting the grand old Maid of the Amstel in all her moods and at key periods in history, from a 1640 Rembrandt etching to Matthias Meyer's *Museumplein*. Art historian Carole Denninger-Schreuder's incisive text accompanies the reproductions, which are by artists as diverse as Pieter Saenredam, George Hendrik Breitner, Isaac Israëls, Claude Monet, Vincent van Gogh, Piet Mondrian, and many more.

The book adds up to an unforgettable trip down Amsterdam's memory lane, in the company of those observers best able to illuminate the journey.

If you want to buy a book about Old Masters, make it **The Glory of the Golden Age**, by Judikje Kiers and Fieke Tissink. Published to coincide with the bicentennial of Amsterdam's Rijksmuseum (p. 139), this weighty tome comprehensively covers the painting, sculpture, and decorative art of Holland's Golden Age (1600–1700). Works by Rembrandt, Vermeer, Frans Hals, and Jacob van Ruisdael are presented along with those of artists not as famous. Roughly chronological, the book contains a wealth of description about the country's vibrant 17th-century art scene.

Maybe you'd rather not be overwhelmed by Golden Age art but would still like an idea of what the heck was going on then. In this case, a good, affordable, and tolerably portable insight is afforded by **100 Memories: Paintings from the Golden Age**, by Ronald de Leeuw—the Rijksmuseum's former director.

For a personal insight into van Gogh's life and art, read Ken Wilkie's **The Van Gogh File: A Journey of Discovery**. What began as a routine magazine assignment in 1972 to coincide with the opening of the Van Gogh Museum became exactly what the book's subtitle indicates: A journey that continued long after the article was published. Wilkie followed van Gogh's trail through the Netherlands, Belgium, England, and France. Along the way, Wilkie met some of the last surviving people to have known or met the artist. In one of many dramatic discoveries, he finds an original van Gogh drawing while rummaging through a pile of old photographs in an English attic. Equally compelling are revelations from Vincent's private life, especially descriptions of his star-crossed search for love and family.

SOCIETY

You may find yourself chuckling over **The UnDutchables**, as you learn more about Dutch attitudes to home, money, children, transport, and much more. Are all Dutch people rude, their children undisciplined, and Dutch drivers abusive? Colin White and Laurie Boucke, Anglo-American expatriates who first published this paperback in 1989, have their tongues firmly in their cheeks throughout, choosing first to amuse and only second to inform.

CUISINE

Heleen Halverhout's postcard-size **The Netherlands Cookbook** (also published as *Dutch Cooking*), might be considered unambitious, but then the same is true of Dutch cooking—nourishing rather than rich, solid rather than subtle. What other cookbook would give recipes for boiled, mashed, and fried potatoes? Halverhout includes winter favorites like pea soup, *hachée* (beef and onion stew), and *hotch-potch* (alongside whimsical illustrations that play on Dutch stereotypes) and explains Dutch eating habits, devoting plenty of space to cakes and traditional desserts such as *Hague bluff* and *John-in-the-bag*.

PHOTOGRAPHY

The 143 pages of photographer Martin Kers's **Amsterdam** dazzle with a mix not only of subjects, but also of vantages and camera angles, panorama and detail. His graceful images depict subjects like morning mist over a canal, abandoned bicycle remains, kids playing soccer in Vondelpark, and explosions of merrymaking on Queen's Day. A master of composition, Kers infuses even demolished buildings and library books with visual magic, capturing the city's atmosphere and those in it as they pose, walk dogs, or mend a bike. The accompanying text is by Dutch poet Willem Wilmink.

Jacob Olie's evocative images of 19th-century Amsterdam have only recently been rescued from oblivion—5,000 of his negatives resurfaced in 1960. A schoolteacher with a passion for photography, Olie shot most of his pictures during the 1860s, when photography was in its infancy, and during the 1890s, when development in technique permitted him to break new ground. Though strictly documentary, the 79 black-and-white photographs in **De Verbeelding,** a small horizontal book, ooze nostalgia. They afford glimpses of recognition and show people going about their business in a semi-rural, unhurried city where canals haven't yet been filled, and where trams are powered by horses, carts by men, and trains by steam.

Films

Amsterdam-born director Paul Verhoeven is probably the best-known Dutch filmmaker—but that's not saying much, and Verhoeven's Hollywood movies, such as *Basic Instinct, RoboCop,* and *Starship Troopers,* don't contain much (if anything) inspired by his hometown. Closer to home is his wartime resistance drama *Soldier of Orange* (1977), starring Jeroen Krabbé and Rutger Hauer.

Among other Dutch World War II films that are worth seeking out is *The Girl With the Red Hair* (1981), starring Renée Soutendijk as controversial Resistance heroine and Communist Hannie Schaft (1920–45), who operated against the German occupiers in the Haarlem area and was executed in the dunes at Bloemendaal, west of Amsterdam, 3 weeks before the war's end. Wartime drama *The Assault* won the Oscar for best Foreign Language Film in 1986.

Chinese restaurant Nam Kee (p. 113) made a name for itself at the movies by playing a notable role in the red-hot romance flick *Oysters at Nam Kee's* (2002), starring Katja Schuurman. Set in Amsterdam and its seacoast resort Zandvoort, *Simon* (2004) hits most of the hot buttons in contemporary Dutch life—sex, drugs, homosexuality, euthanasia—in a moving story of a free-living individual confronted by his own mortality.

Amsterdam starred as the darkly atmospheric setting of the underworld thriller *Puppet on a Chain* (1972), based on the novel of the same name by Scottish writer Alistair MacLean, and which contained a memorable chase sequence on the canals. And the city played a supporting role in the James Bond movie *Diamonds Are Forever* (1971). *Girl With a Pearl Earring* (2003), starring Scarlett Johansson and Colin Firth, is an appropriately moody interpretation of the "back story" to the Vermeer painting, set and partly filmed in Delft.

Music

About the only well-known song in English to feature Amsterdam in a starring role is *Tulips From Amsterdam* (1956), which was originally written in German. This dose of concentrated saccharine keeps unlikely company with pot smoking, sex tourism, and gay parades as popular images of the city. Kids might likely be more familiar with *A Windmill in Old Amsterdam* (1965), which tells a heart-warming tale of "a little mouse with clogs on, going clip-clippety-clop on the stair." If your French is up to snuff, seek out passionate Belgian singer Jacques Brel's hymn to dissipated sailors, *Dans le Port d'Amsterdam* (1964), covered in English as *In the Port of Amsterdam* (1970) by David Bowie.

The city's homegrown music scene runs more to jazz, blues, and experimental electronic music, as can be experienced at the Muziekgebouw aan 't IJ, Bimhuis (p. 238), and a slew of clubs around town. For something a little more traditional, there are schmaltzy bars and clubs around Rembrandtplein and in the Jordaan, where you can sway to songs about stolen kisses behind the windmill, if you've a mind to—but of course they'll be in Dutch. For big international stars, head out to the Heineken Music Hall, and for bigger-than-big names, to the Amsterdam ArenA stadium, both of them in Amsterdam-Zuidoost (Southeast).

EATING IN AMSTERDAM

The concept of **"Dutch cuisine"** is generally considered a contradiction in terms. Dutch national dishes tend to be ungarnished, hearty, and wholesome—solid, stick-to-your-ribs stuff. A perfect example is *erwtensoep*, a thick pork-accented pea soup that provides inner warmth against cold Dutch winters and is filling enough to be a meal by itself. Similarly, *hutspot*, a potato, carrot, and onion "hotchpotch," or stew, is no-nonsense nourishment that becomes even more so with the addition of *klapstuk* (lean beef). *Hutspot* also has an intangible ingredient—a story behind its name that's based on historical fact: Spanish troops besieging Leiden in 1574 left behind a stew pot when a Dutch relief force surprised them in the middle of dinner, and this became a national symbol of freedom for Holland.

Seafood, as you might imagine in this traditionally seafaring country, is a big deal. Common options, depending on season, are Zeeland oysters and mussels (*Zeeuwse oesters* and *Zeeuwse mosselen*), and herring pickled or "new"—fresh from the North Sea and eaten raw. In fact, if you happen to be in Holland for the beginning of the herring season in June, interrupt your sidewalk strolls for a "green" (raw) herring with onions from a fish stall, or *haringhuis*. Look for signs that say HOLLANDSE NIEUWE (HOLLAND'S NEW). Great excitement surrounds the season's first catch, part of which goes to the queen and the rest to restaurateurs amid spirited competition. At fish stalls, you can also get snacks of baked fish, smoked eel, and seafood salads, taken on the run.

Dutch explorers and traders brought back recipes and exotic spices—and the popular **Indonesian** *rijsttafel* (rice table), a feast of 15 to 30 small portions of different dishes eaten with plain rice, has been a national favorite since the 17th century (see "Secrets of the Rijsttafel," in chapter 6). If you've never experienced this minifeast, it should definitely be on your "must-eat" list for Holland. Should you part company with the Dutch and "their" Indonesian food, you'll find the cuisines of China, France, Greece, India, Italy, Japan, Spain, Turkey, Yugoslavia, and other nations.

At the top of the restaurant scale are those posh dining rooms affiliated with the prestigious **Alliance Gastronomique Néerlandaise.** They're likely to be elegant and sophisticated or atmospherically old-world and quaint. They will certainly be expensive. Then there are the numerous moderately priced restaurants and little **brown cafes.** Dutch families gravitate to the restaurants, while brown cafes are cozy social centers with simple but tasty food, often served outside on sidewalk tables. **Sidewalk vendors,** with fresh herring, the ubiquitous *broodjes* (sandwiches), and other light specialties, are as popular as the brown cafes.

For more info on dining in Amsterdam, see chapter 6.

Terminology

The first step in getting to know Dutch gastronomy is to remember that in Holland, *entrees* are appetizers, also known as *voorgerechten,* and main courses, *hoofdgerechten,* are listed separately as *vis* (fish) or *vlees* (meat), and, in some restaurants, as *dagschotel* (dish of the day). Other courses on Dutch menus include *soepen* (soups), *warme* or *koude voorgerechten* (warm or cold appetizers), *groenten* (vegetables), *salade* (salad), *vruchten* (fruits), *nagerechten* (desserts), *dranken* (beverages), and *wijn* (wine).

The next step is to understand that Dutch is a language of compound words, and just as Leiden Street becomes Leidsestraat—one word for two ideas—the same goes for menus: Beef steak becomes *biefstuk,* pork chop becomes *varkenskotelet,* and so on.

Similarly, you'll find listings for *gehakte biefstuk* (chopped beef) or *gebakken worst* (fried sausage). Look for the following key words as you scan menus:

- For modes of preparation: *gekookt* or *gekookte* (boiled), *gebakken* (fried), *gebraden* (roast or fried), *geroosterd* (toasted or grilled), *gerookte* (smoked).
- For meat cooked to your taste: *niet doorbakken* (rare), *half doorbakken* (medium), *goed doorbakken* (well-done).
- For cuts of meat: *-stuk* (steak or, literally, piece), *-kotelet* or *-kotelette* (cutlet).

Menu Choices

BREAKFAST

See "Hotel Orientation," in chapter 5.

LUNCH & SNACK SPECIALTIES

Below are clarifications of dishes you may see on lunch menus:

BAMI/NASI GORENG & NASI RAMES   Miniature versions of an Indonesian *rijsttafel* (see chapter 6); they come in a bowl on either noodles or rice, with spiced meat and possibly a fried egg or satay (a grilled kabob) on top.

BITTERBALLEN   Fried potato balls, or croquettes, that usually come quite spicy.

BROODJES   Small sandwiches on round buttered rolls made with ham, cheese, roast beef, salami, or other fillings. They're often ordered in pairs and eaten standing up or perched at a narrow counter in a *broodjeszaak,* or sandwich shop.

ERWTENSOEP   This pea soup is thick, creamy, and chock-full of ham, carrots, and potatoes—a meal by itself. (This is a winter dish, so it may be hard to find in summer.)

KROKETTEN   Fried croquettes of meat, shrimps, or cheese that may be gooey inside. They're at their best when served piping hot with a blob of mustard for dunking.

NIEUWE HARING   Chasing herring is what got this city started, and Amsterdam folk are still in hot pursuit. Vendors sell new herring—fresh-caught fish that's eaten whole (minus the head and the tail) with minced onion, or chopped if you're squeamish—at stands all over town during summer; you can also eat them pickled as *maatjes*.

PANNENKOEKEN & POFFERTJES   These Dutch pancakes are the equivalent of French crepes, and they're served topped with confectioners' sugar, jam (jelly), syrup, hot apples, or—typically Dutch—hot ginger sauce. Less common are *pannenkoeken* with meat. *Poffertjes* are small fried-pancake "puffs" coated with confectioners' sugar and filled with syrup or liqueur.

SAUCIJZENBROODJE   A hot dog, except the bun's made of flaky pastry and the hot dog is a spicy Dutch *worst*, or sausage.

TOSTIS   Grilled ham-and-cheese sandwiches.

UITSMIJTER   An open-faced sandwich consisting of a buttered slice of bread (or two) topped with cold cuts and fried eggs—tasty, inexpensive, and a good lunch choice. (The name, incidentally, is the same for "bouncer," the burly doorman at nightclubs.)

VLAMMETJES ("LITTLE FLAMES")   These belong to the same family of *borrelhapjes* (drinking snacks) as *bitterballen* (see above), but are more like diminutive spring rolls which, like Napoleon, make up in fiery aggression for what they lack in size.

DINNER SPECIALTIES

With the exception of one excellent treat—the Indonesian *rijsttafel* (see chapter 6)—the Dutch may seem to be less inventive with dinner specialties than they are with lunch and snacks. This is partly because many traditional Dutch dishes closely resemble dishes popular elsewhere in Europe and the U.S. But mostly it's due to Holland's ongoing, ever-growing love affair with French cuisine. Here, however, are a few typical Dutch options you may encounter, particularly in winter, when real Dutch cooking can be best appreciated:

ASPERGES   Asparagus. The thick, white cultivated variety. Most of it comes from Limburg, so it's marketed as "the white gold of Limburg"—but most folks just call it asparagus.

CAPUCIJNERS MET SPEK   Marrow beans with bacon.

GEMBER MET SLAGROOM   A sweet-and-sour dessert of tangy, fresh ginger slices topped with whipped cream.

GEROOKTE PALING   Smoked eel (most of which come from the IJsselmeer—though many are now imported). A typically Dutch appetizer.

HAZENPEPER   Jugged hare.

HUTSPOT   A stew made of beef ribs, carrots, onions, and potatoes, often mashed together. This is a dish with historic significance, particularly for the people of Leiden: It's the Dutch version of the stew found in the boiling pots left behind after the Spaniards were evicted after a long siege during the Eighty Years' War.

KRABBETJES   Dutch spareribs, usually beef rather than pork.

MOSSELEN   Mussels, raised in the clean waters of Zeeland's Oosterschelde (Eastern Scheldt) estuary. Mussel season begins in mid-August with great fanfare (it runs until Apr), and the first crop is eagerly awaited. The mollusks are often steamed and served in a bit of white-wine-and-vegetable stock.

ROLPENS   Homemade sausage stuffed with meat and spices.

STAMPOT   Cabbage with smoked sausage.

ZUURKOOL MET SPEK EN WORST   Sauerkraut with bacon and sausage.

PLANNING YOUR TRIP TO AMSTERDAM

3

Amsterdam isn't hard to get to grips with even if you arrive there cold (in the preparedness sense). The local tourist organization, **VVV Amsterdam,** prides itself on being able to answer any conceivable travel question any conceivable traveler might have, excepting only those who are illegal or of doubtful moral worth. The city is foreign, of course, but not impossibly so; many Dutch speak English.

To really put your best foot forward, you'll want to know how much the essentials will cost; how you're going to get there; what documents, clothing, and other travel necessities you should bring; and when you should go to best take advantage of special events. This chapter provides the information you need to plan your trip before leaving home.

For additional help in planning your trip and for more on-the-ground resources in Amsterdam, please turn to chapter 12, "Fast Facts," on p. 289.

WHEN TO GO

"In season" in Amsterdam means mid-April to mid-October. The tourist season peaks in July and August, when the weather's at its finest. Climate, however, is never really extreme at any time of year; if you favor off-season travel, you'll find the city every bit as attractive during these months. Not only are hotels and restaurants cheaper and less crowded (with more relaxed and personalized service), but some very appealing events also take place. The bulb fields near Amsterdam, for example, burst with color from April to mid-May.

The Weather

Summertime temperatures in Amsterdam don't often rise above 75°F (24°C), making for a pleasant, balmy climate.. Summertime temperatures don't often rise above 75°F (24°C), making for a pleasant, balmy climate. July and August are the best months for in-line skating in Vondelpark, soaking up rays on cafe terraces, dining alfresco in the evening, and going topless on the beach at Zandvoort. September usually has a few weeks of fine late-summer weather.

Mean precipitation—and the precipitation in Holland can be pretty mean—is high enough that rain shouldn't come as a surprise. Although the temperature rarely dips below freezing in winter, remember that Amsterdam and much of Holland is below sea level, making fog, mist, and dampness your too-frequent companions. This damp chill often seems to cut to the bone, so in colder months, layer yourself in Gore-Tex or something similar. There are, however, plenty of bright but cold days in winter, and if the temperature falls far enough, canals, rivers, and lakes freeze to become sparkling highways for skaters throughout the city and the surrounding countryside. Throughout the year, some rain can be expected. Average annual rainfall is 63½ cm (25 in.). Most of it falls November through January, though substantial showers can occur year-round.

Amsterdam's Average Monthly Temperature & Days of Rain

	JAN	FEB	MAR	APR	MAY	JUNE	JULY	AUG	SEPT	OCT	NOV	DEC
Temp. (°F)	38	37	43	47	54	59	62	62	58	51	44	40
Temp. (°C)	3	3	6	8	12	15	17	17	14	11	7	4
Days of rain	21	17	19	20	19	17	20	20	19	20	22	23

The Best Times to Go

There's no worst time to visit Amsterdam: The city provides year-round stimulation to the brain's pleasure center. High season is the spring tulip season (early Apr to mid-May), and school vacations are in July and August. The city is very busy at both times, which means hotel rooms are hard to find and bargains don't exist at all (but who wants to tiptoe through the fallow tulip fields in November, or sit on a sidewalk cafe terrace in a snowstorm?). If you're planning to travel during high season, book several months in advance. Summer is also the best time for cycling, which is an essential Dutch experience; try a canal bike if you're fearful about going on the roads.

In winter, room rates are generally cheaper, and cafes and restaurants are less crowded and feel more genuine. You won't find such a big line to get into the Anne Frankhuis (though a line will still exist), you'll be able to stand longer in front of Rembrandt's *The Night Watch* and your favorite Van Gogh, and you might get a chance to go skating on the canals. You also get a better view of the canals, because the trees bordering them shed their screens of leaves in winter. As an added bonus, the lights from all those canalside windows, whose curtains never close, glow with Japanese-lantern charm on the inky surface.

Impressions

I call to mind a winter landscape in Amsterdam—a flat foreground of waste land, with here and there stacks of timber, like the huts of a camp of some very miserable tribe; the long stretch of the Handelskade; cold, stone-faced quays, with the snow-sprinkled ground and the hard, frozen water of the canal, in which were set ships one behind another with their frosty mooring-ropes hanging slack and their decks idle and deserted . . .
—Joseph Conrad, *The Mirror of the Sea* (1906)

Holidays

A Dutch holiday can add a festive note to your trip, particularly if it involves a parade or special observance. But expect banks, government offices, shops, and many museums to be closed, and public transportation to operate on Sunday schedules for the following holidays: **New Year's Day, Good Friday, Easter Sunday, Easter Monday, *Koninginnedag*** (Queen's Day: Queen Beatrix's official birthday is Apr 30), **Ascension Day** (Thurs, 40 days after Easter), **Pentecost Sunday** (7th Sun after Easter), *Pinksteren* (Pentecost Mon), **Christmas Day,** and **December 26.**

In addition, there are two World War II "Remembrance Days," neither of which is an official holiday, though some establishments close: *Herdenkingsdag* (May 4) honors all those who died in the war; *Bevrijdingsdag* (May 5) celebrates the Liberation.

Amsterdam Calendar of Events

For an exhaustive list of events beyond those given here, check http://events.frommers.com, where you'll find a searchable, up-to-the-minute roster of what's happening in cities all over the world. The websites of Amsterdam's tourist organization, **VVV Amsterdam** (www.iamsterdam.nl), and of the **Netherlands Board of Tourism & Conventions** (www.holland.com), have more information.

JANUARY

New Year, throughout the city center, but mostly at the Dam and Nieuwmarkt. This celebration is wild and not always wonderful. Youthful spirits celebrate the transition from *Oudejaarsavond* (New Year's Eve) to the new year with firecrackers, which they cheerfully—if not drunkenly—throw at the feet of passersby. This keeps hospital emergency rooms busy. January 1.

International Film Festival Rotterdam. More than 300 indie films are screened at theaters around town. Contact ℂ **010/890-9090;** www.filmfestivalrotterdam.com. January 26 to February 6, 2011; similar dates in 2012.

FEBRUARY

Chinese New Year. Celebrations usually take place over one day and centre around Chinatown and the Zeedijk. Expect dragon dances, fireworks and special events. Visit www.iamamsterdam.com for details of this year's event.

MARCH

Windmill Days, Zaanse Schans. All five working windmills (out of eight windmills in total) are open to the public at this re-created old village and open-air museum in the Zanstreek, just north of Amsterdam. Contact **Zaanse Schans** (ℂ **075/681-0000;** www.zaanseschans.nl). March to October.

Stille Omgang. This "silent procession" along Kalverstraat is walked by Catholics every year to celebrate the "Miracle of the Host"—this refers to a Roman Catholic communion wafer that is said to have resisted all attempts to burn it—which occurred in 1345. The procession begins at the Royal Palace on the Dam and goes from midnight to 2:30am. Contact the **Gezelschap voor de Stille Omgang** (www.stille-omgang.nl). March 19, 2011; March 17, 2012.

Opening of Keukenhof Gardens, Lisse. The greatest flower show on earth blooms with spectacular displays of tulips and narcissi, daffodils and hyacinths, bluebells, crocuses, lilies, amaryllis, and many others at this 32-hectare (80-acre) garden in the heart of the bulb country. There's said to be nearly eight million flowers, but who's counting? Contact **Keukenhof** (ℂ **0252/465-555;** www.keukenhof.nl). March 24 to May 20, 2011; similar dates in 2012.

APRIL

National Museum Weekend. A weekend during which most museums in Amsterdam and many throughout the Netherlands offer free or reduced admission, and have special exhibits. Contact **Museumweekend** (ℂ **020/551-2932;** www.museumweekend.nl). April 2 and 3, 2011; similar dates in 2012.

Bloemencorso van de Bollenstreek (Bulb District Flower Parade). Floats keyed to a different floral theme each year parade from Noordwijk, through Sassenheim, Lisse, and Bennebroek, to Haarlem. Contact **Bloemencorso Bollenstreek** (📞 **0252/428-237;** www.bloemencorso-bollenstreek.nl). April 16, 2011; April 21, 2012.

Koninginnedag (Queen's Day). This nationwide holiday for the House of Orange is vigorously celebrated in Amsterdam with a gigantic dawn-to-dawn street carnival, which packs the city center so densely that it's virtually impossible to move. A citywide street market features masses of stalls, run by everyone from kids selling old toys to professional market folk in town to make a killing. Orange ribbons, orange hair, and orange-painted faces are everywhere, as are Dutch flags. Street music and theater combine with probably too much drinking, but Koninginnedag remains a good-natured, boisterous affair. *Tip:* Wear something orange, even if it's just suspenders or a ribbon in your hair. Contact **VVV Amsterdam** (📞 **0900/400-4040;** www.iamsterdam.nl). Gay and lesbian celebrations convene around the city's main gay areas and the Homomonument (p. 156). Expect a variety of entertainment, local gay and lesbian society stall, and food and drink options. April 30.

MAY

Herdenkingsdag (Memorial Day). Countrywide observance honoring World War II victims. Queen Beatrix places a wreath at the Nationaal Monument on the Dam, and 2 minutes of silence begin at 8pm. Contact **VVV Amsterdam** (📞 **0900/400-4040;** www.iamsterdam.nl). May 4.

Bevrijdingsdag (Liberation Day). This citywide event is a less frenetic version of Koninginnedag (see "April," above). It recalls the country's liberation from Nazi occupation at the end of World War II and is celebrated on the anniversary of the German forces' surrender in the Netherlands. Canadian troops made it into the city first (2 days later), so Canadian flags are popular accessories. More street markets, music, and theater.

Contact **VVV Amsterdam** (📞 **0900/400-4040;** www.iamsterdam.nl). Gay and lesbian participation includes stage performances, from belly-dancing to drag, stalls publicizing various gay and lesbian organizations, and food and drink. May 5.

National Windmill Day. Around two-thirds of the country's almost 1,000 windmills—including Amsterdam's eight—spin their sails (if they have them) and a solid number are open to the public. Contact **De Hollandsche Molen** (📞 **020/623-8703;** www.molens.nl). Second weekend in May: May 14–15, 2011; May 12–13, 2012.

JUNE

Vlaggetjesdag (Flag Day), Scheveningen. The fishing fleet opens the herring season with a race to bring the first *Hollandse Nieuwe* herring back to port (the first barrel is auctioned for charity). Some 200,000 people pour into town for the celebrations, and Dutch flags fly everywhere. Contact **Stichting Vlaggetjesdag Scheveningen** (📞 **070/345-3267;** www.vlaggetjesdag. com). June 11, 2011 (unconfirmed, due to a possible conflict of events; check website); June 9, 2012.

Holland Festival, Amsterdam, The Hague, Rotterdam, and Utrecht. Each year, these four cities join forces to present a cultural buffet of music, opera, theater, film, and dance. The schedule includes all the major Dutch companies, plus visiting companies and soloists from around the globe. Contact **Holland Festival** (📞 **020/788-2100;** www.hollandfestival.nl). Throughout June.

Amsterdam Roots Festival. This festival features music and dance from around the world, along with workshops, films, and exhibits in various venues. One part is the open-air **Oosterpark Festival,** a multicultural feast of song and dance held at Oosterpark in Amsterdam-Oost (East). Contact **Amsterdam Roots Festival** (📞 **020/531-8181;** www.amsterdamroots.nl). June 16 to June 19, 2011; similar dates in 2012.

Open Gardens Days. If you wonder what the fancy gardens behind the gables of some of the city's houses-turned-museums look like, this is your chance to find out. Some of the best are open to the public for 3 days. Go to the website of **Grachten Musea** (*☎* **020/ 320-3660;** www.grachtenmusea.nl). Third week in June.

From June to mid-August, catch a performance at the **Vondelpark Open-Air Theater.** Everything goes here: theater, all kinds of music (including full-scale classical concerts by the famed Royal Concertgebouw Orchestra), dance, and even operettas. Contact **Vondelpark Openluchttheater** (*☎* **020/ 428-3360;** www.openluchttheater.nl).

JULY

Over Het IJ Festival. Performers stage avant-garde theater, music, and dance in Amsterdam-Noord, beside the IJ channel, at the old NDSM Wharf, TT Neveritaweg 15. Contact **Over Het IJ Festival** (*☎* **020/492-2229;** www.overhetij.nl). July 7 to July 17, 2011; July 5 to July 15, 2012.

North Sea Jazz Festival, Ahoy, Rotterdam. One of the world's leading gatherings of top international jazz and blues musicians unfolds over 3 concert-packed days at the city's giant Ahoy venue. Last-minute tickets are scarce, so book as far ahead as possible. Contact **North Sea Jazz Festival** (*☎* **0900/ 300-1250** in Holland, or *☎* 31-10/591-9000 from outside Holland; www.northseajazz. com). Mid-July.

AUGUST

Amsterdam Gay Pride. This is a big event in Europe's most gay-friendly city. 150,000 people turn out to watch the highlight: Boat Parade's display of 100 or so outrageously decorated boats cruising the canals. In addition, there are street discos and open-air theater performances, a sports program, and a film festival. Go to the website of **Amsterdam Gay Pride** (www.amsterdam gaypride.nl) for info. First weekend in August: August 4 to August 7, 2011 (Canal Parade Aug 6); similar dates in 2012. Dates to be confirmed; check with website.

Grachten Festival (Canal Festival). This 5-day classical music festival, with a different theme each year, plays at various intimate and elegant venues along the canals and at the Muziekgebouw aan 't IJ. There's always a performance or two designed for children. Part of the festival is the exuberant Prinsengracht Concert (see below), which plays on a pontoon in front of the Hotel Pulitzer (p. 86). Contact **Stichting Grachtenfestival** (*☎* 020/421-4542; www.grachtenfestival. nl). August 13 to August 21, 2011; similar dates in 2012.

Prinsengracht Concert. Chamber music floats up in the evening from an open pontoon moored in front of the Hotel Pulitzer, at Prinsengracht 315–331 (see "The Canal Belt," in chapter 5). Crowds pile in by boat, by bike, and on foot to take it in, jamming up the canal and both banks of the canal. The free concert, the highlight and culmination of the Grachten Festival (see above), usually begins at 9:30pm and lasts an hour. If it rains, there's an alternative indoor venue, which is announced at the time of the concert. Contact **Stichting Grachtenfestival** (*☎* 020/421-4542; www.grachtenfestival. nl). August 21, 2011; similar date in 2012.

Uitmarkt. Amsterdam previews the soon-to-open cultural season with this superb 3-day "open information market," which runs alongside free performances at theaters, concert halls, and impromptu outdoor venues. Professional and amateur groups present shows that run the gamut of music, opera, dance, theater, and cabaret. Visit the website of **Uitmarkt** (www.amsterdam suitburo.nl/uitmarkt) for info. Usually the last weekend in August, but dates are not confirmed until the preceding March.

SEPTEMBER

Jordaan Festival, Westermarkt. This loosely organized festival in the trendy Jordaan neighborhood features various genres of Dutch music played in front of the **Westerkerk** (p. 162). Contact **Stichting Jordaan Festival** (www.jordaanfestival.nl). Mid-September.

Open Monumentendag. A chance to see countrywide historical buildings and monuments usually not open to the public—and to get in free. Contact **Vereniging Open**

Monumentendag (📞 020/422-2118; www.openmonumentendag.nl). Second Saturday and Sunday in September: September 10 and 11, 2011; September 8 and 9, 2012.

Dam tot Damloop (Dam to Dam Run). The country's most popular running event starts at the Dam in the center of Amsterdam, heads out of town through the IJ Tunnel to the center of Zaandam, and back again, for a distance of 16km (10 miles). Contact **Dam tot Damloop** (📞 072/533-8136; www.damloop.nl). Third Sunday in September.

OCTOBER

Leidens Ontzet (Relief of Leiden). These processions and festivities commemorate the defeat of the 1574 Spanish siege that came close to starving Leiden into submission. Citizens distribute *haring en witte brood* (herring and white bread), just as the pirate-like band of Sea Beggars did during the siege, helping to drive the Spaniards away. Contact **VVV Leiden** (📞 071/516-6000; www.vvvleiden.nl). October 3 (Oct 4 when the 3rd is a Sun).

International Horti Fair, Amsterdam. The largest exhibit of autumn-blooming flowers in the Netherlands takes place at the RAI convention center. Contact **Horti Fair** (📞 0297/344-033; www.hortifair.nl). November 1 to 4, 2011; October 30 to November 2, 2012.

Leather Pride is a growing cluster of parties and other events for gays who are into a leather lifestyle. Contact **Leather Pride**

Nederland (📞 020/422-3737; www.leatherpride.nl). Last weekend of October.

NOVEMBER

Sinterklaas Arrives. Holland's equivalent of Santa Claus (St. Nicholas) launches the Christmas season; he arrives by boat at the Centraal Station pier and is accompanied by black-painted assistants, called *Zwarte Pieten* (Black Petes), who hand out sweets to kids. Saint Nick goes in stately procession through Amsterdam before getting to the Dam, where the mayor hands him the keys to the city. Contact **VVV Amsterdam** (📞 0900/400-4040; www.iamsterdam.nl). Third Saturday in November: November 19, 2011, and November 17, 2012.

Crossing Border Festival, Den Haag (The Hague). This 5-day festival in The Hague combines literature, poetry, film, and music. Contact **Crossing Border** (📞 070/346-2355; www.crossingborder.nl). November 17 to 20, 2011; November 22–25, 2012 (unconfirmed; check website).

DECEMBER

Sinterklaas. Saint Nicholas's Eve is the traditional day in Holland for exchanging Christmas gifts. Join Dutch friends or a Dutch family if possible. December 5.

World Christmas Circus. The best acts from the world's circuses go into action under the big top at Koninklijk Theater Carré. Contact **Carré** (📞 020/622-5225; www.theatercarre.nl). December 16, 2010, to January 2, 2011; similar dates in 2011/2012.

WHAT TO pack

Some pointers on being prepared for Amsterdam's often unpredictable weather: First, invest in a fold-up umbrella and hope you never have to use it; likewise, carry a raincoat (with a wool liner for winter). Second, pack a sweater or two (even in July) and be prepared to layer clothing at any time of year. Don't worry: You're allowed to leave space for T-shirts, skimpy tops, and sneakers.

If you own a pair of in-line skates or roller skates, or even one of those dinky self-propelled scooter things, consider bringing them along. You can go around in the bicycle lanes while saving money and staying fit.

ENTRY REQUIREMENTS

Passports & Visas

Citizens of the U.S., Canada, the European Union, Australia, and New Zealand need only a valid passport if visiting the Netherlands for less than 3 months—in the case of visitors who reside in most other E.U. countries, a valid national identity card is sufficient. Citizens of other countries should be sure to check travel regulations before leaving. For them, a valid passport is always required, and in addition, citizens of some countries require a visa. You can get information on these requirements from the Dutch embassy or consulate in your country of birth or residence. A list of these is available from the website of the Ministry of Foreign Affairs in The Hague: **www.minbuza.nl**.

For information on obtaining a passport and a visa, please visit "Fast Facts," on p. 289.

It is advised to always have at least one or two consecutive blank pages in your passport to allow space for visas and stamps that need to appear together. It is also important to note when your passport expires. Many countries require your passport to have at least 6 months left before its expiration in order to allow you into the destination.

Customs

WHAT YOU CAN BRING INTO THE NETHERLANDS

Visitors 17 years and older arriving from countries that are not members of the European Union (E.U.) may bring in duty-free 200 cigarettes or 100 cigarillos or 50 cigars or 250 grams (9 oz.) of tobacco; 1 liter of liquor or 2 liters of sparkling wine or fortified wine (such as port or sherry), and 2 liters of wine; 50 grams (1¾ oz.) of perfume, and 0.25 liters of eau de toilette; 500 grams (18 oz.) of coffee or 200 grams (7 oz.) of coffee extracts or coffee essences; and 100 grams of tea or 40 grams (1½ oz.) of tea extracts or tea essences. Import of most other goods is unlimited, so long as import duty is paid on all dutiable goods above a combined value of 430€; in some circumstances, including entering the European Union by land), this amount is reduced to 300€. Forbidden products include firearms, counterfeit goods, banned narcotic substances, protected animals and plants, and products made from these.

Duty-free shopping has been abolished in the E.U. Therefore, standard allowances do not apply to goods bought in another E.U. country and brought into the Netherlands. In essence, there is no limit on what travelers arriving from an E.U. country can take into the Netherlands, as long as the items are for personal use (this includes gifts), and you have already paid the necessary duty and tax. However, the law sets out guidance levels. If you bring in more than the following, you may be asked to prove that the goods are for your own use: 800 cigarettes, 400 cigars or cigarillos, and 1 kilogram (2⅕ lb.) of smoking tobacco; 10 liters of hard liquor (spirits), 90 liters of wine, 20 liters of fortified wine (such as port or sherry), and 110 liters of beer.

There are no limitations on the amount of foreign currency you can bring into the country.

For more information in English, visit the Netherlands Customs website: **www.douane.nl**.

WHAT YOU CAN TAKE HOME FROM AMSTERDAM

You'll likely get no more than a raised eyebrow back home for schlepping in a pair of brightly colored souvenir clogs, but bulbs, plants, and flowers might not be so welcome. Some countries require a phyto-sanitary certificate, which many Dutch suppliers provide. (Note that the rules from the information sources referred to below also apply to legal residents of the countries concerned, whether they are citizens or not.)

For information on what you're allowed to bring home, contact one of the following agencies:

U.S. Citizens: U.S. Customs & Border Protection (CBP), 1300 Pennsylvania Ave. NW, Washington, DC 20229 (✆ **877/287-8667;** www.cbp.gov).

Canadian Citizens: Canada Border Services Agency, Ottawa, Ontario K1A 0L8 (✆ **800/461-9999** in Canada, or ✆ 204/983-3500; www.cbsa-asfc.gc.ca).

U.K. Citizens: HM Customs & Excise, Crownhill Court, Tailyour Road, Plymouth PL6 5BZ (✆ **0845/010-9000;** from outside the U.K., ✆ 020/8929-0152; www.hmce.gov.uk).

Irish Citizens: Revenue Customs Division, St. Conlon's Road, Nenagh, Co. Tipperary (✆ **1890/666333;** from outside the Republic of Ireland, ✆ 067/63400; www.revenue.ie).

Australian Citizens: Australian Customs Service, Customs House, 5 Constitution Avenue, Canberra City, ACT 2601 (✆ **1300/363-263;** from outside Australia, ✆ 612/6275-6666; www.customs.gov.au).

New Zealand Citizens: New Zealand Customs, The Customhouse, 17–21 Whitmore St., Box 2218, Wellington 6140 (✆ **04/473-6099** or ✆ 0800/428-786; www.customs.govt.nz).

Medical Requirements

No health or vaccination certificates are required for the Netherlands. You won't need travel shots either, but if you have a chronic illness, consult your doctor before your departure. Pack important prescription medications in your carry-on baggage, and carry them in their original containers, with pharmacy labels—otherwise they won't make it through airport security. Carry the generic name of prescription medicines, in case local pharmacists are unfamiliar with the brand name. Don't forget an extra pair of contact lenses or prescription eyeglasses. Also, you might want to visit **www.tsa.com** for up-to-date regulations on what is and isn't permissible to pack in carry-on baggage.

GETTING THERE & GETTING AROUND

Getting to Amsterdam

Amsterdam can be reached from around the world by plane, by boat from Britain, and by train, bus, and car from around Europe.

BY PLANE

Amsterdam Airport Schiphol (✆ **0900/0141** from inside Holland, or ✆ 31-20/794-0800 from outside; www.schiphol.nl; airport code: AMS), 13km (8 miles) southwest of the city center, is not only the airport of Amsterdam, but is also the primary airport of the Netherlands. Major international airlines fly here, and the airport handles just about all of the country's international arrivals and departures. Schiphol (pronounced *skhip*-ol) is 4.5m (15 ft.) below sea level. Where the runway is now was once a lake with access to the sea—the Dutch and Spanish fought a naval battle here in 1573.

To find out which airlines travel to Amsterdam, please see "Airline Websites," p. 294.

Getting Into Town from the Airport

Netherlands Railways (NS) (℗ **0900/9292;** www.ns.nl) trains for Amsterdam Centraal Station depart from Schiphol Station, downstairs from Schiphol Plaza, and stop at De Lelylaan and De Vlugtlaan stations in western Amsterdam along the way. Frequency ranges from six trains an hour at peak times to one an hour at night. The one-way fare to Centraal Station is 3.80€ in second class or 6.50€ in first class; the trip takes about 20 minutes.

An alternative rail route serves both Amsterdam Zuid station and Amsterdam RAI station (at the RAI Convention Center). Be sure to check which route goes closest to your hotel (including any tram or bus interchange). If you're staying at a hotel near Leidseplein, Rembrandtplein, in the Museum Quarter, or in Amsterdam-Zuid (South), this route may be better for you than going to Centraal Station. The one-way fare to Amsterdam Zuid is 2.50€ in second class or 4.30€ in first class; the ride takes 8 minutes; the fare to Amsterdam RAI is the same, and the ride takes 12 minutes. From Amsterdam Zuid, take tram no. 5 for Leidseplein and the Museum Quarter; from Amsterdam RAI, take tram no. 4 for Rembrandtplein.

The **Connexxion Hotel Shuttle** (℗ **038/339-4741;** www.schipholhotelshuttle. nl) runs daily every 10 to 30 minutes from 6am to 9pm, between the airport and some 100 Amsterdam hotels. Reservations aren't necessary, and buses depart from in front of Schiphol Plaza. Tickets can be procured from the Connexxion desk inside Schiphol Plaza or on board from the driver (or, for the return journey, from your hotel). The fare is 15€ one-way and 25€ round-trip; children ages 4 to 14 pay half the adult fare. It takes only 15 minutes from the airport to the Bilderberg Garden Hotel, but almost an hour to the NH Barbizon Palace; going the opposite direction, the timing's reversed. Some hotels have their own shuttle services.

Connexxion line bus service from Schiphol is likely to be less useful for arriving travelers, since line buses are slower than both the train and the Connexxion hotel shuttle. The most useful line, no. 370, departs half-hourly to hourly Monday to Friday, and hourly on Saturdays, Sundays, and holidays from in front of Schiphol Plaza; it goes to Amsterdam's Leidseplein by way of Amsterdam Zuid (South) Station. Connexxion buses also serve other points; comprehensive information is available on the Connexxion website (**www.connexxion.nl**) and at bus stops outside Schiphol Plaza.

Taxis are expensive, but they're the preferred choice if your luggage is burdensome or if there are multiple people to share the cost. You'll find taxis waiting at the **Schiphol Taxi** (℗ **0900/900-6666;** www.schipholtaxi.nl) stands in front of Schiphol Plaza. All taxis from the airport are metered. Expect to pay around 40€ to the center of Amsterdam. Remember, a service charge is already included in the fare.

BY CAR

All of the major international car rental agencies have desks at the airport and offices downtown: **Avis** (℗ **0900/235-2847;** www.avis.nl); **Budget** (℗ **0900/1576;** www.budget.nl); **Europcar** (℗ **0900/0540;** www.europcar.nl); and **Hertz** (℗ **020/201-3512;** www.hertz.nl). Rates vary among companies, as do types of cars, rental plans, and extras (some companies, for example, have free car delivery to your hotel). Rates begin at around 50€ a day for a no-frills, subcompact auto with stick shift and unlimited mileage. A fully equipped luxury car like a BMW can cost as much as 200€ per day. If your car breaks down, call the national auto club, **ANWB Wegenwacht** (℗ **088/269-2888;** www.anwb.nl).

To drive in Holland, drivers need only produce a valid driver's license from their home country. The Netherlands is crisscrossed by a network of major international highways. European expressways E19, E35, E231, and E22 converge on Amsterdam from France and Belgium to the south and from Germany to the north and east. These roads also have Dutch designations; as you approach Amsterdam they become, respectively: A4, A2, A1, and A7. The city's ring road (beltway) is A10. Traffic is invariably heavy—but distances between destinations are relatively short, road conditions are generally excellent, service stations are plentiful, and highways are plainly signposted.

To drive from Britain to Amsterdam, use the efficient **Le Shuttle** (www.eurotunnel. com) automobile transporter through the Channel Tunnel from Folkestone, England, to Calais, France (a 35-min. trip), and drive up from there through Belgium and Holland. Le Shuttle has departures every 15 minutes at peak times, every 30 minutes at times of average demand, and hourly at night. For information and reservations, call ℂ **08443/35-35-35** in Britain, ℂ **0810/63-03-04** in France, or ℂ **0900/504-0540** in Holland. Reserving in advance makes sense at the busiest times, but the system is so fast, frequent, and simple that you may prefer to retain travel flexibility by just showing up, buying your ticket, waiting in line for a short while, and then driving aboard.

The best way to experience most European cities is to drive to the city, park your car, and never touch it again until you leave. In Amsterdam, it's smart not to even bring a car (for reasons, see the "By Car" section under "Getting Around," below).

BY TRAIN

Rail service to Amsterdam from elsewhere in Europe is frequent and fast. International trains arrive at Centraal Station from Brussels, Paris, Berlin, Cologne, and some cities in Austria, Switzerland, Italy, and Eastern Europe.

Nederlandse Spoorwegen (**Netherlands Railways;** ℂ **0900/9292;** www.ns.nl) trains arrive in Amsterdam from towns and cities around Holland. Service is frequent and trains are modern, clean, and punctual. For international trains, call ℂ **0900/9296.**

Schedule and fare information about travel by train and other public transportation (*openbaar vervoer*) in the Netherlands is available by calling ℂ **0900/9292,** or visiting **www.9292ov.nl**.

Britain is connected to mainland Europe via the **Channel Tunnel** (nicknamed "The Chunnel"). On **Eurostar**'s (www.eurostar.com) high-speed train (top speed 300kmph/186 mph), travel time between St. Pancras International, London and Brussels Midi Station in Belgium (the closest connecting point for Amsterdam) is around 2 hours. For Eurostar reservations, call ℂ **08432/186-186** in Britain.

The burgundy-colored **Thalys** (www.thalys.com) high-speed train, with a top speed of 300kmph (186 mph), connects Paris, Brussels, and Cologne to Amsterdam. Travel time from Paris to Amsterdam is 4 hours, 10 minutes; from Brussels, it's 1 hour, 45 minutes. For Thalys information and reservations in France, call ℂ **3635;** in Belgium, ℂ **070/79-79-79;** in Germany, ℂ **11861;** and in Holland, ℂ **0900/9296.** In addition, tickets are available from main railway stations and travel agents.

BY BUS

International buses (sometimes known in Europe as "coaches"), especially those of Eurolines (www.eurolines.com), arrive at the bus terminal outside **Amstel rail station** (Metro: Amstel) in south Amsterdam. Eurolines operates a coach service between

London Victoria Bus Station and Amstel Station, with up to five daily departures in summer. Travel time is just over 12 hours. For reservations, contact **Eurolines** (✆ **08717/818-181** in Britain, or ✆ 020/560-8788 in Holland). From Amstel bus station, go by train and Metro to Centraal Station, and by tram no. 12 to the **Museumplein** area (p. 60), and then to connecting points for trams to the Center. For the **Leidseplein** area (p. 60), take the Metro toward Centraal Station, get out at **Weesperplein,** and go above ground to take tram lines 7 or 10.

BY BOAT

DFDS Seaways (✆ **0871/522-9955** in Britain, or ✆ 0255/546-666 in Holland; www.dfdsseaways.co.uk) has a daily car-ferry service between Newcastle in northeast England and IJmuiden on the North Sea coast, 24km (15 miles) west of Amsterdam. The overnight travel time is 15½ hours. From IJmuiden, you can go by special bus to Amsterdam Centraal Station.

P&O Ferries (✆ **0871/664-2121** in Britain, or ✆ 020/200-8333 in Holland; www.poferries.com) has a daily car-ferry service between Hull in northeast England and Rotterdam (into Europoort's harbor). The overnight trip time is 10¼ hours. Ferry company buses shuttle between the Rotterdam Europoort terminal and Rotterdam Centraal Station, from where there are frequent trains to Amsterdam.

Stena Line (✆ **08447/707070** in Britain, or ✆ 0174/315811 in Holland; www. stenaline.co.uk) has a twice-daily car-ferry service between Harwich in southeast England and Hoek van Holland (Hook of Holland) near Rotterdam. The travel time during the day is 6½ hours, and 8 hours overnight. Frequent trains depart from Hoek van Holland to Amsterdam.

Annually, Amsterdam welcomes some 100 ocean cruise liners from around the world and 700 river cruise boats from Europe's inland waterways. You'll likely arrive at the cruise-liner dock, **Passenger Terminal Amsterdam,** Piet Heinkade 27 (✆ **020/509-1000;** www.ptamsterdam.com; tram: 25 or 26), on the IJ waterway just east of Centraal Station and within easy walking distance of the city center.

Getting Around

The central information and ticket sales point for GVB Amsterdam, the city's public transportation company, is **GVB Tickets & Info,** Stationsplein (✆ **0900/9292** for timetable and fare information, ✆ 0900/8011 for other customer services; www.gvb. nl), in front of Centraal Station, open Monday to Friday from 7am to 9pm, Saturday and Sunday from 8am to 9pm.

Most tram and bus shelters and all Metro stations display maps showing the entire urban transit network. All stops have signs listing the main stops yet to be made by trams or buses at that location. Detailed maps of the network are available free from the GVB Tickets & Info office. Daytime hours of operation for public transportation are from 6am (trams start at 7:30am on Sunday) to around 12:30am. Night buses operate a limited service thereafter, with buses usually on an hourly schedule.

Note: For many of the locations featured in this book, information about the nearest public transportation stop or station is provided, with preference given to the nearest tram (streetcar) stop. The nearest Metro station or bus stop is listed in the few instances that it would be a better option.

CARDS & FARES From 2011, or thereabouts, all public transportation in the Netherlands will be using an electronic stored-value card called the **OV-chipkaart.**

This card has replaced the old system of tickets, "strip cards," and fare zones. "OV" are the initials for *openbaar vervoer,* which is Dutch for public transportation. Three main types of OV-chipkaart are available: Re-loadable "personal" cards that can be used only by their pictured owner; reloadable "anonymous" cards that can be used by anyone; and non-reloadable "throwaway" cards. The personal and anonymous cards, both valid for 5 years, cost 7.50€ and can be loaded and re-loaded with up to 30€. Throwaway cards, which are likely to be the card of choice for short-term visitors, cost 2.50€ for one ride and 4.80€ for two rides. Electronic readers on Metro and train station platforms and on board trams and buses deduct the correct fare; just hold your card up against the reader at both the start and the end of the ride. Reduced-rate cards are available for seniors and children ages 4 to 11; children 3 and under ride free.

A better bet for short-term visitors who plan to use public transportation a lot is a 1-day or a multi-day card: 24 hours (7.50€), 48 hours (11.50€), 72 hours (15€), 96 hours (18€), 120 hours (23€), 144 hours (26€), 168 hours (29€).

Purchase cards from the GVB Tickets & Info office (see above), GVB and Netherlands Railways ticket booths in Metro and train stations, ticket machines (automats) at Metro and train stations, and ticket machines on board some trams. Not every kind of card is available from each of these sources. Note that the cards are valid for use throughout the Netherlands, no matter where you purchase them.

Should you plan to splash out on a 1-, 2-, or 3-day **I amsterdam Card** (see "Your Passport to Amsterdam," later in this chapter), remember that this affords "free" use of public transportation, so you don't need to purchase additional cards. The same applies if you purchase the **All Amsterdam Transport Pass** associated with travel on the Canal Bus (see "On the Water," below).

Teams of roving inspectors do their best to keep everyone honest. The fine for riding without a valid card is 37.50€, plus the fare for the ride, payable on the spot.

BY TRAM

Half the fun of Amsterdam is walking along the canals. The other half is riding the smooth blue-and-gray trams that roll through most major streets. There are 16 tram routes in the city. Ten of these (lines 1, 2, 4, 5, 9, 13, 16, 17, 24, and 26) begin and end at Centraal Station, and one (line 25) passes through, so you know you can always get back to that central point if you get lost and have to start over. The other tram routes are 3, 7, 10, 12, and 14.

Most trams have an access door that opens automatically. Board toward the rear following arrowed indicators outside the tram that point the way to the door. To board a tram that has no such arrowed indicators, push the button on the outside of the car beside any door. Getting off, you may need to push a button with an open-door graphic or the words DEUR OPEN. Tram doors close automatically and they do so quite quickly, so don't dawdle.

BY BUS

An extensive bus network operated by GVB (see above) complements the trams. Many bus routes begin and end at Centraal Station. It's generally faster to go by tram, but many points in the city are served only by bus. A regional and intercity bus service from Amsterdam is operated by **Connexxion** (✆ **0900/266-6399;** www.connexxion.nl), and **Arriva** (✆ **0900/202-2022;** www.arriva.nl). Information about national public transportation is available by calling ✆ **0900/9292** or visiting www.9292ov.nl.

BY METRO

It can't compare to the labyrinthine subway systems of Paris, London, and New York, but Amsterdam does have its own Metro. Four lines—50, 51, 53, and 54—run partly overground and bring people in from the suburbs, but from Centraal Station you can use Metro trains to reach both Nieuwmarkt and Waterlooplein in the central zone. You may want to take them simply as a sightseeing excursion, though, to be frank, few of the sights on the lines are worth going out of your way for. If you do take these lines, be sure to validate your strip card on the platform before boarding.

A new Metro line, the Metro Noord-Zuidlijn (North-South Line), is currently under construction to link Amsterdam-Noord, through the Center, to Station Zuid. It's slated for completion in 2015.

BY TRAIN

The rail network is not as useful within Amsterdam as the tram, bus, and Metro—but sensitive souls might like that they can ride in a first-class car or compartment. In addition to the Centraal Station hub, there are seven train stations in the city: Zuid, RAI (the city's main convention center), Amstel in the south, Muiderpoort in the east, and Lelylaan, De Vlugtlaan, and Sloterdijk in the west. Because the transportation network is tightly integrated, all rail stations are also served by two or more other modes of public transportation.

The excellent Dutch rail network comes into its own for longer distances. It's by far the quickest and best way to get to Schiphol Airport, Haarlem, Zandvoort, Hoorn, and most other points in Holland. Purchase international tickets from an office on platform 2 of Centraal Station, or domestic tickets from an office in the main hall (note that you save .50€ per ticket if you get domestic tickets from the station ticket machines).

ON FOOT

Amsterdam's Centrum (Center) district is small enough for its residents to think of it as a village, but it can be one confusing village until you get the hang of it. It's easy to think you're headed in one direction along the canal belt, only to discover that you're going completely the other way. Those concentric rings of canals, along with several important squares, are the city's defining focal points. This section explains the city's layout, introduces its neighborhoods, tells you how to get around, and squeezes in other useful knowledge.

Walking is the best way to appreciate the city's relaxed rhythm. When you look at an Amsterdam map, you may think the city's too large to explore on foot. Not true: It's possible to see almost every important sight on a 4-hour walk. Be sure to wear

---

📎 Urban Minefield

In a city with so many high and varied gables, there's a temptation to walk along gazing upward. Be careful: There's the possibility you'll walk straight into a canal, but that's a minor danger compared to the one underfoot. Many Amsterdammers have dogs, some of them the size of Shetland ponies. Signs on the sidewalk saying HOND IN DE GOOT (DOG IN THE GUTTER) are mostly ignored. Take your eye off the ground for so much as an instant and you might regret it.

YOUR passport TO AMSTERDAM

To get the most out of your trip, avail yourself of the **I amsterdam Card.** The card, valid for 1 day for 38€, 2 days for 48€, and 3 days for 58€, affords free travel on public transportation, free admission to more than 20 museums and attractions, including the **Rijksmuseum** or the **Van Gogh Museum** (but not both). The card also provides for discounted admission to additional museums and attractions, a free canal-boat cruise, discounted excursions, including reduced rates on the **Hop On Hop Off Museum Line** and the **Canal Bus,** and discounts in certain restaurants and stores. The card comes with a public transportation ticket and a color information booklet. Total possible savings: Around 150€.

Before purchasing, though, consider carefully whether you'll get your money's worth out of this card. Remember, this is Holland, where local fondness for the coin of the realm is proverbial, and bargains are thin on the ground. You'll have to work pretty hard to come out ahead on the cost of the card, jumping on and off trams, buses, and canal boats, and running in and out of museums that fall mostly into the culture class.

Some of Amsterdam's most memorable experiences come from idle strolling, hanging out on cafe terraces, and visiting offbeat stores and attractions. But if a cram course of solid culture is what you're here for, and you're ready to work to achieve it, the card could be a sound investment.

The I amsterdam Card is available from Holland Tourist Information at Schiphol Airport and from VVV tourist information offices in the city. Note that only the person who signs the card can use it. Further details are available from **www.iamsterdamcard.com**.

comfortable walking shoes, as those charming cobbles get under your soles and on your nerves after a time; leave thin-soled shoes and boots at home.

This book's maps depict Amsterdam's basic waterway patterns and the relationships between the major squares and landmarks with their connecting thoroughfares. Once you get the hang of the four major canals' necklace pattern and become familiar with the names of the five principal roads into the Centrum (Center) district, all you need do as you walk along is keep track of whether you're walking toward or away from the Dam—the heart of the city—or simply circling around it.

When walking, remember that cars have the right of way when turning. Don't step in front of one thinking it's going to stop for you. And be aware that many drivers consider road signs and red stoplights to be not much more than occasionally useful suggestions. When crossing a street, watch out for trams, buses, even bikes. Look both ways before crossing a dedicated bike lane—some pedalers get unreasonably irritated if you force them to crash into you.

Kids are irresistibly attracted to water, so watch out for them near any of Amsterdam's 160 canals. Protective fencing rarely exists and the low metal railings meant to keep cars from rolling into the water are ideally positioned for small feet to stumble over.

FINDING AN ADDRESS Wherever possible in this book, addresses include the name of a nearby square, major thoroughfare, adjacent canal, or well-known sight.

Street numbers along the canals ascend from west to east (left to right as you look at the map); on streets leading away from Centraal Station and out from the Center, they ascend from north to south (top to bottom). Now, all you need to know is that, in Dutch, *-straat* means "street," *-gracht* means "canal," *-plein* means "square," *-markt* means "market," *-dijk* means "dike," and *-laan* means "avenue." These suffixes are attached directly to a place name: For example, Princes' Canal becomes Prinsengracht.

BY TAXI

It used to be that you couldn't simply hail a taxi in Amsterdam, but nowadays cabbies stop for most attempts. Alternatively, find one of the taxi stands sprinkled around the city, generally near luxury hotels or at major squares such as the Dam, Stationsplein, Spui, Rembrandtplein, Westermarkt, and Leidseplein. Taxis have rooftop signs and blue license tags, and are metered.

Liberalization of the city's taxis in recent years seems to have all but eliminated those once-typical drivers: Professional machines functioning as smoothly as the Mercedes they drove, who all seemed to have been spat out of the same soulless mold. To a budget traveler, their fares were little short of a mugging. And then they expected a tip. On the plus side, they spoke English and generally didn't exaggerate the price (they didn't need to). The new breed of drivers might drive something less desirable and have varying ideas about fair fares, for better or worse. Some have poor situational awareness, so bring a map or feed directions to the driver—if they understand English.

For generally reliable service, call Taxi Centrale Amsterdam (© **020/777-7777;** www.tca-amsterdam.nl). TCA's base fare begins at 7.50€ when the meter starts and, after 2km (1¼ miles), runs up at 2.20€ a kilometer, or 3.55€ a mile; after 25km (15 miles) at 1.75€ a kilometer, or 2.80€ a mile; and after 50km (30 miles) at 1.45€ a kilometer, or 2.35€ a mile. The fare includes service; you can round it up if you like, or tip for a good service, like help with your luggage, or for a helpful discourse.

ON THE WATER

With all Amsterdam's water, it makes sense to use it for transportation. Though options for canal-based transit are limited (with the exception of cruises and excursions), they do exist, and provide unique and attractive views of the city. Given the ongoing redevelopment in the old harbor areas, where new residential projects sprout like tulips in springtime, it seems likely that water transportation will become increasingly important. See also "Organized Tours," in chapter 7.

Stop & Go

A grand little bus service, the **Stop/Go,** is helping to solve one of Amsterdam's knottiest transit problems: Accessing the long, narrow canalsides of the *Grachtengordel* (Canal Belt). Colorful Stop/Go minibuses go in both directions between the Oosterdok, via Centraal Station and Brouwersgracht, all the way along Prinsengracht, to the Amstel River and Waterlooplein. A bus departs every 12 minutes from each terminus, daily from 9am to 5:30pm—it makes a great mini-sightseeing tour. There are no regular stops; just hold out your hand and the bus stops for you to get on. When you want to get out, just tell the driver. A ticket valid for 1 hour, only on the Stop/Go bus, costs 1€.

Amsterdam's population is 750,000, a figure projected to reach 800,000 by 2020. Since 2010, native Dutch residents have for the first time been outnumbered by ethnic minorities—many of whom are now considered Dutch, of course—and foreign expats. The Old City, inside Singelgracht canal's arc, covers 8 sq. km (3 sq. miles) and contains 44,000 dwellings housing 80,000 people. Residents share this central space with 8,000 historical monuments, 2,000 shops, 1,500 restaurants, and 200 hotels. Every working day, a million people pour into the heart of town by bike, car, and public transportation.

BY WATER BUS Two separate companies operate water buses (rarely, if ever, used by locals) that bring you to, or close to, many of the city's top museums, attractions, sights, and shopping and entertainment districts. **Canal Bus** (℮ **0900/333-4442;** www.canal.nl) has four routes—Green, Red, Blue, and Orange—with a combined total of stops that include Centraal Station, Westermarkt, Leidseplein, Rijksmuseum (with an extension to the RAI Convention Center when big events are on there), Waterlooplein, and East Amsterdam. Hours of operation are daily from 10am to 6:30pm, with two buses an hour at peak times. Day passes for adults cost 22€ for 24 hours, 33€ for 48 hours, and 44€ for 72 hours; children aged 4 to 12 travel for half the adult price, and children 3 and under are free.

An **All Amsterdam Transport Pass,** valid on the Canal Bus, trams, buses, and the Metro, costs 28€ a day, and is available from GVB Tickets & Info, VVV tourist information offices, and the Canal Bus company. It's good value if you make extensive use of the Canal Bus and GVB public transportation.

The **Hop On Hop Off Museum Line** (℮ 020/530-5412; www.lovers.nl) transports weary tourists on their pilgrimages from museum to museum. And for those with limited time, it provides some of the features of a canal-boat cruise. Boats depart from the Rederij Lovers dock in front of Centraal Station daily from 10am to 5pm, every 30 to 45 minutes. They stop at seven key spots that provide access to museums and other attractions, including the Rijksmuseum, the Van Gogh Museum, Anne Frankhuis (Anne Frank House), Leidseplein, Vondelpark, Amsterdam Historisch Museum, Stedelijk Museum, the Flower Market, Museum Het Rembrandthuis, the Jewish Historical Museum, Artis Zoo, Muziektheater, and Tropenmuseum. Tickets, available from the Lovers Canal Cruises counter near the dock, are 20€, 10€ for children ages 4 to 12, and free for children 3 and under. Tickets include discounted admission to some museums and attractions along the route.

BY FERRY Free ferries for passengers and two-wheeled vehicles connect the Center with Amsterdam-Noord (North), across the IJ channel. The short crossings afford fine views of the harbor, which make them ideal micro-cruises for the cash-strapped. Sadly, there's little of interest in Noord, so the free trip may have to be its own attraction. Ferries depart from the Waterplein West dock on De Ruijterkade behind Centraal Station. One route goes to Buiksloterweg on the north shore, with ferries every 6 to 12 minutes round the clock. A second route goes to IJplein, a more easterly point on the north shore, with ferries every 8 to 15 minutes from 6:30pm to around midnight.

Another ferry goes west to NDSM Island, a 20-minute trip that doesn't pass any points of particular interest but still affords a decent view of the harbor.

BY WATER TAXI Since you're in the city of canals, consider splurging on a water taxi. These do more or less the same thing as landlubber taxis, except they do it on the canals, in the harbor, and on the Amstel River. You move faster than on land and you get your very own boat tour. To order one, call **VIP Watertaxi Amsterdam** (© **020/535-6363;** www.water-taxi.nl), or hail one from the dock outside Centraal Station, close to the VVV office. To and from points in the city center, a water taxi for between one and eight passengers costs 20€ per half-hour; to and from points outside the city center, the rate is 50€ per half-hour. In addition, multiple charter options are available.

BY SWIMMING Believe it or not, some folks (perhaps influenced by too many trips to the "coffeeshop") think this is a good way to get around. It isn't. True, the canals have been cleaned up quite a bit in recent years, and the water quality is probably the best it's ever been. Even so, the liquid filling the canals is still something of a witch's brew; swallow some, and a close encounter with a hospital stomach pump may lie in your immediate future.

BY BICYCLE

Instead of renting a car, follow the Dutch example and ride a bike (*fiets*). Sunday, when the city is quiet, is a good day to pedal along sleepy, off-the-beaten-path canals or through Vondelpark, and to practice riding on cobblestones and over bridges before venturing into the fray of an Amsterdam rush hour. There are more than 600,000 bikes in the city, so you'll have plenty of company.

Navigating the city on two wheels is mostly safe—or at any rate, not as suicidal as it looks—thanks to a vast network of dedicated bike lanes. Bikes even have their own traffic lights. Amsterdam's battle-scarred bike-borne veterans make it almost a point of principle to ignore every written safety rule. Though most live to tell the tale, don't think the same necessarily applies to you. (See "Bicycling in Amsterdam," below.)

Bike-rental rates are around 12€ per day or 50€ per week; a deposit of around 50€ is required. **MacBike** (© **020/620-0985;** www.macbike.nl) rents a range of bikes, including tandems and six-speeds. The company has rental outlets at Stationsplein 12 (tram: 1, 2, 4, 5, 9, 13, 16, 17, 24, 25, or 26), Centraal Station; Mr. Visserplein 2 (tram: 9 or 14), Waterlooplein; and Weteringschans 2 (tram: 1, 2, 5, 7, or 10), at Leidseplein. **Bike City,** Bloemgracht 68–70 (© **020/626-3721;** www.bikecity.nl; tram: 13, 14, or 17), near the Anne Frankhuis, is another good choice. **Damstraat Rent-a-Bike,** Damstraat 20–22 (© **020/625-5029;** www.rentabike. nl; tram: 4, 9, 14, 16, 24, or 25), is centrally located near the Dam. Feminists both male and female might want to give their business to **Zijwind Fietsen,** a women's cooperative, at Ferdinand Bolstraat 168 (© **020/673-7026;** www.zijwind.com; tram: 25), though it's a bit out from the Center.

> ### Feeling Flushed
>
> Amsterdam gets a daily purging of sorts. Between 7 and 8:30pm, 600,000 cubic meters (160 million gallons) of fresh IJsselmeer water are pumped through the canal system to prevent the water from becoming stagnant.

A Vicious (Bi)Cycle

One endearing aspect of Amsterdam life is that, instead of mugging passersby, junkies here steal battered old bicycles to fund their next fix. They sell the bikes for around 20€, and plenty of young Amsterdammers—who themselves have had a series of store-bought bikes stolen by junkies—end up sighing and stepping aboard this treadmill, knowing they're only encouraging the crooks. Make this destructive transaction at your own risk; renting will endow you with better karma.

Warning: Because bicycle theft is common, always lock both your bike frame and one of the wheels to something fixed and solid.

BY TAXI-BIKE You can get driven around town on a kind of sophisticated rickshaw, courtesy of **Wielertaxi** (*©* **06/2824-7550**), which operates two-seater units from the Dam. They go in the bike lanes and, like regular taxis, can get you where public transportation doesn't reach. And they make for a pretty good touring option. The fare is 1€ ($1.60) per person for every 3 minutes, or 20€ ($32) for two for 30 minutes; children ages 2 to 12 ride for half-price, and children 1 and under sitting on an adult's lap ride free.

BY CAR

Don't go by car around Amsterdam. You'll likely regret the expense and the hassle. The city is a maze of one-way streets, narrow bridges, and no-parking zones. It's not unheard of for an automobile, left parked with the hand brake carelessly disengaged, to roll through a flimsy foot-high railing into a canal. To park, you need either to feed the parking automat, or have a parking permit prominently displayed in your car.

See "By Car" under "Getting to Amsterdam" above for more info on driving in Amsterdam.

PARKING Street parking in the city center costs 4€ to 5€ per hour, depending on the location, and 3€ per hour, payable at ticket machines (automats). In zones bordering the city center, the rate ranges from 1.40€ to 3€ per hour. In the city center, and in some other parts of Amsterdam, parking ticket machines no longer accept cash payments, but only payment by chip-and-PIN–enabled bank card or credit card, and the number of districts where such is the case is due to increase. Beyond a certain number of hours, it's more economical to buy a day ticket, ranging in price from 17€ to 45€ in the central zone, and for less in the outer zones, and also available from the automats. Reduced-rate permits are available from many hotels. Permits valid for a day, a week, or a month are available from offices of the **Cition** parking management authority (see below).

Amsterdam has become a free-fire zone for marauding parking-enforcement units. Locals have learned to keep their heads down and their automat tickets clearly displayed. If you overstay your time limit or if you park illegally, you're almost sure to fall victim to the swift and merciless patrols. The cost of transgression is high: 51€ plus an hour's parking charge, payable within 48 hours.

bicycling IN AMSTERDAM

What are the rules of the road for going by bicycle in Amsterdam? Apparently, there are none. Bicycle riders can go anywhere they want, whenever they want, however they want. Or so you'd think from the antics of Amsterdam's massed legions of pedal-bikers. They're enough to scare a Hell's Angel. Particularly terrifying is your standard young mother transporting two kids (one on the steering bars and the other in a kid's seat), chatting on her phone while dicing with the Leidseplein trams. Biking is one activity during which you should disregard the maxim, "When in Amsterdam, do as the Amsterdammers do"—you might easily end up injured.

It takes a while to get used to moving smoothly and safely through the whirl of trams, cars, buses, fellow bikers, and pedestrians, particularly if you're on an ancient and much-battered *stadfiets* (city bike), also known as an *omafiets* (grandmother bike)—the only kind that makes economic sense here, since anything fancier will attract a crowd wanting to steal it. Many such bikes don't have handbrakes; instead, you pedal backward to slow down and stop. It works okay, but you may need time to get used to it.

It's better to develop street smarts slowly. The first rule: Don't argue with trams—they push back hard. The second rule: Cross tram tracks perpendicularly so that your wheels don't get caught in the grooves, which could pitch you out of the saddle. And the third rule: Don't crash into pedestrians—the subsequent punch on the chin could be painful. That's about it. Like everyone else, you'll make up the rest of the rules as you go.

If the parking operatives think your car constitutes enough of an obstacle, they tow your car to the **Cition** car-pound at Daniël Goedkoopstraat 7–9 (✆ **14-020** (information line), or 020/251-3737 (reception); www.cition.nl; Metro: Spaklerweg), open 24 hours a day, way out in the boonies of the southeastern Over-Amstel district, and they charge you 58€ for every 24-hour period (or portion thereof) that it's out there, plus the towing charge. You pay parking fines at the car-pound office, or at a second office, De Clercqstraat 42–44 (Tram: 3, 13, or 14).

If you rack up five unpaid parking tickets, you'll be rewarded with a wheel-clamp. If the parking operatives think your car constitutes an obstacle, they'll tow it to the **Dienst Stadstoezicht** car-pound at Daniël Goedkoopstraat 7–9 (✆ **020/251-2121;** Metro: Spaklerweg), open 24 hours a day, the charge is 58€ for every 24-hour period (or portion thereof) that it's out there, plus the towing charge. You can pay parking, clamp, and towing fines at the car-pound office and at a second office, De Clercqstraat 42–44 (✆ **020/553-0333;** tram: 3, 13, or 14). To get a wheel clamp removed fast, call the **Cition** service (✆ **020/251-3322;** www.cition.nl), and pay the fine by credit card.

Additional obstacles to parking on the fly are *Amsterdammertjes* (Little Amsterdammers), those zillions of ubiquitous anti-parking posts that have lined streets and canals across the city probably since Rembrandt was a kid.

To avoid charges, or parking-garage rates, stash your car for 6€ a day on the edge of town at **Park+Ride lots** at some of the outer Metro and rail stations (directions are indicated by blue-and-white P+R signs along the way), and come in by Metro, train, or tram. There are parking garages throughout town; most cost 3€ to 6€ an hour and 25€

to 50€ ($32–$64) a day, depending on the location. The largest lots are at Centraal Station, Damrak, Marnixstraat, under Waterlooplein, and adjacent to Leidseplein.

As if all the parking hassle isn't bad enough, anything left in your car is cash on wheels for every junkie and ne'er-do-well in town. They can withdraw your iPod, phone, and camera faster than you can get cash from an ATM. Cars with foreign tags are most tempting, since they're likeliest to have valuables in the trunk.

MONEY & COSTS

THE VALUE OF THE EURO VS. OTHER POPULAR CURRENCIES

Euro (€)	US$	Can$	UK£	Aus$	NZ$
1.00	$1.23	C$1.27	£.81	A$1.41	NZ$1.73

Amsterdam is by no means inexpensive. Clearly, whether you agree with this statement will depend on how much you can bring to bear—or bear to bring—in the way of financial resources. If you are used to the prices in New York and London, it won't seem too out of whack. But opportunities for scoring genuine bargains run a thin gamut from few-and-far-between to nonexistent. Remember, the Dutch have for centuries been consummate traders and middlemen. You need only look at how well-appointed their country is to appreciate how fair a job they've done extracting money from foreigners.

In your favor is that the Dutch themselves display an almost proverbial reluctance to unnecessarily part with a euro. A sound rule of thumb is that if you lodge, dine, and entertain yourself in the same places where "ordinary" Dutch do, you can limit financial damage.

Currency

The European **euro** (€) is the currency in the Netherlands. There are 100 euro cents to each euro. The euro **coins** are: .01€, .02€, .05€, .10€, .20€, .50€ (1, 2, 5, 10, 20, and 50 euro cents), 1€, and 2€. The euro **notes** are 5€, 10€, 20€, 50€, 100€, 200€, and 500€.

Holland does not produce its own 1 and 2 euro cent coins (except for commemorative issues), and prices in the country are rounded to the nearest 5 cents. The 200€ and 500€ notes are pretty much unusable because few businesses accept them.

Frommer's lists exact prices in the local currency. The currency conversions quoted above were correct at press time. However, rates fluctuate, so before departing consult a currency exchange website such as **www.oanda.com/convert/classic** to check up-to-the-minute rates.

ATMs

The **Cirrus** (© 800/424-7787; www.mastercard.com) and **PLUS** (© 800/843-7587; www.visa.com) networks span the globe; look at the back of your bank card to see which network you're on, then check online for ATM locations in Amsterdam. Be sure you know your personal identification number (PIN) and daily withdrawal limit before you depart. *Note:* Remember that many banks impose a fee every time you use a card at another bank's ATM, and that fee can be higher for international

	€
Taxi from the airport to downtown Amsterdam	40
Double room, moderate	125
Double room, inexpensive	60
Three-course dinner for one without wine, moderate	25–40
Bottle of Heineken beer	2–4
Bottle of Coca-Cola	3
Cup of coffee	2.50–4.50
1 gallon/1 liter of premium gas (petrol)	6 / 1.60
Admission to most museums	6–12

transactions than for domestic ones. In addition, the bank from which you withdraw cash may charge its own fee. For international withdrawal fees, ask your bank.

If you have a five- or six-digit PIN, be sure to obtain a four-digit number from your bank to use in Amsterdam. Some cards with five- or six-digit PINs might work, but this depends on which bank you're with. The best advice is still to get a four-digit number from your bank.

Credit Cards

Credit cards are not as commonly accepted in Amsterdam as they are in the U.S. and Britain. Many restaurants and shops in the city—and some hotels—don't accept them at all. Some establishments tag on a 5% charge for card payment. **Visa** and **MasterCard** (also known as **Eurocard** in Europe) are the most widely used cards in Holland. **American Express** is often accepted, mostly in the middle- and upper-bracket category. **Diners Club** is not as commonly accepted as American Express.

Beware of hidden credit card fees while traveling. Check with your credit or debit card issuer to see what fees, if any, will be charged for overseas transactions. Recent reform legislation in the U.S., for example, has curbed some exploitative lending practices. But many banks have responded by increasing fees in other areas, including fees for customers who use credit and debit cards while out of the country—even if those charges were made in U.S. dollars. Fees can amount to 3% or more of the purchase price. Check with your bank before departing to avoid any surprise charges on your statement.

In Holland, you'll rarely (perhaps never) come across a business that uses the old swipe system for authorizing credit card payments. Instead, payments will either be authorized by a chip system in the card and the cardholder's signature, or by chip-and-PIN, with a four-digit personal identification number replacing the signature. An additional complication is that many card-accepting machines and businesses in Holland, in particular those like parking machines, train ticket machines, self-service gas (petrol) stations, and small shops, take the local *Chip-knip* stored-value cards. Foreign visitors may be obliged to use their cards to a certain extent just for withdrawing funds from bank ATMs, and paying with old-fashioned cold, hard cash.

HEALTH

There are no particular health concerns in Amsterdam—if you don't count the "risk" of occasionally breathing in a whiff of second-hand hashish smoke. Traveling in the Netherlands poses few health problems. The tap water is safe to drink, the milk is pasteurized, blood for transfusions is HIV-screened, and you likely won't need to worry about getting too much sun.

If You Get Sick

If a medical emergency arises, your hotel staff can usually put you in touch with a reliable doctor. If not, contact the **Central Doctors Service (𝄐 020/592-3434)** or go to the emergency room at one of the local hospitals. The U.S. and U.K. consulates in Amsterdam can provide a list of area doctors who speak English (almost every doctor in town). Most Amsterdam hospitals have walk-in clinics for emergency cases that are not life-threatening, though you may not get immediate attention.

We list additional **emergency numbers** in "Fast Facts," p. 289.

GENERAL AVAILABILITY OF HEALTHCARE

The Dutch healthcare system is among the world's best. It's easy in Holland to get over-the-counter medicines and other simple remedies for minor ailments. Local brands and generic equivalents of common prescription drugs are available. Most doctors speak English (though their lingo might be a little disturbing, like when a doctor once told me he knew what "disease" I had when I reported a minor ailment).

SAFETY

In Amsterdam, if it isn't bolted to the floor, somebody *will* try to steal it—and even if it *is* bolted to the floor, somebody will still try to steal it. Watch for pickpockets on trams, buses, Metro trains, and in train and Metro stations. Constant public announcements at Centraal Station and Schiphol Airport warn about pickpockets, and tram signs warn, in a multitude of languages, ATTENTION: PICKPOCKETS. Drivers often recognize a pickpocket who gets on their bus or tram, and announce over the vehicle's PA system that passengers should watch out for their belongings. It's fun to watch the miscreants getting off again at the next stop, foiled. Pickpockets and other thieves often wait until you are occupied or distracted—or act to occupy or distract you—before making their move. Consider wearing a money belt. Women, wear your purse crossed over your shoulder so that it hangs in front, with the clasp or zipper facing in. A backpack worn on the back is an open invitation to thieves, so either don't wear it like that or don't put anything valuable in it (you could consider packing it with loaded mousetraps).

Violence is not unknown to Amsterdam, but it's not at all a violent city. Foreign drug dealers whacking each other doesn't count—unless innocents get caught in the crossfire, this usually merits only a single-sentence news blip on p. 21 of the local paper. Drug-related crime is prevalent, but most of it, like pickpocketing, is nonviolent, relatively minor, and opportunistic. Stealing bicycles is a "big" problem here; see the box on p. 45 for more info. Muggings and armed robberies do happen, but they're not a regular feature of life.

There are some risky areas, especially in and around the Red Light District. Be leery of walking alone after dark through narrow alleyways and along empty stretches of canal. Don't use ATMs at night in quiet areas. It's wise to stay out of Vondelpark at night, but there are cafes on the edge of the park that are busy until closing time.

Amsterdam has its share (more than its share, really) of weird folks, some of whom may lock onto you for one reason or another. If you can't shake them off, go into a cafe or hotel and wait until they leave or call a taxi to take you away.

Beggars are common, although the generous Dutch welfare system ensures that few, if any, locals need to resort to panhandling. Those who do this might be drug addicts, illegal migrants, young visitors trying to make their stay last longer, lazy ne'er-do-wells—and some genuine hardship cases. If you're prepared to hand out money, keep coins handy rather than rummaging through your billfold or purse, which might get grabbed by the intended recipient of your generosity.

In Amsterdam, of all places, there is a rising incidence of gays being verbally abused and even assaulted. The perpetrators often are young Muslim men and teens. In 2006, the editor of the *Washington Blade* gay paper was beaten up in such an incident. Recent surveys show that more gays feel less safe in the city than formerly, and some are turning to self-defense and martial arts classes in an effort to protect themselves. So worrisome has the problem become that the former city mayor commissioned the University of Amsterdam to research the whole question of homophobic attacks.

Tensions caused by the Israeli–Palestinian conflict have led to some anti-Jewish attacks from the same minority-community source. Jewish visitors who dress in a way that clearly identifies them as Jewish should be aware of this, even though the chances of being a victim of such an attack are very small.

Report any crime committed against you to the police *(politie)*, most of whom speak English and are generally helpful to visitors.

See also the section on women travelers in "Specialized Travel Resources," later in this chapter.

Note: Listing some of the possible dangers together like this can give a false impression of the threat of crime in Amsterdam. There is no need to be afraid to do the things you want to do. Amsterdammers aren't. Just remember to exercise the usual rules of caution and observation that apply in any big city.

Dealing with Discrimination

Most Dutch would claim that they don't have the discrimination gene, and in most cases that's probably true. U.S. visitors are welcome but *might* occasionally encounter hostility from some quarters, due primarily to the conflict in Afghanistan. Iraq has faded from the headlines, and seems no longer to be a factor. Even though the Dutch military was strenuously engaged in Afghanistan, prior to its announced withdrawal in 2010, some native Dutch and some of the country's significant Muslim minority might want to take issue with Americans on this subject. The election in 2008 of Barack Obama as U.S. president undoubtedly improved the status of American visitors, if only by association.

British visitors, on the other hand, were being tarred with the brush of drunk and violence-prone compatriots, whose welcome in the Dutch capital had run out to the extent of fervent hopes being expressed that a weak British pound might keep more of them at home.

Meanwhile, Holland is experiencing an increase in votes for political parties opposed, to one degree or another, to mass immigration, and in particular to migrants who do not share "European values." This attitude could at the margin translate into discrimination against non-white visitors, though the majority of Dutch would have nothing to do with this.

SPECIALIZED TRAVEL RESOURCES

In addition to the destination-specific resources listed below, please visit Frommers. com for other specialized travel resources.

Gay & Lesbian Travelers

Amsterdam is Europe's gay epicenter—in fact, it might just be the most gay-friendly city on the planet. It even has a monument, the **Homomonument** (p. 156), dedicated to gays and lesbians who have been persecuted around the world through the ages.

Get local information by visiting **COC,** Rozenstraat 14 (✆ **020/626-3087;** www. cocamsterdam.nl), the Amsterdam branch of the Dutch LGBT organization, open Monday to Friday from 9am to 5pm. COC's national office is just a few doors along, at Rozenstraat 8 (✆ **020/623-4596;** www.coc.nl), open Monday to Friday from 9am to 5pm. The **Gay and Lesbian Switchboard** (✆ **020/623-6565;** www.switchboard. nl), open daily from 10am to 10pm, provides all kinds of information and advice.

Gay and lesbian bars and clubs are well publicized, but for a listing, see "The Gay & Lesbian Scene" under "The Bar Scene," in chapter 10. *Gay News* (www.gaynews. nl), a monthly magazine in both Dutch and English, is available for free in gay establishments around the city.

For more gay and lesbian travel resources visit frommers.com.

Travelers with Disabilities

The old center of Amsterdam—filled with narrow cobbled streets, steep humpback bridges, zillions of little barrier pillars called *Amsterdammertjes,* and bicycles parked all over the place—can be hard going. But many hotels and restaurants provide easy access for people with disabilities, and some display the international wheelchair symbol in their brochures. It's always a good idea to call ahead to find out about accommodations before you book; bear in mind that many older hotels have steep, narrow stairways and no elevators. Many, but not all, museums and other sites are wheelchair accessible, wholly or partly, and some have adapted toilets. Call ahead to check on accessibility at sites you wish to visit.

Schiphol Airport has a service to help travelers with disabilities through the airport. Not all trams in Amsterdam are easily accessible for wheelchairs, but newer trams have low doors that are accessible, and most buses are accessible. The Metro system is fully accessible, but that's not as good as it sounds because few Metro stations are near places where visitors want to go. Taxis are also difficult, but the new minivan taxis are an improvement. Call ahead to book a wheelchair-accessible cab from **Taxi Centrale Amsterdam** (✆ **020/677-7777**).

There's comprehensive assistance for travelers on **Netherlands Railways** trains and in stations. Call ✆ **030/235-7822** for information, or visit www.ns.nl. Give this organization a day's notice of your journey (by visiting a station or calling ahead) and they'll arrange for assistance along the way.

A good source of travel-related information in the Netherlands is the **ANWB Disabled Department** (© **070/314-1420**; www.anwb.nl).

For more on organizations that offer resources to travelers with disabilities, go to frommers.com.

Family Travel

At first glance, Amsterdam is not a great family destination. Who wants to be taking the kids into a hash-smoking den, or traipsing around the Red Light District? Or to a country that permits children from age 12 to have "non-exploitative" sexual relationships? To boot, a legal political party, the Brotherly Love, Freedom, and Diversity Party (PNVD), openly advocates pedophilia and child pornography.

A second glance is likely to be more promising. This the capital of a country in which kids are relatively highly regarded. There's also plenty of wholesome stuff for them to do.

Let's see now: Pedaling a rented bicycle around town, or a water-bike around the canals; riding trams, harbor ferries, and canal boats; visiting Artis Zoo, the Anne Frank House, and one of several children's farms; exploring the beach at Zandvoort; swimming in the IJsselmeer; working off steam at adventure parks. And lots more.

Some of the city's more expensive hotels offer kids' suites, and you might even find that a suite is cheaper than booking two rooms. Many hotels allow children up to a certain age to sleep free or for a reduced rate in their parent's room, and may provide an extra bed.

Arrange ahead of time for such necessities as a crib, bottle warmer, and car seat (in the Netherlands, small children are not allowed to ride in the front seat). For information about babysitters, see "Fast Facts," p. 289.

To locate accommodations, restaurants, and attractions that are particularly kid-friendly, look for the "Kids" icon throughout this guide.

Women Travelers

Although Amsterdam is generally safe, nighttime rules about not walking alone in poorly lit and unpopulated areas apply especially to women. Harassment incidents do occur, and rape is not unheard of. It's safe for groups of women to go around the famed (and notorious) Red Light District—supposing they can stomach seeing other women serving purely as sex objects—but a young woman on her own, particularly after dark, could be subject to at least verbal harassment, and be mistaken for a "working girl." Public transportation is usually busy even late at night, so you generally won't have to worry about being alone in a tram or Metro train. If you do feel nervous, sit close to the driver, if possible. Many local women go around by bicycle at night.

The Netherlands has long enjoyed what one might call a relaxed attitude to the undraped female form—a government-issued DVD, part of a mandatory "education" for would-be migrants, portrays going topless at the beach as an integral part of Dutch culture. But if close personal observation is anything to go by, I can assure you that far fewer women are actually going without at the beach or in the park these days, and those who do aren't likely to be young.

For general travel resources for women, go to frommers.com.

Senior Travel

Sightseeing and entertainment attractions in the Netherlands often offer senior discounts, but some places offer these reductions only to Dutch citizens. Be sure to bring along your passport or other identity document when you want to sign up for reduced-rate fares on public transportation, and other senior benefits. A group of local seniors run so-called *Mee in Mokum* guided tours on foot through the city— "Mokum" is the name Amsterdam's once-thriving Jewish community used for the city, and it's still used informally by the populace. The name means something like *Going With Amsterdam*. People of any age can go on the tours, which are not exclusively for seniors, but are more likely to be run at a slower pace than standard tours. The guides speak English and know their beloved city inside out, as you might expect from people who have lived there for decades. Tours depart Tuesday to Sunday from the **David & Goliath** restaurant, Kalverstraat 92 (at the Amsterdams Historisch Museum); they last 2 to 3 hours and cost 5€. Call ✆ **020/625-4450** or visit www.gildeamsterdam.nl for info.

Frommers.com offers more information and resources on travel for seniors.

Student Travel

Students—and young folk in general—are big in Amsterdam. There are two major universities in the city, the UA (University of Amsterdam) and the VU (Free University), and a number of colleges, schools of this and that, and other institutes of higher learning.

Check out the **International Student Travel Confederation (ISTC)** (www.istc.org) website for comprehensive travel services information and details on how to get an **International Student Identity Card (ISIC),** which qualifies students for substantial savings on rail passes, plane tickets, admission fees, and more. It also provides students with basic health and life insurance and a 24-hour helpline. The card is valid for a maximum of 18 months. You can apply for the card at **STA Travel** (www.statravel.com; ✆ **800/781-4040** in the U.S.; ✆ **888/427-5639** in Canada; ✆ **0871/230-0040** in the U.K.; ✆ **021/427-9188** in Ireland; ✆ **132 782** in Australia; ✆ **0800/474400** in New Zealand), the biggest student travel agency in the world. If you're no longer a student but are still under 26, you can get an **International Youth Travel Card (IYTC)** from the same people, which entitles you to some discounts.

Single Travelers

Amsterdam is Europe's ideal singles city, because it is not that difficult a place to get to and to navigate for a person traveling alone. Plenty of solo travelers visit here every year—you can think of Amsterdam as Europe's singles central. There are lots of hotels and restaurants in all price bands, and it's easy to meet other people around the bars and clubs, on canal-boat tours and bicycle tours, and in other ways. Companies that specialize in solo travel to Amsterdam are thin on the ground, though. One is the **Singles Travel Company,** 56 N. Santa Cruz Ave., Los Gatos, CA 95030 (✆ **888/286-8687** or ✆ 408/354-3871; www.singlestravelcompany.com), which takes in Amsterdam as a part of its European tour.

For more information on traveling in the city as a single, go to frommers.com.

RESPONSIBLE TOURISM

The Dutch take the environment seriously: Understandable for a small country that's so heavily populated it needs to recover land from the sea. More than 60% of household waste is sorted, collected, and recycled. As a visitor in Amsterdam, you are expected to play your part and not to just toss stuff without first checking if it's recyclable, or reusable. For instance, if the word *Statiegeld* is written on the label of a bottle, it means you've paid a deposit on it, which you get back when you return the bottle to any shop that sells it.

All those bicycles you see in the city—around 600,000—may get on your nerves after a time, considering how aggressively many young Amsterdammers ride the things, and how easy it is to stumble into a dedicated bike lane, where you promptly get hit by what seems like a thousand of them. Yet the presence of these bikes keeps plenty of cars off the roads, which makes for cleaner air. You can rent bikes all over the city, including the **Bicycle Hotel** (p. 98).

Anyone who's not riding a bike is also more likely to be walking, or getting around by tram, than driving. Visitors are encouraged to do likewise; a recent university study found that just 1% of the "ecological footprint" tourists brought with them to the city was attributable to using local public transportation. The city's public transportation is easy to use and efficient; for more information see "Getting Around," p. 38.

Green living in Amsterdam extends to what people eat. Restaurants such as **Bol-hoed** (p. 118), **Golden Temple** (p. 120), and **De Kas** (p. 133) use "bio" and vegan ingredients in their meals. Some hotels, among them the **Radisson Blu** (p. 81), have signed on to the Sustainable Hotels Amsterdam Center Agreement, which

---

GENERAL RESOURCES FOR responsible TRAVEL

The following websites provide valuable wide-ranging information on sustainable travel.

o **Responsible Travel** (www. responsibletravel.com) is a great source of sustainable travel ideas; the site is run by a spokesperson for ethical tourism in the travel industry. **Sustainable Travel International** (www.sustainabletravel international.org) promotes ethical tourism practices, and manages an extensive directory of sustainable properties and tour operators around the world.

o **Carbonfund** (www.carbonfund. org), **TerraPass** (www.terrapass. org), and **Cool Climate** (http:// coolclimate.berkeley.edu) provide info on "carbon offsetting," or

offsetting the greenhouse gas emitted during flights.

o **Greenhotels** (www.greenhotels. com) recommends green-rated member hotels around the world that fulfill the company's stringent environmental requirements. **Environmentally Friendly Hotels** (www.environmentallyfriendly hotels.com) offers more green accommodations ratings.

o **Volunteer International** (www. volunteerinternational.org) has a list of questions to help you determine the intentions and the nature of a volunteer program. For general info on volunteer travel, visit **www.volunteerabroad. org** and **www.idealist.org**.

requires hotels to become more energy-efficient in all areas of operation, from conserving water to reducing unsorted waste. Hotels that meet the standard are awarded Green Key certification; see reviews throughout chapter 5 for info.

For info on volunteer and other sustainable travel opportunities in Amsterdam, see "Special Interest & Escorted Trips" below.

SPECIAL INTEREST & ESCORTED TRIPS

Escorted Tours

With a good escorted group tour, you'll know ahead of time what your trip will cost, and you won't have to worry about transportation, luggage, hotel reservations, communicating in foreign languages, and other basics—an experienced guide will take care of all that and lead you through all the sightseeing. The downside of a guided tour is that you trade much of the freedom and personal free time independent travel grants you and often see only the canned postcard-ready side of Amsterdam through the tinted windows of a giant bus. You get to *see* Amsterdam, but rarely do you get the chance to really *know* it. Consult a good travel agent for the latest offerings and advice.

Some unique escorted tour offerings exist in the city, too. **Artifex (✆ 020/620-8112;** www.artifex-travel.nl) offers everything from architecture walks to painting classes on canal boats in the city. Its tailor-made tours aren't exactly cheap (the price depends on what you want to do), but the multilingual guides—trained art historians—can get you into private collections, the Royal Palace even when it's closed to the public, the Amsterdam School's Scheepvaarthuis (never open to the public), and plenty more places. Some clients wind up spending half their day in a cozy brown cafe.

See "Organized Tours" in chapter 7 for more touring options in Amsterdam.

Volunteer Tours

Volunteer travel has become increasingly popular among those who want to venture beyond the standard group-tour experience to learn languages, interact with locals, and make a positive difference while on vacation, and there are a number of options for this type of sustainable travel in Amsterdam. Volunteer travel usually doesn't require special skills—just a willingness to work hard—and programs vary in length from a few days to a number of weeks. Some programs provide free housing and food, but many require volunteers to pay for travel expenses, which can add up quickly.

For general info on volunteer travel, visit **www.volunteerabroad.org** and **www.idealist.org.** Also see the options listed under "Special Interest & Escorted Trips" below.

Here's a list of companies offering educational and volunteer opportunities in Amsterdam:

- **www.jobsabroad.com:** Listings for jobs throughout Europe, as well as links to study and volunteer options.
- **www.idealist.org:** Resources and tips on volunteering abroad, along with volunteer and paid postings.
- **www.volunteerabroad.com:** Extensive listings for European volunteer opportunities.

Language & Cooking Classes

Maybe you've always dreamed of learning Dutch, of dazzling friends with your non-chalantly correct pronunciation of Van Gogh (see "Don't 'Go,'" p. 141), Schiphol Airport, and the many other little delights of the tongue that goes by the name of *Nederlands*. Beware. You'll need to perfect a mode of delivery that will lead both friends and beloved to believe you're choking on a chicken bone. The good news is that it can be done in Amsterdam. All three of the city's universities offer Dutch courses:

○ **Universiteit van Amsterdam,** Spui 21, 1012 WX Amsterdam (© **020/525-9111;** www.uva.nl).

○ **Volksuniversiteit,** Rapenburgerstraat 73, 1011 VK Amsterdam (© **020/626-1626;** www.volksuniversiteitamsterdam.nl).

○ **Vrije Universiteit Amsterdam,** De Boelelaan 1105, 1081 HV Amsterdam (© **020/598-9898;** www.vu.nl).

You can even learn the lingo and whip up some Dutch dishes on the same vacation. "Dutch cooking is not a widely known cuisine," admits a reviewer of *The Art of Dutch Cooking* (1997) by Corry Countess Van Limburg Stirum. This is akin to pointing out that the Pope is a Catholic. Yet all is not lost, as you can discover by making contact with **De Kookfabriek,** De Flinesstraat 2–4, 1099 CB Amsterdam-Duivendrecht (© **020/463-5635;** www.kookfabriek.nl), which (among other things) organizes Dutch cookery classes.

STAYING CONNECTED

Cellphones (Mobile Phones)

If your phone has GSM (Global System for Mobiles) capability and you have a world-compatible phone, you should be able to make and receive calls from Holland. Only certain phones have this capability, though, and you should check with your service operator first. Call charges can be high. Alternatively, you can rent a phone through **Cellhire** (www.cellhire.com; www.cellhire.co.uk; www.cellhire.com.au). After a simple online registration, they will ship a phone (usually with a U.K. number) to your home or office. Usage charges can be astronomical, so read the fine print.

U.K. mobiles work in Holland; call your service provider before departing your home country to ensure that the international call bar has been switched off and to check call charges, which can be extremely high. Also remember that you are charged for calls you *receive* on a U.K. mobile used abroad.

If you have Web access while traveling, consider a broadband-based telephone service (in technical terms, **Voice-over Internet protocol,** or **VoIP**) such as Skype (www.skype.com) or Vonage (www.vonage.com), which allows you to make free international calls from your laptop or in a cybercafe. Neither service requires the people you're calling to also have that service (though there are fees if they do not). Check the websites for details.

Internet & E-mail

Almost all hotels in Amsterdam have Wi-Fi or Internet access either in the rooms or in the public spaces, or both, and either paid-for or free. The full range of connectivity options is possible, including, of course, none at all.

The whole of Schiphol Airport has Wi-Fi connectivity provided by KPN, and Internet access at KPN Internet Centers and KPN Internet Zones. There's a central help number: ☎ 020/653-1852.

Dedicated cybercafes have virtually disappeared from the Amsterdam scene, now that Wi-Fi and Internet connections are available at so many hotels, cafes and coffeehouses, and fast-food restaurants.

Newspapers & Magazines

The main British and Irish daily newspapers, and the *International Herald Tribune*, *The Wall Street Journal Europe*, *USA Today*, *Time*, *Newsweek*, *U.S. News & World Report*, *Business Week*, *Fortune*, *The Economist*, and more are available at the **American Book Center,** Spui 12 (☎ 020/625-5537; tram: 1, 2, or 5), and **Waterstone's,** Kalverstraat 152 (☎ 020/638-3821; tram: 4, 9, 14, 16, 24, or 25). Newsstands at Schiphol Airport and Centraal Station also stock a wide range of international publications.

Telephones

To call Amsterdam from outside the Netherlands:

1. Dial the international access code: **011** in the U.S., and **00** in most other countries.
2. Dial the country code for the Netherlands: **31.**
3. Dial the area code **20** and then the number. So the whole number you'd dial would be 011-31-20-000-0000.

Area Codes: The area code for Amsterdam is **020** (use just **20** when you're calling from outside the Netherlands). When making local calls in Amsterdam, you don't need to use this area code. When making local calls within other cities, you don't need to use the city's area code. You do, however, need to use an area code between towns and cities.

There are two main formats for Dutch phone numbers: For cities and large towns, a three-digit area code is followed by a seven-digit number. For smaller towns and villages, a four-digit area code is followed by a six-digit number. In addition to Amsterdam's, some other area codes used in this book are Haarlem, **023;** The Hague and Scheveningen, **070;** Rotterdam, **010;** Delft, **015;** Leiden, **071;** and Gouda, **0182.**

Operator assistance: Call ☎ 0800/0410.

Information: For numbers inside the Netherlands, call ☎ 0900/8008; for international numbers, call ☎ 0900/8418.

Toll-free numbers: Numbers beginning with 0800 within Holland are toll-free, but calling a 1-800 number in the States from Holland is not toll-free. In fact, it costs the same as an overseas call.

Special numbers: Watch out for the special Dutch numbers that begin with 0900. Calls to these are charged at a higher rate than ordinary local calls. Depending on whom you call, it can be up to .90€ a minute.

International calls: To make international calls from Amsterdam, first dial **00** and then the country code. To call the United States or Canada, dial **00** (the international access code) + **1** (the country code) + the area code + the number. For example, if you wanted to call the British Embassy in Washington, D.C., you would dial 00-1-202-588-7800. Other country codes are United Kingdom, **44;** Ireland, **353;** Australia, **61;** New Zealand, **64.**

International calls, per minute, are **U.S.** and **Canada:** .30€; **U.K.** and **Ireland:** .35€; **Australia** and **New Zealand:** .40€.

You can use payphones in booths all around town with a **KPN,** and at some places with a **Telfort** *telefoonkaart* (phone card)—but note that neither provider's cards work with the other company's phones. KPN cards sell for 5€, 10€, 20€, and 50€, from post offices, train-ticket counters, VVV tourist information offices, GWK Travelex currency exchange offices, and some tobacconists and newsstands. Telfort cards sell for 8€, which includes an additional 2€ worth of time free.

There are, however, alternatives to buying the KPN and Telfort cards: Some payphones take credit cards, and a few take coins of .10€, .20€, .50€, 1€, and 2€.

Tip: Use smaller coins whenever possible, at least until you are connected with the right person, as no change is given from an individual coin—and once the call has begun, excess coins will not be returned when you hang up.

A busy signal sounds like a sustained dial tone, then a beep-beep sound. Should there be no answer, hang up and the coin comes back to you. On both card and coin phones, a digital reading tracks your decreasing balance so that you know when to add another card or more coins. To make additional calls when you still have a coin or card inserted, briefly break the connection; you'll get a new dial tone for another call.

Both local and long-distance calls from a payphone cost .30€ a minute. Note that calls placed through your hotel switchboard or dialed direct from your room phone usually cost more than twice the standard rate.

To charge a call to your calling card, call AT&T (✆ **0800/022-9111**), MCI (✆ **0800/022-9122**), Sprint (✆ **0800/022-9119**), Canada Direct (✆ **0800/022-9116**), British Telecom (✆ **0800/022-9944**), Australia Direct (✆ **0800/022-0061**), or Telecom New Zealand (✆ **0800/022-4295**).

SUGGESTED AMSTERDAM ITINERARIES

W hen in Amsterdam, having a strategy can take you only so far. This is a hang-loose city, and objectives-based planning works against the city's very nature. Yet having no strategy leaves you to the whims and vagaries of chance, and there's no guarantee that all your surprises will be pleasant ones. What's useful is a general plan for allocating your time while leaving time for serendipity to work its magic.

CITY LAYOUT

Amsterdammers will tell you it's easy to find your way around their city. However, when each resident offers you a different pet theory of how best to maintain your sense of direction, you begin to sense that the city's layout can be confusing. Some of the natives' theories actually do work. If you try to "think in circles," "follow the canals," or "watch the way the trams go," you might be able to spend fewer minutes consulting a map or trying to figure out where you are and which way to walk to find the Rijksmuseum, a restaurant, or your hotel.

When you step out of Centraal Station's main entrance, you're facing south toward the *Centrum* (Center). From here, the city is laid out around you along four concentric semicircles of canals, the *Grachtengordel* (Canal Belt): **Singel, Herengracht, Keizersgracht,** and **Prinsengracht.** Along these canals, 16th- and 17th-century merchants lived in elegant homes, most of which are still standing. The largest and most stately canal houses are along Herengracht. Connecting these canals are many smaller canals and streets radiating out from the Center, and effectively dividing the city into an archipelago of tiny islands linked by bridges. The area inside the **Singelgracht** canal, a fifth concentric waterway forming an outer rim to the canal belt (and not to be confused with Singel, the inner concentric canal), is considered the Old City—and it's so compact that a fit person should be able to walk across it in around 30 minutes.

A heavily touristed street, **Damrak,** leads from Centraal Station to the main central square called the **Dam.** In the 17th century, Damrak was a canal, its quays jammed with cargo boats and lined with mapmaker stores and ships' chandlers, coopers and ropemakers. Narrow side streets like **Haringpakkerssteeg** and **Zoutsteeg** recall the herring packers of yore (*haring* means "herring") and where ships used to unload salt (*zout* means "salt"). In the late 19th century, Damrak was lined with fancy stores and filled with elegant shoppers. Today, it's a brash thoroughfare of souvenir stores and noisy cafes. Houses on the bank stand in water, Venice-style.

To the east of the Dam, where the original Amstel River dam stood, and where the Royal Palace is now, is the (in)famous Red Light District, where government-licensed prostitutes sit behind windows, waiting for customers. A block to the west of Damrak is **Nieuwendijk,** a pedestrians-only shopping street that becomes **Kalverstraat** on the far side of the Dam. Follow Kalverstraat to the end, and you're at **Muntplein** beside the old Mint Tower. Cross over Muntplein and continue in the same direction to reach **Rembrandtplein,** one of the city's main nightlife areas, beyond which lies the old *Jodenbuurt* (Jewish Quarter).

The other main nightlife area is **Leidseplein,** on the outer, Singelgracht canal. Leidseplein is close to the end of **Leidsestraat,** a car-free (but not tram-free) shopping street leading from Singel to Singelgracht.

The wide, green **Museumplein,** site of the city's three most famous museums—Rijksmuseum, Van Gogh Museum, and Stedelijk Museum—is a 5-minute walk along Singelgracht from Leidseplein (note that much of the Rijksmuseum is closed until 2013 for refurbishment, but the Stedelijk should be re-opened by 2011.

An area worth a special mention is the **Jordaan** (pronounced yor-*daan*), an old neighborhood filled with inexpensive restaurants, offbeat stores, and small galleries. The Jordaan lies between Brouwersgracht, Prinsengracht, Looiersgracht, and Lijnbaansgracht. To get there, turn right off Damrak at any point between Centraal Station and the Dam, then cross over Prinsengracht.

Returning to Centraal Station—and *everybody* winds up back there eventually—if you exit the station at the rear you'll be standing on the city's fast-changing **Waterfront,** which is the setting for much of the city's redevelopment effort for years to come.

THE PRINCIPAL SQUARES   There are six major squares in central Amsterdam that will be the hubs of your visit:

The **Dam** is the city's heart and the site of the original dam across the Amstel River that gave the city its name. Encircling the square are the Royal Palace, the Nieuwe Kerk national church, and department stores, hotels, and restaurants. On the square is the Nationaal Monument of World War II.

Leidseplein and the streets around the city's signature nightlife square glitter with restaurants, nightclubs, music venues, a casino, and movie theaters. It's a fun scene even if hustle and bustle reigns over style.

Rembrandtplein is another entertainment scene, and bustles with eateries and places to grab a drink.

Museumplein is the main cultural center, containing the Rijksmuseum, Concertgebouw, Van Gogh Museum, and Stedelijk Museum, all in close proximity.

Waterlooplein, another cultural focal point, is home to the Muziektheater and a superb flea market (p. 227).

Muntplein is a busy transportation hub, easily recognizable for its crown-topped 17th-century Munttoren (Mint Tower), one of the city's original fortress towers.

Neighborhoods in Brief

For the purposes of locating the hotels and restaurants reviewed in this book, I've divided the city of Amsterdam into six major neighborhoods and four outlying districts. Keep in mind that some of these could have been further subdivided and there are inevitable "border disputes" about where one area begins and another ends—and in which one a particular establishment properly belongs.

The Center   The *Centrum* is the core area around the Dam and Centraal Station, and through the neighborhood known as De Wallen (the Walls), is the oldest part of the city, and includes the Red Light District. It's home to the main downtown shopping areas and attractions such as the Royal Palace, the Amsterdam Historical Museum, Madame Tussauds, and many canal-boat piers. Note that the Red Light District is only a small part of the Center, so you won't be constantly tripping over hookers and dope-heads. There are plenty of reasons to lodge in the Center, right in the heart of things, and a few reasons not to: It's busy, filled with traffic, noise, and social whirl. If you seek tranquillity, the Center's not the place to find it.

The Waterfront   Centered on Centraal Station and stretching east and west along both banks of the channel known as *Het IJ,* this fast-redeveloping area includes the artificial islands, warehouses, and other installations of Amsterdam's old harbor (the new harbor lies west of the city). A shiny new kind of Amsterdam is taking shape on parts of this waterfront where old facilities have been demolished, marked now by gentrification and vast construction sites. Across the water from Centraal Station is **Amsterdam-Noord** (Amsterdam North), a district that has been little more than a dull dormitory suburb up until now. This is changing, though, with dining and entertainment venues opening up.

The Canal Belt   The semicircular, multi-strand "necklace" of manmade waterways, Herengracht, Keizersgracht, and Prinsengracht (called the *Grachtengordel* in Dutch), was built around the old heart of town during the 17th-century Golden Age. Its vista of elegant, gabled mansions fronting long, tree-lined canals forms the image most often associated with Amsterdam. This zone includes the 16th-century Singel canal, hotels of all sizes, restaurants, antiques shops, and attractions like the canal-house museums and the Anne Frankhuis (p. 138). It would be a shame to visit this watery city without staying in a canal-view hotel, particularly since those lodgings are usually in 300-year-old buildings. So to really experience Amsterdam, splurge a bit, even if it's only for a night or two, to stay at a canal-house hotel.

Leidseplein   The city's most happening nightlife square, its immediate surroundings cover such a small area that perhaps it could have been included under "the Canal Belt." But so distinctive is Leidseplein that it demands to be highlighted on its own. In addition to performance venues, movie theaters, bars, and cafes, there are plenty of good hotels and restaurants in this frenetically busy area, which won't suit those who don't like crowds and bustle.

Rembrandtplein   Like Leidseplein but on a reduced scale, this square boasts a swatch of hotels, restaurants, cafes, and nightlife venues lively enough to justify picking it out from its surroundings.

The Jordaan   This nest of tightly packed streets and canals lies west of the Center, beyond the major canals. Once a neighborhood of tradesmen, artisans and their families, it's become fashionable, and is now filled with artists, students, and professionals, served by trendy boutiques and restaurants. Still, its "indigenous" residents, the *Jordanezen,* are alive and well, and show no signs of succumbing to gentrification. In its long history, the old Jordaan has seen plenty of trends come and go; it'll still be there whether or not the boutiques and

Amsterdam Neighborhoods

NOORD

Het IJ

JAVA-EILAND

Waterplein West

De Ruijterkade

Centraal Station

Centraal Station

IJ-Tunnel

Muziekgebouw aan 't IJ/ Bimhuis

Passenger Terminal Amsterdam

Jan Schaefer Brug

IJhaven

De Ruijterkade

Oostelijke Handelskade

Piet Heinkade

Dijksgracht

Nieuwendijk

Oosterdokskade

Oosterdok

MARINE ETABLISSEMENT (NAVAL COMPLEX)

CENTRUM

Scheepvaarthuis

Science Center NEMO

Oude Kerk

RED LIGHT DISTRICT

Damrak

Warmoes

Zeedijk

Geldersekade

Kromme Waal

Waals Eilandsgracht

Oude Waal

Prins Hendrikkade

Scheepvaartmuseum (Maritime Museum)

Kattenburgervaart

Kattenburgerstraat

Grote Wittenburgerstraat

Wittenburgervaart

Nieuwmarkt

Nieuwmarkt

Recht boomssloot

Oudezijds-Achterburgwal

Oudezijds-Voorburgwal

Binnen-Kadijk

Boomssloot

Oude Schans

Nieuwe Uilenburgerstraat

Valkenburgerstraat

Kattenburger-gracht

Wittenburger-gracht

Oostenburgergracht

Nieuwe Vaart

Oude

Nieuwe

Oudezijds Voorburgwal

Kloveniersburgwal

Groenburgwal

Sint-Antonies-breestraat

Jodenbreestraat

Hooge Kadijk

Laagte Kadijk

JODENBUURT (JEWISH QUARTER)

Wertheim-park

Plantage

Entrepotdok

Doklaan

Sarphatistraat

Stad-huis

Muziek-theater

Zwanenburgwal

Jodenbreestraat

Waterloo-plein

Mr. Visserplein

Planetarium

Geologisch Museum

ARTIS ZOO

Binnenamstel

Amstel

Blauw-brug

Waterlooplein

Nieuwe Herengracht

Hortus Botanicus

Plantage Middenlaan

Mauritskade

Rembrandt-plein

Herengracht

Keizers-gracht

Utrechtsestraat

Hermitage Amsterdam

Nieuwe Keizersgracht

Nieuwe Kerkstraat

Plantage Muidergracht

Plantage Muidergracht

Zoologisch Museum & Aquarium

OOST

Kerk-straat

Amstel

Magere Brug

Nieuwe Prinsengracht

Weesperstraat

Amstelveld

Prinsengracht

Amstel-sluizen

Nieuwe Achtergracht

Singelgracht

Tropenmuseum

Linnaeusstraat

Falckstraat

Frederiks-plein

Weesperplein

Sarphatistraat

Mauritskade

Sajet-plein

Boerhaave-plein

OOSTERPARK

Witsenkade

Stadhouderskade

Sarphati-

Hoge-sluis

's-Gravesande-plein

Oosterpark

Kastanje-plein

Toronto Brug

Mauritskade

Wibautstraat

Ruyschstraat

Blasiusstraat

Eerste Oosterparkstr

Tweede Oosterparkstraat

Eiken-plein

Derde Oosterparkstraat

DE PIJP

Van Woustraat

Amstel

Nieuwe Amstelbrug

Beuken-plein

Vrolikstraat

Populierenweg

SARPHATIPARK

Ceintuurbaan

To Wibautstraat

restaurants survive. Note that this book only lists a couple of Jordaan hotels; this is a great residential neighborhood, but it doesn't have many lodging options.

Museum District & Vondelpark Gracious and residential, this area surrounds the three major museums: The Rijksmuseum, the Van Gogh Museum, and the Stedelijk Museum, which accounts for its Dutch name: *Museumbuurt*. There's also the Concertgebouw (a superb concert hall), many restaurants, Amsterdam's most elegant shopping streets (Pieter Cornelisz Hooftstraat and van Baerlestraat), and the city's best-known park, Vondelpark itself. The U.S. and U.K. consulates are here too, as is a cluster of small, value-oriented hotels.

Amsterdam South A residential area dating from the first half of the 20th century, *Zuid* offers a number of hotels, particularly along Apollolaan, a broad avenue the locals dubbed the "Gold Coast" for its rows of expensive houses.

Amsterdam East The old residential *Oost* district stretching from the right bank of the Amstel River has attractions like the Tropical Museum (p. 148) and Artis, the city's zoo (p. 171). The East, which is rich in ethnic minority groups, also has great views along the Amstel, a status-symbol hotel (the **Inter-Continental Amstel Amsterdam**) and restaurant **(La Rive),** and a top performance venue **(Koninklijk Theater Carré).**

Amsterdam West The district west of the Singelgracht canal covers a lot of ground but doesn't have much in the way of sights and delights.

Amsterdam North Across the IJ channel from Centraal Station, *Noord* has up until now been a largely uninteresting "dormitory" district. That's beginning to change, but for now most of the interesting developments in this area are along what used to be the old harbor, and these are featured under the "Waterfront" heading.

THE BEST OF AMSTERDAM IN 1 DAY

You'll want to limit yourself in what you attempt to accomplish with just a day in Amsterdam. It's better to leave with a few good memories than try for quick, unsubstantial glimpses of everything. That doesn't mean you can't see a lot. The Center is a small enough neighborhood that you'll get around it without much trouble, either on foot or by using public transportation. This itinerary takes you to most of the must-see attractions, and includes the two most popular museums, the Rijksmuseum and the Van Gogh Museum. Still, the route affords plenty of opportunity for diverting to sights that strike your fancy. *Start: Trams 4, 9, 14, 16, 24, or 25 to the Dam.*

1 The Dam ★★★

Amsterdam grew up around a dam on the Amstel River that's now a monumental square. So opulent was the town hall on the Dam, royalty took it over for the Koninklijk Paleis (Royal Palace) ★. Teens can join the young people hanging out at the World War II Nationaal Monument, just across the tram rails. Younger kids might want to feed the pigeons in front of the palace. See p. 149.

2 Canal-Boat Cruise ★★

Sailing is easier on your feet than walking, and the view of this city from the water is the best one. Stroll or take any tram from the Dam south along Rokin to Spui and cross the street to get to the tour-boat dock. Catch you back here in an hour. See p. 172.

3 The Begijnhof ★★

A former religious cloister for women, the Begijnhof, founded in the 14th century, is now a residence for elderly women. You're allowed to stroll (quietly) through the tranquil courtyard. See p. 152.

4 Café Luxembourg 🍺 ★
The best of the "grand cafes" is a place to kick back for coffee, breakfast, lunch, or a cosmopolitan salad or snack. Dine in the dusky interior or on the sidewalk terrace. Spuistraat 24. 𝄐 020/620-6264. See p. 113.

5 Leidseplein

Humpback bridges on Leidsestraat afford views of the Herengracht, Keizersgracht, and Prinsengracht canals: Amsterdam's 17th-century Golden Age Grachtengordel (Canal Belt). In summer, Leidseplein's sidewalks are just about filled with cafe tables. See chapter 10.

6 Café Americain 🍺 ★
This Art Nouveau and Art Deco jewel dating from 1900 has lost none of its visual allure, though tourist popularity has ruined its once-exclusive cachet. Amsterdam American Hotel, Leidsekade 97. 𝄐 020/556-3000. See p. 122.

7 Rijksmuseum ★★★

Renovative work at Holland's National Museum means that most of this trove of Dutch art and culture is behind impenetrable walls until 2013. Yet the vast collection's highlights alone, squeezed into the Philips Wing, under the title *The Masterpieces,* is more than worth a visit. See p. 139.

8 Zeebanket van Altena 🍺 ★
Nowhere is that Dutch specialty, fresh raw herring, better than at this *haringhuis* fish stall next to the Rijksmuseum. Stadhouderskade (at Jan Luijkenstraat). 𝄐 020/676-9139. See p. 124.

9 Museumplein

The **Rijksmuseum** is at the top, the **Van Gogh Museum** and the **Stedelijk Museum** are down one side, and the **Concertgebouw** is at the bottom of this wide open space. In warm weather, picnic under the trees or cool your feet in an oval pond. See p. 60.

10 Van Gogh Museum ★★★

Be prepared to join the line for a museum dedicated to a no-hope 19th-century Dutch artist who sold a single painting during his lifetime and ended his life by suicide. Vincent's admirers are now legion and each of the more than 200 van Goghs hung on the museum's walls is as near priceless as paintings get. See p. 140.

11 The Concertgebouw ★★★

If you've planned ahead, you'll be the one with the smug look and the ticket in your pocket for a concert by the **Royal Concertgebouw Orchestra** at Amsterdam's stellar concert hall. See p. 235.

SUGGESTED AMSTERDAM ITINERARIES

The Best of Amsterdam in 1 Day

Amsterdam Suggested Itineraries

DAY ONE
1. The Dam
2. Canal-Boat Cruise
3. The Begijnhof
4. Café Luxembourg ☕
5. Leidseplein
6. Café Americain ☕
7. Rijksmuseum
8. Zeebanket van Altena ☕
9. Museumplein
10. Van Gogh Museum
11. The Concertgebouw
12. Brasserie Keyzer ☕
13. Vondelpark
14. Vertigo ☕

DAY TWO
1. Anne Frankhuis
2. Westerkerk
3. Homomonument
4. De Prins ☕
5. Houseboat Museum
6. Amsterdams Historisch Museum
7. Kantjil & de Tijger ☕
8. Bloemenmarkt
9. Muntplein
10. Rembrandtplein
11. Café Schiller ☕
12. Magere Brug
13. Muziektheater
14. Breitner ☕

DAY THREE

1. Waterlooplein
2. Museum Het Rembrandthuis
3. Nieuwmarkt
4. In de Waag 🍴
5. Hash Marihuana & Hemp Museum
6. Oude Kerk
7. Centraal Station
8. Grand Café–Restaurant 1e Klas 🍴
9. Muziekgebouw aan 't IJ/Bimhuis
10. Harbor Ferry Ride
11. Wilhelmina Dok 🍴

12 Brasserie Keyzer ☕ ★
Dine adjacent to the Concertgebouw at this venerable, atmospheric, and moderately formal restaurant. Van Baerlestraat 96. ✆ 020/675-1866. See p. 128.

13 Vondelpark ★★
A walk in the park should be a relaxing way to end your explorations on a late afternoon or early evening when it's still light. After dark, it's not so desirable. See p. 167.

14 Vertigo ☕ ★
With its terrace looking out on Vondelpark, the Film Museum's cafe-restaurant sets the scene for some fine-dining action. Vondelpark 3. ✆ 020/612-3021. See p. 131.

THE BEST OF AMSTERDAM IN 2 DAYS

Before you leave your hotel on the second day, try getting tickets to the ballet or opera at the **Muziektheater** for an evening performance. See the **Anne Frankhuis** first and go early because there's always a line (although during summer, when the museum is busiest and open until 10pm, it may be better to go in the evening). *Start: Trams 13, 14, or 17 to Westermarkt.*

1 Anne Frankhuis ★★★
The Prinsengracht canal house where Anne Frank hid from the Nazis during World War II seems haunted by tragic ghosts, yet filled with her brave spirit. See p. 138.

2 Westerkerk ★
A bronze statue of Anne Frank graces the square outside the 17th-century Protestant church where Rembrandt was laid to rest. Head up the steeple for heavenly views of the city. See p. 162.

3 Homomonument
The world's first ever monument to persecuted gays and lesbians takes the form of three rose-colored granite triangles, recalling the shape of the badge the Nazis forced homosexuals to wear. See p. 156.

4 De Prins ☕ ★★
Though it's in a heavily touristed area, De Prins has kept the finest qualities of a quintessential Amsterdam *eetcafé*. Prinsengracht 124. ✆ 020/624-9382. See p. 120.

5 Houseboat Museum
Ever wondered what it would be like to own a houseboat? Find out aboard the vintage canal-barge **Hendrika Maria**. Be sure to duck when you go below. See p. 165.

6 Amsterdams Historisch Museum ★★
Amsterdam manages to stay on the cutting edge of just about every trend even while remaining immersed in more history than is easy to digest. That's where the Historical Museum's breezy traipse through 800 years comes in handy. See p. 143.

7 Kantjil & de Tijger 🍵 ★

Nothing is more typical of Amsterdam than its love affair with Indonesian cuisine. This elegant eatery is a master of the genre. Spuistraat 291–293. ✆ 020/620-0994. See p. 111.

8 Bloemenmarkt (Flower Market) ★

The famed floating flower market stands partly on barges permanently moored on Singel and partly on shore—so that "floating" tag is more marketing-driven than real. By any name, though, the flower market is a colorful sight. See p. 227.

9 Muntplein

This misshaped "square" doesn't quite cut it as a visitor attraction, despite boasting the medieval **Munttoren (Mint Tower)** with its graceful spire and tinkling carillon. Most people are preoccupied with staying alive at this busy tram intersection. See p. 60.

10 Rembrandtplein

A city square (re-modeled in 2009) that makes up in sheer tackiness for what it lacks in sophistication. Actually, that's not quite fair. There are a few decent cafes and the determination to have a good time can be infectious, or at any rate loud. Don't miss Rembrandt's so-so statue in the center of the square. See p. 60.

11 Café Schiller 🍵 ★

While it can seem *too* cool for Rembrandtplein—perhaps the reason it's often empty—Schiller has Art Deco style and a calm-oasis character some locals find engaging. Rembrandtplein 36. ✆ 020/624-9864. See p. 246.

12 Magere Brug ★

The "Skinny Bridge" over the Amstel River has about as many tales associated with its creation as lights that illuminate it at night. In daylight or darkness, the view from this wooden drawbridge is memorable. See p. 155.

13 Muziektheater ★★

A synthetic-modern architecture has earned the city's opera and dance venue the biting epithet of the "False Teeth." The Amsterdam-based Netherlands Opera and National Ballet, and the regularly visiting Netherlands Dance Theater (from The Hague), do their impressive best to keep it real on the inside. See p. 236.

14 Breitner 🍵 ★

For pre- or post-Muziektheater dining, and even during the performance (if you didn't attend), Breitner puts on a pretty refined show. Amstel 212. ✆ 020/627-7879. See p. 117.

THE BEST OF AMSTERDAM IN 3 DAYS

If you want to visit the Red Light District on your third day, morning is the best time. Most of its weird folk have crashed for the day and there's an air almost of innocence to the place, which occupies one of the oldest parts of town. Only the middle segment of this itinerary goes through the Red Light District; the rest is a picture of purity—or as much purity as a smudgy city like Amsterdam ever aspires to. **Start:** *Metro and trams 4, 9, or 14 to Waterlooplein.*

1 Waterlooplein

The flea market here was once a fixture of the old Jodenbuurt (Jewish Quarter). Not much of the Jewish community survived the war, and neither did much of their neighborhood. There's still a flea market on the square, though, and plenty of grungy stuff to buy. See p. 227.

2 Museum Het Rembrandthuis ★★

Rembrandt painted some of the world's finest art, and put on airs and graces at this house—before bankruptcy spoiled the party and he had to leave. Be sure to view his etchings and drawings. See p. 145.

3 Nieuwmarkt

Sint-Antoniesbreestraat curves around to this lively old market square which, partly because its only public transportation link is a Metro station, seems like a place apart from the rest of this old part of town. See p. 228.

4 In de Waag 🍵 ★

Housed in a centuries-old fortified city gate and weigh house, this cafe-restaurant combines a medieval setting with sharp modern cuisine. Nieuwmarkt 4. ☎ 020/422-7772. See p. 111.

5 Hash Marihuana & Hemp Museum ★

The hash museum goes far out of its way, or maybe just far out, to demonstrate that hemp has all manner of useful applications besides being tamped into little pipes. Yeah, right. Look for David Teniers's painting of long-ago hemp-puffing peasants. See p. 169.

6 Oude Kerk ★★

It's somehow symbolic of Amsterdam—a once-Catholic place of pilgrimage turned sober Calvinist—that its Old Church should sit smack in the middle of what's now the Red Light District. Surrounding the church are neat little homes once occupied by pious women. Today, many are still occupied by women, who might well be pious, if not exactly virtuous. See p. 161.

7 Centraal Station

Everyone ends up here sooner or later. The architecturally noteworthy station, a great place for people-watching, is the focal point of the city's public transportation by train, tram, bus, Metro, taxi, water-taxi, ferry, and canal bus. Stroll to the rear of the station for fine harbor views. See p. 200.

8 Grand Café-Restaurant 1e Klas 🍵

Surprising as it might seem, the station restaurant is a decent place to grab a bite, whether or not you're catching a train. Platform 2B, Centraal Station. ☎ 020/625-0131. See p. 115.

9 Muziekgebouw aan 't IJ/Bimhuis ★

Just east of Centraal Station, the waterfront redevelopment zone acquired one of its shiniest works of modern architecture when the Muziekgebouw aan 't IJ concert hall for contemporary music (and the attached Bimhuis jazz club) opened to thunderous applause in 2005, even though both operations had previously occupied grungy premises that seemed to fit better with the city's rep. See p. 236.

10 Harbor Ferry Ride

Free ferries shuttle back and forth across Het IJ waterway from the Waterplein West dock behind Centraal Station. They make for a good way of viewing the city's old harbor. Along its shores, residential, commercial, and cultural properties are surging up in waves of redevelopment. See p. 43.

11 Wilhelmina-Dok 🍵 ★

Taking the free ferry across Het IJ to IJplein in Amsterdam-Noord puts you within easy walking or bicycling distance of this breezy restaurant. Nordwal 1. ℂ 020/632-3701. See p. 115.

WHERE TO STAY

I s your preference old-world charm combined with luxurious quarters? Glitzy modernity with every conceivable amenity? Small, intimate, family-run hotels? An historic canal house reflecting the lifestyle of centuries past? A modern, medium-size hotel on the fringe of inner-city bustle? A bare-bones dorm room that frees up scarce dollars for other purposes? Amsterdam has them all, and more.

5

Some hotels share more than one of these characteristics: A common fusion is that of historic canal house on the outside and glitzy, amenity-laden modernity on the inside.

You probably have your own idea of what makes a great hotel. My advice is to let your choice reflect the kind of city Amsterdam is—democratic, adventurous, quirky, and always in search of that enigmatic Dutch quality, *gezelligheid,* which is the ambience that makes a place warm, cozy, and welcoming (for more, see the "In Search of *Gezelligheid*" box later in this chapter). You can find this quality at all price levels, and especially among moderately priced hotels owned by locals.

Hotel Orientation

Amsterdam is expensive, but don't despair if you need to spend less than 100€ a night for a double room. Most city hotels, whatever their cost, are clean and tidily furnished, and in many cases they've been recently renovated. I've mostly listed hotels with rooms that have private facilities, even in the inexpensive category—and if I've included a hotel where this is not the case, I've only done so for the most compelling of reasons.

Many hotels offer significant rate reductions between November 1 and March 31, with the exception of the Christmas–New Year period. The city is as much a delight during this season as it is during the tourist-packed summer months; you'll enjoy a calendar full of cultural events, many traditional Dutch menu dishes not offered in warm weather, and streets, eateries, and museums filled with more locals than visitors.

If a particular hotel takes your fancy but is out of your price range, inquire whether special off-season, weekend, specific weekday, or other packages will bring prices down to what you can afford.

Smoke Won't Get in Your Eyes

Smoking is forbidden by law in Dutch hotel public areas—such as the lobby, restaurants, and bars—except in separate designated and enclosed spaces, in which staffers are not allowed to provide waiting or other services. Few, if any, hotels plan to establish such a separate space. Each hotel can decide whether or not smoking is legally allowed in its guest rooms. Around 90% of Dutch hotels have implemented a total ban on smoking in guest rooms. Hotels may charge guests who ignore the ban for extra cleaning costs associated with smoking.

You may want to avoid certain neighborhoods that harbor the haunts of drug or sex peddlers—I say "may" because many visitors head for Amsterdam precisely to experience these aspects of the city. Most Amsterdammers accept them as facts of life, and there are really no "no-go" areas, but it's wise to limit ventures into Amsterdam's shady corners to daylight or early-evening hours—there's no reason to spend your nights in a less-than-desirable area. The hotels described here are all decent hotels in decent neighborhoods (for the few on the fringes of dubious neighborhoods, I've mentioned this in the review).

The Netherlands adheres to the Benelux Hotel Classification System. Hotels get stars based on set criteria—having a pool, an elevator, and so on—so the hotel with the most stars isn't necessarily the most comfortable or elegant (though often it is). Each establishment must display a sign indicating its classification, from "1" for those with minimum amenities to "5" for deluxe, full-service hotels.

STANDARD AMENITIES A major element in upgrading low-cost hotels is squeezing bathrooms into guest rooms in the city's canal houses and older buildings. The term *bathroom,* by the way, is used whether the facilities include a tub, tub/shower combination, shower stall, or even one of those silly shower/toilets in the same space that inevitably results in lots of soggy toilet paper. If having a full bathroom is important to you, verify in advance that all you need is included.

Dutch TV channels air American and British programs in English with Dutch subtitles. Cable TV offers CNN International, BBC World News, MTV, Sky, and others. If you're traveling with kids, be warned that some Dutch, German, and Luxembourg stations broadcast soft (and some not-so-soft) porno shows late at night.

RESERVATIONS Should you arrive without a reservation, VVV Amsterdam tourist offices will help you for 4€, plus a refundable room deposit. They can find you something, even during the busiest periods, but it may not be exactly what, or where, you want. To reserve ahead of time, contact the **Amsterdam Tourism & Convention Board,** P.O. Box 3901, 1001 AS Amsterdam (© **020/201-880;** fax 020/201-8850; reservations@atcb.nl; www.iamsterdam.nl). Online reservations are free; those made by phone, fax, and e-mail cost 14€ and it costs an additional 14€ to change a reservation.

RATES Many moderately priced and budget hotels now copy expensive hotels by varying their rates from day to day for both online and phone reservations, according to the level of demand, and whether it's an advance-purchase or a last-minute reservation. A particular hotel reviewed in this chapter might be categorized as "Expensive" or "Very Expensive" even when its lowest possible rate would fit into the "Moderate" or even "Budget" range. If you manage to secure a room at that rate, rejoice in your luck or acumen, but be aware that plenty of your fellow guests will be paying at the higher end of the range.

TAXES Value-added tax (BTW) of 6% and service are included in hotel bills. In addition, a 5% city tax applies to rooms at all Amsterdam hotels. Most hotels add this tax separately to the room rate; others include it in the rate. Be sure to check this when reserving.

VEXATIONS Mosquitoes, which thrive in the damp conditions on and near the canals and on marshy reclaimed land around the city, can be a major nuisance. You can buy various plug-in devices to hold them at bay, and a fly-swatter to bring 'em down, but it's best not to let them into your room in the first place.

The lower down the price scale you go, the more likely you are to find yourself subject to "amenities" such as tiny sinks in which you can just about wash one hand at a time, no soap or shampoo in the bathroom, or a supplementary charge for orange juice at breakfast—talk about being nickel-and-dimed (or dollar-and-pounded).

GAY & LESBIAN HOTELS Though by law no hotel is allowed to turn away same-sex couples—in Amsterdam, such a thing is unimaginable anyway—service will be better-tailored at gay-run hotels, and Amsterdam has gay hotels aplenty. Prices and facilities are pretty unexceptional—the innkeepers' knowledge that most guests will be out enjoying themselves is probably why these hotels don't turn up the luxury level.

COMPLAINTS Standards of service can be, aah . . . "relaxed" . . . in Amsterdam. That doesn't mean you won't get good, friendly service—you will—but there's a subtle subtext: Dutch service providers just naturally assume they're doing you a favor, rather than their job. This attitude surfaces most clearly when you make a complaint. You may be astonished to discover that if you have a problem, you might be blamed for not being satisfied with what's provided.

If you dare to make a heated complaint—such as rearing up on your hind legs and hollering until the staff person gets his or her butt into gear—your effort goes down like the *Titanic*. In big international hotels, where staffers are accustomed to the demanding "foibles" of global business travelers, the response is likely to be glacial but correct. But in a hotel farther down the financial food chain, watch out: You may have a stand-up fight on your hands.

A Down-to-Earth Warning

Elevators are hard to shoehorn into the cramped confines of a 17th-century canal house and cost more than some moderately priced and budget hotels can afford. Many simply don't have them. If lugging your old wooden sea chest up six flights of steep, narrow stairs is liable to void your life insurance, you better make sure an elevator is in place and working. Should there be no elevator and you have trouble climbing stairs, ask for a room on a low floor. Or think positively and regard the stairs as your workout for the day.

BREAKFAST   If breakfast isn't included, expect to pay 5€ to 25€ for a continental, buffet, or full breakfast, depending on the hotel category. A typical morning begins with a selection of breads—whole-grain, nutty, or rye—fresh from the *warme bakker*; rusks (crunchy toasted rounds, like Zwieback); *ontbijtkoek* (spicy gingerbread cake); a platter of cheese and sliced meats (ham, roast beef, salami); coffee (thicker and stronger than American or English coffee, and often served with *koffiemelk*—gunk similar to condensed milk) or tea. Some hotels throw in a boiled egg, yogurt, fruit juice, or all three.

This, at any rate, is the ideal spread, but cheap hotels may present only a few sorry-looking, curled-up-at-the-edges cheese slices, assorted cold meats of indeterminate provenance, and eggs boiled hard enough to sink an enemy sub.

Saving on Your Hotel Room

The **rack rate** is the maximum rate that a hotel charges for a room. However, hardly anybody pays this price, except in high season or on holidays. To lower your cost:

- **Ask about special rates or discounts.** You may qualify for corporate, student, military, senior, frequent-flyer, union, or other discounts.
- **Dial direct.** When booking a room in a chain hotel, you'll often get a better deal by calling the individual hotel rather than the chain's main number.
- **Book online.** Many hotels offer Internet-only discounts or deals on Priceline, Hotwire, or Expedia; these rates are much lower than those available through the hotel itself.
- **Remember the law of supply and demand.** Resort hotels are most crowded and therefore most expensive on weekends, so discounts are usually available for midweek stays. Business hotels in downtown locations are busiest during the week, so expect big discounts over the weekend. Many hotels have high- and low-season prices; booking even a day after high season ends can mean big discounts.
- **Look into group or long-stay discounts.** If you come as part of a large group, you should be able to negotiate a bargain rate. Likewise, if you're planning a long stay (at least 5 days), you may qualify for a discount. As a general rule, expect 1 night free after a 7-night stay.
- **Avoid excess charges and hidden costs.** When you book a room, ask whether the hotel charges for parking. Use your own cellphone or prepaid phone card instead of dialing direct from hotel phones, which usually charge exorbitant rates. Don't be tempted by the room's minibar offerings. Finally, ask about local taxes and service charges, which can increase a room's cost by 15% or more.
- **Book an efficiency.** A room with a kitchenette allows you to shop for groceries and cook your own meals. This is a big money saver, especially for families on long stays.
- **Enroll in hotel frequent-stay programs,** which are upping the ante lately to win repeat customers' loyalty. Frequent guests can accumulate points or credits to earn free hotel nights, airline miles, in-room amenities, merchandise, tickets to concerts and events—and even credit toward stock in the participating hotel, in the case of the Jameson Inn hotel group. It's not only the many chain hotels and motels (**Hilton HHonors, Marriott Rewards,** to name but two) that award perks, but also individual inns and B&Bs. Many chain hotels partner with other hotel chains, car-rental firms, airlines, and credit card companies to give consumers additional incentive to do repeat business.

Landing the Best Room

Somebody has to get the best room in the house, and it might as well be you. Start by joining the hotel's frequent-guest program, which may make you eligible for upgrades. A hotel-branded credit card usually gives its owner "silver" or "gold" status in frequent-guest programs for free. Always ask for a corner room—they're usually larger and quieter, with more windows and light, and they often cost the same as standard rooms. When making your reservation, ask if the hotel is renovating; if it is, request a room away from the construction. Ask about nonsmoking rooms, rooms with views, rooms with twin, queen-, or king-size beds. If you're a light sleeper, request a quiet room away from vending machines, elevators, restaurants, bars, and discos. Ask for a room that has been most recently renovated or redecorated. If you're not happy with your room when you arrive, ask for another one. Most hotels will accommodate.

For tips on surfing for hotel deals online, visit frommers.com.

BEST HOTEL BETS

For additional recommendations, see "The Best Splurge Hotels" and "The Best Moderately Priced Hotels," in chapter 1.

- **Best Value:** Taking all factors into account—price, location, facilities, hospitality, Dutchness, and that indefinable element that makes a stay memorable—the **Estheréa,** Singel 303–309 (𝄞 **020/624-5146**), is the best value in town. See p. 86.
- **Best for Tradition: Die Port van Cleve,** Nieuwezijds Voorburgwal 176–180 (𝄞 **020/714-2000**), is one of Amsterdam's oldest hotels, but has entirely modernized rooms, so you can celebrate the 17th century in 21st-century comfort. See p. 80.
- **Best for Families:** The **Amstel Botel,** NDSM-Werf 3 (𝄞 **020/626-4247**). It's hard to beat a floating hotel that you reach by boat. Among its neighbors are a retired Soviet attack sub, a Greenpeace warrior of the seas, and the "Pancake Boat." See p. 85.
- **Best for Business Travelers:** The **NH Barbizon Palace,** Prins Hendrikkade 59–72 (𝄞 **020/556-4564**), is modern, luxurious, stylish, efficient, and has an excellent location—opposite Centraal Station—and a full range of business facilities. See p. 84.
- **Best Unknown Hotel:** This accolade goes to **Seven Bridges,** Reguliersgracht 31 (𝄞 **020/623-1329**), for its combination of location, decor, personal service, enthusiastic owners, and general all-round quality. See p. 88.
- **Best Budget Hotel:** Many cheap hotels in Amsterdam leave a lot to be desired. Not so the **Museumzicht,** Jan Luijkenstraat 22 (𝄞 **020/671-2954**), a plain, clean, and friendly hotel at a superb location across from the Rijksmuseum. See p. 96.

THE OLD CENTER

Very Expensive

Hotel de l'Europe ★★★   Change is afoot at this grande dame of Amsterdam hotels, which dates from 1896 and occupies a stretch of prime waterfront where the Amstel River flows into the city's canal net. While it keeps the airs and graces of a

5

WHERE TO STAY | The Old Centre

> ## No Stomach for Art
>
> So repelled were diners by the Karel Appel mural *Inquisitive Children* in the then-Town Hall's staff restaurant—now the Sofitel Amsterdam The Grand hotel's elegant restaurant **Bridges**—that it was covered up for 10 years. Today, modern-art devotees visit just to view the mural.

dignified, *fin de siècle* style behind its pastel-red and white facade, beginning in 2010 the hotel is undergoing major renovations and upgrades to all guest rooms (until now they have been furnished in classic style, spacious and bright, and with marble bathrooms). And this is in addition to a new, exclusive annex, dubbed the **De l'Europe Dutch Masters,** containing 23 suites that are the last word in contemporary luxury. Try for a room with a balcony overlooking the river. At mealtimes, choose from the laid-back French menu in the brasserie or more formal dining in the **Excelsior** restaurant (p. 107). **Note**: This hotel has been awarded a Green Key certificate for its environmental awareness and sustainable practices.

Nieuwe Doelenstraat 2–8 (facing Muntplein), 1012 CP Amsterdam. ℂ **800/223-6800** in the U.S. and Canada, or ℂ 020/531-1777. Fax 020/531-1778. www.leurope.nl. 100 rooms. 450€–550€ double; from 750€ suite. AE, DC, MC, V. Valet and self-parking 53€. Tram: 4, 9, 14, 16, 24, or 25 to De Munt. **Amenities:** 2 restaurants; 2 bars; babysitting; concierge; health club; pool (heated indoor); room service; sauna. *In room:* A/C, TV, hair dryer, minibar, Wi-Fi (free).

Sofitel Amsterdam The Grand ★★ In a fully modernized (most recently in 2009) courtly building that was a 15th-century convent, a 16th-century royal guesthouse, the 17th-century Amsterdam Admiralty headquarters, and the city's 19th-century Town Hall, the Grand is grand indeed, with its courtyard fountain and brass-and-wood revolving door. Enjoy afternoon tea in the lounge amid Art Deco and stained-glass windows; Oriental rugs grace black-and-white marble floors. Such elegance, and only a few blocks south of the Red Light District. Individually styled and furnished rooms reflect the different phases of the building's past and are the last word in plush. Most have couches and armchairs. Views are of 17th-century canals, the garden, or the courtyard. The contemporary French restaurant **Bridges** sports an abstract expressionist mural, *Inquisitive Children* (1949), by Cobra artist Karel Appel. **Note:** This hotel is nonsmoking, and has been awarded a Green Key certificate for its environmental awareness and sustainable practices.

Oudezijds Voorburgwal 197 (off Damstraat), 1012 EX Amsterdam. ℂ **800/515-5679** in the U.S. and Canada, or ℂ 020/555-3111. Fax 020/555-3222. www.thegrand.nl. 177 rooms. 550€–650€ double; from 800€ suite. AE, DC, MC, V. Valet parking 50€. Tram: 4, 9, 14, 16, 24, or 25 to Spui. **Amenities:** Restaurant; snack bar; lounge; bar; airport transfer; babysitting; concierge; health club and spa; pool (heated indoor); room service. *In room:* A/C, TV, hair dryer, minibar, Wi-Fi (free).

Expensive

Crowne Plaza Amsterdam City Centre ★ Relaxed luxury is pe[...] way to describe this fine hotel two blocks from Centraal Station. [...] the wooden beams typical of canalside houses in Amsterda[...] equipped with a trouser press, comfortable armchairs, and g[...] want to work. This hotel is a good bet for tourists as well [...] ers. A recent renovation program has brought the rooms [...] up-to-date. The **New Dorrius Brasserie** is a decent imp[...]

Where to Stay in Central Amsterdam

5

WHERE TO STAY | The Old Center

Dutch restaurant. **Note**: This hotel has been awarded a Green Key gold certificate for its environmental awareness and sustainable practices.

Nieuwezijds Voorburgwal 5 (at Hekelveld), 1012 RC Amsterdam. ☎ **877/227-6963** in the U.S. and Canada, or ☎ 020/620-0500. Fax 020/620-1173. www.amsterdam-citycentre.crowneplaza.com. 270 rooms. 200€–300€ double; from 450€ suite. Rates for executive rooms and suites include continental breakfast. AE, DC, MC, V. Valet parking 40€. Tram: 1, 2, 5, 13, or 17 to Martelaarsgracht. **Amenities:** 2 restaurants; lounge; bar; babysitting; concierge; executive rooms; health club and spa; room service. *In room:* A/C, TV, hair dryer, minibar, Wi-Fi (7€/hr., 20€/day).

Die Port van Cleve ★   One of the city's oldest hotels—it actually started life in 1864 as the first Heineken brewery—stands right across the street from the Royal Palace on the Dam. The ornamental facade, with its turrets and alcoves, is original and has been fully restored. Likewise, the interior was completely renovated a few years back. The guest rooms are relatively small, and in general are furnished in a plain way that doesn't quite complement the building's handsome looks. Watch out for noise from the busy (or bustling, if you prefer) street, in rooms at the front, especially in summer when you may want the windows open due to the absence of air-conditioning. You won't eat much more traditionally Dutch than in the **Brasserie de Poort,** and you can drink in the **Bodega de Blauwe Parade** watched over by a feast of Delft blue tiles.

Nieuwezijds Voorburgwal 176–180 (behind the Royal Palace), 1012 SJ Amsterdam. ☎ **020/714-2000.** Fax 020/714-2001. www.dieportvancleve.com. 121 rooms. 175€–350€ double; from 425€ suite. AE, DC, MC, V. No parking. Tram: 1, 2, 5, 13, or 17 to the Dam. **Amenities:** Restaurant; bars; babysitting; concierge; executive rooms; room service. *In room:* TV, hair dryer, Wi-Fi (free).

Hotel Amsterdam-De Roode Leeuw   A stone's throw from the Dam, this hotel, founded in 1911, has an 18th-century facade. Its rooms are super-modern, though, with thick carpets and ample wardrobe space. Rooms at the front of the hotel tend to get more light, but are also subject to more street noise; some have balconies. The award-winning **De Roode Leeuw** restaurant serves traditional Dutch cuisine, and the glassed-in heated terrace overlooking the Dam is a pleasant spot for a beer (open daily 11am–11:30pm). **Note:** This hotel has been awarded a Green Key certificate for its environmental awareness and sustainable practices.

Damrak 93–94 (beside the Dam), 1012 LP Amsterdam. ☎ **800/44-UTELL** in the U.S. and Canada, or ☎ 020/555-0666. Fax 020/620-4716. www.hotelamsterdam.nl. 79 rooms. 110€–325€ double. AE, DC, MC, V. No parking. Tram: 4, 9, 14, 16, 24, or 25 to the Dam. **Amenities:** Restaurant; cafe; room service. *In room:* A/C, TV, hair dryer, Internet (7.50€/hr., 15€/day), minibar, Wi-Fi (free).

5

WHERE TO STAY | The Old Center

NH Grand Hotel Krasnapolsky   The "Kras," located right on the Dam, began as the Wintertuin (Winter Garden) restaurant, founded in 1866 by a Polish tailor turned entrepreneur. Victorians sipped wine and nibbled pancakes beneath the hanging plants and lofty skylight ceiling, where breakfast and lunch are now served. Since then, it has spread amoeba-like over four buildings, including one with a Japanese garden and another with a Dutch roof garden. Some rooms are small, while others have been converted into individually decorated apartments. Their state varies from worn to tastefully renovated. Since there are so many, take a look at one first and retain an option to change one that's not suitable. The street alongside the hotel leads into the Red Light District, which may not be everyone's idea of the perfect evening stroll. *Note:* This hotel has been awarded a Green Key certificate for its environmental awareness and sustainable practices.

Dam 9 (facing Royal Palace), 1012 JS Amsterdam. ℂ **020/554-9111.** Fax 020/622-8607. www.nh-hotels.com. 468 rooms. 194€–204€ double; from 475€ suite. AE, DC, MC, V. Parking 50€. Tram: 4, 9, 14, 16, 24, or 25 to the Dam. **Amenities:** 2 restaurants; lounge; bar; babysitting; concierge; executive rooms; health club; Jacuzzi; room service. *In room:* A/C, TV, hair dryer, minibar, Wi-Fi (6€/hr., 11€–18€/day).

Radisson Blu ★   You can't get much closer to Old Amsterdam than at this stylish hotel in the higgledy-piggledy heart of the city. When you walk into the dazzling atrium, you face a vicarage dating from 1650. Radisson couldn't knock the building down, so they incorporated it into the new structure. Two 18th-century merchants' houses and a former paper factory complete the renovated ensemble. The hotel offers four types of themed rooms: Typical Dutch, with oak furnishings and orange curtains; Scandinavian; Asian; and Art Deco. All offer a standard of comfort and style that has made this hotel a firm Amsterdam favorite. Each room has a writing desk, and king-, queen-, or twin-size beds. Dine in the Dutch restaurant **De Palmboom.** The oak-beamed **De Pastoriebar** in the old vicarage handles drinks and snacks. *Note*: This hotel has been awarded a Green Key certificate for its environmental awareness and sustainable practices.

Rusland 17 (at the University of Amsterdam), 1012 CK Amsterdam. ℂ **800/333-3333** in the U.S. and Canada, or ℂ 020/623-1231. Fax 020/520-8200. www.radissonsas.com. 247 rooms. 150€–350€ double; from 600€ suite. Buffet breakfast included in business class, executive, and suite rates. AE, DC, MC, V. Parking 50€. Tram: 4, 9, 14, 16, 24, or 25 to Spui. **Amenities:** Restaurant; bar; babysitting; executive rooms; concierge; health club; room service; sauna. *In room:* A/C, TV, hair dryer, minibar, Wi-Fi (free).

Renaissance Amsterdam ★   Van Gogh liked this setting well enough to paint part of it in his *View of Amsterdam from Centraal Station* (1885). Built around an open central courtyard in an area of old warehouses, the six-story Renaissance blends with the gabled facades nearby. Antiquity's influence stops at the front door, however: The Renaissance is highly modern, offering big beds, color TVs with in-house movies, electronic security, and message-retrieval systems. It's a matter of opinion whether the hotel's transformation of the adjacent domed Lutheran **Koepelkerk** into an ultra-modern conference center is appropriate. The restored old church, which dates from 1671 (and was painted in 1885 by Vincent van Gogh), occasionally serves as a dining room for special events. The hotel's regular restaurant was closed for rebuilding at the time of writing; in the meantime, there's still the brown cafe–style **Koepelcafé,** which serves light meals. *Note:* This hotel is smoke-free, and has been awarded a Green Key certificate for its environmental awareness and sustainable practices.

Kattengat 1 (at Spuistraat), 1012 SZ Amsterdam. ℂ **888/236-2427** in the U.S. and Canada, or ℂ 020/621-2223. Fax 020/627-5254. www.renaissancehotels.com. 396 rooms. 275€–345€ double; from 595€ suite. Club Room rates include continental breakfast. AE, DC, MC, V. Parking 50€–55€. Tram: 1, 2, 5, 13, or 17 to Martelaarsgracht. **Amenities:** Restaurant; bar; babysitting; concierge; executive rooms; health club and spa (nearby); room service. *In room:* A/C, TV, hair dryer, minibar, Wi-Fi (7€/hr., 20€/day).

Moderate

Avenue Hotel ★   Part of this recently renovated hotel is a converted Golden Age warehouse that belonged to the V.O.C., the United East India Company. The rooms aren't huge, but they're bright and have clean furnishings and good-size bathrooms, some with a double sink. The location is pretty central and convenient for getting to and fro by tram—the downside is the clackety-clack of outside traffic. If this is likely to disturb you, ask for a room at the back or at least not on a low floor. Or simply look for a hotel in a location with less action. The Dutch buffet breakfast is more than decent, and the St. Jacobsstreet Café, around the corner in Sint-Jacobsstraat, takes care of dinner in reasonable style.

Nieuwezijds Voorburgwal 33 (near Centraal Station), 1012 RD Amsterdam. ℂ **020/530-9530.** Fax 020/530-9599. www.emb-hotels.nl. 80 rooms. 115€–160€ double. Rates include buffet breakfast. AE, DC, MC, V. Limited street parking. Tram: 1, 2, 5, 13, or 17 to Nieuwezijds Kolk. **Amenities:** Cafe/bar. *In room:* A/C (some rooms), TV, hair dryer, Wi-Fi (free).

Best Western Dam Square Inn   This hotel is another example of putting an old building to good use. This time, the old building—and a magnificent building it is— was a distillery. It's behind **Nieuwe Kerk** (p. 150), and its granite details accentuate the brickwork and massive curve-topped doors with elaborate hinges. The location is superb, just footsteps off the Dam. Inside, the rooms (all renovated in 2009) are all you'll want: Modern, bright, comfortable, and reasonably priced for the location.

Gravenstraat 12–16 (at the Dam), 1012 NM Amsterdam. ℂ **800/344-1212** in the U.S. and Canada, or ℂ 020/623-3716. Fax 020/638-1156. www.bestwesterndamsquareinn.com. 38 rooms. 155€–195€ double. Rates include continental breakfast. AE, DC, MC, V. No parking. Tram: 1, 2, 4, 5, 9, 13, 14, 16, 17, 24, or 25 to the Dam. **Amenities:** Bar. *In room:* A/C, TV, hair dryer, Wi-Fi (7.50€/day).

Rho Hotel   Once you find it, you'll bless this hotel for its generally quiet-yet-central location, surely one of the best in town, and a friendly staff, which together make up for some deficiencies in other attributes. Tucked away on a side street just off the Dam's **Nationaal Monument** (p. 149), the Rho's building was once the offices of a gold company and, before that, a theater from around 1908 (which is now the reception and breakfast area). Most rooms in the nonsmoking hotel are modern and comfortable, if not overly inspired in the looks department, and some are on the small side. Check out a few rooms, if you can, before committing.

Nes 5–23 (at the Dam), 1012 KC Amsterdam. ℂ **020/620-7371.** Fax 020/620-7826. www.rhohotel. com. 165 rooms. 100€–165€ double. Rates include buffet breakfast. AE, MC, V. Parking 35€. Tram: 4, 9, 14, 16, 24, or 25 to the Dam. **Amenities:** Lounge; bikes. *In room:* TV, fridge, hair dryer, Wi-Fi (free).

Sint Nicolaas ★★ 🛎   Named after Amsterdam's patron saint, this hotel is conveniently near Centraal Station, in a prominent corner building at the apex of two converging streets. Heavy tram, bus, and car traffic passing by outside is the downside to this location. Originally, the building was a factory that manufactured ropes and carpets from sisal imported from the then-Dutch colonies; it later housed harbor offices. New owners have upgraded the interior to near-boutique status, affording a level of comfort that's rarely achieved by Amsterdam hotels in this price range. This applies especially if you score a rate at the lower end of wide scale rates—skewed upwards by the "de luxe doubles"—and bear in mind a thin amenities roster. Each room has a different character, with the regular ones emphasizing classic comforts, warm colors, prints, and exposed wood beams; and the deluxe doubles all cool blacks, grays, and whites.

Spuistraat 1A (at Nieuwendijk), 1012 SP Amsterdam. ℂ **020/626-1384.** Fax 020/623-0979. www.centre hotels.nl. 27 rooms. 95€–250€ double. Rates include continental breakfast. AE, DC, MC, V. Limited street parking. Tram: 1, 2, 5, 13, or 17 to Martelaarsgracht. **Amenities:** Lounge; bar. *In room:* TV, hair dryer, Wi-Fi (free).

Inexpensive

Budget Hotel Clemens Amsterdam ★   A 2-minute walk from the **Anne Frankhuis** (p. 138), this friendly, recently refurbished and modernized hotel spreads over four floors in one of those typical steep-staired Dutch buildings, with the reception and breakfast room up one flight of stairs. There's no elevator. Both the fairly spacious "deluxe" rooms (which have bathrooms) and the fairly tight budget rooms (which are without bathrooms) are kept in good trim. All are bright, clean, and homely rather than stylish. Nos. 7 and 8 each have a balcony facing the **Westerkerk** (p. 162). Three rooms are triples. There are a few laptops available to rent at reception to guests who haven't lugged their own along. Raadhuisstraat is a busy street during the day, though generally not so at night; keep this in mind if any amount of noise is a deal-breaker for you.

Raadhuisstraat 39 (near the Westerkerk), 1016 DC Amsterdam. ℂ **020/624-6089.** Fax 020/626-9658. www.clemenshotel.nl. 9 units (5 with bathroom). 120€ double with bathroom; 75€–80€ double without bathroom. Rates include buffet breakfast. AE, MC, V (for budget rooms, only cash is accepted). Limited street parking. Tram: 13, 14, or 17 to Westerkerk. **Amenities:** Room service. *In room:* TV, hair dryer, Internet (free), minifridge.

Winston   Maybe too close to the Red Light District for some people's taste, and on a slightly seedy street, the Winston is a step up from grungy and has a hang-loose, alternative rep. You might even hear some (fanciful) comparisons made to New York's Chelsea Hotel. Local artists created paintings, photographs, and other works of what you might call art, for the halls, rooms, doors, and bathrooms. The sparely furnished rooms vary in size, contain from two to six beds, and are tolerably clean and maintained.

   Summer Stays: Reserve Ahead

July and August are tough months for finding rooms in Amsterdam; you're advised to reserve as far ahead as possible. If you have problems getting a room, contact the **VVV Amsterdam** tourist office, which will find you one somewhere, though it might not be in the kind of hotel you want. It can be particularly hard to find hoteliers willing to give away rooms for a single night when that might cost them a longer booking. In this circumstance, a last-minute search might be called for, since a hotel that's had a last-minute cancellation is more likely to consider single-night occupancy. This is a *possible* exception to the rule that a last-minute search is the wrong way to go about finding a hotel room in Amsterdam.

None of them has a view that's worth looking out the window for. Bathrooms are small, but have most of the requisite bits and pieces in them, and most rooms that don't have a bathtub do have a shower. The **Belushi's** bar is a fun meeting place and the next-door **Winston Kingdom** club has daily live music or DJs.

Warmoesstraat 129 (off Damrak), 1012 JA Amsterdam. ✆ **020/623-1380.** Fax 020/639-2308. www. winston.nl. 69 rooms. 69€–136€ double. Rates include buffet breakfast. AE, DC, MC, V. No parking. Tram: 4, 9, 14, 16, 24, or 25 to the Dam. **Amenities:** Restaurant; bar; bikes; Wi-Fi (free). *In room:* TV (some rooms), no phone.

THE WATERFRONT

Expensive

Lloyd Hotel ★ Located in the redevelopment zone of the old harbor east of Centraal Station, the Lloyd was an emigrants' hotel from 1921 to 1935. Each of its rooms has a different shape, style, and modern decor, and with rooms of various classes, the hotel straddles all categories except "Very Expensive." Its most expensive rooms, which are the largest, have a view of the water or a specially designed interior (or both). The mattresses are firm, but only a few rooms have king-size doubles—one does, however, have a bed that "sleeps" eight. The hotel's **Culturele Ambassade** houses art exhibits, modern artworks are scattered around the property, and there's an attic library. Two restaurants aim to make it cool to dine in a hotel: **Snel**, fast and affordable, is open 24/7; **Sloom** is leisurely and expensive, and you can order whatever you desire and the kitchen will aim to cook it.

Oostelijke Handelskade 34, 1019 BN Amsterdam (at IJhaven). ✆ **020/561-3636.** Fax 020/561-3600. www.lloydhotel.com. 117 rooms (106 with bathroom). 95€ double without bathroom; 140€–450€ double with bathroom. AE, DC, MC, V. Parking 25€. Tram: 10 or 26 to Rietlandpark. **Amenities:** 2 restaurants; bar; babysitting; bikes; room service. *In room:* TV, Wi-Fi (free).

NH Barbizon Palace ★ Centrally located, within easy walking distance of Centraal Station and the Dam, this sparkling establishment meets every criterion for an ideal Amsterdam hotel. Built behind the facades of 19 traditional canal houses, it's fully modern and efficient inside, and loaded with amenities. Many rooms feature split-level designs and antique oak beams. A Roman forum may come to mind as you step into the hotel; the lobby is a long promenade of highly polished black-and-white marble floor tiles, with a massive skylight arching above. The excellent French restaurant **Vermeer** earns frequent praise from food critics. **Hudson's,** serving a la carte meals, and a late breakfast of juice, two eggs, a *broodje*, and coffee or tea from 10:30am to noon, is also good. **Note**: This hotel has been awarded a Green Key certificate for its environmental awareness and sustainable practices.

Prins Hendrikkade 59-72 (facing Centraal Station), 1012 AD Amsterdam. ✆ **020/556-4564.** Fax 020/624-3353. www.nh-hotels.com. 274 rooms. 135€–225€ double; from 475€ suite. AE, DC, MC, V. Parking 48€. Tram: 1, 2, 4, 5, 9, 13, 16, 17, 24, 25, or 26 to Centraal Station. **Amenities:** 2 restaurants; bar; babysitting; concierge; health club; Jacuzzi; room service; sauna. *In room:* A/C, TV, hair dryer, minibar, Wi-Fi (11€/day).

Park Plaza Victoria Amsterdam ★ The proprietors' idea is to give guests a five-star hotel at four-star rates—and a great location. Since 1890, the elegant Victoria has been a turreted landmark at the head of the street called Damrak. It overlooks canal-boat piers and it can be noisy and tacky out on the busy, neon-lit street, but you won't notice that inside due to the double-glazed panes in the windows. This is as close as you can be to Centraal Station, where most of Amsterdam's trams begin and end their routes, and where you can board a train to other parts of Holland. The spacious rooms have been refurbished. Those in the new block inevitably lack some of the atmosphere of those in the old. Enjoy dinner at **Park Plaza Brasserie's** glassed-in terrace beside Damrak, or a quick lunch in **Seasons Garden** restaurant, with its Scandinavian decor.

Damrak 1–5 (facing Centraal Station), 1012 LG Amsterdam. ✆ **800/814-7000** in the U.S. and Canada, or ✆ 020/623-4255. Fax 020/625-2997. www.parkplaza.com. 306 rooms. 160€–360€ double; from 500€ suite. AE, DC, MC, V. No parking. Tram: 1, 2, 4, 5, 9, 13, 16, 17, 24, 25, or 26 to Centraal Station. **Amenities:** 2 restaurants; bar; babysitting; concierge; executive rooms; health club and spa; pool (small heated indoor); room service. *In room:* A/C, TV, hair dryer, minibar, Wi-Fi (9.50€/day).

Inexpensive

Amstel Botel ☺ Where better to experience a city on the water than on a boat-hotel moored permanently to a dock on the IJ waterway northwest of Centraal Station? The Botel is popular largely because of that extra thrill added by sleeping on the water—its modest (for Amsterdam) rates don't hurt either. This retired inland waterways cruise boat has cabins on four decks that are connected by an elevator. The bright, modern rooms are no-nonsense but comfortable, the showers small. Be sure to ask for a room with a view on the water, to avoid the uninspiring quay. To get here, take the NDSM Ferry for foot passengers and two-wheel transportation from behind Centraal Station to the NDSM dock and you'll see it floating in front of you. A free shuttle bus goes between the Botel and the station when the ferry's not running.

NDSM-Werf 3, 1033 RG Amsterdam. ✆ **020/626-4247.** Fax 020/639-1952. www.amstelbotel.com. 175 rooms. 69€–94€ double. AE, DC, MC, V. Limited free parking on quay. Boat: NDSM Ferry from Centraal Station. **Amenities:** Bar; bikes; Internet (in bar, .20€/min.). *In room:* TV.

THE CANAL BELT

Very Expensive

The Dylan Amsterdam ★★★ The Asian-influenced decor at this prestigious canalside boutique hotel is arguably the most stylish in town. Its setting started out as a 17th-century theater (Vivaldi once conducted here, and the serene **Dylan Lounge** still sports the theater's original brick floor). It later became a Catholic almshouse. All the guest rooms and suites have the usual array of luxury amenities and are individually decorated with different colors and themes. No. 5 is a blue Japanese-style room with a deep soaking tub and traditional sliding screens. Only three rooms have a canal view, so if this is important to you, specify it—and be ready to pay for the privilege. Style here occasionally trumps substance: The water-fountain-style sinks in a few of the rooms look grand, but their design makes them somewhat hard to use. The superlative French restaurant **Vinkeles** (p. 117) draws admirers on its own account.

Keizersgracht 384 (at Runstraat), 1016 GB Amsterdam. ✆ **020/530-2010.** Fax 020/530-2030. www.dylanamsterdam.com. 41 rooms. 395€–695€ double; from 900€ suite. AE, DC, MC, V. Limited street parking. Tram: 1, 2, or 5 to Spui. **Amenities:** Restaurant; lounge; bar; bikes; boat rental; concierge; exercise room; room service. *In room:* A/C, TV, hair dryer, minibar, Wi-Fi (free).

Hotel Pulitzer ★   This hotel spreads through 25 old adjoining canal houses dating from the 17th and 18th centuries. It has frontage on the historic Prinsengracht and Keizersgracht canals. With the exception of bare beams or brick walls here and there, the Pulitzer's interior is modern, and the multiplicity of buildings means that rooms have different sizes, shapes, and desirability in terms of location, from elegant salons to attic garrets. The rooms with the best views look out over either the canals or the hotel garden. The Pulitzer maintains its own art gallery, and every August it sponsors the classical-music **Prinsengracht Concert,** performed by musicians on canal barges (p. 32). As icing on the cake, the Pulitzer owns a restored 1909 motor launch, which awaits you at the hotel's own jetty. The international **Restaurant Keizersgracht 238** is both trendy and highly regarded.

Prinsengracht 315-331 (near Westermarkt), 1016 GZ Amsterdam. ℂ **800/325-3535** in the U.S. and Canada, or ℂ 020/523-5235. Fax 020/627-6753. www.starwoodhotels.com. 230 rooms. 250€–450€ double; from 650€ suite. AE, DC, MC, V. Valet parking 45€. Tram: 13, 14, or 17 to Westermarkt. **Amenities:** Restaurant; cafe; bar; babysitting; bikes; concierge; exercise room; room service. *In room:* A/C, TV, hair dryer, minibar, Wi-Fi (19€/day).

Expensive

Estheréa ★★★ ☺   If you like to stay at elegant, not-too-big hotels, you're sure to be pleased by the Estheréa. It's been owned by the same family since its beginnings and, like many Amsterdam hotels, was built within a group of neighboring 17th-century canal houses. The family touch shows in attention to detail and a breezy yet professional approach. It has an elevator, a rarity in these old Amsterdam homes. In the 1940s, the proprietors spent a lot of money on wood paneling, crystal chandeliers, and other structural additions; younger family members who took over the management have had the good sense to leave it all in place. Wood bedsteads and dresser-desks lend warmth to the constantly renovated and upgraded guest rooms, which vary considerably in size; a few are quite small. Most rooms accommodate two guests, but some rooms have more beds, which makes them ideal for families.

Singel 303-309 (near Spui), 1012 WJ Amsterdam. ℂ **800/223-9868** in the U.S. and Canada, or ℂ 020/624-5146. Fax 020/623-9001. www.estherea.nl. 92 rooms. 191€–314€ double. AE, DC, MC, V. Parking 55€. Tram: 1, 2, or 5 to Spui. **Amenities:** Lounge; bar; babysitting; concierge; room service. *In room:* TV, hair dryer, minibar, Wi-Fi (10€/24 hr.).

The Toren ★★   With its antique elegance in two side-by-side buildings dating from 1617 on a posh stretch of canal, this relatively small family-run boutique hotel, completely restyled in 2008 by local interior design guru Wim van de Oudeweetering, is justifiably considered one of Amsterdam's "hidden treasures." If you're a devotee of less-is-more design, though, you might feel that it's more than a tad overdone. The style varies hugely from room to room—which makes a visit before signing up a useful exercise. It's decorated in a medley of reds, golds, and black, from plush Italianate to something that comes perilously close to resembling a classy 19th-century bordello, but with a whirlpool bathtub. There's no restaurant, but if you have the means to lodge here, you should have no problems picking up the tab for room service from elegant French partner restaurant **Christophe** (see p. 117), just around the corner on Leliegracht.

Keizersgracht 164 (near Leliegracht), 1015 CZ Amsterdam. ℂ **020/622-6352.** Fax 020/626-9705. www.thetoren.nl. 38 rooms. 180€–275€ double; 350€–400€ suite. AE, DC, MC, V. Limited street parking. Tram: 13, 14, or 17 to Westermarkt. **Amenities:** Bar; babysitting; room service. *In room:* A/C, TV, high-speed Internet, hair dryer, minibar, Wi-Fi (16€/day).

Moderate

Agora ★ Old-fashioned friendliness is the keynote at this efficiently run and well-maintained lodging, a block from the **Flower Market** (p. 227). Proprietors Yvo Muthert and Els Bruijnse like to keep things friendly and personal. Bouquets greet you as you enter, and a distinctive color scheme creates a simultaneous effect of peacefulness and drama. Though the hotel occupies a canal house built in 1735, it's been fully restored in an eclectic style. Furniture from the 1930s and 1940s mixes with fine mahogany antiques. There's an abundance of overstuffed furniture; nearly every room has a puffy armchair you can sink into after a wearying day of sightseeing. Rooms with a canal view cost the most, but the extra euros are worth it—though the street's hustle and bustle can make them somewhat noisy by day. Rooms without a canal view look out onto a pretty garden at the back. There's no elevator.

Singel 462 (at Koningsplein), 1017 AW Amsterdam. ℂ **020/627-2200.** Fax 020/627-2202. www.hotel agora.nl. 16 rooms. 75€–159€ double; add 5% city tax. Rates include buffet breakfast. AE, DC, MC, V. Limited street parking. Tram: 1, 2, or 5 to Koningsplein. *In room amenities:* TV, hair dryer, Wi-Fi (free).

Ambassade ★★ 🛎 Perhaps more than any other hotel in Amsterdam, this one, in 10 17th- and 18th-century houses on the Herengracht and Singel canals, re-cre-ates what it must have felt like to live in an elegant canal house. The pastel-toned rooms are individually styled, and their size and shape vary according to the indi-vidual houses' characters. Everyone who stays here can enjoy the view each morning with breakfast in the bi-level chandeliered breakfast room, or each evening in the adjoining parlor, amid Persian rugs and a stately grandfather clock. To get to some guest rooms, you cope with a steep and skinny staircase, though other rooms are accessible by elevator. For the nimble-footed who can handle the stairs, the reward is a spacious room with large windows overlooking the canal. There's a hushed Empire-style library room and a free-to-use Internet room.

Herengracht 341 (near Spui), 1016 AZ Amsterdam. ℂ **020/555-0222.** Fax 020/555-0277. www. ambassade-hotel.nl. 59 rooms. 195€–275€ double; 325€–375€ suite. AE, DC, MC, V. Limited street park-ing. Tram: 1, 2, or 5 to Spui. **Amenities:** Lounge; babysitting; bikes; room service; spa (nearby). *In room:* TV, hair dryer, Wi-Fi (free).

Amsterdam Wiechmann ★ It takes only a moment to feel at home in the antiques-adorned Wiechmann, a classic, comfortable sort of place, despite the suit of armor you encounter just inside the front door. Its location is one of the best you'll find in this or any price range: 5 minutes in one direction is the Kalverstraat shopping street; 5 minutes in the other, Leidseplein. Most of the rooms—all of them nonsmok-ing—are standard, with twin or double beds, and some have big bay windows. Room furnishings are modern, and Oriental rugs grace many of the floors in public spaces. The higher-priced doubles have a view of the Prinsengracht canal. The breakfast room has hardwood floors, lots of greenery, and white linens. There's no elevator.

Prinsengracht 328–332 (at Looiersgracht), 1016 HX Amsterdam. ℂ **020/626-3321.** Fax 020/626-8962. www.hotelwiechmann.nl. 37 rooms. 90€–165€ double. Rates include continental breakfast. MC, V. Lim-ited street parking. Tram: 1, 2, or 5 to Prinsengracht. **Amenities:** Lounge; bikes. *In room:* TV, Wi-Fi (free).

Dikker & Thijs Fenice On the Prinsengracht canal, where it intersects lively Leidsestraat, is this small, homey hotel, a business that started out here in 1921, and whose smart but cozy character emanates from the marble-rich lobby and stylish facade. Upstairs, spacious and tasteful rooms cluster in groups of two or four around small lobbies, which makes this feel more like an apartment building than a hotel. Welcoming touches are flowers in the rooms, a subtle but elegantly modern Art Deco decor, and double-glazed windows to eliminate the noise rising up from Leidsestraat. Rooms at the front have a super view of classy Prinsengracht.

Prinsengracht 444 (at Leidsestraat), 1017 KE Amsterdam. 📞 **020/620-1212.** Fax 020/625-8986. www.dtfh.nl. 42 rooms. 115€–275€ double; add 5% city tax. AE, DC, MC, V. Limited street parking. Tram: 1, 2, or 5 to Prinsengracht. **Amenities:** Lounge; bar; bikes; concierge; room service. *In room:* TV, hair dryer, minibar, Wi-Fi (2.50€/hr., 10€/day).

Mercure Amsterdam Arthur Frommer   This recently refurbished hotel, once owned by (full disclosure) Arthur Frommer, is tucked away in the canal area off Vijzelgracht. Its entrance opens onto a small courtyard off a side street that runs behind Prinsengracht; someone painted a canalside mural along the facing wall. This nonsmoking hotel, though not easy to locate, is well worth finding. A top-to-bottom renovation has transformed its rooms, giving them a stylish decor in a soft pastel palette. All rooms have big double or single beds. The small, cozy **Golden Age Bar** is a pretty decent re-creation of an olde-worlde Dutch bar.

Noorderstraat 46 (off Vijzelgracht), 1017 TV Amsterdam. 📞 **800/515-5679** in the U.S. and Canada, or 📞 020/622-0328. Fax 020/620-3208. www.accorhotels.com. 93 rooms. 125€–175€) double. AE, DC, MC, V. Parking 20€–25€. Tram: 16, 24, or 25 to Weteringcircuit. **Amenities:** Bar; sauna. *In room:* A/C, TV, hair dryer, minibar, Wi-Fi (15€–20€/day).

Rembrandt Classic ★   Built anew within a wide 18th-century building on a canal above Raadhuisstraat and four small 16th-century houses directly behind it on the Singel canal, this hotel has recently been modernized and all guest rooms upgraded to a bright, contemporary style. But the rooms (which come in a variety of sizes and shapes) tend to be large. Some still have their old fireplaces adorned with elegant wood or marble mantels, though these furnaces no longer function. Those that have views on the grand "Gentlemen's Canal" cost a bit more and are generally snapped up early. As you walk around, you'll occasionally pass through a former foyer on the way to your room, or glimpse an old beam.

Herengracht 255 (at Hartenstraat), 1016 BJ Amsterdam. 📞 **020/622-1727.** Fax 020/625-0630. www.rembrandtclassic.com. 111 rooms. 120€–225€ double. AE, DC, MC, V. Limited street parking. Tram: 1, 2, 5, 13, 14, or 17 to the Dam. **Amenities:** Bar; room service. *In room:* TV, hair dryer, Wi-Fi (5€/hr.).

Seven Bridges ★★ 💼   Proprietors Pierre Keulers and Günter Glaner have made the Seven Bridges, named for its view of seven arched bridges, one of Amsterdam's canal-house gems. Each room is individual, but furnished with antiques from the 17th to the 20th centuries, plush carpets, handmade Italian drapes, hand-painted tiles, wood-tiled floors, and Impressionist art reproductions. The biggest room, a quad on the first landing, has high ceilings, a big mirror over the fireplace, an Empire onyx table, antique leather armchairs, an array of potted plants, and a huge marble-floored bathroom. Attic rooms have sloped ceilings and exposed wood beams, and basement rooms are big and bright. Rooms at the front overlook a canal, and those at the rear overlook a garden. There's no elevator, and no breakfast room; breakfast is served in the room in 8 out of the 11 rooms, and not at all in the remaining 3.

Reguliersgracht 31 (at Keizersgracht), 1017 LK Amsterdam. 📞 **020/623-1329.** Fax 020/624-7652. www.sevenbridgeshotel.nl. 11 rooms. 90€–250€ double. Rates include full breakfast served in room (in 8 rooms only). AE, MC, V. Limited street parking. Tram: 4 to Keizersgracht. *In room:* TV, hair dryer, Wi-Fi (free).

Singel Hotel Style marries tradition in the elegant little Singel, near the Brouwersgracht's head in one of Amsterdam's most pleasant and central locations. Three renovated canal houses, part of which functioned as spice warehouses back in the 17th century, were harmoniously united to create this hotel. Decor is bright and welcoming, and the modern rooms are spacious for a small hotel; some have an attractive view of the Singel canal. An elevator services the building's four floors.

Singel 13–17 (near Centraal Station), 1012 VC Amsterdam. © **020/626-3108.** Fax 020/620-3777. www.singelhotel.nl. 32 rooms. 95€–175€ double. Rates include continental breakfast. AE, DC, MC, V. Limited street parking. Tram: 1, 2, 5, 13, or 17 to Martelaarsgracht. **Amenities:** Bar; babysitting; room service. *In room:* TV, hair dryer, Wi-Fi (free).

Inexpensive

Hegra Housed in a narrow 17th-century canal house a 5-minute walk from the Dam, this cozy little hotel has been under the same management for two generations. Robert de Vries, the proprietor, is extremely helpful and friendly. Rooms are small but tastefully furnished and have beamed ceilings. There's no elevator, so you have to climb four stories if you get a room at the top. Breakfast is served in a cozy space.

Herengracht 269 (near Hartenstraat), 1016 BJ Amsterdam. © **020/623-7877.** Fax 020/623-8159. www.hotelhegra.nl. 11 rooms, 9 with bathroom. 85€–105€ double with bathroom; 70€–90€ double without bathroom. Rates include Dutch breakfast. MC, V. Valet parking 20€ (plus 10€ pickup charge). Tram: 1, 2, 5, 13, 14, or 17 to the Dam. **Amenities:** Bikes. *In room:* No phone, Wi-Fi (free).

Hoksbergen At a tranquil point on the historic Singel canal, this inexpensive hotel in a 300-year-old canal house isn't flashy or elegant, but it is bright and fresh, which makes it appealing to budget-conscious travelers who don't want to give up at least the simplest creature comforts. Its central location makes for easy access to all the surrounding sights and attractions. Rooms at the front have a canal view. There's no elevator.

IN SEARCH OF *gezelligheid*

When in Amsterdam, do as the Dutch do: Look for someplace *gezellig,* and treasure it if you find it.

So what is *gezellig,* or *gezelligheid* (the state of being *gezellig*)?

Ah . . . it's a simple idea, yet one that underlines everyday life. Indeed, it's one of those imprecise, enigmatic, and finally untranslatable-in-a-single-word concepts for a mood and attitude that you'll recognize right away when you find it, and then you'll say with quiet satisfaction, "This looks *gezellig.*"

So what *is* it then?

The special something that makes a place comfortable, congenial, cozy, familiar, friendly, intimate, memorable, tolerant, warm, and welcoming. Dutch, in short. You find it in abundance in brown cafes, in candlelit restaurants where the atmosphere is unforced and there's a view of a softly illuminated canal, in a Dutch home where you're made to feel like one of the family, even on a packed-to-bursting tram where everyone is in good humor and sees the funny side of the situation.

The great thing about *gezelligheid* is that it's free. Box some up and take it home with you.

Singel 301 (near Spui), 1012 WH Amsterdam. 📞 **020/626-6043.** Fax 020/638-3479. www.hotel hoksbergen.nl. 19 rooms. 72€–129€ double. Rates include buffet breakfast. AE, DC, MC, V. Limited street parking. Tram: 1, 2, or 5 to Spui. *In room:* TV.

Keizershof ★ 🍴 Owned by the genial de Vries family, this hotel in a four-story canal house from 1672 has just four beamed rooms, named after old Hollywood stars—though a greater claim to fame is that members of the Dutch royal family were regular visitors in its pre-hotel days. Several other touches make a stay at this nonsmoking hotel memorable: From the street-level entrance, a steep wooden spiral staircase built from a ship's mast leads to guest rooms—there's no elevator. There are, however, a television and a grand piano in the cozy lounge. In good weather, take breakfast, which includes excellent omelets and pancakes, in the flower-bedecked courtyard. Because the hotel has so few rooms, you need to book well ahead.

Keizersgracht 618 (at Nieuwe Spiegelstraat), 1017 ER Amsterdam. 📞 **020/622-2855.** Fax 020/624-8412. www.hotelkeizershof.nl. 4 rooms. 90€–105€ double with bathroom; 65€ double without bathroom. Rates include Dutch breakfast. MC, V. Limited street parking. Tram: 16, 24, or 25 to Keizersgracht. *In room:* Hair dryer, no phone.

Prinsenhof ★ This modernized canal house near the Amstel River offers rooms with beamed ceilings and basic—yet tolerably comfortable—beds. The place was recently refurbished with, among other additions, new showers and carpets. Front rooms look out onto Prinsengracht, where colorful houseboats are moored. Breakfast takes place in an attractive blue-and-white dining room. The proprietors, Rik and André van Houten, take pride in their hotel and will make you feel welcome. There's no elevator, but a pulley hauls your luggage up and down the stairs.

Prinsengracht 810 (at Utrechtsestraat), 1017 JL Amsterdam. 📞 **020/623-1772.** Fax 020/638-3368. www.hotelprinsenhof.com. 11 rooms, 6 with bathroom. 95€ double with bathroom; 65€ double without bathroom. Rates include buffet breakfast. AE, MC, V. Limited street parking. Tram: 4 to Prinsengracht..

LEIDSEPLEIN

Expensive

Eden Amsterdam American ★★ One of the most fanciful buildings on Amsterdam's long list of monuments, this castle-like mix of Venetian Gothic and Art Nouveau has been a prominent landmark and a popular meeting place for Amsterdammers since 1900. While the exterior must always remain an architectural treasure curiosity of turrets, arches, and balconies, the interior (except that of the cafe, which is also protected) is modern and chic. Rooms are subdued and refined, superbly furnished, and gifted with great vistas: Some have a view of the Singelgracht, while others overlook kaleidoscopic Leidseplein. All are nonsmoking. The location, in the thick of the action and near many major attractions, is one of the best in town. Famous **Café Americain** is one of Europe's most elegant eateries (p. 122). There is also the **Bar Americain,** which has a closed-in terrace looking out on Leidseplein.

Leidsekade 97 (at Leidseplein), 1017 PN Amsterdam. 📞 **020/556-3000.** Fax 020/556-3001. www. edenamsterdamamericanhotel.com. 175 rooms. 130€–290€ double; from 415€ suite. AE, DC, MC, V. No parking. Tram: 1, 2, 5, 7, or 10 to Leidseplein. **Amenities:** Restaurant; bar; concierge; electric scooters; exercise room; room service; sauna. *In room:* A/C, TV, hair dryer, Internet (1€/hr.), minibar.

Moderate

Orfeo   One of the city's longest-standing gay hotels has been providing basic, practical facilities and friendly, helpful service at low rates for over 30 years. The front desk is in a cozy and sociable lounge, and the breakfast room has marble flooring. Only three guest rooms have a full bathroom; others share a shower or toilet or both. A perk is the small in-house Finnish sauna; it doesn't hurt either that the largest concentration of city-center restaurants is right on the doorstep.

Leidsekruisstraat 12–14 (off Leidseplein), 1017 RH Amsterdam. ✆ **020/623-1347.** Fax 020/620-2348. www.hotelorfeo.com. 19 rooms, 3 with bathroom. 120€–150€ double with bathroom; 55€–95€ double without bathroom. Rates include continental breakfast. AE, MC, V. Limited street parking. Tram: 1, 2, or 5 to Prinsengracht. **Amenities:** Restaurant; bar; Wi-Fi (free). *In room:* TV, minibar.

REMBRANDTPLEIN

Expensive

NH Schiller Hotel ★   An Amsterdam gem from 1912, this hotel, now fully restored, blends Art Nouveau and Art Deco in its public spaces and in its guest rooms' tasteful decor and furnishings. Its sculpted facade, wrought-iron balconies, and stained-glass windows stand out on the often brash Rembrandtplein. The hotel is named for the painter Frits Schiller, who built it in 1912. His outpourings of artistic expression, in the form of 600 portraits, landscapes, and still lifes, are displayed in halls, rooms, stairwells, and public areas. Experience classic French and Dutch cuisine and the hotel's own beer, Frisse Frits, in the Art Nouveau **Brasserie Schiller** (p. 124), or join the in-crowd next door for a drink amid the Art Deco splendor of **Café Schiller** (p. 246), one of Amsterdam's trendiest watering holes. *Note*: This hotel has been awarded a Green Key certificate for its environmental awareness and sustainable practices.

Rembrandtplein 26, 1017 CV Amsterdam. ✆ **020/554-0700.** Fax 020/624-0098. www.nh-hotels.com. 92 rooms. 95€–203€ double; from 161€ suite. AE, DC, MC, V. Limited street parking. Tram: 4, 9, or 14 to Rembrandtplein. **Amenities:** Restaurant; lounge; 2 bars; babysitting; executive rooms; room service. *In room:* TV, hair dryer, minibar, Wi-Fi (11€/24 hr).

Moderate

Eden Hotel Amsterdam   The biggest city-center hotel in its class has a great setting in several converted 17th-century merchants' houses (and a chocolate factory) beside the Amstel River, just behind Rembrandtplein. Rooms vary quite a lot in size, with some of them on the small side. Still, they're all well cared-for and have bright, modern furnishings. Many have a fine view of the river, and these are the most desirable—and most expensive. The **Pipa's** bar, overlooking the river, is a good place to kick back after a day's sightseeing. *Note*: This hotel has been awarded a Green Key certificate for its environmental awareness and sustainable practices.

Amstel 144 (across the river from the Muziektheater), 1017 AE Amsterdam. 📞 **020/530-7888.** Fax 020/623-3267. www.edenhotelgroup.com. 218 rooms. 155€–225€ double. AE, DC, MC, V. Parking 35€. Tram: 4 or 9 to Rembrandtplein. **Amenities:** Restaurant; bar; concierge; Wi-Fi (free). *In room:* A/C, TV, hair dryer.

THE JORDAAN

Inexpensive

Acacia ★ The hotel faces an unfashionable canal just a block from Prinsengracht. The friendly couple who run the fully smoke-free Acacia have worked hard to make it welcoming and clean, and they're justifiably proud of the result. The simple, well-kept, and comfortable rooms, all of which have canal views, have been equipped with new beds, writing tables, and chairs. The large front-corner rooms, shaped like pie slices, sleep as many as five and have windows on three sides. A couple of studios have tiny kitchenettes. Breakfast is served in a cozy Old Dutch room with windows on two sides and a nice canal view. There's no elevator.

Lindengracht 251 (at Lijnbaansgracht), 1015 KH, Amsterdam. 📞 **020/622-1460.** Fax 020/638-0748. www.hotelacacia.nl. 14 rooms. 80€–90€ double. Rates include continental breakfast. MC, V (5% charge). Limited street parking. Tram: 3 or 10 to Marnixplein. *In room:* TV, Wi-Fi (free).

Van Onna 🍴 Consisting of three canal houses, the center one dating from 1644, this hotel has grown over the years, but genial owner Loek van Onna continues to keep prices reasonable. Mr. van Onna has lived here since he was a boy and will gladly regale you with tales about the building's history. Rooms vary considerably, with the best options in the newest building. However, even the oldest, plainest rooms have character, and all are both neatly furnished and clean. Whichever building you wind up in, request a front room overlooking the canal. The hotel is smoke-free. There's no elevator.

Bloemgracht 102-104 and 108 (off Prinsengracht), 1015 TN Amsterdam. 📞 **020/626-5801.** No fax. www.hotelvanonna.com. 41 rooms. 90€ double. Rates include continental breakfast. No credit cards. Limited street parking. Tram: 13, 14, or 17 to Westermarkt.

MUSEUM DISTRICT & VONDELPARK

Expensive

Bilderberg Hotel Jan Luyken One block from the Van Gogh Museum and from the elegant Pieter Cornelisz Hooftstraat shopping street, the Jan Luyken is a small boutique hotel with many of the amenities and facilities of a large one—though without the large rooms. Everything here is done with perfect attention to detail; there's a

Where to Stay in the Museum District & Amsterdam South

Acro **11**
Apollofirst-Hampshire
  Classic **15**
Atlas **4**
Bicycle Hotel
  Amsterdam **17**
Bilderberg Garden
  Hotel **14**

Bilderberg Hotel
  Jan Luyken **10**
citizenM Amsterdam
  City **16**
De Filosoof **3**
Fusion Suites **5**
Museumzicht **12**
Owl Hotel **7**
Piet Hein **9**
Stayokay Amsterdam
  Vondelpark **8**
Toro **1**
Van de Kasteelen **13**
Vondel **6**
Zandbergen **2**

balance between sophisticated facilities (double sinks and bidets, an elevator, a lobby bar with fireplace, and meeting rooms for business) and an intimate and personalized approach that's apropos for this 19th-century residential neighborhood. That residential feel extends to the rooms, which look much more like they belong in a well-designed home than a hotel. The proprietors are proud of the atmosphere they've created—and it's smoke-free, too—and are constantly improving the hotel's appearance.

Jan Luijkenstraat 58 (near the Rijksmuseum), 1071 CS Amsterdam.⟨ℰ 020/573-0730. Fax 020/676-3841. www.janluyken.nl. 62 rooms. 99€–159€ double; from 500€ suite; add 5% city tax. AE, DC, MC, V. Limited street parking. Tram: 2 or 5 to Hobbemastraat. **Amenities:** Wine bar; lounge; babysitting; bikes; concierge; room service; spa (small). *In room:* A/C, TV, hair dryer, minibar, Wi-Fi (17€/24 hr.).

Moderate

Acro ★
The Acro, in a town house on a fairly quiet street near Vondelpark and close to the main museums, appeals especially to young travelers. The hotel is modern on the inside, with crisp-and-clean bedspreads and light-blue-gray walls. Most rooms have twin beds—some have three and some four. The hotel bar has more ambience than many street cafes. The Acro definitely offers value for your money.

Jan Luijkenstraat 44 (near the Rijksmuseum), 1071 CR Amsterdam.⟨ℰ 020/662-0526. Fax 020/675-0811. www.acro-hotel.nl. 65 rooms. 80€–160€ double. Rates include buffet breakfast. AE, DC, MC, V. Limited street parking. Tram: 2 or 5 to Hobbemastraat. **Amenities:** Bar; bikes, Wi-Fi (free). *In room:* TV, hair dryer.

Atlas ★
Off van Baerlestraat, the recently renovated and modernized Atlas is a converted Art Nouveau house with a convenient location for shoppers, concertgoers, and museum lovers. The update has put oodles of coordinated color, in both the decor and the bedspreads and pillows, into a hotel that formerly preferred cool grays and blues. Most of the guest rooms are on the small side, but tolerably decent modern paintings seem to open things up a bit. Leather chairs fill the front lounge, where a grandfather clock ticks away in the corner next to a flatscreen television.

Van Eeghenstraat 64 (near Vondelpark), 1071 GK Amsterdam.⟨ℰ 020/676-6336. Fax 020/671-7633. www.hotelatlas.nl. 23 rooms. 100€–180€ double. Rates include continental breakfast. AE, DC, MC, V. Limited street parking. Tram: 2, 3, 5, or 12 to van Baerlestraat. **Amenities:** Bar; concierge; room service. *In room:* TV, hair dryer, Wi-Fi (3.50€/½ hr.–25€/10 hr.).

De Filosoof ★★ 🎒
On a quiet street facing Vondelpark, this hotel might be your place if you fancy yourself something of a philosopher. One of the proprietors, a philosophy professor, has chosen posters, painted ceilings, framed quotes, and gathered unusual objects to represent philosophical and cultural themes; the garden is a grove of academe. Each room is dedicated to a mental maestro—Aristotle, Plato, Goethe, Wittgenstein, Nietzsche, Marx, and Einstein among them—or is based on motifs like Eros, the Renaissance, astrology, or femininity. To join the intellectual melee, consult your private bookshelf or join in a weekly philosophy debate. Rooms in an annex across the street are larger, and some open onto a private terrace. Regular improvements keep the property up-to-date.

Anna van den Vondelstraat 6 (off Overtoom, at Vondelpark), 1054 GZ Amsterdam.⟨ℰ 020/683-3013. Fax 020/685-3750. www.sandton.eu. 38 rooms. 105€–180€ double. Rates include buffet breakfast. AE, MC, V. Limited street parking. Tram: 1 to Jan Pieter Heijestraat. **Amenities:** Lounge. *In room:* TV, Wi-Fi (free).

Fusion Suites ★★★ 🎒
It seems almost a crime of *lèse majesté* to describe this superb luxury guesthouse-residence, hosted by a devoted couple, as a B&B, though

technically that's what it is. On two floors of an 1893 mansion, a block from the northern edge of Vondelpark's panhandle, the four spacious suites have chic designer furniture mixed with antiques, and views that look out on similar 19th-century mansions at the front, or on lush gardens at the rear. Each suite is individually styled, using natural materials as far as possible, a characteristic emphasized by the use of Coco-Mat beds.

Roemer Visscherstraat 40 (at Eerste Constantijn Huygensstraat), 1054 EZ, Amsterdam. ✆/fax **020/618-4642.** www.fusionsuites.com. 4 rooms. 245€–275€ suite. Rates include full breakfast. AE, DC, MC, V. Tram: 1 to Eerste Constantijn Huygensstraat; 3 or 12 to Overtoom. *In room amenities:* minibar, Wi-Fi (free).

Owl Hotel 🦉 If small but chic and reasonably priced describes the sort of hotel you prefer, you'll be pleased at the Owl, in the pleasant residential area around Vondelpark. One of Amsterdam's better values, the hotel has been owned by the same family since 1972 and is bright, tidy, and well looked after. The guest rooms aren't very big, but they're not cramped either, and they've all been kept up to date, with furnishings and decor that aim at being cozy rather than chic. For families that don't mind sharing a room, the quads are a particularly good deal. There's a pleasant lounge bar, and a stroll in the small garden makes for a nice way to soothe the strains of a stressful day's sightseeing.

Roemer Visscherstraat 1 (off Stadhouderskade), 1054 EV Amsterdam. ✆ **020/618-9484.** Fax 020/618-9441. www.owl-hotel.nl. 34 rooms. 105€–130€ double. Rates include buffet breakfast. AE, DC, MC, V. Limited street parking. Tram: 1 to Stadhouderskade. **Amenities:** Lounge; bar; babysitting; room service. *In room:* TV, hair dryer, Wi-Fi (3€/hr., 10€/5 hr.).

Piet Hein Facing Vondelpark, and close to Amsterdam's important museums, this appealing, well-kept Art Nouveau villa hotel is named after a 17th-century Dutch admiral who captured a Spanish silver shipment. Its spacious rooms have all been modernized recently and are furnished with a subtle nautical theme. Half the rooms overlook the park; two second-floor double rooms have semicircular balconies. Lower-priced rooms are in an annex behind the main hotel. In summer the bar sets tables and chairs out on the garden terrace.

Vossiusstraat 52–53 (off van Baerlestraat), 1071 AK Amsterdam. ✆ **020/662-7205.** Fax 020/662-1526. www.hotelpiethein.nl. 65 rooms. 135€–250€ double. Rates include continental breakfast. AE, DC, MC, V. Limited street parking. Tram: 3, 5, or 12 to Van Baerlestraat. **Amenities:** Bar; room service. *In room:* TV, hair dryer, Wi-Fi (free).

Toro ★ On Vondelpark's edge in a quiet residential district, this hotel in a renovated Art Nouveau mansion (ca. 1900) is a good choice. Both inside and out, it's as near as you can get in Amsterdam to staying in a country villa. Furnishings and decor are tasteful, and combine Louis XIV and Liberty styles while featuring stained-glass windows and Murano chandeliers. The house also has a private garden and terrace. It's about a 10-minute walk through Vondelpark to Leidseplein.

Koningslaan 64 (off Oranje Nassaulaan), 1075 AG Amsterdam. ✆ **020/673-7223.** Fax 020/675-0031. www.hoteltoro.nl. 22 rooms. 130€–240€ double. AE, MC, V. Limited street parking. Tram: 2 to Valeriusplein. **Amenities:** Lounge; bikes; Wi-Fi (free). *In room:* A/C, TV/DVD, hair dryer, minibar.

Van de Kasteelen On a quiet side street not far from the **Van Gogh Museum** (p. 140), this hotel is owned by a gracious Indonesian family. The smallish guest rooms are outfitted with a minor-key classic elegance. Wood furnishings, bright and adjustable lighting, firm mattresses, and fine drapes all indicate that the proprietors have taken great care to create a comfort zone. Bathrooms, which have a combination tub/shower, are large in relation to room size; there's space enough for two at morning *toilette,* provided neither has sharp elbows. A small patio-garden out back is a pleasant place to relax in fine weather. Van de Kasteelen lies between two tram stops, but isn't too far from either of them.

Frans van Mierisstraat 34 (off van Baerlestraat), 1071 RT Amsterdam. ✆ **020/679-8995.** Fax 020/670-6604. www.hotelvandekasteelen.com. 14 rooms. 120€–250€ double; add 5% city tax. Rates include continental breakfast. AE, MC, V. Limited street parking. Tram: 16 to Johannes Vermeerplein. **Amenities:** Lounge. *In room:* TV, hair dryer, minibar (except in 1 single room), Wi-Fi (free).

Vondel ★★   Named after the 17th-century Dutch poet Joost van den Vondel, this nonsmoking hotel in six connected town houses, in a quiet area close to the main city museums and Leidseplein, has become one of Amsterdam's leading four-star hotels, following a recent upgrade to full boutique status. Even the smallest rooms—some are small even by Dutch standards—utilize clever design to maximize the available space, so they don't feel cramped. Subdued color schemes and restrained lighting in some rooms might either make them appear slightly gloomy, or simply restful, according to taste; a few others have maybe too much of an Ikea-style feel. The variety is enough that it makes sense to check out a few rooms, if possible, before choosing. The cool **Joost** restaurant has a garden terrace in summer.

Vondelstraat 26 (off Stadhouderskade), 1054 GE Amsterdam. ✆ **020/515-0455.** Fax 020/505-0451. www.hotelvondel.nl. 85 rooms. 170€–205€ double; 295€ suite. Rates include buffet breakfast. AE, DC, MC, V. Limited street parking. Tram: 1 to Eerste Constantijn Huygensstraat; 3 or 12 to Overtoom. **Amenities:** Restaurant; bar; babysitting; bikes; room service. *In room:* TV, hair dryer, minibar, Wi-Fi (4.50€/hr., 10€/day).

Zandbergen ★   The style is simple but bright and clean at the fully nonsmoking Zandbergen, and a proud proprietor, Henk de Lugt, does his best to keep it that way. Wall-to-wall carpets and a light-toned color scheme make the rooms seem more spacious and inviting; all are outfitted with some flair and have comfortable beds. There's a great family-size room for up to four guests, and it has a garden patio. Recent improvements include new bathrooms and air-conditioning in the reception and breakfast areas.

Willemsparkweg 205 (at Vondelpark), 1071 HB Amsterdam. ✆ **020/676-9321.** Fax 020/676-1860. www.hotel-zandbergen.com. 18 rooms. 95€–160€ double; add 5% city tax. Rates include buffet breakfast. AE, DC, MC, V. Limited street parking. Tram: 2 to Emmastraat. **Amenities:** All rooms smoke-free. *In room:* TV, hair dryer, minibar (most rooms), Wi-Fi (free).

Inexpensive

Museumzicht ★   This hotel, in a town house that dates from 1890 across from the Rijksmuseum's rear, is ideal for museumgoers on a budget. The breakfast room, which has numerous stained-glass windows, commands an excellent view of the museum. Proprietor Robin de Jong has filled guest rooms with eclectic furniture that spans from the 1930s (think English wicker) to the present day. Note that there's no elevator and the staircase up to reception is quite steep.

Jan Luijkenstraat 22 (facing the Rijksmuseum), 1071 CN Amsterdam. ✆ **020/671-2954.** Fax 020/671-3597. www.hotelmuseumzicht.nl. 14 rooms, 3 with bathroom. 115€ double with bathroom; 55€–85€ double without bathroom. Rates include continental breakfast. AE, DC, MC, V. Limited street parking. Tram: 2 or 5 to Hobbemastraat. **Amenities:** Lounge; room service (coffee and tea); Wi-Fi (free).

Stayokay Amsterdam Vondelpark ☺ "The new generation of city hostel" is how the Dutch youth hostel organization NJHC describes this marvelous budget lodging just inside Vondelpark. The location, facing Leidseplein, could hardly be better for youthful spirits who want to be near the action. At the hostel's core is a former girls' school that's now a protected monument. All of the simple-but-modern rooms are brightly furnished, clean, and have an en-suite bathroom. The four- and six-bed rooms are ideal for families traveling on a limited budget and for groups of friends. Some rooms are suitable for people with disabilities. Although the hostel is open 24 hours a day, security is taken seriously, and all guests have key cards. The **Backpacker's Lounge** is a pleasant place to meet fellow travelers. In summer, a low-cost Schiphol Airport shuttle is available.

Zandpad 5 (in Vondelpark), 1054 GA Amsterdam. ℂ **020/589-8996.** Fax 020/589-8955. www.stay okay.com/vondelpark. 105 rooms (536 beds). 20€–30€ dorm bed; 25€–35€ per person in 4- to 8-bed rooms; 75€–195€ per room for 2- to 8-bed rooms; 2.50€ reduction for IYHF/HI members. Rates include buffet breakfast. AE, MC, V. No parking. Tram: 1, 2, 5, 7, or 10 to Leidseplein. **Amenities:** Restaurant; bar/ lounge; bikes; Wi-Fi (3€/hr.).

AMSTERDAM SOUTH

Expensive

Bilderberg Garden Hotel ★ Amsterdam's most personal five-star hotel is set in a leafy corner along the Amstelkanaal. Because of its excellent restaurant, the Garden considers itself a "culinary hotel," an idea that extends to the rooms, whose color schemes are salad-green, salmon-pink, cherry-red, and grape-blue—you can choose whichever suits you best. The rooms themselves are furnished and equipped to a high standard and with refined taste. Bathrooms are marble, and each executive room has a Jacuzzi tub. The spectacular lobby has a wall-to-wall fireplace with a copper-sheathed chimney. A deserved reputation attaches to the superb French-Mediterranean **Mangerie de Kersentuin** (**Cherry Orchard**) restaurant (p. 133); all things considered, its menu is reasonably priced. The **Kersepit** (**Cherry Pit**) is a cozy bar with an open fireplace and a vast range of Scotch whiskeys.

Dijsselhofplantsoen 7 (at Apollolaan), 1077 BJ Amsterdam. ℂ **020/570-5600.** Fax 020/570-5654. www.gardenhotel.nl. 124 rooms. 225€–325€ double. AE, DC, MC, V. Limited street parking. Tram: 5 or 24 to Apollolaan. **Amenities:** Restaurant; bar; babysitting; bikes; concierge; room service. *In room:* A/C, TV, hair dryer, minibar, Wi-Fi (10€/hr., 17€/day).

Moderate

Apollofirst–Hampshire Classic The small and elegant Apollofirst, a family-owned hotel set amid the Amsterdam-school architecture of Apollolaan, advertises itself as the "best quarters in town in the town's best quarter." Their claim may be debatable, but the Venman family's justifiable pride in their intimate establishment is not. All rooms are quiet, spacious, and grandly furnished. Bathrooms are fully tiled, and rooms at the hotel's rear overlook well-kept gardens and the summer terrace where guests have cocktails and snacks.

Apollolaan 123 (off Minervalaan), 1077 AP Amsterdam. ℂ **020/577-3800.** Fax 020/675-0348. www. hampshire-hotels.com. 40 rooms. 135€–185€ double; 295€ suite. Rates include continental breakfast. AE, DC, MC, V. Limited street parking. Tram: 5 or 24 to Apollolaan. **Amenities:** Bar; babysitting; room service. *In room:* TV, hair dryer, Wi-Fi (8.50€/day).

citizenM Amsterdam City ★   If you consider yourself a mobile citizen—better make that net-citizen, since only online reservations are accepted—of the world, this hotel could be the perfect Amsterdam node for you. Admittedly, a location in the business-orientated World Trade Center zone in Amsterdam-Zuid (South) means you'll miss out on lodging in the bustling heart of one of the world's most exciting cities. But the hotel's ultra-modern design (which wouldn't look too out of place on the fictional Star Wars planet Coruscant), touch-control room installations, king-size double beds, and moderate prices, and the area's relative tranquillity, are among a bunch of persuasive plus-points. Besides, there's a fast-tram connection into the city center. TripAdvisor.com readers named this the world's trendiest hotel in 2010, which makes one wonder how they'll beat that, if at all, in 2011. The inhouse eatery is called **canteenM**—how's that for self-confidence.

Prinses Irenestraat 30 (at Beethovenstraat), 1077 WX Amsterdam. ✆ **020/811-7090.** www.citizenm amsterdamcity.com. 215 rooms. 72€–166€ double. AE, DC, MC, V. Limited street parking. Tram: 5 to Prinses Irenestraat/Beethovenstraat or Station-Zuid. **Amenities:** Restaurant; bar. *In room:* TV, Wi-Fi (free).

Inexpensive

Bicycle Hotel Amsterdam ★   This establishment's young owners hit on a cool idea: Cater to visitors who wish to explore Amsterdam by bike. They're helpful in planning biking routes through and around the city. You can rent bikes for 7.50€ daily, no deposit, and stable your trusty steed indoors. The recently renovated rooms have new carpets and plain but comfortable modern furnishings; some have kitchenettes and small balconies, and there are large rooms for families. The hotel is a few blocks from the popular **Albert Cuyp street market** (p. 228), in the hip De Pijp neighborhood. Two old bicycles hang 6m (20 ft.) high on the hotel's facade, and there are always bikes parked in front. There's no elevator.

Van Ostadestraat 123 (off Ferdinand Bolstraat), Amsterdam 1072 SV. ✆ **020/679-3452.** Fax 020/671-5213. www.bicyclehotel.com. 16 rooms, 8 with bathroom. 60€–120€ double with bathroom; 50€–80€ double without bathroom. Rates include Dutch breakfast. AE, MC, V (4% charge). Parking 25€. Tram: 3, 12, or 25 to Ceintuurbaan/Ferdinand Bolstraat. **Amenities:** Lounge; bikes; Wi-Fi (free). *In room:* TV.

AMSTERDAM EAST
Very Expensive

InterContinental Amstel Amsterdam ★★★   The stately Amstel has been the grande dame of Amsterdam hotels since its 1867 opening. It offers the ultimate in luxury, which is why you might spy visiting royalty and superstars hiding from eager fans here. The Amstel's only possible fault is that it may seem to run a bit *too* smoothly, with a level of perfection that's almost uncanny. The hotel sports a mansard roof and wrought-iron window guards, a graceful Grand Hall, and rooms that boast all the elegance of a country manor, complete with antiques and genuine Delft blue porcelain. The Italian marble bathrooms have separate toilets and showers, and staffers note each guest's personal preferences for his or her next visit. The French **La Rive** restaurant is one of the hallowed temples of Amsterdam cuisine (p. 132). The **Amstel Bar & Brasserie** and terraces overlooking the river are more informal.

Prof. Tulpplein 1 (at the Torontobrug over the Amstel River), 1018 GX Amsterdam. ✆ **800/327-0200** in the U.S. and Canada, or ✆ 020/622-6060. Fax 020/622-5808. www.interconti.com. 79 rooms. 520€–650€ double; from 900€ suite. AE, DC, MC, V. Valet parking 60€. Tram: 7 or 10 to Weesperplein.

Amenities: Restaurant; lounge; bar-brasserie; concierge; executive suites; health club and spa; pool (heated indoor); room service. *In room:* A/C, TV/DVD/VCR, high-speed Internet, CD player, hair dryer, minibar, Wi-Fi (25€/day).

Moderate

Arena ★   A converted Roman Catholic orphanage from 1890 houses a friendly, stylish, youth-oriented hotel. Although the exterior bears a passing resemblance to Dracula's castle, the interior proves they really knew how to do orphanages in those days. Monumental marble staircases, cast-iron banisters, stained-glass windows, marble columns, and original murals have all been faithfully restored. The rambling spaces where the dormitories once were now house stylish doubles and twins. Spare modern rooms, some that are split-level, and some that sport timber roof beams and wooden floors, are individually decorated by young up-and-coming Dutch designers. The Continental cafe-restaurant **To Dine** looks a little like an upgraded cafeteria, but has a great alfresco terrace in the garden and an attached bar, **To Drink.** Hotel guests get discounted admission to the nightclub **To Night,** which spins music from the 1960s onward in the old orphanage chapel.

's-Gravesandestraat 51 (at Mauritskade), 1092 AA Amsterdam. ℂ **020/850-2410.** Fax 020/850-2415. www.hotelarena.nl. 127 rooms. 100€–175€ double; 225€–325€ suite. Rates include buffet breakfast. AE, DC, MC, V. Parking 25€. Tram: 7 or 10 to Korte 's-Gravesandestraat. **Amenities:** Restaurant; bar. *In room:* TV, Wi-Fi (3.50€/hr., 10€/day).

Bridge Hotel ★   The bridge in question is the famous **Magere Brug (Skinny Bridge)** over the Amstel River (p. 155). This small, tastefully decorated hotel likely provides guests with more space per euro than any other hotel in town. Its pine-furnished rooms seem like studio apartments, with couches, coffee tables, and easy chairs arranged in lounge areas in such a way that there's plenty of room left between them and the beds for you to do your morning exercises. There's no elevator.

Amstel 107–111 (near Koninklijk Theater Carré), 1018 EM Amsterdam. ℂ **020/623-7068.** Fax 020/624-1565. www.thebridgehotel.nl. 46 rooms. 105€–175€; double; 195€–295€ apt. Rates include continental breakfast. AE, DC, MC, V. Limited street parking. Tram: 7 or 10 to Weesperplein. **Amenities:** Lounge. *In room:* TV, Wi-Fi (free).

AT & NEAR THE AIRPORT
Very Expensive

Sheraton Amsterdam Airport ★   You could only be more convenient to the airport by lodging on the runway. All the comfort you would expect of a top-flight Sheraton is here, including soundproof rooms with big, comfortable beds, marble bathrooms with separate shower, and the well-equipped Oasis health club with pool. That said, the Sheraton is no fount of Dutch tradition. Blocky and modern is the kindest description I can muster about the exterior, which is what you'd expect of a hotel at this location. The inside story is better, with rooms that bring a touch of style to their mission of lodging itinerant businesspeople. Room styles range from modern and functional to unashamed luxury in the suites. The **Voyager** restaurant has an international a la carte menu. The Dutch-style **Runway Café** serves drinks and snacks.

Schiphol Blvd. 101 (outside Schiphol Plaza), 1118 BG Amsterdam. ☏ **800/325-3535** in the U.S. and Canada, or ☏ 020/316-4300. Fax 020/316-4399. www.starwoodhotels.com. 406 rooms. 175€–360€ double; from 800€ suite. AE, DC, MC, V. Parking 40€. **Amenities:** 2 restaurants; 2 bars; babysitting; concierge; health club; pool (heated indoor); room service. *In room:* A/C, TV, hair dryer, minibar, Wi-Fi (19€/day).

Expensive

Ibis Amsterdam Airport   A more reasonably priced alternative to the Sheraton (see above), and still close to the airport, is the Ibis, a standard modern chain hotel housed in a tinted-glass cube. It may have little in the way of character—none at all, really—but this French-run property provides perfectly good facilities for travelers in transit, and is comfortable in an efficient kind of way. Relax over a drink in the **Red Baron Bar.**

Schipholweg 181, 1171 PK Badhoevedorp. ☏ **800/515-5679** in the U.S. and Canada, or ☏ 020/502-5100. Fax 020/657-0199. www.ibishotel.com. 644 rooms. 165€–250€ double. AE, DC, MC, V. Parking 12€. **Amenities**: Restaurant; airport transfers (free); concierge; health club; room service. *In room:* A/C, TV, hair dryer, minibar, Wi-Fi (6€/hr.).

Inexpensive

Etap   A worthwhile option for budget travelers, this bare-bones facility, one of a French-owned chain, misses no opportunity to leave luxury at the door. Etap hotels used to sport a front-door notice (or warning): "You are now entering a luxury-free zone." And what Benjamin was told in *The Graduate*—that plastics are the future—could have been taken from the Etap manual. But the rooms can accommodate three people, in twin beds and a bunk bed, making them ideal for a one-kid family. The hotel is just 7 minutes from Schiphol by way of a free hotel shuttle.

Schipholweg 185, 1171 PK Badhoevedorp ☏ **800/515-5679** in the U.S. and Canada, or ☏ 020/348-3533. No fax. www.etaphotel.com. 118 rooms. 65€ double. AE, DC, MC, V. Parking .75€/hr. (1st 4 hr. free; 6€/day from 3rd day). **Amenities:** Airport transfers (free). *In room:* TV, Wi-Fi (6€/hr., 18€/day).

WHERE TO DINE

I f cities get the cuisine they deserve, Amsterdam's ought to be liberal, multiethnic, and adventurous. Guess what? It is. A port and trading city with a true melting-pot character, this city has absorbed culinary influences from far, wide, and yonder, and rustled them all up to its own satisfaction.

Just about every international cuisine type can be found on the city's restaurant roster. In Amsterdam, they say, you can eat in any language. More than 50 national cuisines are represented in restaurants here—and many of these eateries satisfy the sturdy Dutch insistence on getting maximum value out of every euro.

From elegant 17th-century dining rooms to cozy canalside bistros, to boisterous taverns with exuberant Greek waitstaff to exotic Indonesian rooms attended by turbaned waiters, to the *bruine kroegjes* (brown cafes) with smoke-stained walls and friendly table conversations, Amsterdam's eateries confront visitors with the exquisite agony of being able to choose only one or two from their vast numbers each day. Dutch cooking, of course, is part of all this, but you won't be stuck with *biefstuk* (beefsteak) and *kip* (chicken) every night.

RESTAURANT ORIENTATION

DINING HOURS   Most restaurants are open from noon to 2:30pm for lunch, and from 6 or 7 to 10 or 11pm. Many kitchens are closed by 10pm. It's wise not to make reservations for 8pm or after, if you want to enjoy a relaxed, unhurried meal. Even if a restaurant is open until 11pm or midnight, you won't get served unless you arrive well before then—how much before varies with the restaurant, and maybe with the mood of the staff, but it should be at least 30 minutes in moderate and budget places, and at least an hour in more upscale venues. Still, more and more restaurants stay open later these days.

RESERVATIONS   On weekends, unless you eat especially early or late, reservations are recommended at top restaurants and at those on the high end of the moderate price range. Call ahead to check; restaurants are often small and may be crowded with neighborhood devotees. Note that restaurants with outside terraces are always in big demand on pleasant

Good-Eats Cafes

For decent, low-cost food, look for examples of that Dutch dining institution, the *eetcafé* (pronounced *ayt*-caff-ay). Many of these—some of which are reviewed below—are essentially brown cafes (bars) with a hardworking kitchen attached. The food is unpretentious, mainstream Dutch (though some are more adventurous). The *dagschotel* (plate of the day), which might come with meat, vegetable, and salad on one plate, is usually 10€ to 16€.

summer evenings and fill up fast; make a reservation, if the restaurant will let you—if not, get there early or forget it.

INFORMATION   Good eating-out info is available online at www.specialbite. com, www.iens.nl, www.diningcity.nl, and www.dinnersite.nl.

TIPPING   A 15% service charge *and* taxes (BTW) are included in all prices. For more, see "Fast Facts," p. 289.

BUDGET DINING   Eating cheaply in Amsterdam is not an impossible dream. And, happily, in some cases you can even eat cheaply in style. And though there's no such thing as a free lunch, there might be a *dagschotel* (plate of the day) and a *dagmenu* (menu of the day), for usually decent food at a bargain rate. Almost every neighborhood has a modestly priced restaurant or two, and new budget places are popping up all over town.

LUNCH & SNACK COSTS   Lunch doesn't have to be an elaborate affair (save that for evening). Typical Dutch lunches are light, quick, and cheap (see "Eating in Amsterdam," in chapter 2). A quick midday meal can cost 6€ to 12€. An afternoon pit stop for a pastry and coffee will set you back 4€ to 6€.

WINE   Estate-bottled imported wines are expensive in Holland, and even a bottle of modest French wine can add 12€ to 20€ to a dinner tab. House wine, on the other hand, likely will be a more economical choice in restaurants of any price level. Wine by the glass costs anywhere from 3€ to 10€.

SMOKING   Smoking is not permitted in restaurants and cafes, except in a separate room or partitioned enclosure where staff will not serve customers.

BEST DINING BETS

o **Best for Opulence:** Royalty eats at **La Rive,** in the InterContinental Amstel Amsterdam Hotel, Professor Tulpplein 1 (© **020/520-3264**), as do business magnates, opera divas, and even ordinary folks with well-padded pocketbooks. It's highly opulent, the location is great, and the food is outstanding. See p. 132.

o **Best Value:** It breaks my heart to write this, because I know it will only make it harder to find a seat at **De Prins,** Prinsengracht 124 (© **020/624-9382**). But duty calls. When you eat in this handsome, friendly, cozy, warm—in a Dutch word, *gezellig*—brown cafe–restaurant, you'll wonder why you paid twice as much for food half as good as that in that other place last night. See p. 120.

o **Best Grand Cafe:** A *New York Times* reviewer went so far as to call **Café Luxembourg,** Spuistraat 24 (© **020/620-6264**), "one of the world's great cafes."

But Luxembourg is great on an Amsterdam scale. That is to say, it's cozy and kind of intimate, with little, if any, of the pretension that would normally go along with world-class status. See p. 113.

o **Best Traditional Dutch:** It sounds contradictory to say that **D'Vijff Vlieghen** ("The Five Flies"), Spuistraat 294–302 (© **020/530-4060**), is touristy and still traditionally Dutch, yet somehow it manages to be both. See p. 107.

o **Best Mexican: Rose's Cantina,** Reguliersdwarsstraat 38–40 (© **020/625-9797**), is more a popular institution than truly great eatery, though the food can be quite good. There will likely be a wait for a table, during which Rose's deploys its secret weapon—marvelous margaritas. See p. 114.

o **Best Vegetarian: Bolhoed,** Prinsengracht 60–62 (© **020/626-1803**), takes this title for its *joie de vivre,* romantic atmosphere, and excellent, imaginative vegetarian cuisine. See p. 118.

o **Best Sandwich:** The only problem with **Sal Meijer,** Scheldestraat 45 (© **020/673-1313**), is that it's a bit removed from the action. They deliver, but their delicious authentic kosher sandwiches are well worth a tram ride. See p. 124.

o **Best Indonesian:** Every Amsterdammer has his or her own favorite place for that "traditional" Dutch dinner treat: Indonesian food. With so many Indonesian restaurants in the city, it's hard to pick just one. Still, **Kantjil & de Tijger,** Spuistraat 291–293 (© **020/620-0994**), has a restrained, refined character and consistently good food. See p. 111.

o **Best Brunch:** At **Café Luxembourg,** Spuistraat 24 (© **020/620-6264**), you can read international newspapers while drinking coffee that actually tastes like coffee and munching your way through an extensive range of breakfast plates, sandwiches, and snacks. See p. 113.

o **Best Business Lunch:** If it's a casual affair, many Amsterdam businesspeople will be perfectly happy with a snack from a seafood stall, but if you aim to impress, try the **Excelsior,** in the Hotel de l'Europe, Nieuwe Doelenstraat 2–8 (© **020/531-1705**). The cuisine perfectly complements the elegant surroundings. See p. 107.

o **Best Kids' Spot:** For small diners with big appetites, there can be no better experience than the **Kinderkookkafé,** Vondelpark 6B (© **020/625-3257**), where kids (carefully supervised) get to cook their own meals. See p. 114.

o **Best Late-Night Dinner:** You can't help feeling a little sorry for the staff at **De Knijp,** Van Baerlestraat 134 (© **020/671-4248**), when you saunter in around midnight. They've been going hard for hours, but are ready, willing, and just about able to do it one more time. See p. 130.

What's in a Name

There's Chinese food and there's Indonesian food. In Holland, there's *Chinees-Indisch* (Chinese-Indonesian) food, too. Watch out for this not-here-and-not-there genre. *Chinees-Indisch* restaurants are rarely, if ever, any good (there are plenty of these restaurants in Amsterdam, and I can't think of a single one worth recommending). Places that attempt this crossover style can't get either one right.

📷 SECRETS OF THE *rijsttafel*

The Indonesian **rijsttafel** is Holland's favorite feast; it has been ever since the United East India Company sea captains introduced it to the wealthy Amsterdam burghers in the 17th century. The *rijsttafel* (literally, "rice table") originated with Dutch plantation overseers in Indonesia, who liked to sample selectively from Indonesian cuisine. It became a tradition upheld by Indonesian migrants to Holland who opened restaurants and, knowing the Dutch fondness for *rijsttafel*, made it a standard menu item. *Rijsttafels* are only a small part of an Indonesian restaurant's menu, and there's a trend among the Dutch to look down on them as "just for tourists": The Dutch generally have a good understanding of Indonesian cuisine and prefer to order an individual dish rather than the mixed hash of a *rijsttafel*. However, *rijsttafels* remain popular, and many Chinese, Japanese, Vietnamese, and Thai restaurants have copied the idea.

The basic concept of a *rijsttafel* is to eat a bit of this and a bit of that, blending flavors and textures. A simple, unadorned bed of rice is the base and mediator between spicy meats and bland vegetables or fruits, between sweet-and-sour tastes and soft-and-crunchy textures. Although a *rijsttafel* for one is possible, it's better shared by two or more people. In the case of a solitary diner or a couple, a 17-dish *rijsttafel* will be enough; with four or more, order a 24- or 30-dish *rijsttafel* and experience the total taste treat.

RESTAURANTS BY CUISINE

AFRICAN
Kilimanjaro ★ (The Waterfront, $, p. 116)

BISTRO
't Stuivertje (The Jordaan, $$, p. 127)

CHINESE
Dynasty (The Old Center, $$$, p. 110)
Nam Kee ★ (The Old Center, $, p. 113)
Treasure (The Old Center, $$, p. 112)

CONTINENTAL
Amsterdam ★ (Amsterdam West, $$, p. 134)
Brasserie Keyzer ★ (Museum District & Vondelpark, $$$, p. 128)
Café Americain ★ (Leidseplein, $$, p. 122)

Café-Restaurant Van Puffelen (The Canal Belt, $$, p. 118)
De Belhamel ★★ (The Canal Belt, $$, p. 118)
De Jaren (The Old Center, $, p. 113)
De Kas ★★ (Amsterdam South, $$$, p. 133)
Excelsior ★★ (The Old Center, $$$$, p. 107)
Grand Café-Restaurant 1e Klas (Eerste Klas) (The Waterfront, $$, p. 115)
In de Waag ★ (The Old Center, $$, p. 111)
Lof ★ (The Old Center, $$, p. 112)
Sluizer (The Canal Belt, $$, p. 119)
Spanjer & van Twist ★ (The Canal Belt, $$, p. 119)
't Blaauwhooft (The Waterfront, $, p. 116)

KEY TO ABBREVIATIONS:
$$$$** = Very Expensive **$$$** = Expensive **$$** = Moderate **$ = Inexpensive

Before you begin to imagine 30 dinner-size plates of food, it's important to note that the dishes are small and the portions served are gauged by the number of people expected to share them. Remember, the idea is to taste many things rather than hunker down with any single item. Also, an Indonesian *rijsttafel* has no separate courses. Once your table has been set with a row of low plate warmers, all 17, 24, or 30 dishes arrive all at once, like a culinary avalanche. The sweets come alongside the sours and the spicy, so you're left to plot your own course through the extravaganza.

Among the customary dishes and ingredients of a *rijsttafel* are *loempia* (Chinese-style egg rolls); *satay,* or *sateh* (small pork kebabs, grilled and served with spicy peanut sauce); *perkedel* (meatballs); *gado-gado* (vegetables in peanut sauce); *daging smoor* (beef in soy sauce); *babi ketjap* (pork in soy sauce); *kroepoek* (crunchy, puffy shrimp toast); *serundeng* (fried coconut); *roedjak manis* (fruit in sweet sauce); and *pisang goreng* (fried banana).

Caution: When something on the menu is described as *pedis,* meaning spicy, that's exactly what it is. Beware in particular of one very appealing-looking dish of sauce with small chunks of what looks to be bright-red onion—that's *sambal badjak,* or just *sambal,* and it's hotter than hot. A fire extinguisher would be a useful table accessory; for an equally effective alternative, order a *witbier* (white beer).

FUSION
Fifteen Amsterdam ★ (The Waterfront, $$$, p. 114)

Le Garage ★★ (Museum District & Vondelpark, $$$, p. 130)

GREEK
Aphrodite (Leidseplein, $$, p. 122)

Grekas Griekse Traiterie ★ (The Canal Belt, $, p. 121)

INDIAN
Akbar (Leidseplein, $, p. 123)

Memories of India (Rembrandtplein, $$, p. 125)

INDONESIAN
Bojo ★ (Leidseplein, $, p. 123)

Kantjil & de Tijger ★★ (The Old Center, $$, p. 111)

Sama Sebo ★ (Museum District & Vondelpark, $$, p. 131)

Tempo Doeloe ★★ (The Canal Belt, $$, p. 119)

INTERNATIONAL
Atrium (The Old Center, $, p. 113)

Brasserie De Poort ★ (The Old Center, $$, p. 110)

Breitner ★ (The Canal Belt, $$$, p. 117)

Café Luxembourg ★ (The Old Center, $, p. 113)

Café-Restaurant De Duvel ★ (Amsterdam South, $$, p. 130)

De Luwte ★★ (The Canal Belt, $$, p. 118)

Grand Café De Balie (Leidseplein, $$, p. 123)

Grand Café l'Opera (Rembrandtplein, $$, p. 125)

Pier 10 ★ (The Waterfront, $$, p. 115)

Supperclub ★ (The Old Center, $$$, p. 110)

ITALIAN
Hostaria ★ (The Jordaan, $$, p. 127)

Toscanini ★ (The Jordaan, $$, p. 127)

JAPANESE
Osaka ★ (Amsterdam North, $$$, p. 134)

Umeno ★ (Amsterdam South, $$, p. 133)

MEDITERRANEAN
Christophe ★★ (The Canal Belt, $$$, p. 117)

Gare de l'Est ★★ (The Waterfront, $$, p. 114)

La Rive ★★★ (Amsterdam East, $$$$, p. 132)

Mangerie De Kersentuin ★ (Amsterdam South, $$$, p. 133)

Vertigo ★★ (Museum District & Vondelpark, $$, p. 131)

Wilhelmina-Dok ★★ (The Waterfront, $$, p. 115)

MEXICAN
Rose's Cantina (The Old Center, $, p. 114)

NEPALESE
Sherpa (Leidseplein, $, p. 123)

PANCAKES
Pancake Bakery (The Canal Belt, $, p. 121)

SEAFOOD
Albatros Seafoodhouse & Vis Restaurant ★ (The Jordaan, $$, p. 126)

Le Pêcheur ★ (The Old Center, $$, p. 111)

Sluizer (The Canal Belt, $$, p. 119)

Visrestaurant Lucius (The Old Center, $$$, p. 110)

SOUTHEAST ASIAN
Dynasty (The Old Center, $$$, p. 110)

SPANISH
Duende (The Jordaan, $, p. 128)

THAI
Rakang (The Jordaan, $$, p. 127)

TIBETAN
Sherpa (Leidseplein, $, p. 123)

VEGETARIAN
Bolhoed ★ (The Canal Belt, $$, p. 118)

Golden Temple ★ (The Canal Belt, $, p. 120)

THE OLD CENTER

Very Expensive

Excelsior ★★ FRENCH/CONTINENTAL Located in the tony Hotel de l'Europe (p. 76), one of Amsterdam's finest restaurants derives its reputation from French master chef Jean-Jacques Menanteau's Michelin-starred cuisine coupled with superb service. It's formal by Amsterdam standards. Crystal chandeliers, elaborate moldings, crisp linens, fresh flower bouquets, and picture-frame windows with Amstel River views typify this classically grand establishment. A meal here is an exercise in refinement, aided by diligent and discreet waitstaff. Respectable attire is required. If your budget can't quite compete with that of the royalty and showbiz stars who dine here, try the three-course *middagmenu* (lunch menu), or the evening *menu du théâtre* (theater menu), both of which make fine dining a touch more affordable. The appetizer menu includes foie gras, smoked eel with dill, and marinated sweetbreads of lamb with salad. Choices for main courses include halibut filet with caper sauce or filet of veal with leek sauce.

In the Hotel de l'Europe, Nieuwe Doelenstraat 2–8 (facing Muntplein). ✆ **020/531-1705.** www.leurope. nl. Reservations recommended on weekends. Main courses 34€–38€; fixed-price menus 55€–95€. AE, DC, MC, V. Mon–Fri 7–11am, 12:30–2:30pm, and 7–10:30pm; Sat–Sun 7–11am and 7–10:30pm. Tram: 4, 9, 14, 16, 24, or 25 to Muntplein.

Expensive

De Silveren Spiegel MODERN DUTCH/FRENCH The menu at "The Silver Mirror," one of the oldest and best-known restaurants in Amsterdam, offers updated preparations of traditional seafood and meat dishes, such as baked sole filets with wild spinach, and trilogy of lamb with ratatouille—but just as in the old days, the lamb (from Texel, one of Holland's Frisian Islands) is still Holland's finest. Be sure to try the Zaanse mustard (from windmill village Zaanse Schans, see p. 267). The two houses that form the premises were built in 1614 for a wealthy soap maker, Laurens Jansz Spieghel. It's typical Old Dutch inside, with a bar downstairs and dining rooms where bedrooms used to be. The whole place emanates a Dutch tidiness that's very welcoming. There's a garden at the back, and adjacent is the 17th-century, domed Ronde Lutherse Kerk (Round Lutheran Church).

Kattengat 4–6 (off Singel). ✆ **020/624-6589.** www.desilverenspiegel.com. Main courses 27€–29€; fixed-price menus 40€–53€. AE, MC, V. Mon–Sat 5:30–10:30pm. Tram: 1, 2, 5, 13, or 17 to Martelaarsgracht.

D'Vijff Vlieghen ★ MODERN DUTCH The "Five Flies" has nine separate dining rooms spread over five canal houses decorated with objects from Holland's Golden Age—among them four original Rembrandt etchings. Each dining room has a different character. There's the Rembrandt Room; the Glass Room, with a collection of antique handmade glassware; and the Knight's Room, adorned with 16th-century armor and accoutrements, to name just three. Chef René Cramer is passionate about what he calls "New Dutch" cuisine, which aims to convey the culinary excellence inherent in many traditional Dutch recipes and products, but in an updated, French-influenced form, employing organic ingredients as often as possible. Enjoy quite a mouthful by choosing the *geroosterde tamme eend op een bedje van appeltjes en tuinboontjes overgroten met een vinaigrette van rode en groene pepers*

Where to Dine in Central Amsterdam

NORTH

JAVA-EILAND

Het IJ

IJ-Tunnel

De Ruijterkade

Centraal Station

Muziekgebouw aan 't IJ/ Bimhuis

Passenger Terminal Amsterdam

IJhaven

Stationsplein

Centraal Station

De Ruijterkade

Piet Heinkade

Prins Hendrikkade

Nieuwendijk

Damrak

Damrak straat

Warmoes-straat

Zeedijk

Gelderskade

Kromme Waal

Oosterdokskade

Dijksgracht

OLD CENTER

Oude Kerk

Scheepvaarthuis

Oosterdok

Science Center NEMO

MARINE ETABLISSEMENT (NAVAL COMPLEX)

RED LIGHT DISTRICT

Nieuw-markt

Nieuwmarkt

Binnenkant

Waals-Eilandsgracht

Oude Waal

Prins Hendrikkade

Rechtboomssloot

Scheepvaartmuseum (Maritime Museum)

Kattenburgerstraat

Voorburgwal

Oudezijds Achterburgwal

Sint-Antonies-breestraat

Kromboomssloot

Oude Schans

Kattenburger-gracht

Kattenburger-vaart

Raamgracht

Nieuwe Uilenburgerstraat

Schans

Uilenburgergracht

Valkenburgerstraat

Rapenburg

Wittenburger-gracht

Nieuwe Vaart

Klovenierburgwal

Jodenbreestraat

Rapenburgerstraat

Hoogte Kadijk

Laagte Kadijk

Zwanenburgwal

Waterlooplein

Mr. Visser-plein

Muider-straat

Wertheim-park

Entrepotdok

Plantage Doklaan

Stadhuis, Muziek-theater

Waterlooplein

Hortus Botanicus

Plantage

Planetarium

Geologisch Museum

ARTIS ZOO

Binnenamstel

Amstel

Blauw-brug

Nieuwe Herengracht

Plantage Middenlaan

Rembrandtplein

Hermitage Amsterdam

Nieuwe Keizersgracht

Plantage Muidergracht

Zoologisch Museum & Aquarium

Herengracht

Amstel

Nieuwe Kerkstraat

Nieuwe Prinsengracht

Roetersstraat

Utrechtsestraat

gracht

Keizersgracht

Magere Brug

Nieuwe Weesperstraat

Achter-gracht

Sarphatistraat

EAST

Keizersestraat

Kerkstraat

Amstel-sluizen

Reguliersgracht

Amstel-veld

Prinsengracht

Nieuwe

Weesperplein

Utrechtsedwarsstraat

Frederiks-plein

Hoge-straat

Singelgracht

Mauritskade

Sarphati-sluis

Toronto Brug

Rose's Cantina **8**	Tempo Doeloe **68**
Sherpa **2**	Toscanini **38**
Sluizer **67**	Treasure **27**
Soupkitchen **48**	't Stuivertje **22**
Spanjer & van Twist **31**	Vinkeles **16**
Stubbe's Haring **46**	Visrestaurant Lucius **19**
Supper Club **24**	Walem **12**
't Blaauwhooft **41**	Wilhelmina-Dok **52**

(roasted tame duck on a layer of apples and broad beans drizzled with a vinaigrette of red and green peppers).

Spuistraat 294-302 (at Spui; entrance at Vliegendesteeg 1). ✆ **020/530-4060.** www.d-vijffvlieghen.com. Main courses 22€–39€; seasonal menu 26€–53€. AE, DC, MC, V. Daily 5:30pm–midnight. Tram: 1, 2, or 5 to Spui.

Dynasty CHINESE/SOUTHEAST ASIAN   It's an unlikely mix: Tropical Asia at a formal Louis XV–style canal house. But it works. Dining in this cozy cavern of exotic colors, cushioned rattan chairs, fine table settings, and upturned Chinese paper umbrellas won't disappoint. In fine weather, enjoy your meal outdoors in the courtyard garden. Dynasty offers an array of dishes, an extravaganza of flavors—Cantonese, Thai, Malay, Filipino, and Vietnamese—that take you on a culinary tour through Southeast Asia. Among the intriguing possibilities is Promise of Spring, an appetizer of crisp pancakes filled with bamboo shoots and minced meat, and the delightfully named "drunken prawn," which is jumbo shrimp marinated in *shooshing* wine and Chinese herbs. Recommended main courses include the lobster lightly seasoned with ginger and scallions, and the Szechuan beef.

Reguliersdwarsstraat 30 (off Leidsestraat). ✆ **020/626-8400.** www.restaurantdynasty.nl. Main courses 15€–36€; fixed-price menus 33€–52€. AE, DC, MC, V. Wed–Mon 5:30–11pm. Tram: 1, 2, or 5 to Koningsplein.

Supper Club ★ INTERNATIONAL   Kick back in this ultra-modern, blindingly white, hypertrendy restaurant-club-cabaret, where the gorgeously brain-dead lie recumbent on sofas and cushions, and groove along to whatever the DJ is spinning. There's no telling what the chefs (called "food magicians") will whip up—you inform your waiter of any dietary restrictions and wait to see what arrives on your table. Typical dishes might include pea soup or Parma ham with melon for an appetizer, and seared tuna on greens or chicken with a sweet and sour sauce with roasted vegetables for a main course. The atmosphere (not the food) is the highlight here.

Jonge Roelensteeg 21 (near the Dam). ✆ **020/344-6400.** www.supperclub.nl. Reservations recommended on weekends. Fixed-price menus 65€–75€. AE, DC, MC, V. Daily 6–11pm. Tram: 1, 2, 5, 13, 14, or 17 to the Dam. Map p 108.

Visrestaurant Lucius SEAFOOD   Lucius, which means "pike" in Latin, has earned a reputation for fine seafood at fairly reasonable prices. Oysters and lobsters imported from Norway and Canada are the specialties. The three-course menu is very popular. Among the six or so choices featured on the chalkboard menu, you might find fish soup to start, followed by grilled plaice, Dover sole, bass, or John Dory. The spectacular seafood plate includes six oysters, 10 mussels, clams, shrimp, and half a lobster. The long, narrow dining room features an aquarium. In summer, you can dine out on the sidewalk.

Spuistraat 247 (near Spui). ✆ **020/624-1831.** www.lucius.nl. Main courses 19€–28€; fixed-price menu 38€. AE, DC, MC, V. Daily 5pm–midnight. Tram: 1, 2, or 5 to Spui.

Moderate

Brasserie De Poort ★ DUTCH/INTERNATIONAL   In a former beer hall across from the Royal Palace, this restaurant has been serving up steaks and typically Dutch fare—though now backed by a cast of international dishes—since 1870. Beamed and tiled with Delft blue from Koninklijke Porcelyne Fles, the Dutch-tavern dining room has been fully restored along with its parent hotel, called Die Port van Cleve (p. 80). De Poort maintains a tradition that's become legendary among regular patrons: Each steak is numbered, and if the number on yours is a round thousand, you win a bottle of wine. They've already served close to 6 million steaks! The restaurant is equally known for its Dutch pea soup.

In the Hotel Die Port van Cleve, Nieuwezijds Voorburgwal 176–180 (behind the Dam). ☏ **020/622-6429.** www.dieportvancleve.com. Main courses 18€–28€; fixed-price menus 30€–35€. AE, DC, MC, V. Daily 7am–10:30pm. Tram: 1, 2, 5, 13, 14, or 17 to the Dam.

Haesje Claes ★ DUTCH   If you're yearning for a cozy Old Dutch environment and hearty Dutch food at moderate prices, try this inviting place. Lots of nooks and crannies decorated with wood paneling, Delftware, wooden barrels, brocaded benches, and traditional Dutch hanging lamps with fringed covers create an intimate, comfortable setting. The menu covers a lot of ground, from canapés to caviar, but you'll have the most luck with Dutch stalwarts ranging from omelets to tournedos. Take in *hutspot* (stew), *stamppot* (mashed potatoes and cabbage), and various fish stews, including those with IJsselmeer *paling* (eel), along the way.

Spuistraat 273–275 (at Spui). ☏ **020/624-9998.** www.haesjeclaes.nl. Main courses 16€–26€; *Neerlands Dis* menu 28€. AE, DC, MC, V. Daily noon–10pm. Tram: 1, 2, or 5 to Spui.

In de Waag ★ CONTINENTAL   In the 14th century, this building was the Sint-Antoniespoort Gate in the city walls; by the Golden Age, a couple of centuries later, it had become a public weigh house: De Waag. Dissections were once carried out on the top-floor Theatrum Anatomicum. Nowadays, any dissection that occurs is of a culinary nature; this castle-like structure holds one of Amsterdam's most stylish and social eateries, and it's in an area that's becoming hipper by the day. It's romantic, with long banquet-style tables that are, in the evenings, lit with hundreds of candles, and it serves organic food. Look for lamb from Texel (one of Holland's Frisian Islands) and blonde d'Aquitaine steaks. You can also just drop by for coffee or a drink and to peruse the international newspapers and magazines available.

Nieuwmarkt 4. ☏ **020/422-7772.** www.indewaag.nl. Main courses 17€–25€; fixed-price menu 34€. AE, DC, MC, V. Daily 10am–1am. Metro: Nieuwmarkt.

Kantjil & de Tijger ★★ INDONESIAN   Unlike Holland's many Indonesian restaurants that wear their ethnic origins on their sleeves, with staffers decked out in traditional costume, The Antelope and The Tiger is popular, chic, and modern. Moreover, it attracts customers who like their Indonesian food not only chic and modern, but also prepared well. Two bestsellers in this popular place are *nasi goreng Kantjil* (fried rice with pork kebabs, stewed beef, pickled cucumbers, and mixed vegetables), and the 20-item *rijsttafel* for two. Other choices include stewed chicken in *soja* sauce, tofu omelet, shrimp with coconut dressing, Indonesian pumpkin, and mixed steamed vegetables with peanut-butter sauce. Finish your meal with multilayered cinnamon cake or (try this at least once) coffee with ginger liqueur and whipped cream.

Spuistraat 291-293 (beside Spui). ☏ **020/620-0994.** www.kantjil.nl. Reservations recommended on weekends. Main courses 11€–16€; *rijsttafels* 40€–50€ for 2. AE, DC, MC, V. Mon–Fri 4:30–11pm; Sat–Sun noon–11pm. Tram: 1, 2, or 5 to Spui.

Le Pêcheur ★ SEAFOOD   Popular and appealing, and in a frenetic neighborhood where establishments are more commonly either one or the other, Le Pêcheur has long combined elegant simplicity of presentation with a steely focus on freshness and taste. Flowers adorn tables set on a marble floor in the airy, tranquil dining room. There's also a mural ceiling, and enough space between tables to stretch a little. A romantic courtyard garden is perfect for summer dining. Dishes are prepared in Dutch, continental, and international styles. In season, come for the *coquilles Saint-Jacques* scallops, the mussels and oysters from the southern Dutch province of Zeeland, and the house-smoked salmon. You could also try poached brill with onion sauce, fried wolf-fish with light mustard sauce, or sashimi. Beef tournedos are available as an alternative to seafood, and the wine list is extensive.

Reguliersdwarsstraat 32 (behind the Flower Market). ✆ **020/624-3121.** www.lepecheur.nl. Main courses 21€–40€; fixed-price menu 40€. AE, MC, V. Mon–Fri noon–midnight; Sat 5pm–midnight. Tram: 1, 2, or 5 to Koningsplein.

Lof ★ 🍴 CONTINENTAL It's hard to pin down this fashionable, vaguely French–Italian eatery. For one thing, there's no menu. Its youthful chefs describe their creations as *cuisine spontane*—they go to the markets, spontaneously pick out whatever's fresh and catches their fancy, and equally spontaneously figure out what to do with it back at base. But *lof* means "praise" in Dutch, and it's an apt name, since the results are invariably admirable. The choice is deliberately limited, not quite take-it-or-leave-it, yet not far from that. Oysters are a regular feature among two or three starters; then choose from three main courses: Meat, fish, or vegetarian and finish with a *torte*. You dine on one of two levels, at plain tables in a cozy setting with bare brick walls, or with a view of proceedings in the open kitchen.

Haarlemmerstraat 62 (near Centraal Station). ✆ **020/620-2997.** Main course 23€; fixed-price menu 35€. AE, DC, MC, V. Tues–Sat 7–11pm (or later). Tram: 1, 2, 5, 13, or 17 to Maartelaarsgracht.

Treasure CHINESE In a city with a passion for Indonesian food, it can be difficult to find traditional Chinese cuisine, let alone *good* traditional Chinese cuisine. Don't despair—make a beeline for this legendary restaurant. It offers a wide array of classic Chinese choices in a classic Chinese setting: Lots of lanterns, watercolor paintings, and Chinese scripts adorn the place. You can eat dishes from any of the four main styles of Chinese cooking—Beijing, Shanghai, Cantonese, and Szechuan. Look for specialties such as Beijing duck, Szechuan-style shrimps (very spicy), and steamed dumplings.

Nieuwezijds Voorburgwal 115–117 (near the Dam). ✆ **020/623-4061.** Main courses 9€–16€; fixed-price menus 26€–39€. AE, MC, V. Daily noon–11pm. Tram: 1, 2, 5, 13, 14, or 17 to the Dam.

Grand Cafes

A popular Amsterdam scene is that of the grand cafes in the, well, grand tradition of Paris, Vienna, and Rome, with lots of style, ambience, and balconies or terraces—see-and-be-seen places. Grand cafes are distinguished by their emphasis on food and drink, architecture, production values, and style. The definition is an elusive one: The grand cafes listed below truly are grand, but be aware that others use the name even though they may not be particularly impressive.

Inexpensive

Atrium 🔳 DUTCH/INTERNATIONAL   Students, professors, and regular humans in search of cheap, sustaining nosh congregate in the casual self-service *mensa* (student restaurant) at the University of Amsterdam. A courtyard between restored buildings has been covered with a glass roof that lets in plenty of light. To reach the food lines, walk up the stairs and, just inside the door, cross over the pedestrian bridge. The menu mixes standard Dutch fare like salads and pea-and-ham soup with exotic influences like filled Indonesian *bami* (noodle) and *nasi* (rice) croquettes that have themselves become Dutch standards. None of these, it must be stated, are produced to any unforgettable effect, but they're all perfectly edible, and the knowledge that they're costing close to nothing goes a long way toward compensating for any culinary shortcomings. An added value is the nature of the place, which makes it easy to share tables and strike up conversations.

Oudezijds Achterburgwal 237 (at Grimburgwal). ℂ **020/525-3999.** Most items under 6€. No credit cards. Mon–Fri noon–2pm and 5–7pm. Tram: 4, 9, 14, 16, 24, or 25 to Spui.

Café Luxembourg ★ INTERNATIONAL   "One of the world's great cafes," the *New York Times* called this bohemian, see-and-be-seen grand cafe, where waitstaff wear starched white aprons. Unlike other Amsterdam cafes, which often draw distinctive clientele, Luxembourg attracts all kinds of people because it offers amazingly large portions of food at reasonable prices. Soups, sandwiches, and dishes such as meatloaf are available. Especially appealing are specials like the Chinese dim sum and the *satay ajam* (Indonesian grilled chicken in peanut sauce). Sundays in particular, but also on other days, it's a relaxing place to do breakfast with one of the many international papers available here and a cup of strong coffee; diners are encouraged to linger. In summer, there's sidewalk dining.

Spuistraat 24 (at Spui). ℂ **020/620-6264.** www.cafeluxembourg.nl. Salads and specials 7.50€–13€; lunch 4.90€–9.90€; main courses 9.50€–16€. AE, DC, MC, V. Sun–Thurs 9am–1am; Fri–Sat 9am–2am. Tram: 1, 2, or 5 to Spui.

De Jaren CONTINENTAL   This cafe-restaurant with picturesque surroundings is fashionable without being pretentious. It occupies a solid-looking former bank; ceilings are unusually high and flooring is multicolored tiled mosaic. Students from the nearby University of Amsterdam lunch here, and it's popular with the media crowd. De Jaren's unique selling point is its two marvelous open-air patios beside the Amstel River, sunny spots that, in fine weather, are much in demand. Occupants of those prime seats settle into them with a firmness of purpose, but it's worth checking out the outdoor decks, in case one of these permanent-seeming patrons might have fallen—or been pushed—into the river. Enjoy ham and eggs for breakfast, a salad from the extensive salad bar for lunch, or spaghetti Bolognese, couscous, or rib-eye steak for dinner. Sip on coffee, beer, or *jenever* (gin) while perusing the English-language newspapers.

Nieuwe Doelenstraat 20–22 (near Muntplein). ℂ **020/625-5771.** www.cafe-de-jaren.nl. Main courses 14€–20€; lunch menu 9.50€. V. Sun–Thurs 10am–1am; Fri–Sat 10am–2am. Tram: 4, 9, 14, 16, 24, or 25 to Muntplein.

Nam Kee ★ CHINESE   In the heart of Amsterdam's small but growing Chinatown, Nam Kee has a long interior with few obvious graces and little in the way of decor. Don't let the drab, neon-lit dining room dissuade you from trying the very good, fresh food here. People come for authentic, excellent, modestly priced food from a 140-item menu. Those steamed oysters with black bean sauce and the duck with plum sauce are to die for. The Peking duck—always an indicator of quality in a Chinese restaurant—is satisfyingly crisp-skinned. Service is fast, so you won't have long to wait for a table, and they're open late.

Zeedijk 111-113 at Nieuwmarkt. ✆ **020/624-3470.** www.namkee.nl. Main courses 5.75€-16€. AE, DC, MC, V. Daily 11:30am-midnight. Metro: Nieuwmarkt.

🎁 Chef Child

Children are both the chefs and the waiters at the self-service bar (daily, 10am–5pm) in the **Kinderkookkafé**, Vondelpark 6B (✆ **020/625-3257**; www.kinderkookkafe.nl; tram: 1), in the Vondelpark. With the help and supervision of adults, children can do everything here—cook, bake cookies, wait tables, wash up, serve behind the bar (soft drinks only), and write checks.

Rose's Cantina MEXICAN A meal starting with tortilla chips and salsa, followed by a *plato mixto* or fried *gallinas* (roast hen with fries and red peppers), and accompanied by a Mexican beer should hit the spot. The tables are oak, the service is decent but slow—the basic rate of continental drift is a good comparison—and the atmosphere is Latin American and buzzing with cheer. Beware of long waiting times for a table that'll have you at the bar downing one after another of Rose's deadly margaritas. There's a small sidewalk terrace on feverish Reguliersdwarsstraat for summer dining.

Reguliersdwarsstraat 38-40 (off Leidsestraat). ✆ **020/625-9797.** www.rosescantina.com. Main courses 14€-24€. AE, DC, MC, V. Mon-Fri 5-10:30pm; Sat-Sun 5-11:30pm. Tram: 1, 2, or 5 to Koningsplein.

THE WATERFRONT

Moderate

Fifteen Amsterdam ★ FUSION British celeb-chef Jamie Oliver has brought his unique restaurant concept from London to the old Brazilië building in the harbor redevelopment zone east of Centraal Station. His Amsterdam hotspot has both a full-menu restaurant and an adjoining trattoria serving less-elaborate fare. Drop-dead gorgeous staff serve the equally gorgeous clientele dishes like a salad of the day with figs, prosciutto, Gorgonzola, and toasted almonds on field greens; seafood risotto; and pan-fried calves' liver with balsamic figs. Though Jamie doesn't often preside in person, you can try out his eclectic-fun cooking concept in the vast dining room. You can also dine outdoors on a waterside terrace.

Pakhuis Amsterdam, Jollemanhof 9 (at Oostelijke Handelskade). ✆ **0900/343-8336.** www.fifteen.nl. Main courses 18€-21€. AE, MC, V. Mon-Sat noon to 3pm and 5:30pm-1am. Tram: 25 or 26 to Passenger Terminal Amsterdam.

Gare de l'Est ★★ FRENCH/MEDITERRANEAN This distinctive detached house with a conservatory extension and a large sidewalk terrace was built in 1901 as a coffeehouse for longshoremen (dockworkers). A meal at this restaurant is an altogether good reason to take a ride to what's now a fashionable part of town. As the restaurant's name indicates (it means "East Station"), the cuisine is traditional French—but its chefs do incorporate Mediterranean touches. Service is relaxed and knowledgeable, and the fixed-price menu is excellent value: Surprises appear on your plate rather than on the check. The strict three-course formula leaves no room for choice—except for the main course—but plenty for market-fresh ingredients and culinary creativity. There's literally no way to know what'll be on the daily-changing menu.

Cruquiusweg 9 (at the Oosterdok/Eastern Harbor). © **020/463-0620.** www.garedelest.nl. Reservations recommended on weekends. Fixed-price menu 32€. AE, DC, MC, V. Daily 6–11pm. Tram: 7 or 10 to Zeeburgerdijk.

Grand Café-Restaurant 1e Klas ♠ CONTINENTAL   Should you have both a train to catch and some eating to get done, Centraal Station's brasserie is a good choice; it's no run-of-the-mill buffet. The dining room, in the station's former 1881 first-class waiting room, has been restored to its original Art Nouveau elegance. Despite high ceilings, wood paneling, tall windows, chandeliers, painted pilaster columns, and potted plants, 1e Klas is rather gloomy. Drop by for just a coffee or a beer, and you'll sit at a table along the wall; for a meal, you get a table in the central dining area. The soup of the day is usually good and quick, as is the club sandwich. To squelch more substantial hunger pangs, there are Caesar salad, Dover sole with salad and fries, beef stroganoff, and more.

Spoor (Platform) 2B, Centraal Station. © **020/625-0131.** www.restaurant1eklas.nl. Main courses 20€–35€. No credit cards. Daily 8:30am–11pm. Tram: 1, 2, 4, 5, 9, 13, 16, 17, 24, 25, or 26 to Centraal Station.

Pier 10 ★ FRENCH/INTERNATIONAL   Perched as it is on an old pier on Het IJ behind Centraal Station, this restaurant can hardly help being romantic. It has great views of the IJ waterway from its big outdoor terrace and from the *serre* (glassed-in room) at the end of the pier. If the views of Waterplein-West, the ferry dock next door, are not quite as fantastic, then at least the ferries' comings and goings add a dash of nautical bustle to the scene. When cruise liners head to sea and workaday barges make for the inland waterways, they sail down the ship channel within view, making this one of only a few restaurants where you can see the sea and port traffic that was once Amsterdam's lifeblood. Candlelight softens the funky diner decor, and the food is fanciful international-eclectic—there are salads of all sorts, steak, and fish (including new herring), among other offerings.

De Ruyterkade, Steiger 10 (behind Centraal Station). © **020/427-2310.** www.pier10.nl. Reservations recommended on weekends. Main courses 20€–22€. AE, DC, MC, V. Daily noon–3pm and 6:30pm–1am. Tram: 1, 2, 4, 5, 9, 16, 17, 24, 25, or 26 to Centraal Station.

Wilhelmina-Dok ★★ 🍴 ☺ MEDITERRANEAN   Just across the IJ waterway from Centraal Station, this restaurant is more than worth a short, free ferryboat ride followed by a 5-minute walk. It's on three floors (the chandeliered top floor is for groups only), and plain wood, candlelit tables, wood floors, and oak cabinets give the interior an old-fashioned maritime look. Large windows serve up views across the narrow channel. Most tables on the outdoor terrace are sheltered from the wind in a glass-walled enclosure. The thin dinner menu favors plain cooking and organic products; and concentrates on a few broadly Italian, French, or Spanish items with an occasional dash of the Maghreb. Or settle back with just a beer and a snack. On Monday evenings in summer, you can take in movies on an outdoor screen.

Nordwal 1 (at IJplein). © **020/632-3701.** www.wilhelmina-dok.nl. Reservations recommended on weekends. Main courses 18€–21€; chef's menu 28€. AE, DC, MC, V. Daily 11am–midnight. Ferry: IJveer from Waterplein-West behind Centraal Station to the dock at IJplein, then go right, along the dike-top path.

FROMMER'S FAVORITE local SPOTS

- Raw herring is a Dutch specialty, and there are dozens of *haringhuis* fish stands in town. The top place is (arguably) the centrally located **Stubbe's Haring,** Haarlemmersluis (✆ **020/623-3212;** tram: 1, 2, 5, 13, or 17), at Singel. It's a great spot for "new herring" and other seafood snacks.
- There aren't many better outdoor terraces than that of **Klein Kalfje,** Amsteldijk 355 (✆ **020/644-5338;** www.restaurantkleinkalfje. nl; bus: 62). This atmospheric little

Dutch cafe-restaurant's waterside terrace is at a tranquil spot along the Amstel River, just outside the city limits. It's easier to get here by car or by bike.
- Sabrina and Denise of **Basilico,** Willemsstraat 29A (✆ **020/627-2685;** www.basilico.nl; tram: 3), in the Jordaan, rustle up some ace homemade Italian food, but only for takeout. If you have somewhere to eat an Italian meal, or are looking for picnic makings, go for it.

Inexpensive

Kilimanjaro ★ AFRICAN   This chic restaurant on the ground floor of a narrow old house not far from the Maritime Museum has few tables, and it serves such authentically good food—a variety of African specialties, such as Senegalese lamb curry, crocodile steak (very snappy), and *doro wat* (spicy Ethiopian chicken sautéed in red pepper sauce and served with a spinach salad). And the simple decor of high ceilings, white walls, and colorful tablecloths smartly manages to avoid the usual colonial jungle-cabana look.

Rapenburgerplein 6 (at Prins Hendrikkade). ✆ **020/622-3485.** www.restaurantkilimanjaro.com. Reservations required. Main courses 11€–17€; *dagschotel* 15€. AE, DC, MC, V. Tues–Sun 5–10pm. Bus: 22, 42, or 43 to Kadijksplein.

't Blaauwhooft 🍴 DUTCH/CONTINENTAL   A plain neighborhood brown cafe in the gentrified Westelijke Eilanden (Western Islands) district has been transformed into a great *eetcafé* by the simple expedient of adding a kitchen and a menu. It partakes of the villagey setting on these tranquil islands—which feel isolated despite a location just west of Centraal Station—and brings its own cozy atmosphere to the party. The clientele is drawn mainly from locals who can afford to occupy one of the bijou apartments in transformed old warehouses, yet who don't want to look like it or to lose touch with their roots. There's a nice sidewalk terrace on the square, though with an uninspiring view of trains coming and going into Centraal Station on the adjacent elevated rail line. The kitchen finds its comfort zone in Dutch standbys like Zeeland mussels, but runs to ostrich steak and some adventurous salads.

Hendrik Jonkerplein 1 (Bickerseiland, off Haarlemmerhouttuinen). ✆ **020/623-8721.** www.blaauwhooft. nl. Main courses 9€–18€; *dagschotel* 12€. No credit cards. Daily 3–10pm. Bus: 18 or 22 to Haarlemmerhouttuinen.

THE CANAL BELT

Expensive

Breitner ★ FRENCH/CONTINENTAL A fast, last-minute dash from here should get you to the Muziektheater or **Koninklijk Theater Carré** just in time for the evening curtain rise, but that would involve dining in unseemly haste, and undervalues the performance of the excellent kitchen and knowledgeable waitstaff. The plush red carpet, chandelier, and wine cupboard suggest classical timelessness, yet modern decor and paintings tell a different story. Named after Amsterdam's Impressionist painter George Hendrik Breitner, this restaurant finds a way to fuse a classic French foundation with this city's cosmopolitan spirit. The menu changes four times a year, tracking the seasons. Light floods in from big riverside and canal-side windows, so a window seat guarantees fine views on the water. Ordering the three-course menu is the way to go for theatergoers.

Amstel 212 (at Herengracht). © **020/627-7879.** www.restaurant-breitner.nl. Reservations recommended at theater time. Main courses 25€–36€; fixed-price menus 35€–58€. AE, DC, MC, V. Mon–Sat 6–10:30pm. Tram: 9 or 14 to Waterlooplein.

Christophe ★★ MODERN FRENCH/MEDITERRANEAN French chef Jean-Joel Bonsens has a penchant for wielding tangy Mediterranean flourishes to create a version of classic French cuisine. His ultra-refined food, served in a main dining room of modern flair, employs traditional Mediterranean ingredients—figs, truffles, olives, anchovies, peppers, saffron, and more—in exciting new ways. North African *tajine* and Italian *pata negra* ham have a place on the menu, alongside French "staples" like roast Vendée duck. Bonsen rings the changes seasonally, so what you might get depends on when you visit. You get a flavor of what's on offer from dishes like the tuna carpaccio with salted lemon, the roasted pheasant in a crust of green peppers and cardamom, and the roasted turbot with turnip and a tartare of oysters, spinach, and samphire in a Noilly Prat sauce. Sommelier Ellen Mansfield has a nose for intriguing finds from French vineyards.

Leliegracht 46 (btw. Prinsengracht and Keizersgracht). © **020/625-0807.** www.restaurantchristophe. nl. Main courses 29€–36€; fixed-price menus 36€–66€. AE, DC, MC, V. Tues–Sat 6:30–10:30pm. Tram: 13, 14, or 17 to Westermarkt.

Vinkeles ★★★ MODERN FRENCH If you dress up in black to celebrate (and I don't mean a tux) then head for this ultra-hip, Michelin-star restaurant in an unlikely setting: The converted bakery of a 17th-century almshouse. Named after Amsterdam engraver Reinier Vinkeles (1741–1816), who made an etching of the building's monumental gateway, its restrained tones soften some of the harsher edges of the über-chic designer hotel, the Dylan Amsterdam (p. 85). The decor includes a bare section of the bakery's brick wall, along with ovens and other fittings. Master chef Dennis Kuipers, who has an instinct for taste combinations and the know-how to put them together so they hit the spot, whips up dishes such as roasted Anjou pigeon with five spices and dried apricots. Dining outside in fine weather in the tree-shaded courtyard is an added bonus.

In the Dylan Amsterdam Hotel, Keizersgracht 384 (at Runstraat). © **020/530-2010.** www.dylan amsterdam.com. Reservations required. Main courses 29€–44€; fixed-price menu 45€. AE, DC, MC, V. Mon–Fri 7–11am, noon–2pm, and 6:30–11pm; Sat 7–11am and 6:30–11pm. Tram: 13, 14, or 17 to Westermarkt.

Moderate

Bolhoed ★ VEGETARIAN   Forget the sweetcorn-and-brown-rice image affected by some vegetarian restaurants. Instead, garnish your healthful habits with tangy flavors and a dash of zest. This former hat store—*bolhoed* is Dutch for bowler hat—has Latin style, aboriginal art, world music, ethnic exhibits, evening candlelight, and a fine canal view from each of the two plant-bedecked, cheerful rooms. Service is delivered with equal helpings of gusto and attention. Try pumpkin soup, *ragout crois-sant* (pastry filled with leeks, tofu, seaweed, and curry sauce), a variety of salads, and *zarzuela* (a cold Spanish soup). Even the entrees with brown rice and tofu taste good. If you want to go whole hog, so to speak, and eat vegan, most dishes can be prepared that way upon request. Ingredients and wine are organic, and in fine weather, you can dine at tiny tables on a small sliver of sidewalk right beside the canal.

Prinsengracht 60–62 (near Noordermarkt). ✆ **020/626-1803.** Main courses 13€–17€; fixed-price menus 13€–19€. No credit cards. Sun–Fri noon–11pm; Sat 11am–11pm. Tram: 13, 14, or 17 to Westermarkt.

Café-Restaurant Van Puffelen DUTCH/CONTINENTAL   A young profes-sional crowd gets to choose between brown-cafe–style eating and drinking, and a slightly more sophisticated experience in a separate dining room. Some menu dishes don't add up to much more than regular steak with accompaniments. Others, like the baked seawolf wrapped in Serrano ham and served with olive risotto and a lime sauce, display greater, Mediterranean-inspired flair. In any case, as far as possible they use locally sourced organic produce and meat from free-range animals. Save room for the handmade chocolates that are house specialties. The sidewalk terrace with a view of the Prinsengracht is—like most similar canalside assets—much in demand when the weather's fine.

Prinsengracht 377 (facing Lauriergracht). ✆ **020/624-6270.** www.goodfoodgroup.nl. Main courses 15€–19€; fixed-price menu 19€. AE, DC, MC, V. Mon–Wed 3pm–1am; Fri–Sat noon–2am; Sun noon–1am. Tram: 13, 14, or 17 to Westermarkt.

De Belhamel ★★ 🛍 CONTINENTAL   Soft classical music complements a grace-ful Art Nouveau setting at this bi-level restaurant overlooking the photogenic junction of the Herengracht and Brouwersgracht canals. Tables fill up quickly most evenings, so make reservations or go early. The menu changes seasonally (game is a big deal here in the fall). Look for these—or something as good as these—on the list: Puffed pastries layered with salmon, shellfish, and crayfish tails to start; and, for a main course, beef tenderloin in Madeira sauce with zucchini (courgette) rösti and puffed garlic. You can also order vegetarian dishes. Try for a window table and take in the superb canal views. Although generally excellent, De Belhamel does have two potential deal-breakers: The waitstaff can be too relaxed on occasion, and when the restaurant's full, as it often is, the place's acoustic peculiarities mean that it can get noisy.

Brouwersgracht 60 (at Herengracht). ✆ **020/622-1095.** www.belhamel.nl. Main courses 11€–27€; fixed-price menus 34€–45€. AE, MC, V. Sun–Thurs 6–10pm; Fri–Sat 6–10:30pm. Tram: 1, 2, 5, 13, or 17 to Martelaarsgracht.

De Luwte ★★ INTERNATIONAL   *Graceful* is the word that seems best to sum up this fine restaurant, though that quality never descends into stiffness. Grace comes from Florentine wall murals, floor-to-ceiling Art Deco lamps, drapes, hangings, ceiling mirrors painted with flowers and vines, a candle on each table, and not least of all, its elegant canalside location. And it avoids being starchy by a characteristically

Amsterdam exuberance and buzz. In either of the twin rooms, try for a window table looking out on the handsome little Leliegracht canal. The menu ranges across the globe, from Dutch and Mediterranean, look to items such as the vegetarian coconut curry crepes filled with spinach, lentils, and nuts; and stir-fried guinea fowl with nuts and *bok choy*.

Leliegracht 26–28 (btw. Keizersgracht and Herengracht). ℂ **020/625-8548.** www.restaurantdeluwte.nl. Main courses 16€–20€; fixed-price menu 32€. AE, MC, V. Daily 6–11pm. Tram: 13, 14, or 17 to Westermarkt.

Sluizer CONTINENTAL/SEAFOOD   Two notable restaurants (sadly, not for the price of one), both called Sluizer, stand side by side in convivial harmony. No. 45 is an old-fashioned brasserie with an eclectic, slightly French-biased menu. Try such items as *entrecôte Dijon* (steak with mustard sauce) and *poulet à la Provençal* (chicken with olives, sage, rosemary, and tomato). Next door, at nos. 41–43, the vaguely Art Deco *visrestaurant* (fish restaurant), with ceiling fans and fringed table-lamps, has at least 10 daily specials, ranging from simple cod or eel to *coquille Saint-Jacques* (scallops), crab casserole, Dover sole, halibut, and octopus. Meat dishes, such as beef stroganoff and chicken supreme, also appear on the menu. With kitchens open until midnight, both these places qualify as late-dining restaurants.

Utrechtsestraat 41–45 (btw. Herengracht and Keizersgracht). ℂ **020/622-6376.** www.sluizer.nl. Main courses 15€–25€; fixed-price menus 22€–32€. AE, DC, MC, V. Daily 5–11pm. Tram: 4 to Utrechtsestraat.

Spanjer & van Twist ★ 🍴 CONTINENTAL   This place would almost be worth a visit for its unusual name alone, so it's doubly gratifying that the food is good, too. The interior is typical neighborhood-*eetcafé* style, with the day's specials chalked on a blackboard, a long table with newspapers at the front, and the kitchen visible at the back. High cooking standards, however, put this place above others of its kind. The eclectic menu changes seasonally, but its range has included Thai fish curry and *pandan* rice; *saltimbocca* of trout in white-wine sauce; and artichoke mousseline with tarragon sauce and green asparagus. In fine weather, eat under the trees on an outdoor terrace beside the tranquil Leliegracht canal.

Leliegracht 60 (off Keizersgracht). ℂ **020/639-0109.** www.spanjerenvantwist.nl. Main courses 14€–17€. MC, V. Sun–Thurs 10am–1am; Fri–Sat 10am–2am (only light snacks after 10pm). Tram: 13, 14, or 17 to Westermarkt.

Tempo Doeloe ★★ INDONESIAN   For authentic Indonesian cuisine (the name means "The Old Days" in Javanese) from Java, Sumatra, and Bali, this place has it. It's got a *batik* ambience that's restrained Indonesian, and fine china. Try the

---

📎 All in Good Taste

As the waitperson removes your plate, he or she may ask: *Heeft het gesmaakt?* (Did it taste good?). If it did, the appropriate answer is: *Ja, lekker* (Yes, tasty), or *heel lekker* (very tasty). And if you had an unparalleled experience of gustatory pleasure, you can roll your eyes, pat your stomach contentedly, and purr: *Mmmm, ja, heerlijk* (wonderful). If you didn't enjoy your experience, however, you won't likely be able to, or need to, explain it in Dutch. Still, if you're adamant about expressing your displeasure, you could say: *Nee, het heeft niet gesmaakt* (No, it didn't taste good).

many little meat, fish, and vegetable dishes of the three different *rijsttafel* (rice table) options: The 15-plate vegetarian *rijsttafel sayoeran,* the 15-plate *rijsttafel stimoelan,* or the sumptuous 25-plate *rijsttafel istemewa.* In the big one, you get dishes like *gadon dari sapi* (beef in mild coconut sauce and fresh coriander/cilantro), *ajam roedjak* (chicken in a strongly seasoned chili-pepper-and-coconut sauce), *sambal goreng oedang* (small shrimps with Indonesian spices), and *atjar* (sweet-and-sour Indonesian salad). For great individual dishes, go for *udang raksasa* (a large grilled shrimp bathed in coconut-curry sauce), the *nasi koening* (spiced yellow rice), or any of the vegetarian options. Finish with the *spekkoek,* a layered spice cake.

Utrechtsestraat 75 (btw. Prinsengracht and Keizersgracht). ✆ **020/625-6718.** www.tempodoeloe restaurant.nl. Reservations required. Main courses 15€–26€; *rijsttafel* 28€–36€; fixed-price menu 27€–45€. AE, DC, MC, V. Mon–Sat 6–11:30pm. Tram: 4 to Keizersgracht.

Walem CONTINENTAL   Walem may have lost a few of its brownie points since the time when it was one of the hottest addresses in town, but that only means it's easier to get a seat on one of its two wonderful terraces: One outside beside the canal and the other at the rear in a sheltered, quiet garden patio. The space between them isn't bad either; it was designed by Philippe Starck, with small tables in front of and beside the long bar, where daily newspapers are provided. This cafe-restaurant's standards have not slipped at all, so don't worry about being seen in yesterday's in-spot. Menu items include pasta specialties, steak, chicken, and salads.

Keizersgracht 449 (at Leidsestraat). ✆ **020/625-3544.** www.walem.nl. Main courses 15€–17€. AE, DC, MC, V. Sun–Thurs 10am–1am; Fri–Sat 10am–2am. Tram: 1, 2, or 5 to Leidsestraat.

Inexpensive

De Prins ★★ ✦ DUTCH/FRENCH   This friendly restaurant, in a 17th-century canal house across the canal from the Anne Frankhuis, has a smoke-stained, brown-cafe style and food that could easily grace a much more expensive place. De Prins offers an unbeatable price-to-quality ratio for Dutch–French menu items, and long may it continue to do so. The youthful clientele is loyal and enthusiastic, so the relatively few tables fill up quickly. This is a quiet neighborhood place—nothing fancy or trendy, but very appealing in a human way. There's a bar on a lower level, and from March to September you can eat on the canalside terrace.

Prinsengracht 124 (at Egelantiersgracht). ✆ **020/624-9382.** www.deprins.nl. Main courses 11€–17€; *dagschotel* 12€. AE, DC, MC, V. Daily 10am–1 or 2am (kitchen to 10pm). Tram: 13, 14, or 17 to Westermarkt.

Golden Temple ★ VEGETARIAN   In its fourth decade of tickling meat-shunning palates, this temple of organic taste is still one of the best vegetarian (and vegan) options in town. If anything, the atmosphere is a tad too hallowed, an effect enhanced by a minimalist absence of decorative flourishes. The menu livens things up, though, with its unlikely roster of Indian, Middle Eastern, and Mexican dishes. This could make for a rewarding mix-and-match game if only the small print didn't all but instruct you to keep flavors apart. Multiple-choice platters are a good way to go. For the Indian *thali,* you select from constituents like *sag paneer* (homemade cheese), vegetable *korma,* and *raita* (cucumber and yogurt dip); the Middle Eastern platter has stalwarts like falafel, chickpea (garbanzo)-and-vegetable stew, and *dolmas* (stuffed grape leaves). A variety of side dishes range from guacamole to couscous to *pakora* (deep-fried fritters).

Utrechtsestraat 126 (2 blocks south of Prinsengracht). ✆ **020/626-8560.** www.restaurantgolden temple.com. Main courses 14€–16€; mixed platter 16€. MC, V. Daily 7am–10pm. Tram: 4 to Prinsengracht.

Grekas Griekse Traiterie ★ 🎁 GREEK   With just five tables and a small sidewalk terrace for summertime, Grekas would be more of a frustration than anything else, except that its main business is takeout service. If you're staying at one of the hotels in this neighborhood—particularly next door at the Estheréa (see p. 86), to which Grekas provides room service—this place can become your local diner. If there are no free tables, you can always take your choices back to your room, or eat alfresco on the canalside. Menu items are standard Greek but with freshness and taste that's hard to beat. The moussaka and pasticcio are heavenly; the roast lamb with wine, herbs, olive oil, and bouillon is excellent; the seafood in the calamari salad seems to have come straight out of Homer's wine-dark sea; and there's a good Greek wine list, too. Takeout dishes cost a euro or two less.

Singel 311 (near Spui). ℂ **020/620-3590.** No reservations. Main courses 9€–15€. No credit cards. Wed–Sun 5–10pm. Tram: 1, 2, or 5 to Spui.

Pancake Bakery ☺ PANCAKES   Located in a 17th-century canal warehouse, this two-story restaurant with winding staircases and exposed beams is a firm local favorite that serves some of the most delicious and unusual pancakes you'll ever taste. There are several dozen varieties, almost all of which make for a full meal. The satisfyingly large—you might even find them heavy—pancakes come adorned with all sorts of toppings, both sweet and spicy. Choices include salami and cheese, cheese and ginger, curried turkey with pineapple and raisins, honey nuts and whipped cream, and ice cream and *advokaat* (a Dutch eggnog-like cocktail). A bestseller is the American pancake: It comes topped with fried chicken, sweetcorn, peppers, carrots, Cajun sauce, and salad. In summer, there's outdoor seating overlooking the canal, but beware: All the syrup, honey, and sugar tends to attract bees and hornets.

☺ FAMILY-FRIENDLY restaurants

Kinderkookkafé   Amsterdam's only place where children not only get to do the eating, but the cooking and the serving too. Since young Dutch children don't speak much English, you may want to query the organizers about any possible language issues. See p. 114.

Pancake Bakery   I have yet to meet a kid who doesn't love pancakes, and this is *the* best pancake source in town. Pancakes come with various inventive toppings, both sweet and savory. Suitably colorful ornaments such as umbrellas and clowns accompany child-oriented meals and desserts. Toys, children's chairs, and special menus complete the picture. See p. 121.

Wilhelmina-Dok   Though not conceived as a kid-friendly place, this waterside cafe-restaurant does have a few things going for it. You get there and return by harbor ferry, which ought to add some interest to the proceedings. Once there, either outside on the breezy terrace or snug and warm inside, young folks can see barges, ferries, yachts, and other vessels coming and going on the IJ ship channel, and maybe even spot a cruise liner docked at Passenger Terminal Amsterdam. If you have young kids in tow, this is likely a better jaunt at lunchtime. See p. 115.

Prinsengracht 191 (at Prinsenstraat). ℂ **020/625-1333.** www.pancake.nl. Reservations required for large groups. Pancakes 5.95€–14€, 4.95€–6.95€ for kids. AE, MC, V. Daily noon–9:30pm. Tram: 13, 14, or 17 to Westermarkt.

Piet de Leeuw 🍴 DUTCH   Think of it as "Piet's Place," the kind of joint where you feel right at home. Its dark, cozy interior, in a residential street a block behind Prinsengracht, smells slightly of beer and was probably last decorated around 1955. The famous, cholesterol-rich, artery-clogging killer beefsteaks, pan-fried in margarine with onions, come with a slice of white bread and are fantastic. Waiters check you out before bringing you toothpicks with tiny national flags to spear your raw herring, sweet pickles, and triangles of toast. On weekends, you can get a pan-fried steak or a plate of herring until midnight.

Noorderstraat 11 (at Vijzelgracht). ℂ **020/623-7181.** www.pietdeleeuw.nl. Main courses 13€–20€. AE, MC, V. Mon–Fri noon–11pm; Sat–Sun 5–11pm. AE, MC, V. Tram: 16, 24, or 25 to Prinsengracht.

LEIDSEPLEIN
Moderate

Aphrodite GREEK   In an area awash with Greek restaurants that do a pretty routine island-taverna impersonation, Aphrodite stands out for putting more emphasis on taste and less on dazzling Aegean colors, fishing nets, and Olympian deities. Its single room is modern, restrained in its decor, and softly lit. The specialties—*afelia* (lamb cubes in coriander/cilantro-and-wine sauce), moussaka, *kleftiko* (oven-baked lamb), and others—are not much different in principle from those of other local Greek restaurants, but are generally better prepared and served—which, after all, is difference enough.

Lange Leidsedwarsstraat 91 (off Leidseplein). ℂ **020/622-7382.** Main courses 11€–20€. No credit cards. Daily 5–11pm. Tram: 1, 2, 5, 7, or 10 to Leidseplein.

Café Americain ★ CONTINENTAL   The lofty dining room is a national monument to Art Nouveau and Art Deco. Since its opening in 1900, this has been a hangout for Dutch and international artists, writers, dancers, and actors. *Tout Amsterdam* once liked to be seen here. Now it's mostly for tourists. Don't let that worry you, though: It's still great. Leaded stained-glass windows, newspaper-littered reading tables, bargello-patterned velvet upholstery, frosted-glass Tiffany chandeliers from the 1920s, and tall carved columns are all part of the dusky sit-and-chat atmosphere. Seafood specialties include monkfish, perch, salmon, and king shrimps; meat dishes include rack of Irish lamb and rosé breast of duck with creamed

> ### The Knives Are Out
>
> In the 1960s, satirist Gerrit Komrij described Café Americain's famously brusque waiters as "unemployed knife-throwers."

potatoes. Jazz lovers can stock up on good music and food at the Sunday jazz brunch, from 12:30 to 3:30pm (reservations needed), and if you're starved for news, settle down at a long reading desk with the international press.

In the Amsterdam American Hotel, Leidsekade 97 (at Leidseplein). ℭ **020/556-3000.** www.eden amsterdamamericanhotel.com. Main courses 16€–23€. AE, DC, MC, V. Daily 10:30am–midnight. Tram: 1, 2, 5, 7, or 10 to Leidseplein.

Grand Café De Balie INTERNATIONAL   In what was once a jail, this chic theater cafe-restaurant pulls in an arty, theatergoing crowd and serves them an inexpensive lunch and some great snacks along with beers, wines, and coffee, in a stylish, high-ceilinged, ground-floor cafe. Simple but fine meals are served in a restaurant upstairs, which has an ever-changing menu that's short on choice but long enough on taste. A Dutch option might be a zippy variation on something traditional, like *lamsfilet met mierikswortelsaus* (lamb filet with a horseradish sauce). There's invariably a vegetarian plate, maybe something like the Mediterranean-style *mozarellataartje met gedroogde tomaten, broccoli en olijvensaus* (mozzarella pie with dried tomatoes, broccoli, and an olive sauce). De Balie is well placed for a dinner before or after a visit to its own theater, the nearby Stadsschouwburg (p. 237), or one of the movie multiplexes around Leidseplein.

Kleine-Gartmanplantsoen 10 (off Leidseplein). ℭ **020/553-5131.** www.debalie.nl. Main courses 14€– 17€; fixed-price menus 20€. AE, MC, V. Cafe daily 11:30am–10pm. Restaurant daily 6–10pm. Tram: 1, 2, 5, 7, or 10 to Leidseplein.

Inexpensive

Akbar INDIAN   The best Indian restaurant in the Leidseplein area has been here (though not always at this address) since 1981, as one of the city's first Indian restaurants. It's a consistently good performer across the range of Punjabi cuisine—tandoori, curry, balti, vegetarian, and seafood—without being exactly outstanding in any category. The set meals are a good value, and service is friendly and prompt. There's also a takeout service.

Korte Leidsedwarsstraat 15 (off Leidseplein). ℭ **020/624-2211.** www.akbar.nl. Main courses 12€–22€; set menus 20€–25€ per person. AE, DC, MC, V. Daily 4:30pm–12:30am. Tram: 1, 2, 5, 7, or 10 to Leidseplein.

Bojo ★ 🍴 INDONESIAN   For quick, cheap, and tasty dishes served until the wee hours, head for long-established Bojo, a cheap and cheery eatery near Leidseplein. If hunger strikes after a late night on the town, drop in for a flavorful *longtong rames* (special boiled rice served with chewy rice cakes). If it looks too crowded, be sure to check the adjoining dining room, which has a separate entrance.

Lange Leidsedwarsstraat 49–51 (off Leidsestraat). ℭ **020/622-7434.** www.bojo.nl. Main courses 6€–14€; *rijsttafels* 12€–22€. No credit cards. Mon-Thurs 4pm–2am; Fri-Sat noon–4am; Sun noon–2am. Tram: 1, 2, 5, 7, or 10 to Leidseplein.

Sherpa NEPALESE/TIBETAN   Sherpa may be a little short on the mystical tranquillity that characterizes its Himalayan homeland, but that's to be expected—it's hard for tranquillity to survive in this brash restaurants-and-bars district. Anyway, Sherpa adds a bit of culinary diversity to the area and its prices are reasonable. What's more, it's the only restaurant of its kind in Holland. You can eat "Yeti's food" (fried noodles with fried chicken and sautéed vegetables) or sample various other Nepalese and Tibetan favorites, including traditional grills.

Korte Leidsedwarsstraat 58 (off Leidseplein). ℭ **020/623-9495.** www.sherpa-restaurant.nl. Main courses 9€–17€. AE, DC, MC, V. Daily 4-11pm. Tram: 1, 2, 5, 7, or 10 to Leidseplein.

✎ QUICK bites

Raw herring is a Dutch specialty, and there are dozens of *haringhuis* fish stands in town. The best of all is **Zeebanket van Altena** ★, Stadhouderskade at Jan Luijkenstraat (✆ **020/676-9139;** tram: 7 or 10), a class-act operation across from the Rijksmuseum. Connoisseurs stock up on Pieter van Altena's raw or pickled herring (peppered with Piet's acerbic observations), and lunch on salmon or crab salad, or a dozen other fishy delights, on warm wholegrain buns. You'll use proper stainless-steel flatware and drink chilled white wine from a stemmed glass. It is basically a stand, but a few lucky diners can even sit down to dine at a couple of tiny tables (though local style is to eat standing). It's open Tuesday to Sunday from 11am to 7pm.

To eat a genuine Dutch *broodje* (sandwich) in a real *broodjeswinkel* (sandwich shop), go to the ever-crowded **Eetsalon Van Dobben,** Korte Reguliersdwarsstraat 5–9 (✆ **020/624-4200;** www.vandobben.nl; tram: 4, 9, or 14), off Rembrandtplein, where you

might try a smoked-eel sandwich. Locals come here for these and herring, liverwurst, croquets, or ox-tongue sandwiches. Simpler roast beef and Gouda sandwiches are also available. Some patrons swear by the platter of giant meatballs. It's open Monday to Saturday from 9:30am to 1am (Sat to 2am), and Sunday from 11:30am to 8pm.

Should Amsterdam's shortage of good pastrami on rye get to you, head out to Amsterdam-Zuid (South), to the great kosher sandwich shop **Sal Meijer** ★, Scheldestraat 45 (✆ **020/673-1313;** www.sal-meijer.com; tram: 12 or 25), off Churchill-laan. The sandwiches go for from 2.95€; the plate of the day begins at 15€. Sal's is open Sunday to Thursday from 10am to 7:30pm, and Friday from 10am to 2pm.

If you thought Amsterdam was a bagel-free zone, think again. Some of the best bagels come from **Gary's Deli,** Kinkerstraat 140 (✆ **020/412-3025;** www.garysdeli.nl; tram: 7 or 17). Choose from plain, sesame, whole-wheat, poppy-seed, pumpernickel, cinnamon

REMBRANDTPLEIN

Moderate

Brasserie Schiller FRENCH/DUTCH   Beamed and paneled in well-aged oak and graced with etched-glass panels and stained-glass skylights, this Art Nouveau landmark from 1892 (not to be mistaken for the equally notable Café Schiller next door; see p. 246) is a splendid sight. Paintings by the artist who built the hotel, Frits Schiller, adorn the walls. Former chefs supplied the restaurant with the exact recipes and techniques used in the old days. On the menu, which now includes a selection of modern dishes, you'll find everything from stewed eel and potato-and-cabbage casserole to T-bone steak, roast leg of lamb with mint sauce, and spaghetti Bolognese. A Breton crustacean and shellfish buffet is served daily, featuring lobster, oysters, crab, mussels, and more.

In the NH Schiller Hotel, Rembrandtplein 26–36. ✆ **020/554-0723.** www.brasserieschiller.nl. Main courses 15€–22€; fixed-price menu 28€. AE, DC, MC, V. Daily 7am–10:30pm. Tram: 4, 9, or 14 to Rembrandtplein.

raisin, onion, and garlic bagels, which range from 2.95€ to 4.95€. The 20 different kinds of toppings include pesto, cream cheese, goat's cheese, guacamole, tomato, smoked salmon, and honey and walnuts. Gary's—which uses organic ingredients whenever possible, brews a range of herbal teas, and offers takeout service—is open Monday to Friday from 8:30am to 7pm, Saturday from 9am to 7pm, and Sunday from 10am to 7pm.

For tasty organic soups, like red-lentil and coconut soup, head to **Soupkitchen,** Nieuwendijk 50 ((ⓒ **020/528-7175;** www.soupkitchen.nl; tram: 1, 2, 5, 6, 13, 17, or 20). While you're there, you might want to sample the bagels, like the bagels with pastrami, roasted sweet peppers, iceberg salad, basilicum vinaigrette, and cream cheese, and other accompaniments, along with coffee and fresh fruit juices.

As in most European cities, you find the best meal bargains are the offerings of the most recent immigrants. In Amsterdam's case, the Middle Eastern snack bars and Surinamese fast-food restaurants have the cheapest meals. The former specialize in shwarma and falafel, and can be found in high concentrations around Leidseplein and Rembrandtplein; the latter are known for their chicken roti, mildly curried pieces of chicken served with a pancake-like bread, and can be found in the vicinity of Albert Cuypstraat, the site of a popular daily market. About 4€ to 8€ gets you a filling meal in either type of place.

Another quick-bite alternative, particularly for seriously cash-strapped budget travelers, are the branches of **Febo Automatiek** that you'll find all around town. They open directly on the sidewalk and look like giant street-side vending machines. Drop a few euro coins in the appropriate slots and—*voilà!*—you have a lunch of Indonesian *nasi goreng* or *bami goreng,* hamburger, fries, and a milkshake. I wouldn't say the portions are small, but they do have a compact form factor.

Grand Café l'Opera INTERNATIONAL   The main advantage of l'Opera is that beyond its Art Nouveau facade is probably the best, most restrained terrace on Rembrandtplein (though others are more centrally located). On busy days in good weather, the Art Deco interior is a cool and quiet brasserie-style retreat, but of course on such days, no one wants to go inside, and the sidewalk terrace is the place to be. The food in this cafe-restaurant is fine, if nothing to write home about. Menu items include such standards as salads, steak and mushrooms, croquettes, and mussels, and even Thai chicken curry for variation. Service, though friendly, is at times a bit erratic.

Rembrandtplein 27-29. ⓒ **020/620-4754.** www.l-opera.nl. Main courses 14€–18€. AE, DC, MC, V. Sun–Thurs 10am–1am; Fri–Sat 10am–2am. Tram: 4, 9, or 14 to Rembrandtplein.

Memories of India INDIAN   The proprietor Khan family earned their spurs in the crowded and intensely competitive London market for Indian cuisine and then brought their award-winning formula to Amsterdam. That formula is simple, really: Serve top-flight Indian cuisine in a setting that gives traditional Indian motifs a

Late-Night Eateries

Since the majority of restaurant kitchens in Amsterdam are closed by 10:30pm, it's good to keep these late-night addresses handy in case the munchies strike: **Fifteen** and **Pier 10** (see "The Waterfront," earlier in this chapter); **Sluizer** (see "The Canal Belt," earlier in this chapter); **Bojo** (see "Leidseplein," p. 123); and **De Knijp** (see "Museum District & Vondelpark," p. 130).

modern slant, charge moderate prices, and employ attentive waitstaff. The menu is pretty straightforward, too, and contains the usual tandoori and curry dishes, but pushes the boat out a bit with some fish items, like the Indian Ocean pomfret in roasted cilantro (coriander)-seed sauce. The restaurant somehow manages to combine the hallowed silence of diners intent on their plates with a buzz of friendly conversation. Takeout service is available.

Reguliersdwarsstraat 88 (at Vijzelstraat). © **020/623-5710.** www.memoriesofindia.nl. Main courses 12€–22€; fixed-price menus 18€–28€ per head. AE, DC, MC, V. Daily 5–11:30pm. Tram: 4, 9, or 14 to Rembrandtplein.

THE JORDAAN
Expensive

Bordewijk ★★ FRENCH This pleasantly located restaurant is often regarded as one of the best in the city. The decor is tasteful, with green potted plants offsetting the severity of the white walls and metallic black tables. Service is relaxed yet attentive, and on mild summer evenings you can't beat dining alfresco on the canalside terrace. But the real treat is the food. An innovative chef accents French standards with Mediterranean and Asian flourishes to create an elegant fusion of flavors. The menu changes often, but a typical expression of this mix is found in the Bresse pigeon with fresh morel mushrooms and polenta. In the *bouillabaisse Marseillaise,* you can just about scent the Provençe coast's heady air, and the *geroosterde coquilles Saint-Jacques* (roasted scallops) are divine. Dinner is followed by a fine selection of cheeses, and the wine list is superb.

Noordermarkt 7 (at Prinsengracht).© **020/624-3899.** www.bordewijk.nl. Reservations required. Main courses 24€–29€; fixed-price menu 39€–72€. AE, MC, V. Tues–Sun 6:30–10:30pm. Tram: 1, 2, 5, 13, or 17 to Martelaarsgracht.

Moderate

Albatros Seafoodhouse & Vis Restaurant ★ SEAFOOD The Atlantic and North Sea fish served here have the great virtue of being grilled, poached, or fried in the simplest manner possible, then served in a relaxed neighborhood atmosphere amid ship-ahoy decor. In summer, you can dine on a narrow sidewalk terrace and watch seagulls and albatrosses flying overhead, while soaking up the atmospheric Jordaan, where there's little traffic and locals chat on stoops. Try the mixed seafood salad, the raw herring, or the sea bass.

Westerstraat 264 (at Lijnbaansgracht). © **020/627-9932.** www.restaurantalbatros.nl. Reservations recommended on weekends. Main courses 16€–23€ (some prices set daily). AE, DC, MC, V. Thurs–Mon 6–11pm. Tram: 3 or 10 to Marnixplein.

Hostaria ★ ITALIAN Owners Marjolein and Massimo Pasquinoli have transformed this tiny space on a lively cafe-lined Jordaan street into a little piece of authentic Italy, and a showcase for the kind of cuisine Italian mothers only wish they could equal. When you sit down, Marjolein brings garlicky *tapenade* and warm bread. As an appetizer, you might select a perfectly balanced fish soup with a slice of salmon or lightly grilled eggplant (aubergine) slices with fresh herbs. The *zuppa di gamberone con l'acquetta,* a plate of shrimps and shellfish from the market, is terrific, and there's also a choice of wonderful homemade pastas—the tagliatelle with arugula (rocket) and truffles is a particular treat—and *secondi piatti* such as sausage-stuffed veal or Roman-style duck.

Tweede Egelantiersdwarsstraat 9 (off Egelantiersgracht). ✆ **020/626-0028.** Reservations recommended on weekends. Main courses 17€–23€; fixed-price menu 34€. No credit cards. Tues–Sun 6–10pm. Tram: 13, 14, or 17 to Westermarkt.

Rakang THAI A meal here is a delight to more than just the sense of taste. The dishes, many of them authentic regional specialties, come in generous portions and are seasoned with Thai spices, carefully blending fierce chili peppers with delicate flavors like ginger, coriander (cilantro), and Thai basil, to suit any palate, whether the preference is for fiery or mild. Bowls of lightly perfumed pandang rice, yellow curry, light-textured sauces, and pad Thai noodles are just some accompaniments. A variety of sorbets is on hand to draw the sting from the sharpest flavors. In the dining room's fragrant cocoon, colorful silk fabrics drape along pastel-toned walls, and chairs are swathed in cool, soft cottons. Takeout service is available.

Elandsgracht 29–31 (off Prinsengracht). ✆ **020/627-5012.** www.rakang.nl. Main courses 17€–23€; fixed-price menus 36€–41€. AE, DC, MC, V. Daily 6–11:30pm. Tram: 7, 10, or 17 to Marnixstraat.

Toscanini ★ SOUTH ITALIAN This small restaurant has a warm, welcoming ambience and excellent southern Italian food (at least that's the point of emphasis, but most regional Italian dishes are available—though not pizza). Popular with the artists and bohemians who inhabit the neighborhood, Toscanini has unembellished country-style decor, and an open kitchen, that speak of authenticity. Cooking is home-style and there's a long-as-your-arm list of Italian wines. Service is congenial and chatty but can be slow, though that doesn't deter loyal regulars, who clamor for specialties like the delicious veal lasagna and *fazzoletti* (green pasta stuffed with ricotta, mozzarella, and mortadella). Fish, risottos, and pastas in wondrous shapes and sizes all deserve consideration. For dessert, the Italian ice cream is as good as it looks, and the cheeses run a close second.

Lindengracht 75 (off Brouwersgracht). ✆ **020/623-2813.** www.toscanini.nu. Main courses 18€–23€; fixed-price menu 45€. AE, DC, MC, V. Mon–Sat 6–10:30pm. Tram: 3 to Nieuwe Willemsstraat.

't Stuivertje BISTRO Tucked down a narrow Jordaan side street, this small and personable neighborhood eatery is invariably filled with locals. Meals come from an open kitchen in an agreeably plain, intimate room, with wood chairs and tables, and a small bar. Black-and-white photographs of American stars, like Ol' Blue Eyes, combine unusually on the walls with Old Dutch prints. The limited menu reflects the restaurant's authentic Amsterdam style, featuring classic Dutch dishes with that extra tasty little something, as in the *gegrilde lamsfilet met honing en tijm* (grilled lamb filet with honey and thyme) and the *roode poon filet in pittige kokos-kerriesaus*

A crowded Saturday-morning spot is **Kwekkeboom,** Reguliersbreestraat 36 (ℂ **020/623-1205;** www.kwekkeboom banket.nl; tram: 4, 9, 14, 16, 24, or 25), between Muntplein and Rembrandtplein. It's a coffeeshop/candy store (sweet shop)/pastry shop/ice-cream stand, where everything's freshly made and management proudly displays awards won for everything from fruit pies, bon-bons, and butter cookies to "fantasy cakes." Two other Kwekkeboom outlets in the city are at Ferdinand Bolstraat 119 (ℂ **020/673-7114;** tram: 3, 12, or 25), and Linnaeusstraat 80 (ℂ **020/665-0443;** tram: 9).

You may have to push your way to the back and wait for a table at

Greenwoods, Singel 103 (ℂ **020/623-7071;** tram: 1, 2, 5, 13, or 17), which brings English flavor to its tea, home-made scones with jam and clotted cream, and lemon meringue pie.

Notable ice cream is created at **Jordino,** Haarlemmerdijk 25 (ℂ **020/420-3225;** www.jordino.nl; tram: 1, 2, 5, 13, or 17), where 30 flavors of Italian ice cream, plus chocolate cake and desserts, appeal to anyone with a sweet tooth.

See also **La Ruche,** in De Bijenkorf, and **M'Café,** in Metz&Co, both under "Department Stores," and **Patisserie Pompadour,** under "Food & Drink," in chapter 9.

geserveerd (red tub gurnard filet in a hot coconut-curry sauce). There are vegetarian choices, daily specials, and a seasonal menu.

Hazenstraat 58 (off Lauriergracht). ℂ **020/623-1349.** www.hetstuivertje.nl. Main courses 13€–25€; fixed-price menu 24€. AE, MC, V. Tues–Sun 5:30–11pm. Tram: 7 or 10 to Marnixstraat.

Inexpensive

Duende SPANISH   Dark, atmospheric, friendly—there's no better place than Duende to experience the varied palette of small plates that are Spanish tapas. Take just one or two and you have a nice accompaniment to a few drinks; put five, six, or more together and you have a full-scale meal. Pick from dozens of choices, including *tortilla española, champiñones al ajillo* (garlic mushrooms), and *calabacín a la marmera* (eggplant/aubergine with seafood). Accompany them with sangria, jump into the arena of friendly conversation, and before long you'll be clapping your hands rhythmically and stamping your feet—and if not, you might want to sign up for Duende's *flamenco* lessons. Bear in mind that though tapas are cheap individually, their cost soon adds up.

Lindengracht 62 (off Brouwersgracht). ℂ **020/420-6692.** www.cafeduende.nl. Tapas 4€–15€. MC, V. Mon–Fri 5pm–1am; Sat–Sun 4pm–1am. Tram: 1, 2, 5, 13, or 17 to Martelaarsgracht.

MUSEUM DISTRICT & VONDELPARK

Expensive

Brasserie Keyzer ★ CONTINENTAL   Whether or not you attend a concert at the Concertgebouw, visit its next-door neighbor, Brasserie Keyzer. An Amsterdam

Where to Dine in the Museum District & Amsterdam South

Brasserie Keyzer **11**

Café-Restaurant
De Duvel **7**

De Kas **4**

De Knijp **10**

Gary's Deli **15**

Kinderkookkafé **12**

Klein Kalfje **2**

Kwekkeboom **6**

Le Garage **9**

Mangerie de
Kersentuin **5**

Sal Meijer **3**

Sama Sebo **14**

Umeno **1**

Vertigo **13**

Wildschut **8**

landmark since 1903, Keyzer has enjoyed a colorful joint heritage with the world-famous concert hall. Among the many stories still told here is the one about the night a customer mistook a concert soloist for a waiter and tried to order whiskey from him. The musician, not missing a beat, lifted his violin case and said graciously, "Would a little Paganini do?" The traditional dark, dusky decor and starched pink linens add elegance, while the menu leans heavily to fish from Dutch waters and, in season, to game specialties such as hare and venison.

Van Baerlestraat 96 (beside the Concertgebouw). ℂ **020/675-1866.** www.brasseriekeyzer.nl. Main courses 22€–35€; fixed-price menus 25€–43€. AE, DC, MC, V. Mon–Sat 9am–midnight; Sun 11am–midnight. Tram: 3, 5, 12, 16, or 24 to Museumplein.

Le Garage ★★ FUSION Even local VIPs have to beg for a reservation here, one of the hottest restaurants in town. Flamboyant restaurateur Joop Braakhekke is a TV celeb. The service is a circus act, but the fare is worth it. Think cubed tuna tartare with curry and a crisp spinach pancake, or flaming-hot Thai chicken with green chili sauce. The decor would be a hit in Vegas—bright lights, big mirrors, red vinyl banquettes, and black wraparound wooden chairs. Nonetheless, the wildly creative food is virtuoso stuff. The menu shuttles between a Parisian brasserie and a Tuscan trattoria with stopovers in Tokyo, Mumbai, and Vegetariania. The kitchen will serve until about midnight, and the tables are still crowded well after the witching hour.

Ruysdaelstraat 54-56 (at Van Baerlestraat). ℂ **020/679-7176.** www.restaurantlegarage.nl. Reservations required. Main courses 23€–33€; fixed-price menu 50€. AE, DC, MC, V. Mon–Fri noon–2pm and 6–11pm; Sat–Sun 6–11pm. Tram: 3, 5, 12, or 24 to Roelof Hartplein.

Moderate

Café-Restaurant De Duvel ★ ☺ INTERNATIONAL Invariably packed with hip locals, "The Devil" is a friendly neighborhood *eetcafé* (bar with eats) that serves more-than-decent food in a cozy red dining room in the trendy De Pijp district, close to Sarphatipark. Indonesian chicken saté, salad with shrimps tempura, and beef filet in a mustard mousseline are some of the typical dishes—so, a bit wider-ranging than your standard Continental fare, but nothing overly adventurous—on a menu that changes every three months yet rarely goes without some kind of pasta, seafood, and chicken offerings. This is one of the few modish Amsterdam eateries that embraces kids, and there are games and coloring books to keep little ones engaged. The bar side of things is at least as important as the restaurant, and the kitchen closes before midnight.

Eerste van der Helststraat 59-61. ℂ **020/675-7517.** www.deduvel.nl. Main courses 13€–17€. AE, DC, MC, V. Mon 4pm–1am, Tues–Thurs 11am–1am, Fri–Sat 11am–3am, Sun noon–1am. Tram: 3, 12, or 25 to Ceintuurbaan/Ferdinand Bolstraat.

De Knijp DUTCH/FRENCH One of this fine restaurant's advantages is that it's open late—its kitchen still takes orders when chefs at many other Amsterdam restaurants are tucked up in bed. This would not count for much, of course, if the food weren't good, but De Knijp is definitely worth staying up for, or worth stopping by for after a performance at the nearby Concertgebouw; many concertgoers and assorted other late-nighters do so. The menu is not wildly inventive, the standard offerings being something like oysters, grilled lamb, or roast duck, but you might find a few adventurous items, such as carpaccio with pesto, poached salmon with tarragon sauce, and goose breast with pink pepper sauce. Service is friendly, if sometimes a tad worn-out (this is a hardworking place) in this intimate bi-level bistro with lots of wood furnishings. In summer, a sidewalk terrace is available.

Van Baerlestraat 134 (near the Concertgebouw). © **020/671-4248.** www.deknijp.nl. Reservations required for lunch and for more than 5 people. Main courses 17€–25€. AE, DC, MC, V. Mon–Fri noon-3pm and 5:30pm-12:30am; Sat-Sun 5:30pm-12:30am. Tram: 3, 5, 12, 16, or 24 to Museumplein.

Sama Sebo ★ INDONESIAN In a place that's often packed with locals, the 23-plate *rijsttafel* sets a standard others try to match, and environs are very Indonesian, with rush mats and *batik*. Some items are hot and spicy, but in general the memorable end result comes from effectively blending spices and sauces rather than adding rocket fuel. You can make your own mini-*rijsttafel* by selecting from the a la carte menu, or take one big menu dish, like the superb *nasi goreng* or *bami goreng*. When you order either of the two lunch specials, you get a heaping mound of food. The restaurant has two sections: The main dining room with its Indonesian motif, and the bar area for more casual dining. If the restaurant's busy (it often is), you can think of the quarters as either convivial or cramped. A sidewalk terrace is equally short on space.

Pieter Cornelisz Hooftstraat 27 (close to the Rijksmuseum).© **020/662-8146.** www.samasebo.nl. Main courses 3.75€–8€; lunch menu 16€; *rijsttafel* 30€. AE, DC, MC, V. Mon–Sat noon–2pm and 6–10pm. Tram: 2 or 5 to Hobbemastraat.

Vertigo ★★ MEDITERRANEAN In the vaulted basement of a monumental, late-19th-century villa on Vondelpark's edge, this tree-shaded, animated cafe-restaurant shares premises with the Film Instituut Nederland and its EYE film theater (see p. 253), which is due to move to Amsterdam-Noord (North) at the end of 2011. Hence the portraits of screen legends on the walls and the classic scenes of movie dining on the menu. On summer days, the terrace is a favored time-out spot for in-line skaters and joggers, and you can expect to share your table and make the instant acquaintance of just about everyone within earshot. On summer evenings, you might even be able to take in an open-air movie. At other times, enjoy the south-Europe cuisine in an intimate indoor candlelit setting. The menu, which changes every 6 to 8 weeks, lists fish, meat, and vegetarian options, plus some fresh pasta varieties.

Vondelpark 3 (at Vondelstraat). © **020/612-3021.** www.vertigo.nl. Reservations recommended on weekends. Main courses 12€–20€; fixed-price menu 25€. AE, MC, V. Daily 10am–1am. Tram: 1 to Eerste Constantijn Huygensstraat; 2, 3, 5, or 12 to Van Baerlestraat.

Picnic Picks

You can pick up almost anything you might want for a picnic, from Dutch cheeses like Edam and Gouda to cold cuts to freshly packed sandwiches at **AH (Albert Heijn)** supermarkets around town. From the AH supermarket at the corner of Leidsestraat and Koningsplein (tram: 1, 2, or 5), you can head over to Vondelpark, only a 10-minute walk. At AH's Museumplein supermarket, across the street from the Concertgebouw (tram: 2, 3, 5, 12, or 16), you can haul your brown bag right up onto the sloping, grass-covered roof, a prime spot for sunbathing, hanging out, and picnicking. Don't forget a bottle of wine.

For more sophisticated picnic makings, see **Basilico,** under "Frommer's Favorite Local Spots," earlier in this chapter.

Wildschut CONTINENTAL One of those places that keeps its chic reputation through thick and thin, Wildschut occupies a curved dining room at the junction of van Baerlestraat and Roelof Hartstraat, not far from the Concertgebouw. Amsterdam's bold and beautiful from the arts and media crowd like to see and be seen on the fine terrace, particularly on a summer evening as the setting sun lights all those carefully presented faces. In winter, the crowd congregates inside the Art Deco brasserie. Friday and Saturday evenings get crowded here, so be prepared to join the standing throng while waiting for a table. The food is straightforward but good, ranging from BLTs (bacon, lettuce, and tomato sandwiches) to vegetarian lasagna to American rib-eye with green pepper sauce. If possible, try to wear something that gets you noticed—but not *too* noticed, if you get the idea.

Roelof Hartplein 1-3 (off Van Baerlestraat). © **020/676-8220.** www.goodfoodgroup.nl. Main courses 15€–18€. MC, V. Mon–Thurs 9am–1am; Fri 9am–3am; Sat 10:30am–3am; Sun 9:30am–midnight. Tram: 3, 5, 12, or 24 to Roelof Hartplein.

AMSTERDAM EAST
Very Expensive

La Rive ★★★ MODERN REGIONAL FRENCH/MEDITERRANEAN Cradling a Michelin star, La Rive is Amsterdam's high temple of culinary art. Master chef Rogér Rassin combines French cuisine with influences from around the Mediterranean and farther afield. Royalty, leading politicians and captains of industry dine here at discretely spaced tables (and hew to the dress code). The dining room overlooks the Amstel River through French windows, and in summer it opens onto a waterside terrace. Cherry-paneled walls punctuated with book-filled cabinets suggest a private library called into service for a dinner party. The menu changes seasonally, so I can't guarantee the presence of palate-pleasers like the Bresse pigeon with pistachio and sweetcorn, or the grill-roasted rack of lamb with dates and Zaanse mustard. The service, while impeccable, manages to keep just on the right side of stuffy, and the wine list is formidable.

In the InterContinental Amstel Amsterdam Hotel, Professor Tulpplein 1 (off Weesperstraat). © **020/520-3264.** www.restaurantlarive.com. Main courses 55€–75€; lunch menu 49€; fixed-price menus 85€–112€. AE, DC, MC, V. Mon–Fri noon–2pm and 6:30–10:30pm; Sat 6:30–10:30pm. Tram: 7 or 10 to Sarphatistraat.

A Dinner Cruise

A delightful way to combine sightseeing and leisurely dining is on a dinner cruise. During these 2½-hour canal cruises, you enjoy a five-course dinner that includes a cocktail and wine with dinner, coffee with bonbons, and a glass of cognac or liqueur to finish. Reservations are required. These cruises cost around 60€–100€, and 30€–50€ for children ages 4 to 12. See "Organized Tours," in chapter 7, for details on tour-boat lines.

AMSTERDAM SOUTH
Expensive

De Kas ★★ CONTINENTAL   Despite its see-and-be-seen attitude, a traipse out to this hip restaurant in a converted hothouse on the edge of town is well merited. The 1926 edifice with a brick smokestack stands on open green ground; it's light and spacious beneath a glass ceiling. You get just a couple of variations on a three-course fixed menu that changes daily. Organic, Mediterranean-style greens and herbs come fresh from an adjacent working hothouse and garden and from the restaurant's own farm; meat is sourced daily from nearby animal-friendly organic producers; the seafood comes from the sea, I guess. In the kitchen, persnickety attention to detail is the norm. The service is attentive enough that the waitstaff seem to be personally acquainted with every item on your plate—those who dine in glass houses shouldn't throw stones, but you might want to bring along a few rocks to chase them away.

Kamerlingh Onneslaan 3 (close to Amstel Station). ✆ **020/462-4562.** www.restaurantdekas.nl. Reservations required. Fixed-price lunch 38€; fixed-price dinner 50€; chef's table 125€. AE, DC, MC, V. Mon-Fri noon–2pm and 6:30–10pm; Sat 6:30–10pm. Tram: 9 to Hogeweg.

Mangerie de Kersentuin ★ FRENCH/MEDITERRANEAN   All cherry red and gleaming brass, the "Cherry Orchard" has floor-to-ceiling windows looking onto the residential street outside and partly screened interior windows looking into the glimmering kitchen inside. Attention to detail (think Christofle silver-plated flatware) has made this restaurant a mecca for visiting stars. From nouvelle cuisine and a strictly French approach, Mangerie has progressed to its own unique culinary concept, based on a French foundation with Mediterranean influences. The menu changes every 2 months, but these samples should give you some idea of what to expect: Lamb filet prepared in goose fat with creamy salsify and cilantro (coriander)-scented vanilla sauce; and sea bass sautéed with peppers, garlic, sea salt, and sesame seeds, served on stir-fried bok choy and tofu, with lemon grass butter.

In the Bilderberg Garden Hotel, Dijsselhofplantsoen 7 (at Apollolaan). ✆ **020/570-5600.** www.mangerie dekersentuin.nl. Reservations recommended on weekends. Main courses 25€–45€; fixed-price menus 43€–50€. AE, DC, MC, V. Mon–Fri noon–2pm and 6–10pm; Sat 6–10pm. Tram: 5 or 24 to Apollolaan.

Moderate

Umeno ★ JAPANESE   This intimate eatery, somewhat off the beaten track near Olympic Stadium, is popular with local Japanese residents—you get only chopsticks to eat with. Both the food and the service make the tram ride out here worthwhile. Decor is traditional and delicate, with rice-paper windows and a menu that comes in a wooden box. It's generally no problem to find a seat, but as the restaurant seats only 32, it makes sense to call ahead. The sushi and sashimi are always fresh, and their quality is high. Other traditional dishes include *shabu-shabu, sukiyaki, yakitori,* and *tonkatsu.*

Agamemnonstraat 27 (off Olympiaplein). ✆ **020/676-6089.** www.umeno.nl. Main courses 15€–35€. No credit cards. Tues-Sun noon–2pm and 6–11pm. Tram: 24 to Olympiaplein.

AMSTERDAM WEST

Moderate

Amsterdam ★ 🎁 CONTINENTAL   Based in a century-old water-pumping station, complete with diesel-powered engine, the inventively-named Amsterdam has taken this monument of Victorian industrial good taste and made of it a model of contemporary good eats. You dine amid a buzz of conviviality in the large, brightly lit former pumping hall, which had been so carefully tended by the water workers that some of its elegant decoration didn't even need repainting. Service is friendly. If you're sharing and feeling flush, spring for a seafood platter of lobster, crab, clams, and more. For dessert, the fried sweetbreads are popular. The Amsterdam is a little bit out from the Center, but easily worth the tram ride.

Watertorenplein 6 (off Haarlemmerweg). ℂ **020/682-2666.** www.cradam.nl. Reservations recommended on weekends. Main courses 12€–18€; seafood platters 33€–65€ (for 2). AE, DC, MC, V. Sun–Thurs 11am–1am; Fri–Sat 11am–2am (meals served to 11:30pm). Tram: 10 to Van Hallstraat.

AMSTERDAM NORTH

Expensive

Osaka ★ JAPANESE   Traditional Japanese food and *teppanyaki* are served here. No matter which you choose, the food's both excellent and modestly priced, as Japanese restaurants go—which together make the somewhat onerous trip to undistinguished Amsterdam-Noord (North) worthwhile. Osaka has borrowed the Indonesian *rijsttafel* concept. Order one (menus are named after various Japanese cities), and you get a little of this, a little of that. Otherwise, the menu is standard Japanese, with sushi among extensive seafood listings. In the *teppanyaki* section, chefs are fast on the draw with carving knives and salt and pepper shakers.

Rode Kruisstraat 22A (off Waddenweg in Amsterdam-Noord). ℂ **020/632-2380.** www.osaka-amsterdam.com. Fixed-price menus 34€–77€; *teppanyaki* buffet 21€–24€. AE, DC, MC, V. Mon–Fri noon–midnight; Sat–Sun 6pm–midnight. Bus: 32, 33, 38, 105, 109, 336, 361, 362, 611, 614, or 693 to Rode Kruisstraat.

EXPLORING AMSTERDAM

Amsterdam affords sightseers an embarrassment of riches. There are miles of canals to cruise, hundreds of narrow streets to wander, 7,000 historical buildings to see in the heart of town, around 40 museums of all types to visit, and diamond cutters and craftspeople to watch as they practice generations-old skills. The list is as long as every tourist's individual interests, and then some.

The first thing you should do is join the 2.5 million people every year who take a canal ride on a tour boat. Why? Because the water-level view of those gabled canalside houses and the picturesque bridges lends meaning and color to everything else you do in Amsterdam.

Yet most of Amsterdam's attractions are hidden, and they're not even attractions in any conventional sense. They're part of a fabric of life, a special but elusive atmosphere that's been slowly evolving for centuries. There are few open vistas or bombastic buildings; rather, the city is enclosed within itself. You'll need to dig a certain amount to get at these hidden-in-plain-sight features. Above all, maintain that certain attitude: A willingness to slow down, open up, and mentally unbutton.

THE BIG THREE

Two of Amsterdam's big three attractions—the Rijksmuseum and the Van Gogh Museum—are around **Museumplein** ("Museum Square"), just south of the oldest part of town (see the "Museum District & Amsterdam South Attractions" map, later in this chapter). Most of the "square" consists of open green areas bordered by avenues of linden trees and gardens and crisscrossed by walking and bike paths. At Museumplein's north end is a long pond that serves as a handy foot-cooler in summer and has served as a skating rink in winter. The third attraction of the top trio, the Anne Frankhuis, is in the historic **Centrum** (Center) district, on Prinsengracht.

By no means should you hit all three in a single day. You'll wind up emotionally battered by the Anne Frankhuis, bedazzled by the Van Gogh Museum, and, well, Rijksmuseum-ed by the Rijksmuseum. One per day is enough.

Central Amsterdam Attractions

Allard Pierson Museum **7**
Amsterdam Tulip Museum **25**
Amsterdams Historisch Museum **12**
Anne Frankhuis **23**
Athenaeum Illustre **8**
Begijnhof **9**
Beurs van Berlage **38**
Bijbels Museum **10**
Blauwbrug **53**
Bloemenmarkt **4**
Brilmuseum **15**
Centraal Station **34**
De Waag **43**
Erasmuspark **24**
Erotic Museum **42**
Hash Marihuana & Hemp Museum **44**
Homomonument **21**
Huis De Pinto **51**
Huis Marseille **11**
KattenKabinet **3**
Kinderboerderij De Dierencapel **31**
Klein Trippenhuis **46**
Koffie en Thee Museum **39**
Koninklijk Paleis **17**
Korenmetershuisje **27**
Madame Tussauds **16**
Magere Brug **55**
Makelaers Comptoir **26**
Montelbaanstoren **56**
Munttoren **5**
Museum Van Loon **1**
Museum Willet-Holthuysen **54**
Muziekgebouw aan 't IJ/ Bimhuis **58**
Nationaal Monument **18**
Nieuwe Kerk **19**
Noorderkerk **30**
Ons' Lieve Heer op Solder **40**
Oost-Indisch Huis **48**
Oude Hoogstraat 22 **49**
Oude Kerk **41**
Pianola Museum **29**
Pijpenkabinet **2**
Poppenhuis **52**
Remonstrantsekerk **28**
Schreierstoren **37**

JAVA-EILAND

Het IJ

IJ-Tunnel

De Ruijterkade

Prins Hendrikkade

Centraal Station
34

Stationsplein
Centraal Station

De Ruijterkade

Muziekgebouw aan 't IJ/ Bimhuis
58

Passenger Terminal Amsterdam

IJhaven

Piet Heinkade

Nieuwendijk

35

Dijksgracht

Damrak

36

37

Oosterdokskade

Oosterdok

Kromme Waal

Zeedijk

Geldersekade

38

39

40

Oude Kerk
41

RED LIGHT DISTRICT

42

43

Nieuw-markt

44

45

46

Sint-Antoniesbreestraat

47

48

49

Nieuwmarkt

51

50

Voorburgwal

Oudezijds Achterburgwal

Rechtboomssloot

Oude Waal

Waals-Eilandsgracht

Binnenkant

Scheepvaarthuis

Binnenkant

Prins Hendrikkade

Oude Schans

56

Nieuwe Uilenburgerstraat

Rapenburg

Valkenburgerstraat

Science Center NEMO
57

MARINE ETABLISSEMENT (NAVAL COMPLEX)

Kattenburgerstraat

Scheepvaartmuseum (Maritime Museum)

Kattenburger-vaart

Kattenburger-gracht

Wittenburger-gracht

Nieuwe Vaart

Ramgracht

Kloveniersburgwal

Groenburgwal

Zwanenburgwal

Jodenbreestraat

Waterlooplein

JODENBUURT (JEWISH QUARTER)

Mr. Visser-plein

Muider-straat

Wertheim-park

Hoogte Kadijk

Laagte Kadijk

Entrepotdok

Plantage Doklaan

Planetarium

Geologisch Museum

ARTIS ZOO

Binnenamstel

Amstel

Stadhuis Muziek-theater

Blauw-brug
53

Rembrandt-plein

54

Herengracht

Keizersgracht

Utrechtsestraat

Waterlooplein

Nieuwe Herengracht

Hermitage Amsterdam

Nieuwe Keizersgracht

Hortus Botanicus

Plantage Middenlaan

Plantage Muidergracht

Plantage Muidergracht

Zoologisch Museum & Aquarium

Roetersstraat

Amstel

Prinsengracht

Kerkstraat

Magere Brug
55

Nieuwe Kerkstraat

Nieuwe Prinsengracht

Nieuwe Weesperstraat

Nieuwe Achter-gracht

Weesperplein

Amstelveld

Utrechtsedwarsstraat

Reguliersgracht

Frederiks-plein

Amstel-sluizen

Hoge-sluis

Sarphatistraat

Toronto Brug

Mauritskade

Singelgracht

Stadhouderskade

Science Center NEMO	57
Sexmuseum Amsterdam	35
Singel 7	33
Sint-Nicolaaskerk	36
SMBA	14
Torensluis	20
Torture Museum	6
Trippenhuis	47
Westerkerk	22
West-Indisch Huis	32
Wijnkopersgildehuis	45
Woonbootmuseum	13
Zuiderkerk	50

Canal-boat cruises
Ⓜ Metro station
ⓘ Information
✉ Post office
- - - - Ferry route

THE canals

Amsterdam would not be the same without its canals. There might still be Golden Age architecture, trams, "brown cafes," and museums, and maybe locals would retain their iconoclastic outlook on life—but without a mirror of water to reflect its soul, the city would be a shrunken glory. The city has 160 canals—more than Venice—with a combined length of 76km (47 miles), spanned by 1,281 bridges.

The best-known canals are those of the 17th-century *Grachtengordel* (Canal Belt, or Canal Ring): Herengracht, Prinsengracht, and Keizersgracht. To these three, UNESCO in 2010 added the 15th-century Singel when it inscribed the *Grachtengordel* on the list of World Heritage Sites.

To get up close and personal with Amsterdam's canals, you could start out by taking **The Golden Age Canals** tour in chapter 8. Or sail forth on a DIY "cruise," by pedaling your way around the canals on a water bike (*pedalo*) from Canal Bike. Or stroll along the canals after dark, when they're lit up. For details of canal-boat cruises, water bikes, and more, see "Organized Tours," later in this chapter.

Anne Frankhuis ★★★   You shouldn't miss seeing and experiencing this typical Amsterdam canal house, with steep interior stairs, where eight people from three separate Jewish families lived together in near silence for more than 2 years during World War II. The hiding place in *Het Achterhuis*—literally "the back house," but more commonly translated as "The Annex"—that Otto Frank found for his family, the van Pels family, and Fritz Pfeffer, kept them safe until tragically close to the end of the war, when it was raided by Nazi forces and its occupants deported to concentration camps. It was in this house that Anne, whose ambition was to be a writer, kept her famous diary as a way to deal with both the boredom and her youthful array of thoughts, which had as much to do with personal relationships as with the war and the Nazi terror raging outside. Visiting the rooms in which she found refuge is a moving experience.

During the war, the building was an office and warehouse, and its rooms are still as bare as they were when Anne's father returned, the only survivor of the eight *onderduikers* (divers, or hiders). Nothing has been changed, except that Plexiglas panels now protect the wall on which Anne pinned up photos of her favorite actress, Deanna Durbin, and of the little English princesses Elizabeth and Margaret. As you tour the building, it's possible to imagine Anne's experience growing up in this place, awakening as a young woman, and writing down her secret thoughts.

In summer, you may have to wait an hour or more to get in. To avoid lines, get there as early as possible—and while this advice isn't as useful as it used to be, it should still save you some waiting time. A better strategy if you're in town from mid-March to mid-September, when the museum is open until 9 or 10pm, is to go in the evening; it's usually quiet then. You won't need, or get, much time inside, but a half-hour should be enough to see what little there is to see—and to pause for a moment to feel Anne's spirit in the rooms. Next door, at no. 265–267, is a modern wing for temporary exhibits.

Prinsengracht 263 (at Westermarkt). ℂ **020/556-7105.** www.annefrank.org. Admission 8.50€ adults, 4€ children 10-17, free for children 9 and under. Mid-Mar to June and 1st 2 weeks Sept Mon–Fri 9am-9pm, Sat 9am-10pm; July-Aug daily 9am-10pm; mid-Sept to mid-Mar daily 9am-7pm (Jan 1 noon-7pm; Dec 25 noon-5pm, Dec 31 9am-5pm). Closed Yom Kippur. Tram: 13, 14, or 17 to Westermarkt.

Rijksmuseum ★★★ The country's premier museum, the Rijksmuseum, is still working through a decade-long refurbishment project that's due to be completed in 2013. Most of it is closed, but key paintings and other works from the 17th-century Dutch Golden Age can be viewed in the museum's Philips Wing, under the banner of *De Meesterwerken* (The Masterpieces). Even in its drastically reduced circumstances, the State Museum is still one of the leading museums in the land. The three-star rating given here is justified for the Golden Age highlights alone, but remember that most of the museum's collection, which totals some 7 million objects (only a fraction of which is displayed at any given time), will be invisible to visitors for some time to come. Still, you'll need to allocate a half-day to get around everything.

> ### Impressions
>
> *From my favorite spot on the floor I look up at the blue sky and the bare chestnut tree, on whose branches little raindrops glisten like silver, and at the seagulls and other birds as they glide on the wind.*
> —Anne Frank, February 25, 1944

Architect Petrus Josephus Hubertus Cuypers (1827–1921), the grandfather of modern Dutch architecture, designed the brick museum in a monumental, gabled Dutch neo-Renaissance style. Cuypers, a Catholic, slipped in more than a dab of neo-Gothic, too, causing the country's thoroughly Protestant King William III to scorn "that cathedral." The building opened in 1885 to a less-than-enthusiastic public reception. Since then, much has been added to both the building and the collection.

The Rijksmuseum contains the world's largest collection of paintings by the Dutch Old Masters, including the most famous of all, a single work that all but defines Holland's Golden Age. That painting is Rembrandt's *The Militia Company of Captain Frans Banning Cocq and Lieutenant Willem van Ruytenburch* (1642), better known as **The Night Watch.** The scene it so dramatically depicts is surely alien to most of the people who flock to see it: Gaily uniformed, but not exactly warrior-looking, militiamen checking their weapons and accoutrements before moving out on patrol. Captain Cocq (once described as the stupidest man in the city, and whose house at Singel 140–142 still stands), Lieutenant van Ruytenburch, the troopers, and observers (including Rembrandt himself) gaze out at us along the corridor of time, and we're left wondering what's going on underneath the paint, inside their minds. One sentiment might be irritation with this upstart artist, who painted some of their faces in profile or partly hidden, yet charged the full-face fee per man—the

---

Following Anne's Footsteps

From 1933, when the Frank family left Germany to escape the Nazis, until they entered their Prinsengracht refuge in 1942, Anne lived at Merwedeplein 37 (tram: 4, 12, or 25), in the south Amsterdam Rivierenbuurt (River District). A bronze statue of Anne was unveiled on the square in 2005. Her father Otto bought Anne's diary as a present for her 13th birthday around the corner in a shop at Rooseveltlaan 62 (the street was known as Zuider Amstellaan at the time).

militiamen hated the artistic freedom Rembrandt had exercised on their group portrait. In 1975, the masterpiece was restored after having been attacked and slashed.

Vermeer, Frans Hals, Jan Steen, Jacob van Ruisdael, Maarten van Heemskerck, Paulus Potter, Pieter de Hooch, Gerard ter Borch, and Gerard Dou are among many other artists represented at the Rijksmuseum. The range is impressive—individual portraits, guild paintings, landscapes, seascapes, domestic scenes, religious subjects, allegories, and the incredible (and nearly photographic) Dutch still lifes. If you are visiting during winter, look out for paintings of fascinating Dutch winter scenes and landscapes, like Hendrick Avercamp's *Winter Landscape with Ice-Skaters* (ca. 1608). In 2009, the museum acquired four masterly watercolors by Jacob Cats, of landscapes in the Gooi district east of Amsterdam. Painted around 1795, they afford interesting points of comparison with similar works by Golden Age masters a century and a half earlier.

In addition, the museum exhibits fine pieces of antique Delftware and silver. Two rare furnished 17th-century dollhouses should be a highlight for children, by bringing the Dutch Golden Age to life for them in a way no amount of "real" stuff could. The dollhouses' owners commissioned craftsmen to copy objects and ornaments, and the contents are exactly as they were in those days, only in miniature. Tiny seashells occupy a display cabinet. The tapestry room walls are covered with silk, the ceiling and the fireplace mantel are painstakingly painted, and Italian marble paves the hall floor. Silver spoons rest on the dining table and the family initials are embroidered on the napkins. Look carefully, and you'll even see pins stuck in pincushions.

In the Rijksmuseum Garden, you can breathe scented air and view interesting sculptural elements and other fragments from old buildings.

Philips Wing, Jan Luijkenstraat 1B (at Museumplein). (C) **020/674-7000.** www.rijksmuseum.nl. Admission 13€ adults, free for children 18 and under. Daily 9am–6pm. Closed Jan 1. Tram: 2 or 5 to Hobbemastraat.

Van Gogh Museum ★★★   More than 200 paintings by Vincent van Gogh (1853–90), along with nearly every sketch, print, etching, and piece of correspondence the artist ever produced have been housed here since the museum opened in 1973. Van Gogh's sister-in-law and a namesake nephew presented the collection to Holland with the provision that the canvases not leave Vincent's native land. To the further consternation of van Gogh admirers and scholars elsewhere in the world, all but a few of the artist's works that aren't in this museum hang at the Kröller-Müller Museum in the Hoge Veluwe National Park, near Arnhem, in the east of the Netherlands.

> ### The Day Watch?
>
> Rembrandt's *The Night Watch* (1642) actually shows a daytime scene. Centuries of grime dulled its luster until restoration revealed sunlight glinting on the militia's weapons.

You can trace this great artist's artistic development and psychological decline by viewing the paintings displayed in chronological order according to the seven distinct periods and places of residence that defined his short career. (He painted for only 10 years and was on the threshold of success when he committed suicide at age 37.) Only one of van Gogh's paintings sold during his lifetime (his brother Theo sold it), but he did give others out to pay for food, drink, and lodgings—some perhaps went for little more than a song.

The Potato Eaters (1885) was van Gogh's anxious and sensitive first masterpiece. Dark and crudely painted, it depicts a group of Dutch peasants gathered around the table for their evening meal after a long day of manual labor, impressing upon the viewer a sense of the hard, rough conditions of their lives. Gone are the beauty and serenity of traditional Dutch genre painting.

In 1888, van Gogh traveled to Arles in Provence. He was dazzled by the Mediterranean sun, and his favorite color, yellow (it signified love to him), dominated such landscapes as *Wheatfield with a Reaper* (1889). Until his death 2 years later, van Gogh remained in the south of France painting at a frenetic pace, between bouts of madness. In *The Night Café* (1888), a billiards hall's red walls and green ceiling combine with a sickly yellow lamplight to charge the scene with an oppressive, almost nightmarish air. (With red and green, Vincent wrote, he tried to represent "those terrible things, men's passions.") We see the halos around the lights swirl as if we, like some of the patrons slumped over their tables, have had too much to drink.

One particularly splendid wall on the second floor has 18 paintings produced during that 2-year period in the south of France, generally considered to be his artistic high point. It's a symphony of colors and contrasts that includes *Gauguin's Chair, The Yellow House, Self-Portrait with Pipe and Straw Hat, Vincent's Bedroom at Arles, Wheatfield with Reaper, Bugler of the Zouave Regiment,* and the very famous *Still Life Vase with Fourteen Sunflowers,* best known simply as *Sunflowers.* By the time you reach the vaguely threatening painting of black crows rising from a waving cornfield, you can almost feel the mounting inner pain the artist was finally unable to bear.

> ### 📎 Don't "Go"
>
> Gogh is not pronounced *go or goff,* as many Anglophones would have it, but *khokh* (the *kh* sound is like *ch* in the Scottish pronunciation of *loch*—a kind of clearing-your-throat sound).

Works by some of van Gogh's friends and contemporaries, including Toulouse-Lautrec, Gauguin, and Monet, bolster this collection. A new wing (1999), elliptical and partly underground, designed by Japanese architect Kisho Kurokawa, houses temporary exhibits of works by van Gogh and other artists.

Note: Lines at the museum can be very long, especially in summer—try going on a weekday morning. Once inside, allow 2 to 4 hours to see everything.

Paulus Potterstraat 7 (at Museumplein). ℂ **020/570-5200.** www.vangoghmuseum.nl. Admission 13€ adults, 2.50€ children 13–17, free for children 12 and under. Sat–Thurs 10am–6pm; Fri 10am–10pm. Closed Jan 1. Tram: 2, 3, 5, or 12 to Van Baerlestraat.

MORE TOP MUSEUMS & GALLERIES

With more than 40 museums, Amsterdam suffers from no lack of cultural institutions, several of which are just a shade less worthy than the big three listed above.

Allard Pierson Museum   The University of Amsterdam's archaeological collection is permanently on view here, though the frequent temporary exhibits are more likely to have truly memorable pieces. In the Egyptian department is a model of the pyramids at Giza, along with mummies, funerary and ritual objects—and a computer that prints your name in hieroglyphics. Of other cultures, ancient Greece, Rome, Etruria, and Cyprus are among the best represented, through their pottery, sculpture, glassware,

Museum District & Amsterdam South Attractions

Albert Cuypmarkt **9**	Electrische Museumtramlijn	Rembrandtpark **1**
Amsterdamse Bos **13**	Amsterdam **11**	Rijksmuseum **6**
Beatrixpark **15**	Geitenboerderij	Sarphatipark **10**
Cobra Museum **14**	Ridammerhoeve **13**	Sportcentrum Amstelpark **16**
Concertgebouw **3**	Heineken Experience **8**	Stedelijk Museum **4**
De Appel **7**	Kinderboerderij De Pijp **12**	Van Gogh Museum **5**
De Rieker **16**	Martin Luther Kingpark **16**	Vondelpark **2**

jewelry, coins, household objects, and more. A touching Greek funerary stela from 420 B.C. depicts a young woman who likely died during childbirth reaching out toward a baby in the arms of a maid. You can see most of the museum in an hour or two.

Oude Turfmarkt 127 (facing Muntplein). © **020/525-2556.** www.allardpiersonmuseum.nl. Admission 6.50€ adults; 3.25€ seniors, students, and children 4–16; free for children 3 and under. Tues–Fri 10am–5pm; Sat–Sun and holidays 1–5pm. Closed Jan 1, Easter Sunday, Apr 30, May 5, Pentecost Sunday, and Dec 25. Tram: 4, 9, 14, 16, 24, or 25 to Spui.

Amsterdams Historisch Museum (Amsterdam Historical Museum) ★★

For a better understanding of everything you'll see while exploring the city on your own, a visit of 3 to 4 hours to this brilliantly executed museum is more than worthwhile. Its location, the restored 17th-century former Burger Weeshuis (City Orphanage), is already notable. Gallery by gallery, century by century, you'll learn how a small fishing village founded around 1200 became a major sea power and trading center. The focus is on the city's 17th-century Golden Age, when Amsterdam was the world's wealthiest city, and some of the most interesting exhibits are of the trades that made it rich. You can also view famous paintings by the Dutch Old Masters in context.

Pop into Café 't Mandje, a typical, if tiny, Amsterdam neighborhood bar. Sadly, you can't order a beer or a *jenever* from this museum exhibit. For real-life alimentation, visit the museum's **David & Goliath** restaurant. It has a high-beamed ceiling and a wooden sculpture (ca. 1650) of David and Goliath that's 5m (16 ft.) high, and salvaged from a local amusement garden that was a feature of Amsterdam's landscape for more than 200 years until 1862. In summer, you can dine outdoors in the shade of courtyard trees.

If you don't feel like visiting the museum yet and are craving some historic art and architecture, stroll through the **Schuttersgalerij (Civic Guards Gallery)**. It's not easy to find this narrow, two-story, sky-lit passageway linking Kalverstraat to the hidden Begijnhof courtyard (p. 152), even though it is just outside the museum and is signposted at various points around it. Under the walkway's glass roof, you'll see 15 bigger-is-better, 17th-century paintings showing the city's heroic musketeers, the Civic Guards. Elegantly uniformed and of doubtful military effectiveness, these militia companies once played an important role in the city's defense but degenerated into little more than banqueting societies. The paintings are in the same tradition, if not quite the same league, as Rembrandt's *The Night Watch,* but you don't have to line up and pay to view them. And seen in this relaxed context, without crowds, they are well worth the detour. One of the best is *Captain Joan Huydecoper's Company Celebrating the Peace of Münster* (1648), by Govert Flinck. Admission is free, and hours are the same as for the museum.

Kalverstraat 92, Nieuwezijds Voorburgwal 357, and Sint-Luciënsteeg 27 (next to the Begijnhof). © **020/523-1822.** www.ahm.nl. Admission 10€ adults, 7.50€ seniors, 5€ children 6–18, free for children 5 and under. Mon–Fri 10am–5pm; Sat–Sun and holidays 11am–5pm. Closed Jan 1, Apr 30, and Dec 25. Tram: 1, 2, 4, 5, 9, 14, 16, 24, or 25 to Spui.

Bijbels Museum (Biblical Museum)

Taking the Good Book as a starting point, visitors here move on to explore biblical history and geography in objects, images, and installations. The setting—twin patrician canal houses from 1662, designed by noted architect Philips Vingboons for timber merchant Jacob Cromhout—is well worth visiting for a couple of hours, both for historical interest and for the rare opportunity to tour a 17th-century canal house (though most of its decor dates from later periods). There are elegant stucco reliefs, and a dizzying elliptical grand staircase. Two ground-floor rooms have magnificent (and neck-stressing) painted ceilings depicting the four seasons, ancient mythological scenes, Greco-Roman gods, and the zodiac signs—all painted by Jacob de Wit in 1718 and 1750. There are fine views of the lovely courtyard garden from some upper-floor windows; stroll through the garden to see a pond and sculptures.

The museum collection includes a superb set of dioramas representing historical and religious scenes. One from the mid-1800s, made from wood, fabric, and gold leaf, depicts the Tabernacle—a desert tent containing the Ark of the Covenant (which holds the Ten Commandments). A model from 1725 is of the Temple of Solomon; another from 1879 evokes the Temple Mount/Haram-al-Sharîf in Jerusalem with the Dome of the Rock. There's one showing how Jerusalem looked in the 1st century A.D., and another that's a Temple of Herod. Replica archaeological finds from Israel, Palestine, and Egypt also feature Jerusalem prominently, as do paintings of biblical scenes. Among the Bibles on display are the first Bible printed in the Low Countries, dating from 1477, and the first edition of the authorized Dutch translation, from 1637.

Herengracht 366–368 (near Spui). ✆ 020/624-2436. www.bijbelsmuseum.nl. Admission 8€ adults, 4.75€ students, 4€ children 13–17, free for children 12 and under. Mon–Sat 10am–5pm; Sun and holidays 11am–5pm. Closed Jan 1 and Apr 30. Tram: 1, 2, or 5 to Spui.

> ### 📎 Money Saver
>
> One way to save money on museums, attractions, and more is to buy the VVV Amsterdam tourist office's I amsterdam Card (p. 41).

Cobra Museum You have to head out to dull suburban Amstelveen south of Amsterdam to find this exciting museum—exciting, that is, if you admire the Cobra group's post–World War II, abstract-expressionist art. The group took its name from the initials of the original players' home cities: Copenhagen, Brussels, and Amsterdam. Folks like **Karel Appel,** Asger Jorn, and Lucebert weren't instantly popular in their day, and it's probably still a stretch to describe them as such today, but they undoubtedly changed the face of art. Appel (1921–2006), a controversial painter, sculptor, and graphic artist who in 1950 co-founded the experimental movement, was the Dutchman of the trio. His work, including *Child and Beast II* (1951), has a childlike quality, employing bright colors and abstract shapes. He once said, "I paint like a barbarian in a barbarous age." View works by Appel here and at the Stedelijk Museum (see below).

Sandbergplein 1–3, Amstelveen. ✆ 020/547-5050. www.cobra-museum.nl. Admission 9.50€ adults, 6.50€ seniors, 5€ students and children 6–18, free for children 5 and under. Tues–Sun 11am–5pm. Closed Jan 1, Apr 30, and Dec 25. Tram: 5 to Binnenhof; Metro: Beneluxbaan.

Hermitage Amsterdam A visit to Amsterdam can offer you some of the experiences of a trip to St. Petersburg. Opened in 2004 in the neoclassical Amstelhof, the Amsterdam branch of Russia's renowned State Hermitage museum recalls links between the two canal-threaded cities that date back centuries. During a visit to Amsterdam in 1697, Czar Peter the Great, an admirer of Holland, visited the Amstelhof, which dates from 1681 to 1683 and was built as a home for seniors (at first only for Protestant women). Surrounding a central courtyard, it's flanked on two sides by canals, and on a third by the Amstel River. Holland even gets some of its own cultural patrimony back again here, if only on loan, since the Hermitage has

600 paintings by Dutch and Flemish Old Masters. The Neerlandia Building, which was built next to the Amstelhof in 1888 as a home for indigent married couples, houses a Hermitage for Children exhibit.

Nieuwe Herengracht 14 (at the Amstel River). © **0900/4376-48243.** www.hermitage.nl. Admission 7.50€ adults, free for children 16 and under. Thurs-Tues 10am-7pm, Wed 10am-8pm. Closed Jan 1 and Dec 25. Tram: 9 or 14 to Waterlooplein.

Joods Historisch Museum (Jewish Historical Museum) ★   In the heart of what was once Amsterdam's thriving Jewish Quarter (see later in this chapter), this museum occupies a restored Ashkenazi synagogue complex. Its cluster of four synagogues—the **Grote Synagoge** (1671), **Obbene Sjoel** (1685), **Dritt Sjoel** (1700–78), and **Nieuwe Synagoge** (1752)—survived the Nazi occupation of Amsterdam during World War II more or less intact. In 1987, they became home to a collection of paintings and decorative ceremonial objects, including magnificent gold and silver ritual vessels. Through these objects, along with photographs, artworks—including paintings by Amsterdam artist Jozef Israëls (1824–1911)—interactive displays, and a study room with a library of books, the museum tells the intertwining stories of Jewish identity, Jewish religion and culture, and Jewish history in the Netherlands. Extended in 2006, it provides insights into the Jewish way of life over the centuries, incorporating both good times and bad. Take a morning or an afternoon, and leave time to appreciate the beauty and size of the buildings themselves, which include Europe's oldest public synagogue. This is a museum for everyone, Jewish or otherwise, and there are frequent temporary exhibits of international interest.

Tip: The museum cafe is a great place to have a cup of coffee and a pastry, or a light kosher meal. It's quiet, inexpensive, and the food is good. You don't need to visit the museum to dine at the cafe.

Nieuwe Amstelstraat 1 (at Waterlooplein). © **020/531-0310.** www.jhm.nl. Admission 9€ adults, 6€ seniors and students, 4.50€ children 13–17, free for children 12 and under. Combined admission with the Portuguese Synagogue (see later in this chapter): 12€ adults, 6€ children 13–17, free for children 12 and under. Daily 11am-5pm (Jan 1 noon-5pm). Closed Jewish New Year (2 days) and Yom Kippur. Tram: 9 or 14 to Waterlooplein.

Museum Het Rembrandthuis (Rembrandt House Museum) ★★   To view the greatest masterpieces by Rembrandt van Rijn (to give the artist his full name), you must visit the Rijksmuseum, but in this house (ca. 1606), you get a more intimate sense of Rembrandt—it's a shrine to one of the greatest artists the world has ever known. Rembrandt bought the three-story, 10-room house in 1639 when he was Amsterdam's most fashionable portrait painter. In this house, his son Titus was born and his wife Saskia died. Due to his extravagant lifestyle, the artist was bankrupt when he left it in 1658 and moved with his son Titus and his mistress Hendrickje to a plain house (that no longer exists) on Rozengracht.

Not until 1906 was the building rescued from a succession of subsequent owners and restored as a museum. More recent restoration has returned the old house to the way it looked when Rembrandt lived and worked here, complete with the artist's art-and-curiosities cabinet, his combined living room and bedroom, the upstairs studio in which he created, among other famous works, *The Night Watch,* a ground-floor kitchen, and the maid's bedroom.

The rooms are furnished with 17th-century objects and furniture that, as closely as possible, match the descriptions in Rembrandt's 1656 petition for bankruptcy. His printing press is back in place, and you can view 250 of his etchings and drawings on the walls, along with works by some of his contemporaries, like Jan Lievens, and his teacher, Pieter Lastman. These include self-portraits and landscapes, and several that relate to the neighborhood's traditionally Jewish character—like the portrait of Rabbi Menassah ben Israel, who lived across the street and was an early teacher of another illustrious Amsterdammer, Baruch Spinoza. Temporary exhibits are mounted in a modern wing next door, and you'll need at least 2 hours to get around the two places. Opposite the Rembrandthuis, appropriately, is the Amsterdam High School for the Arts.

Jodenbreestraat 4 (at Waterlooplein). ✆ 020/520-0400. www.rembrandthuis.nl. Admission 9€ adults, 6€ students, 2.50€ children 6–17, free for children 5 and under. Daily 10am–5pm. Closed Jan 1. Metro: Waterlooplein. Tram: 9 or 14 to Waterlooplein.

Museum Van Loon ★ The van Loon family owned this magnificent patrician house between 1884 and 1945. One of a matched pair dating from 1672, its first occupant was the artist Ferdinand Bol, a student of Rembrandt. On its walls hang more than 80 family portraits, including those of Willem van Loon, one of the founders of the Dutch East India Company; Nicolaas Ruychaver, who liberated Amsterdam from the Spanish in 1578; and another, later, Willem van Loon, who became mayor in 1686. Among many other treasures you'll see on a visit, which should last an hour or two, are a family album containing tempera portraits of van Loons living in the 1600s, and commemorative coins struck to honor seven different golden wedding anniversaries celebrated between 1621 and 1722. A marble staircase with an ornately curlicued brass balustrade leads up through the house, connecting restored period rooms filled with richly decorated paneling, stuccowork, mirrors, fireplaces, furnishings, porcelain, medallions, chandeliers, rugs, and more. The garden boasts carefully tended hedges and a coach house modeled on a Greek temple.

> ## A Familiar Face
>
> Rembrandt painted about 100 self-portraits, more than any other great artist.

Keizersgracht 672 (near Vijzelstraat). ✆ 020/624-5255. www.museumvanloon.nl. Admission 7€ adults, 5€ students and children 6–18, free for children 5 and under. Wed–Mon 11am–5pm. Tram: 16, 24, or 25 to Keizersgracht.

Museum Willet-Holthuysen ★ Take advantage of another rare opportunity to visit an elegant 17th-century canal house with an ornamental garden. This house, built in 1687, was renovated several times before its last owner, Mrs. Willet-Holthuysen, willed her mansion and all its contents, including a fine-arts collection, to the city in 1885. Its various owner and servant quarters allow you to compare the glittering lifestyles of the wealthy and those of the ordinary folk who took care of them. Among the most interesting rooms: A Victorian-era bedroom on the second floor, a large reception room with tapestry wall panels, and an 18th-century basement kitchen that's still so completely furnished and functional you could swear the cook had merely stepped out to go shopping. You'll easily tour this museum in 1 or 2 hours.

Herengracht 605 (near the Amstel River). ✆ 020/523-1822. www.willetholthuysen.nl. Admission 7€ adults, 5.25€ seniors, 3.50€ children 6–18, free for children 5 and under. Mon–Fri 10am–5pm; Sat–Sun and holidays 11am–5pm. Closed Jan 1, Apr 30, and Dec 25. Tram: 4, 9, or 14 to Rembrandtplein.

Ons' Lieve Heer op Solder (Our Lord in the Attic) ★ Though Amsterdam's been known as a tolerant city for many centuries, after the 1578 Protestant *Alteratie* (Changeover), Roman Catholics fell into disfavor. Forced to worship in secret, they devised ingenious ways of gathering for Sunday services. This museum in the heart of the Red Light District's den of iniquity incorporates the most amazing and best preserved of these clandestine places of worship. The church is in the attic of one of the oldest canal houses you can visit, which was transformed in 1661–63 by wealthy Catholic merchant Jan Hartman to house a church. Worshipers entered by a door on a side street and climbed a narrow flight of stairs to the hidden third-floor church. Seeing a rambling old canal house furnished much as it would have been in the mid-18th century, with heavy oak furniture, Delft tiles, and period paintings, makes a visit of an hour or two here worthwhile by itself.

After Hartman died in 1668, Jan Reynst, a Protestant merchant, bought the house. Reynst planned to rent the attic as storage space, but realized he could make more money charging Catholic worshipers for continued use of their secret church. An 18th-century redecoration created the chapel-size church you see now, with its large baroque altar, religious statuary, pews to seat 150, an 18th-century spinet-size pipe organ, vaulted ceiling, two narrow upper balconies, and a side chapel dedicated to the Virgin Mary. It's still used for services and concerts. Other rooms contain a trove of magnificent religious vessels, like 17th-century monstrances in gold and silver. An hour here should do it.

See also **De Rode Hoed,** under "More Historical Buildings," later in this chapter.

Oudezijds Voorburgwal 40 (near the Oude Kerk). © **020/624-6604.** www.opsolder.nl. Admission 7€ adults, 5€ students, 1€ children 5–18, free for children 4 and under. Mon–Sat 10am–5pm; Sun and holidays 1–5pm. Closed Jan 1 and Apr 30. Tram: 1, 2, 4, 5, 9, 13, 16, 17, 24, 25, or 26 to Centraal Station.

Scheepvaartmuseum ★★ ☺ *Note:* Amsterdam's Maritime Museum is closed for renovation until the summer of 2011; some of the service information provided below is likely to change when the museum reopens. A bonanza for anyone who loves ships and the sea, the Maritime Museum overlooks the busy harbor and is housed in a former Amsterdam Admiralty arsenal from 1656. All the exhibits chronicle the country's abiding ties to the sea through commerce, fishing, yachting, exploration, and war. Room after room is filled with boats and ship models, seascapes and ship paintings, prints, navigational instruments, cannons and other weaponry, and old maps and charts. Among the cartographic highlights are a 15th-century Ptolemaic atlas and a sumptuously bound edition of the *Great Atlas, or Description of the World,* produced over a lifetime by Jan Blaeu, the master cartographer of Holland's Golden Age. An expansive model diorama depicts 17th-century shipping in the Texel Roads, with artist Willem van de Velde the Elder (1611–93) and his son Willem van de Velde the Younger (1633–1707) sketching the scene from a small boat.

A major preoccupation here is the history of the Vereenigde Oostindische Compagnie (United East India Company). Moored at the wharf is a full-size replica of the V.O.C. merchant ship *Amsterdam,* which foundered off Hastings, England, in 1749 on her maiden voyage to the fabled Spice Islands (Indonesia). Actors create scenes on the ship: "Sailors" fire cannons, sing sea shanties, mop the deck, hoist cargo aboard, and attend a solemn burial at sea. You can also watch as sail-makers and rope-makers work; in the galley, the cook prepares a real shipboard meal, which you might be invited to taste. *Note:* See "Sail Ahoy," under "Multimedia Attractions," later in this chapter, for the location of the *Amsterdam* until the Maritime Museum reopens.

Other ships available for viewing are a steam icebreaker, a motor lifeboat, and a herring lugger. The fantastical Dutch royal barge and two towing barges are housed indoors. Environmentalists will want to go onboard Greenpeace's *Rainbow Warrior,* a gladiator of environmental protection on the high seas.

Kattenburgerplein 1 (in the Oosterdok). ℂ **020/523-2222.** www.scheepvaartmuseum.nl. Admission 9€ adults, 7€ seniors, 4.50€ children 6–17, children under 6 free. Tues–Sat 10am–5pm (also Mon during school vacations), Sun noon–5pm. Closed Jan 1, Apr 30, and Dec 25. Bus: 22, 42, or 43 to Kattenburgerplein.

Stedelijk Museum ★★ *Note:* Amsterdam's modern-art Municipal Museum is closed for renovation and expansion until 2011; some of the service information provided below is likely to change when the museum reopens. The city's modern-art museum has works by Dutch painters such as Karel Appel, Willem de Kooning, and Piet Mondrian, and by Calder, Oldenburg, Rosenquist, Warhol, and more. It houses the largest collection outside Russia of Kasimir Malevich's abstract paintings, but centers its exhibits around the De Stijl, Cobra, post-Cobra, nouveau réalisme, Pop Art, color-field painting, zero, minimalist, and conceptual schools. The museum cafe features a giant Appel mural from 1956. Depending on your level of interest in modern art, you could spend from 4 hours to all day here.

Paulus Potterstraat 13 (at Museumplein). ℂ **020/573-2911.** www.stedelijk.nl. Admission 9€ adults; 4.50€ seniors, students, and children 7–16; children 6 and under free; 23€ family. Daily 10am–6pm. Closed Jan 1. Tram: 2, 3, 5, 12, 16, or 24 to Museumplein.

Tropenmuseum (Tropical Museum) ★ ☺ One of the city's most intriguing museums belongs to the Royal Institute for the Tropics, a foundation devoted to studying the cultures of tropical areas around the world. Its focus reflects Holland's centuries as a landlord in areas such as Indonesia, Surinam (on South America's northern coast), and the Caribbean islands of St. Maarten, Saba, St. Eustatius, Aruba, Bonaire, and Curaçao. The Tropical Institute building complex alone is worth the tram ride to Amsterdam East; its heavily ornamented 19th-century facade is an amalgam of Dutch architectural styles: Turrets, stepped gables, arched windows, delicate spires, and the monumental galleried interior court—a popular spot for concerts.

The museum's approach to its subject has matured considerably from its original 19th-century colonial pride and condescension—indeed, it's become an antidote to those kinds of views. Its representation of contemporary issues such as the causes of poverty in the developing world and the depletion of the world's tropical rainforests is both considered and balanced. The most interesting exhibits are the walk-through model villages and city-street scenes that, except for the lack of genuine inhabitants, capture daily-life moments. Stroll through a Nigerian village, wander an Arab *souk,* sit in a Mexico City bar or in a traditional *yurt* home of central Asian nomads. Examine the tools and techniques used to produce *batik* (distinctively dyed Indonesian fabrics) and the instruments and ornaments that comprise a tropical residence.

Before leaving the Tropenmuseum—and you could easily spend a full day here—take a snack or a drink at its tropically inspired cafe, Ekeko. The museum shop sells products from the Tropics and developing countries.

Linnaeusstraat 2 (at Mauritskade). ℂ **020/568-8200.** www.tropenmuseum.nl. Admission 9€ adults, 7.50€ seniors, 5€ students and children 6–17, free for children 5 and under, 25€ family. Daily 10am–5pm (3pm Dec 5, 24, 31). Closed Jan 1, Apr 30, May 5, and Dec 25. Tram: 9, 10, or 14 to Alexanderplein.

Verzetsmuseum Amsterdam (Resistance Museum)   Take a trip back in time to Holland's dark World War II days, during the Nazi occupation (1940–45). With authentic photographs, documents, weapons, communications equipment, spy gadgets, and other materials actually used by the Dutch Resistance, exhibits show the ingenuity—along with courage—the freedom-fighters brought to bear on German occupation forces. A pedal-powered printing press is a good example of items that evoke the period and bring it to life. The fate of Amsterdam's Jewish community, herded into a ghetto, then rounded up for deportation to concentration camps, has a prominent place, as do the actions of workers who in 1941 went on strike to protest the first deportation of 400 Jewish Amsterdammers. Yet the museum doesn't shrink from less palatable aspects of Holland's wartime record, like the actions of collaborators, including those who joined Dutch Nazi SS units. The museum, which has a cafe, is in the 1876 neoclassical Plancius Building, which once housed a Jewish social club. A changing program of exhibits takes the story beyond Holland's foreign occupation to feature resistance struggles of recent times.

> ### Impressions
>
> *This city seems to be double: One can also see it in the water; and the reflection of these distinguished houses in these canals makes this spot a fairyland.*
> —Jean-François Regnard,
> French writer, 1681

Plantage Kerklaan 61 (facing Artis Zoo). © **020/620-2535.** www.verzetsmuseum.org. Admission 7.50€ adults, 4€ children 7–15, free for children 6 and under. Tues–Fri 10am–5pm; Sat–Mon and holidays 11am–5pm. Closed Jan 1, Apr 30, and Dec 25. Tram: 9 or 14 to Plantage Kerklaan.

THE DAM ★★★

In English, the city's monumental main square is generally referred to as "Dam Square." Amsterdammers call it just de Dam (the Dam)—some even find it amusing to direct hapless foreigners to "the Dam Square": by taking "this damn street and then crossing over at that damn canal." You'll look in vain for any sign of a dam on the Dam, but this is the likely site of the original dam built around 1200 on the Amstel River, which allowed Amsterdam to begin the growth trajectory that took it from backwater village to world-class watering hole.

Dedicated in 1956 to honor the World War II dead, the **Nationaal Monument,** an obelisk 22m (72 ft.) high on the square's east side, is embedded with three sculptures: *War,* symbolized by four male figures; *Peace,* represented by a woman and child; and *Resistance,* signified by two men with howling dogs, all flanked by two stone lions symbolizing the Netherlands. In the base are 12 urns, containing soil from the 11 Dutch provinces (before the 12th, Flevoland, was established), and the former Dutch East Indies (Indonesia). A memorial ceremony happens here every May 4, when the queen places a wreath on the spot. For the rest of the year, it's a hangout for teens.

See also the descriptions of **NH Grand Hotel Krasnapolsky** in chapter 5 (p. 81) and **De Bijenkorf** department store in chapter 9 (p. 218).

The Royal Palace & New Church

Koninklijk Paleis (Royal Palace) ★   One of the Dam's heavier features is the solid, neoclassical facade of the Royal Palace (1648–55). Jacob van Campen designed it as a *stadhuis* (town hall) to replace the decayed old Gothic one that in 1652 did everyone a favor by going up in flames. Van Campen intended to showcase the city's burgeoning prosperity, so the interior is replete with white Italian marble, sculptures, and painted ceilings. Poet Constantijn Huygens called it the eighth world wonder, and indeed it was among Europe's largest secular buildings at the time, built on a precisely tabulated foundation of 13,659 timber pilings.

Not until 1808, when Napoleon Bonaparte's younger brother Louis reigned as king of the Netherlands, did it become a palace, filled with imperial furniture courtesy of the French ruler. Since the Dutch House of Orange's return to the throne in 1813, this has been the official palace of the reigning king or queen of the Netherlands. Few of them, however, have used it for more than their *pied-à-terre* in the capital or an occasional state celebration, such as Queen Beatrix's inauguration reception—she prefers living at Huis ten Bosch in The Hague, but can on occasion be seen waving from the balcony here to crowds of onlookers below on the Dam.

In the **Vierschaar (Court of Justice),** until the 18th century, magistrates pronounced death sentences under images of Justice, Wisdom, and Mercy. Atlas holds up the globe in the high-ceilinged **Burgerzaal (Citizens Chamber),** and maps inlaid on the marble floor show Amsterdam at the center of the world. Ferdinand Bol's painting *Moses with the Tablets of the Law* (1664) hangs in the **Schepenzaal (Council Chamber),** where city aldermen met. On the pediment overlooking the Dam, Flemish sculptor Artus Quellinus carved a stone tribute to Amsterdam's maritime preeminence; it depicts the *Maid of Amsterdam* and figures symbolizing the oceans paying the city homage. The weathervane on the cupola is shaped like a Dutch sailing ship. Every now and then, the 17th-century Hemony carillon tinkles out a melody.

Tip: Don't miss the excellent video presentation (in English) that's shown continuously, usually in the second-floor Magistrate's Court.

Dam. ✆ **020/620-4060.** www.paleisamsterdam.nl. Admission 7.50€ adults; 6.50€ seniors, students, and children 5–16; children 4 and under free. Generally July–Aug Tues–Sun 11am–5pm; Sept–June Tues–Sun noon–5pm (open days and hours vary; check before going). Closed during periods of royal residence and state receptions. Tram: 1, 2, 4, 5, 9, 13, 14, 16, 17, 24, or 25 to the Dam.

Nieuwe Kerk (New Church)   Many of this originally Catholic church's priceless treasures were removed and its colorful frescoes painted over in 1578 when it passed into Protestant hands, but since 1814, when the king first took the oath of office here (Dutch royalty are inaugurated, not crowned), much of its original grandeur has been restored. Queen Beatrix was inaugurated here in 1980. The church boasts a stately arched nave, an elaborately carved altar, a great pipe organ by Jacob van Campen dating from 1645 that's still in regular use for concerts, and several noteworthy stained-glass windows. Look for the carved, gilded ceiling above the choir, which survived a disastrous fire in 1645. The church holds sepulchral monuments for many of Holland's most revered poets, among them Joost van den Vondel, and naval heroes. A sculpture depicts the 17th-century Admiral Michiel de Ruyter amid sea-battle wreckage. You should make it in and out of here in as little as a half-hour. After your tour, dine on 't Nieuwe Kafé's sidewalk terrace, which has fine Dam views.

Dam (next to the Royal Palace). ✆ **020/638-6909.** www.nieuwekerk.nl. Admission varies with different events; free when there's no exhibit. Daily 10am–6pm (Thurs to 10pm during exhibits). Tram: 1, 2, 4, 5, 9, 13, 14, 16, 17, 24, or 25 to the Dam.

SPECIAL events

April 30 is *Koninginnedag* **(Queen's Day)**; locals and out-of-towners crowd the streets to enjoy performances, parades, markets, and general merrymaking. The area around the Homomonument becomes a huge outdoor dance club.

The **August Gay Pride Festival** in Europe's gay-friendliest city is a big event. A crowd of 150,000 turns out to watch its highlight: The Boat Parade's display of 100 or so outrageously decorated boats cruising the canals. Other draws are street discos, open-air theater performances, a sports program, and a film festival.

In September, the **Jordaan Festival** showcases this old neighborhood peppered with small inexpensive restaurants, second-hand stores, and unusual boutiques and galleries.

The single most important event in the Netherlands is the **flowering of the bulb fields** each spring from March to mid-May. Two-thirds of all the cut flowers sold in the world come from the Netherlands. The best flower-viewing areas are between Haarlem and Leiden and between Haarlem and Den Helder.

The Dam's Lighter Side

Madame Tussauds ☺ If you like your celebrities with a waxen stare, don't miss the Amsterdam version of the famous London attraction. It has its own cast of Dutch characters (Rembrandt, Queen Beatrix, Mata Hari), among a parade of international favorites (Kennedy, Churchill, Gandhi, Obama). Exhibits bring you face to face with waxwork images of the powerful and famous and allow you to step into the times, events, and moments that made them so. The Dutch 17th-century display is magnificent. Cannons roar in the war of liberation against Spain; Rembrandt and Vermeer get busy with their paints; and you can stroll through the streets of Golden Age Amsterdam. More recent Dutch figures get a nod, too, like van Gogh with his sunflowers and Piet Mondrian and a red-yellow-and-blue canvas. Among the characters portrayed—and often brought to life with memorabilia such as paintings or a smoking cigarette—are world leaders, religious leaders, stars, artists, and writers: Nelson Mandela, the Dalai Lama, Michael Jackson, Madonna, David Bowie, Kylie Minogue, Aretha Franklin, Bob Marley, Arnold Schwarzenegger, Sean Connery, Harrison Ford, and many more. Don't miss the great views of the Dam from the building's enormous "round window." Having paid the steep admission, you'll likely want to spend a morning or afternoon here.

Dam 20. ✆ **020/523-0623.** www.madametussauds.nl. Admission 21€ adults, 16€ children 5–15, free for children 4 and under. Generally from 10 or 11am to btw. 4.30 and 8:30pm, depending on the season and the day. Closed Apr 30. Tram: 4, 9, 14, 16, 24, or 25 to the Dam.

HISTORICAL BUILDINGS & MONUMENTS

In a city with almost 7,000 officially recognized historical buildings and monuments, you'll find you're just about tripping over them. That Amsterdam has such a great mass of historical structures gives the city its overall character, but a few stand out head and gables above the crowd. See also the **Koninklijk Paleis (Royal Palace),** above.

Follow the Money

A massive edifice of colored brick and stone enclosing three arcades with glass-and-iron roofs just off the Dam, the **Beurs van Berlage (Berlage Exchange),** or as it was originally known, the Koopmansbeurs (Merchants' Exchange, or Stock Exchange), Beursplein 1 and Damrak 243 (✆ **020/530-4141;** www.beursvanberlage.nl; tram: 4, 9, 14, 16, 24, or 25), represented a revolutionary break with 19th-century Dutch architecture. Designed by Hendrik Petrus Berlage (1856–1934), the father of modern Dutch architecture and an admirer of Frank Lloyd Wright, the old exchange's refined style illustrates Berlage's theories advocating a return to simplicity of form and clarity of line and structure. Now retired as an exchange, the refurbished building, constructed between 1896 and 1903, is used as a space for concerts, conferences, and exhibits. It's well worth visiting as an architectural masterpiece and a prime inspiration for the Amsterdam School of Architecture, but unless you're a fan of this period you won't need to spend much time getting the general idea. Climb the 156 steps (there's no elevator) of the Beurs tower for fine views of Old Amsterdam. Open hours and admission vary for exhibits, concerts, and other events.

A Pious Retreat

A cluster of small homes around a garden courtyard, the **Begijnhof ★★,** Spui (www.begijnhofamsterdam.nl; tram: 1, 2, or 5), dates from the 14th century and is one of the best places to appreciate the city's earliest history, when Amsterdam was a destination for religious pilgrims and an important Catholic center. The Begijnhof was not a convent, but a cloister founded in 1346 for pious women—*begijnen*—involved in religious and charitable work. These kinds of institutions gave options for women who wanted to live without a husband and children, but didn't want to become a nun, at a time when there were few alternatives. Originally, the Begijnhof was surrounded by water, with access via a bridge over a canal that was called the Begijnensloot. Even after the city's 1578 changeover from Catholicism to Protestantism, the Begijnhof remained in operation. The last *begijn* died in 1971, but you can still pay homage to these pious women by pausing a moment at the small flower-planted mound that lies at the center garden's edge and across from the **Engelse Kerk (English Church).** Despite its name, this church, built in 1607 and enlarged in 1665, was actually used by Scottish Presbyterians.

Opposite the church, at no. 30, is the **Begijnhofkapel,** a "secret" Catholic chapel from 1671. It's still in use, and dedicated to the Begijnhof's patron saints, John and Ursula. It wasn't all that much of a secret, since the city's Protestant fathers authorized its construction. It just couldn't be visible as a church from the outside, and the noted Catholic architect Philips Vingboons drew up the plans accordingly. The interior stained-glass windows depict scenes from the Miracle of the Host in 1345, a religious event that led to Amsterdam becoming a place of pilgrimage. Only one of the old (ca. 1425) timber houses, Het Houten Huys, at no. 34, remains.

Visit the Begijnhof daily from 9am to 5pm—but take note that senior citizens now reside in the 47 homes, most of which date from the 17th and 18th centuries, and their privacy and tranquillity must be respected. Access is on Gedempte Begijnensloot, an alleyway off Spui. Admission is free. In fine weather, you might easily want to let a couple of hours slip by here.

More Historical Buildings

You may be starting to get the impression that Amsterdam is one big historical monument. Still, some buildings are more historic and monumental than others and therefore more worth going out of your way for. You won't have to go far out of your way to see **Centraal Station** (Metro: Centraal Station). Designed by architect Petrus Josephus Hubertus Cuypers, the city's main rail station was built between 1884 and 1889 on three artificial islands (supported on 30,000 pilings) in the IJ channel. Amsterdammers thoroughly disliked it at the time. Now it's an attraction, partly for its extravagant Dutch neo-Renaissance facade, partly for the permanent liveliness that surrounds it. The left one of the two central towers has a gilded weathervane; on the right one, there's a clock. Take time to soak up the buzz that swirls around the station in a blur of people, backpacks, bikes, trams, buses, vendors, pickpockets, and junkies. There might even be a street organ—perhaps a century-old Perlee hand-ground barrel-organ, made from richly carved and painted wood.

Not far away, across Prins Hendrikkade at the corner of Geldersekade, stands the **Schreierstoren** (Metro: Centraal Station), built in 1480, and once a strong point in the city wall. Its name, which means Tower of Tears, comes from the tears allegedly shed by wives as their men sailed away on voyages from which they might never return. A stone tablet on the wall shows a woman with her hand to her face. She might be weeping, but who knows what emotion that hand is really covering? Another tablet, placed in 1945, records the 350th anniversary of the *Eerste Schipvaart Naar Oostindië 1595* (First Ocean Voyage to the East Indies 1595). The tower's ground floor now houses a traditional bar, the **V.O.C. Café,** Prins Hendrikkade 94–95 (✆ **020/428-8291;** www.schreierstoren.nl;), named for the Dutch initials of the United East India Company.

The **Munttoren** (tram: 4, 9, 14, 16, 24, or 25), on Muntplein, sits at a busy traffic intersection on the Rokin and Singel canals. In 1487, the Mint Tower's base was part of the Reguliers Gate in the city wall. In 1620, Hendrick de Keyser topped it with an ornate, lead-covered tower, from which a carillon of Hemony brothers bells sings out gaily every hour and plays a 1-hour concert on Fridays at noon. The tower got its present name in 1672, when it housed the city mint.

The tilting **Montelbaanstoren** (Metro: Nieuwmarkt), the "leaning tower of Amsterdam," a fortification at the juncture of the Oude Schans and Waalseilandsgracht canals,

> ### New York Loves Ya, Henry
>
> In 1609, English navigator Henry Hudson set out from the Tower of Tears aboard the sailing ship *Halve Maen.* He was under contract to the United East India Company to find a Northeast Passage to Asia. Instead, he sailed west and "discovered" Long Island, the Hudson River, and the future Nieuw Amsterdam, which would later become New York. The Greenwich Village Historical Society attached a memorial marker to the tower in 1927.

dates from 1512. It's one of few surviving elements of the city's once-powerful defensive works. In 1606, Hendrick de Keyser added an octagonal tower and spire. The building now houses local Water Authority offices.

The 14th-century **De Waag (Weigh House),** Nieuwmarkt (© **020/557-9898;** www.waag.org; Metro: Nieuwmarkt), is the city's only surviving medieval fortified gate. It later became a guild house; among the guilds lodged here was the Surgeon's Guild, immortalized in Rembrandt's painting *The Anatomy Lesson of Dr. Nicolaes Tulp* (1632), which depicts a dissection underway in the upper-floor Theatrum Anatomicum (the painting's on display at the **Mauritshuis** in The Hague; see "The Hague," in chapter 11). Most of De Waag now houses a specialized educational and cultural institute, and is rarely open; admission (when possible) is free, except in the case of occasional special exhibits. You can, however, visit the exceptional cafe-restaurant **In de Waag** on the ground floor (see p. 111).

Most of Golden Age Amsterdam's wealth was generated by trade, and most of that trade was organized by the Vereenigde Oostindische Compagnie (V.O.C.), based at **Oost-Indisch Huis (East India House),** Oude Hoogstraat 24, off Kloveniersburg-wal (Metro: Nieuwmarkt). Dating from 1606, the former headquarters of the first multinational corporation now belongs to the University of Amsterdam. Stroll into the courtyard and there's no problem with going inside, where corridors are hung with paintings depicting the 17th-century Dutch trading settlement of Batavia—today's Jakarta, Indonesia.

Not far from East India House is Amsterdam's first university, the **Athenaeum Illustre,** at Oudezijds Voorburgwal 231 (tram: 4, 9, 14, 16, 24, or 25). Founded in 1631, the Athenaeum moved here in 1632 to occupy the 1470 Gothic **Agnietenka-pel (Church of St. Agnes).** The building now houses the underwhelming Univer-sity of Amsterdam Museum. In a 17th-century lecture room are portraits of the Dutch humanist and theologian Erasmus and of the Florentine strongman Lorenzo de' Medici. Across the Kloveniersburgwal canal from the university, at Kloveniers-burgwal 95, is the opulent **Poppenhuis** (1642), designed by that indefatigable Golden Age architect Philips Vingboons in an Italianate style for Joan Poppen, a wealthy merchant's grandson and heir. It has a classically influenced triangular pediment and ornamental pilasters.

West-Indisch Huis (West India House), at Herenmarkt 93–99, off Brouwers-gracht (tram: 1, 2, 5, 13, or 17), is also interesting. On the north side of this little square is a redbrick building, built as a meat-trading hall in 1615. In 1623, it became the headquarters of the Dutch West India Company, which controlled trade with the Americas. A current tenant is the **John Adams Institute** (© **020/624-7280;** www.john-adams.nl), a U.S.-oriented philosophical and literary society that has hosted lectures by guest speakers like J. K. Galbraith, Gore Vidal, and Norman Mailer. In the courtyard is a bronze statue of Peter Stuyvesant, the one-legged gov-ernor of Nieuw Amsterdam (later New York) from 1647 until the British took over in 1664. A wall sculpture depicts the Dutch settlement on Manhattan Island.

There are just three surviving guildhouses in Amsterdam. These lavish headquarters of artisanal, mercantile, and professional guilds with roots going back to the Middle Ages are worth seeking out, though all three buildings have new functions, and you'll only be able to view the outside. The **Makelaers Comptoir** (1634), Nieuwezijds Voorburgwal 75 (tram: 1, 2, 5, 13, or 17), on the corner of Nieuwe Nieuwstraat, was the guildhouse of the city's mercantile brokers. Nearby, the **Korenmetershuisje**

(1620), Nieuwezijds Kolk 28 (tram: 1, 2, 5, 13, or 17), housed the grain dealers. Finally, head to the Nieuwmarkt area to view the triple-gabled **Wijnkopersgildehuis** (1630), Koestraat 10–12 (Metro: Nieuwmarkt), where the wine dealers hung out.

For more than 2 centuries after Amsterdam's 1578 Protestant revolution, the *Alteratie,* other Christian denominations were forbidden to worship openly. Clandestine places of worship sprang up around the city. The best known of these was the Catholic **Ons' Lieve Heer op Solder** (see "More Top Museums & Galleries," earlier in this chapter). Another, which is in fact Holland's oldest and largest, is the **Remonstrantsekerk (Remonstrant Church)** in a one-time hat store called **De Rode Hoed (the Red Hat),** Keizersgracht 102 (✆ **020/638-5606;** www.rode hoed.nl; tram: 13, 14, or 17), in a fine canalside building—look for the little red hat on the gable stone. The chapel at the back, with a balcony and an impressive organ, dates from 1630 and is now a venue for meetings and debates.

The Smallest Houses

The narrowest house in Amsterdam is at **Singel 7** (tram: 1, 2, 5, 13, 14, or 17). It's just a meter (3½ ft.) wide, barely wider than the front door. It is, however, a cheat. Only the front facade is really so narrow; behind that, it broadens out to more normal proportions. The real narrowest house is at **Oude Hoogstraat 22** (Metro: Nieuwmarkt), next door to Oost-Indisch Huis (see above). It has a bell gable and is 2.02m (6⅔ ft.) wide and 6m (20 ft.) deep. A close rival, at 2.4m (7¾ ft.) wide, is nearby at Kloveniersburgwal 26 (Metro: Nieuwmarkt); this is the cornice-gabled **Klein Trippenhuis,** also known as Mr. Trip's Coachman's House. It faces the elegant **Trippenhuis** at no. 29, which, at 22m (72 ft.), is the widest Old Amsterdam house. The wealthy merchant Trip brothers had it built for themselves in 1660, and the story goes that their coachman exclaimed one day: "Oh, if only I could be so lucky as to

> ### 💬 Floating Cat House
>
> The Poezenboot (Cat Boat), on the Singel canal facing no. 38 (✆ **020/ 625-8794;** www.poezenboot.nl), is a temporary home to dozens of stray cats.

have a house as wide as my master's door!" His master overheard this, and the coachman's wish was granted. The small house is now a fashion boutique, **Webers Holland** (see "Shopping A to Z," in chapter 9).

Notable Bridges

Made of African azobe wood, the famous **Magere Brug (Skinny Bridge)** ★, a double drawbridge, spans the Amstel between Kerkstraat and Nieuwe Kerkstraat (Metro: Waterlooplein). This is the latest successor, dating from 1969, to the 1672 original, which legend says was built to make it easier for the two wealthy Mager sisters, who lived on opposite banks of the river, to visit each other. The footbridge, one of the city's 60 drawbridges, is a big draw, especially after dark, when it's illuminated by hundreds of lights. A bridge master raises it to let boats through.

Though most of the **Blauwbrug (Blue Bridge)** over the Amstel at Waterlooplein (Metro: Waterlooplein) looks gray, renovation reinstated blue lanterns. Now Blauwbrug, at least at night, is once again as blue as when Impressionist artist George Hendrik Breitner (1857–1923) painted it in the 1880s. The cast-iron bridge (1884), inspired by Paris's Pont Alexandre III, is named after a 16th-century timber bridge painted Nassau blue after the 1578 Protestant takeover. The columns that bear the lamps are surmounted by sculpted copies of the Habsburg imperial crown.

The widest bridge in the old town, the **Torensluis,** Singel (at Oude Leliestraat; tram: 1, 2, 5, 13, or 17), stands on the site of a 17th-century sluice gate flanked by twin towers that were demolished in 1829. Its foundations were used for what must have been a particularly damp and gloomy prison. Sidewalk terraces from nearby cafes encroach onto the span, and the bronze statue on the bridge is of Multatuli, a 19th-century author.

From the bridge over Reguliersgracht at Keizersgracht (tram: 16, 24, or 25), you get a view of seven parallel bridges, which are floodlit at night.

Windmills

Once upon a time, when Amsterdammers clomped around in clogs, there were hundreds of windmills right in town. Now there are only half a dozen, two of which are worth visiting. The **De Gooyer,** Funenkade 7 (tram: 10 or 14), at Sarphatistraat, a former corn mill built in 1725, still towers over the Nieuwevaart canal northeast of Artis Zoo. In it is **Bierbrouwerij 't IJ** (see p. 244), a terrific microbrewery. A century older (1636), but a total rebuild job, the thatched **De Rieker,** Amsteldijk at De Borcht in the Amstelpark (bus: 62), was moved to its current site way out on the banks of the Amstel River. Now an elegant private house (not open to the public) it was originally built to drain the Rieker polder, a tract of low, reclaimed land a few miles south of Amsterdam. You've doubtless seen this mill in all those Rembrandt paintings and engravings you know by heart; just to make sure you don't miss the connection, there's a statue here of Rembrandt at work.

Modern Monuments

On Westermarkt (tram: 13, 14, or 17) is the world's first-ever monument to the gays and lesbians killed during World War II and to those persecuted down the ages. The **Homomonument** (1987), by sculptor Karin Daan, and formally titled *To Friendship,* consists of three pink triangular granite blocks (the color and shape of the badge the Nazis forced homosexuals to wear), that together form a larger triangular outline. One block, symbolizing the future, points to the Keizersgracht canal; a second, at ground level, points toward the nearby Anne Frank House—a bronze sculpture of Anne stands on the square; the third, a kind of plinth, points toward the offices of COC, a gay cultural organization.

An equally thought-provoking memorial honors another group of persecuted individuals—black African slaves, of whom the Dutch did their share of abducting, transporting to the Americas, and setting to unrequited labor. The pleasant but undistinguished surroundings of the **Oosterpark** (tram: 3 or 7), a 19th-century park (modeled after a pristine English landscape style) in Amsterdam-Oost (East), experienced quite a jolt in 2002 with the installation of the spectacular **Slavernijmonument (Slavery Monument).** The lengthy sculpture recounts in bronze a journey toward freedom. At the rear, a group of African men, women, and children trudge along, roped together. In the center, one of them passes under a winged arch and enters freedom. At the front, a large figure with outstretched arms greets those emerging from the arch.

NEIGHBORHOODS TO EXPLORE

All of Amsterdam is worth exploring—naturally, some parts more than others.

The Jordaan ★

Few traditional sights clutter the old Jordaan district that lies just west of the Canal Belt's northern reaches—though 800 of its buildings are protected monuments. But the area does provide an authentic taste of Old Amsterdam. The neighborhood of tightly packed houses and narrow streets and canals was built in the 17th century for craftsmen, tradesmen, and artists. Its name may have come from the French *jardin* (garden), from Protestant French Huguenot refugees who settled here in the late 17th century. Indeed, many streets and canals are named for flowers, trees, and plants. Some of today's streets used to be canals until they were filled in during the 19th century (there's talk of reversing that and bringing back some of the lost canals).

> ### Mirrors on the Walls
>
> The Dutch use the little mirrors you'll see on many house fronts to see from upper-story windows who's knocking at their door.

The neighborhood's modest nature persists even though renewal and gentrification has brought in an influx of offbeat boutiques, quirky stores, cutting-edge art galleries, and trendy restaurants. For a close encounter with the district's unconventional character, see "Walking Tour 3: The Jordaan," in chapter 8, p. 192.

The Red Light District

The warren of streets and old canals of the **Rosse Buurt (Red Light District),** around Oudezijds Achterburgwal and Oudezijds Voorburgwal—also known as **De Wallen (the Walls)** or **De Walletjes (the Little Walls)**—is on most people's sightseeing agenda for its open attitude to the world's oldest profession. This is one of the few traditional Amsterdam "industries" still practiced in its original setting, and the first guide to the district's peculiar attractions dates from the 17th century.

However, a visit to this area is not for everyone. If you're liable to be offended by the sex trade exposed in all its garish colors, don't go. If you do choose to go, exercise caution; the area is a center of crime, vice, and drugs. As always in Amsterdam, there's no need to exaggerate the risks. Plenty of tourists visit the Rosse Buurt and suffer nothing more serious than a come-on from one of the prostitutes. Stick to busy streets and be leery of pickpockets at all times. There can be a sinister air to the weird-looking men who gather on the canal bridges; there's a sadder aura around the "heroin whores" who wander the dark streets. Finally, do not take photographs of the women in the windows. Large, observant men are on the lookout, and they won't hesitate to throw your camera (and maybe your person) into the canal.

Still, it's extraordinary to view the prostitutes in leather and lace sitting in storefronts listening to their iPods as they knit or adjust their makeup, waiting patiently for customers. The district seems to reflect Dutch pragmatism; if you can't stop prostitution, you can at least confine it to a particular area and impose health, tax, and other regulations on it.

WHIPPED INTO shape

Back in the 17th century, the City Fathers were disposed to be strict with "fallen women"—when they weren't availing themselves of their services. Some were sent to the **Spinhuis,** a females-only corrections house on Spinhuissteeg, off Oudezijds Achterburgwal, just beyond the Red Light District's southern edge. Here they were returned to the straight and narrow path by a strict regimen of spinning cloth. A relief above the entrance shows women being whipped, accompanied by the inscription: *Schrik niet ik wreek geen quaat maar dwing tot goet. Straf is mijn hand maar lieflyk myn gemoet* (Cry not, I avenge no wrong but compel to the good. Stern is my hand but kind is my aim). The building now houses the University of Amsterdam's Faculty of Politics and Social and Cultural Studies.

The fact is that underneath its tacky glitter, the Red Light District contains some of Amsterdam's prettiest canals and loveliest old architecture, plus some excellent bars and restaurants, second-hand bookstores, and other specialty stores (not all of which aim at erogenous zones). To get there, take tram no. 4, 9, 14, 16, 24, or 25 to the Dam, then pass behind the Grand Hotel Krasnapolsky. See also "Walking Tour 2: The Old Center," in chapter 8, p. 186; and "The Red Light District," in chapter 10, which covers the district as an after-dark attraction.

The Jewish Quarter

Amsterdam was once renowned as the "Jerusalem of the West," and there remain mementos and memorials of what was a thriving Jewish community. For more than 350 years, the city was a center of Jewish life—you still hear locals calling the city Mokum, from the Hebrew word *makom,* meaning "sacred place"—and its Jewish community was a major contributor to the city's vitality and prosperity. The **Jodenbuurt (Jewish Quarter)** was centered on Waterlooplein and neighboring streets such as Jodenbreestraat (Broad Street of the Jews). In this area, they built their synagogues and held their market. Of the five synagogues built during the 17th and 18th centuries, only the **Portuguese Synagogue** (see below) continued to serve as a house of worship after the devastating depletion of the Jewish population during World War II.

The Jewish Quarter has changed almost beyond recognition since then. Wartime damage followed by postwar redevelopment eliminated much of its physical character. The Holocaust decimated most of the area's Jewish population, and wartime damage followed by postwar redevelopment eliminated much of its physical character.

Jodenbreestraat was for centuries the center of Amsterdam's Jewish life. Now, its north side consists of mostly modern buildings with little in the way of distinctive character. On the south side, though, at nos. 4–6, is the stellar **Museum Het Rembrandthuis** (p. 145). Across the handsome **Sint-Antoniesluis bridge,** on the south bank of Oude Schans canal, lies an island that from the 17th century until World War II was home to many Jewish diamond workshops and other small crafts houses. Walk a little way along Sint-Antoniesbreestraat, to no. 69, to view the magnificent **Huis De Pinto,** a mansion that dates from the early years of the 17th century. In 1651, it came into the possession of the Jewish businessman and scholar

Isaäc de Pinto, and later in the century was remodeled in the ornate Italian Renaissance style. It now houses a branch of the Amsterdam Public Library.

In the middle of **Waterlooplein,** the square that hosts the Waterlooplein Flea Market, are the city's modern opera and ballet house, the **Muziektheater** (p. 236), and the **Stadhuis (Town Hall).** You can assess the likelihood of getting your feet wet in Amsterdam, at the **Normaal Amsterdams Peil (Normal Amsterdam Level),** a fixed point against which experts measure sea level—NAP is Europe's standard for altitude measurements. Next to a bronze plaque in the passageway between the Muziektheater and the Town Hall are three acrylic columns filled with water. The first two show the current sea level at Vlissingen in the province of Zeeland and IJmuiden on the North Sea coast west of Amsterdam; the third, 4.6m (15 ft.) high, shows the high-water mark during the disastrous Zeeland floods of 1953. **Grand Café Dantzig aan de Amstel,** Zwanenburgwal 15 (✆ 020/620-9039), is a large, modern, trendy place built into a corner of the Stadhuis (City Hall) complex, with an alfresco terrace beside the Amstel River where you can soak up sunrays.

Also on Waterlooplein is the **Mozes en Aäronkerk (Moses and Aaron Church),** which started as a secret church for Catholics who were forbidden to worship in public when the Calvinists rose to power in the 16th century, and (on the corner of Zwanenburgwal) the **Monument Joods Verzet (Jewish Resistance Memorial),** a black marble monument to the Dutch Jews who engaged in armed struggle against the Nazi oppression during World War II.

Just before the **Blauwbrug** (Blue Bridge), look for the outline of **Megadlei Yethomin,** an orphanage established in 1836 for German and East European Jewish boys. During World War II, the boys were deported to Sobibor concentration camp. After the war, the orphanage reopened, this time as a home for boys who wanted to get to Israel; it successfully placed many orphans in Israel before closing in 1955. Only the building's outline remains today, as a memorial to the orphans and their caretaker who died in Sobibor. The rest was demolished in 1977 to make way for the Metro and, later, for the new Town Hall and the Muziektheater.

The district's main focal points are the **Portuguese Synagogue** (see p. 162) on Mr. Visserplein, and the **Joods Historisch Museum** (see p. 145) on Nieuwe Amstelstraat. Across the street from the main museum is the **Arsenal,** which served as a munitions storage space in the 19th century, and now forms part of the museum. On nearby Jonas Daniël Meijerplein, pause to view **De Dokwerker (The Dockworker;** 1952). This bronze statue by Mari Andriessen was erected in 1952 to commemorate the 1941 February Strike by Amsterdam workers protesting the Nazis' persecution of the city's Jews. The strike, one of the biggest collective anti-Nazi actions in all of occupied Europe, was ruthlessly suppressed.

Along Weesperstraat is a small garden, a resting spot that contains a monument to the Dutch people who protected their Jewish compatriots during World War II. The memorial, known as the **Monument van Joodse Erkentelijkheid (Monument of Jewish Gratitude;** 1950), is a white limestone altar, and has five reliefs of mourning men, women, and children.

A plaque at the offices of **Artis Zoo** (see p. 171) commemorates Jewish resistance fighters who attempted to destroy the city registers to prevent the Nazis from discovering how many Jews were in Amsterdam and where they lived. This brave effort could have kept thousands of Amsterdam Jews from dying in concentration camps. But tragically, the attempt failed and 12 resistance fighters were executed.

Only the shell remains of the **Hollandsche Schouwburg (Dutch Theater),** Plantage Middenlaan 24 (© **020/626-9945;** www.hollandscheschouwburg.nl; tram: 9 or 14). Behind the facade of this former Yiddish theater is a memorial plaza of grass and walkways. Nazis used the theater as an assembly point for Dutch Jews—60,000–80,000 of whom passed through here on their way to death camps. A granite column rising out of a Star of David emblem commemorates "those deported from here 1940–45." On a marble memorial, watched over by an eternal flame, are inscribed 6,700 family names of the 104,000 Dutch Jews who perished in the Holocaust. An educational exhibit shows how the Nazis gradually isolated Amsterdam's Jewish community before beginning to exterminate its members. The site is open daily from 11am to 4pm. Admission is free. Some deportees' children were able to sneak across the street to a kindergarten—these lucky ones were saved by residents in the attached houses. A plaque on the school building celebrates the children's escape. Opposite the theater, notice the bright primary colors of architect Aldo van Eyck's **Moederhuis** (1978), a residence for single mothers.

The **Verzetsmuseum Amsterdam (Resistance Museum)** at Plantage Kerklaan 61A (see p. 149) eerily evokes the dark years of Amsterdam's Nazi occupation and the slow but sure implementation of Hitler's "Final Solution" to rid Europe of Jews. Though really more like a large garden with benches, the small **Wertheimpark** on the corner of Plantage Parklaan and Plantage Middenlaan is a good place for a rest. At its heart is a memorial (1993) to Auschwitz victims by Dutch sculptor Jan Wolkers. Six large broken-seeming mirrors laid flat on the ground reflect a shattered sky and cover a buried urn containing ashes of those who died in the concentration camp. NOOIT MEER AUSCHWITZ (Never Again Auschwitz), reads the dedication. An information board lists in impersonal round numbers some of the Holocaust's gruesome statistics: Of Holland's 140,000 Jews, 107,000 were deported to concentration camps. Just 5,200 returned. One of those who perished (at Bergen-Belsen) was Anne Frank. At the park's far end, there's a street named after her.

The Waterfront ★★

Visitors suffering from a kind of linguistic seizure could be forgiven for wishing Amsterdam's waterfront had been given a different name. What to make of Het IJ? The first word is the neuter form of the word "the," and pronounced more or less as it looks. But IJ? (Yes, that is two upper-case letters.) *Idge? Eyedge?* Say *Aye,* as in "Aye aye, skipper," and you'll be close enough. The narrow ship channel takes its name from a river that used to flow into the Zuider Zee hereabout until, centuries ago, its course was washed away by an expanding sea. Then, last century, the Zuider Zee transformed into a freshwater lake called the IJsselmeer (after the IJssel River that still flows into it farther east).

Amsterdam's biggest redevelopment project is underway in the IJ channel's **Oostelijk Havengebied (Eastern Harbor),** once a major part of Amsterdam Port. City government touts the project as "a new life on the water." Java-Eiland, KNSM-Eiland, and other artificial islands and peninsulas have been cleared of most of their warehouses and other harbor installations. Modern housing and infrastructure take their place. A visit here is a good way to see how Amsterdam sees its future, away from its Golden Age heart.

A fast tram service (line 26) connects Centraal Station with the old Eastern Harbor's redeveloped districts along Het IJ. Among its stops are ones for the **Muziekgebouw aan 't IJ** and **Bimhuis** concert halls, the Passenger Terminal Amsterdam cruise-liner dock, and the Eastern Islands' new residential, shopping, and entertainment zones. The service goes out as far as the new IJburg suburb, on an artificial island in the IJsselmeer's southern reaches. See also **Science Center NEMO,** p. 163, and the **Scheepvaartmuseum (Maritime Museum),** p. 147.

Some of the redevelopment focus has switched to the area west of Centraal Station.

To get around in the harbor without treading water, see "Tour 4: The Waterfront," in chapter 8, p. 196.

SIGHTS OF RELIGIOUS SIGNIFICANCE

Religion has always been an important part of Amsterdam's history; hundreds of churches are testimony to the great variety of religious beliefs still alive—if not always thriving—in the city. Most can be visited during regular services; some have open doors during weekdays so that visitors may have a look.

In addition to the churches and a synagogue reviewed below, you can find information about the **Nieuwe Kerk (New Church)** under "The Dam," earlier in this chapter. The **Biblical Museum,** the **Jewish Historical Museum,** and the secret church **Our Lord in the Attic** are covered under "More Top Museums & Galleries," earlier in this chapter. For another secret church, in a building called **De Rode Hoed,** and for the city's medieval **Begijnhof,** look under "Historical Buildings & Monuments," earlier in this chapter.

Noorderkerk (North Church)   A Greek cross-shaped church, designed by Hendrick de Keyser and dating from 1620, Noorderkerk was built for the Jordaan's poor Calvinist faithful. The four triangular houses tucked into the cross's angles weren't part of de Keyser's original plan; architect Hendrick Staets, unwilling to see so much useful space go to waste, added them after de Keyser died in 1621. This is still a working church with an active congregation. A plaque on the facade recalls the 1941 strike protesting Nazi deportation of the city's Jews. Between May and September, for 15€, you can take in a classical music recital every Saturday at 2pm. A brief visit (when that's possible) and a turn around the outside should suffice.

Noordermarkt 44–48 (off Prinsengracht). *℄* **020/626-6436.** www.noorderkerk.org. Free admission. Mon 10:30am–12:30pm; Sat 11am–1pm; Sun (services) 10am and 7pm. Tram: 1, 2, 5, 13, or 17 to Martelaarsgracht; Stop/Go minibus.

Oude Kerk (Old Church) ★★   This triple-nave, late-Gothic church—its official name is Sint-Nicolaaskerk (St. Nicholas's Church), but nobody ever calls it that—was begun in 1250 and essentially completed with the extension of the bell tower in 1566. Then, in 1578, Protestant reformers destroyed much of its Catholic ornamentation. On the southern porch, to the right of the sexton's house, is a coat of arms belonging to Maximilian of Austria, who, with his son Philip, contributed to the porch's construction. Rembrandt's wife is entombed in vault 28K, which bears the simple inscription "Saskia Juni 1642." The church contains a magnificent Christian Müller organ (1728) that's regularly used for recitals. An inscription over the entrance to the marriage chapel warns all who enter: *'t is haest getrout dat lange rout (Marry in haste, repent at leisure)*. Nowadays, the pretty gabled almshouses around the Oude Kerk feature red-fringed windows through which can be seen the scantily clad ladies of the Red Light District. On a guided tour, climb the 70-m (230-ft.) church tower, which holds a carillon of 17th-century Hemony bells, for great views of Old Amsterdam.

Oudekerksplein 23 (at Oudezijds Voorburgwal). ℂ **020/625-8284** church; ℂ 020/689-2565 tower. www.oudekerk.nl. Church: Admission 7.50€ adults; 5.50€ seniors, students, and children 5-13; free for children 4 and under. Mon-Sat 11am-5pm; Sun 1-5:30pm. Tower: Admission 6€; minimum age 12. Sat-Sun 1-5pm; tours every 30 min. Metro: Nieuwmarkt.

Portugese Synagoge (Portuguese Synagogue)   Sephardic Jews fleeing Spain and Portugal during the 16th and early 17th centuries established a neighborhood east of the center known as the Jewish Quarter. In 1665, they built an elegant synagogue, modeled on the Temple in Jerusalem, within an existing courtyard facing what's now a busy traffic circle. The total cost of the magnificent building was 186,000 florins, a king's ransom in those days but a small price to pay for the Sephardic Jews, whose community could worship openly for the first time in 200 years. The building was restored in the 1950s, and today it looks essentially as it did almost 350 years ago, with the women's gallery supported by 12 stone columns to represent the Twelve Tribes of Israel, and the large, low-hanging brass chandeliers that together hold 1,000 candles, all of which are lighted for the private weekly services.

Mr. Visserplein 3 (at Waterlooplein). ℂ **020/624-5351**. www.esnoga.com. Admission 6.50€ adults, 5€ seniors and students, 4€ children 13-17, free for children 12 and under. Combined admission with the Jewish Historical Museum (see earlier in this chapter): 12€ adults, 6€ children 13-17, free for children 12 and under. Apr-Oct Sun-Fri 10am-4pm; Nov-Mar Sun-Thurs 10am-4pm, Fri 10am-2pm. Closed Jewish holidays. Tram: 9 or 14 to Mr. Visserplein.

Sint-Nicolaaskerk (St. Nicholas's Church)   Opened in 1887, the city's somewhat gloomy, neo-baroque main Catholic church has twin towers and a high domed cupola. At the heart of what was once the old harbor, it started out as a place of worship for seafarers (of whom St. Nicholas is the patron). Inside, murals illustrate themes from the saint's life; the 1345 Miracle of Amsterdam; and the execution of the Catholic martyrs of Gorcum (Gorinchem).

Prins Hendrikkade 73 (facing Centraal Station). ℂ **020/330-7812**. www.nicolaas-parochie.nl. Free admission. Mon and Sat noon-3pm; Tues-Fri 11am-4pm. Tram: 1, 2, 4, 5, 9, 13, 16, 17, 24, 25, or 26 to Centraal Station.

Westerkerk (West Church) ★   The Renaissance-style Westerkerk holds the remains of Rembrandt, his mistress Hendrickje Stoffels, and probably his son Titus, all in unmarked graves. It's also where, in 1966, Princess (now Queen) Beatrix and Prince Claus said their marriage vows. The church was begun in 1620 and opened in 1631, with Hendrick de Keyser as the initial designer, whose son Pieter took over after Hendrick's death in 1621. In the church's light and spacious interior is a fine organ.

Get Amsterdam's best views by climbing the 186-step stairway or taking the elevator to the top of the Westertoren, on a guided tour. The 85-m (277-ft.) church tower, nicknamed "Lange Jan" (Long John), is Amsterdam's tallest, providing a spectacular panoramic view of the city—and a 3-centimeter (1-in.) sway on a windy day. On its top is the Holy Roman Empire's blue, red, and gold imperial crown, a symbol bestowed on the then-Catholic city in 1489 by the Habsburg emperor Maximilian. The tower's carillon of 17th-century Hemony brothers bells is among the city's most lyrical.

Westermarkt. (© **020/624-7766** church; (© 020/689-2565 tower. www.westerkerk.nl. Church: Free admission. Apr–Sept Mon–Sat 11am–3pm. Tower: Admission 6€. Apr–Oct Mon–Sat 10am–5:30pm; tours every 30 min. Tram: 13, 14, or 17 to Westermarkt.

Zuiderkerk (South Church) Three of Rembrandt's children were buried here, in the city's first Protestant church, designed by Hendrick de Keyser and built between 1603 and 1614. In recent years, it's succumbed to a shortage of worshipers and today houses a permanent exhibit on modern urban planning, which shows where Amsterdam's headed and is well worth investing an hour or two in. You can climb the church tower, the Zuiderkerktoren, on a tour; its Hemony carillon still peals out in clear tones every hour, and the city carilloneur plays a 1-hour concert here on Thursdays at noon.

Zuiderkerkhof 72 (btw. Nieuwmarkt and Waterlooplein). (© **020/552-7987** church; (© 020/689-2565 tower. www.zuiderkerk.amsterdam.nl. Church: Free admission. Mon–Fri 9am–4pm; Sat noon–4pm; Tower: 6€ adults, 3€ children 6–12, free for children 5 and under. Apr–Sept Mon–Sat noon–4:30pm (every half-hour). Tram: 9 or 14 to Waterlooplein.

MULTIMEDIA ATTRACTIONS

Amsterdam is not only about history and heavy-duty culture. Here's a selection of places with a modern bent.

Heineken Experience Five minutes into the self-guided multimedia tour at Heineken's old Amsterdam brewery, I was already mentally pinning Frommer's "Overrated" icon to this review. Two things persuaded me not to: First, the further you go, the better it gets; second, the other visitors (mostly young males) were having a whale of a time. But admission is steep—even if you do get two "free" fills of Heineken beer and a keepsake Heineken glass. The experience unfolds inside former Heineken brewing facilities, which date from 1867. Before the brewery stopped functioning in 1988, it produced more than 100 million liters (26 million gal.) annually. Fermentation tanks, each capable of holding a million glassfuls of Heineken, are still there, along with multistory malt silos and all manner of vintage brewing equipment. You "meet" Dr. Elion, the 19th-century chemist who isolated the renowned Heineken "A" yeast, which gives the beer its taste. In one amusing attraction, you stand on a moving floor, face a large video screen, and get to see and feel what it's like to be a Heineken beer bottle—one of a half-million every hour—careening on a conveyor belt through a modern Heineken bottling plant.

> **Prohibition? No Thanks.**
>
> In April 1933, 100 gallons of beer from the Heineken brewery in Rotterdam arrived in Hoboken, New Jersey. This was the first legal shipment of beer to the U.S. in 13 years.

Stadhouderskade 78 (at Ferdinand Bolstraat). (© **020/523-9222.** www.heinekenexperience.com. Admission 15€; children 17 and under admitted only when accompanied by an adult. Daily 11am–7pm (last admission 5:30pm). Closed Jan 1, Apr 30, Dec 25 and 26. Tram: 16, 24, or 25 to Stadhouderskade.

Science Center NEMO ★ ☺ A fount of science and technology, NEMO is housed in a swooping modern building in the Eastern Dock, designed by Italian architect Renzo Piano. It seems to reproduce the graceful lines of an oceangoing ship. The center is a hands-on experience, through games, experiments, and demonstrations—

Amsterdam East Attractions

Artis Zoo **17**
De Dokwerker **8**
De Gooyer Windmill **18**
Flevopark **20**
Hermitage Amsterdam **10**
Hollandsche Schouwburg **16**
Hortus Botanicus **12**
Joods Historisch Museum **9**
Monument Joods Verzet **3**
Monument van Joodse Erkentelijkheid **11**
Mozes en Aäronkerk **6**
Museum Het Rembrandthuis **2**
Muziektheater/Stadhuis **4**
Oosterpark **21**
Portugese Synagoge **7**
Scheepvaartmuseum **14**
Sint-Antoniesluis bridge **1**
Tropenmuseum **19**
Verzetsmuseum Amsterdam **15**
Waterlooplein markt Flea Market **5**
Wertheimpark **13**

Sail Ahoy

Moored alongside NEMO is a full-size replica of the United East India Company (V.O.C.) merchant ship *Amsterdam,* which foundered off Hastings, England, in 1749 on its maiden voyage to Indonesia. The replica was moved here from its usual berth across the water at the temporarily closed Scheepvaartmuseum (Maritime Museum; see "More Top Museums & Galleries," earlier in this chapter), which is due to reopen in 2011. The ship has the same opening hours as NEMO. Admission is 6€, and free for children 3 and under.

the motto is: *Forbidden Not to Touch.* Admission, though not exactly cheap, is worth it, and most kids will want to spend hours here.

You'll learn how to steer a supertanker safely into port, boost your earnings on the floor of the New York Stock Exchange, execute a complicated surgical procedure, blow a soap bubble large enough to stand inside, boil potatoes, and play the drums. One exhibit even tries to help you understand the basis of sexual attraction. Questions are asked and answered: Why is water clear but the ocean blue? Why does toothpaste contain sugar? In NEMO's digital world, don a virtual-reality helmet and play with images, sounds, and your own imported material. Internet-linked computers on every floor provide additional insights, as do workshops and theater and video productions.

The broad, sloping stairway to NEMO's roof is an attraction unto itself, a place to hang out and (when the sun cooperates) soak up some rays. At the top, you're 30m (98 ft.) above the IJ waterway, with fine views over the city's redeveloped harbor.

Oosterdokskade 2 (off Prins Hendrikkade, over the south entrance to the IJ Tunnel). © **020/531-3233.** www.e-nemo.nl. Admission 13€, free for children 3 and under. July–Aug daily 10am–5pm; Sept–June Tues–Sun 10am–5pm (also Mon during school vacations). Closed Jan 1, Apr 30, and Dec 25. Bus: 22, 42, or 43 to Kadijksplein.

MINOR MUSEUMS

The following is only a sampling of the city's many small museums. See the world through cats' eyes in sculptures, paintings, and prints at the **KattenKabinet (Cat Cabinet),** Herengracht 497 (© **020/626-5378;** www.kattenkabinet.nl; tram: 16, 24, or 25). The museum is open Monday to Friday from 10am to 4pm, and Saturday, Sunday, and holidays from noon to 5pm (closed Jan 1, Apr 30, and Dec 25, 26, and 31). Admission is 5€ for adults, 2.50€ for children ages 4 to 12, and free for children 3 and under.

In Amsterdam, no one ever tosses away an old boat. Some 2,400 legally occupied houseboats float on the city's waters—but you won't be able to go aboard most of them unless you know the owner. The *Hendrika Maria,* a former commercial sailing barge built in 1914, is an exception. It's now the **Woonbootmuseum (Houseboat Museum),** facing Prinsengracht 296 (© **020/427-0750;** www.houseboatmuseum. nl; tram: 13, 14, or 17), at Elandsgracht. Visit the original deckhouse where the skipper and his family lived, the cupboard bed in which they slept, and the cargo hold, now equipped as remarkably spacious and comfortable living quarters. You can go aboard March to October, Tuesday to Sunday from 11am to 5pm; and November, December, and February, Friday to Sunday from 11am to 5pm; it's closed most of

January, April 30, and December 25, 26, and 27. Admission is 3.50€ for adults, and 2.75€ for children under 1.52m (5 ft.).

The **Amsterdam Tulip Museum,** Prinsengracht 112 (© **020/421-0095;** www.amsterdamtulipmuseum.com; tram: 13, 14, or 17), at Egelantiersgracht, tells the history of Holland's fascination with a flower. It takes in the bizarre speculative bubble during the 17th century known as *Tulipomania,* when fortunes were won and lost on the price of a handful of rare bulbs. You can spend a far smaller fortune to purchase bulbs in the museum shop.

Surely the most rollicking museum in town is the **Pianola Museum,** Westerstraat 106 (© **020/627-9624;** www.pianola.nl; tram: 3 or 10), at Tweede Boomdwarsstraat in the Jordaan. Aficionados congregate in a front-room brown cafe to sip coffee and to listen to, and sing along with, vintage tunes played on some of the three dozen old player-pianos and automated music machines—around half of them still in working order—in this private collection. Among some 14,000 "recordings" on perforated-paper rolls are works by Debussy and Gershwin. The museum is open Sunday from 2 to 5pm, and for groups by appointment. Admission is 5€ for adults, 4€ for seniors, 3€ for children ages 5 to 12, and free for children 4 and under.

Geels & Co., a coffee-roasting and tea-importing store in the Red Light District (see "Shopping A to Z," in chapter 9), has been around for more than a century. It has a marvelous collection of antique grinders, roasters, tea canisters, and all sorts of coffee-and-tea–brewing paraphernalia in its small, atmospheric upstairs **Koffie en Thee Museum (Coffee and Tea Museum),** Warmoesstraat 67 (© **020/624-0683;** www.geels.nl; tram: 4, 9, 14, 16, 24, or 25), at Oude Brugsteeg. The museum is open Saturday 2 to 4:30pm, and for groups by appointment. Admission is free.

If pipes are your thing, check out the **Pijpenkabinet (Pipe Cabinet),** Prinsengracht 488 (© **020/421-1779;** www.pijpenkabinet.nl; tram: 1, 2, 5, 13, 14, or 17), at Leidsestraat. Housed at Smokiana, a pipe museum-store with a remarkable collection of tribal, antique, and ultra-modern puffing equipment (p. 227), the Pijpenkabinet is open Wednesday to Saturday from noon to 6pm, and by appointment. Admission is 5€.

A boutique known for selling modern, fashionable (and occasionally bizarre) eyeglasses is the **Brilmuseum (Eyeglass Museum),** Gasthuismolensteeg 7 (© **020/421-2414;** www.brilmuseumamsterdam.nl; tram: 1, 2, 5, 13, 14, or 17), between Singel and Herengracht. It lives up to its billing by displaying a collection of antique eyeglasses and taking you on an eye-opening tour through 700 years of impaired-vision aids. It's quite a spectacle. It's open Wednesday to Friday from noon to 5:30pm, and Saturday from noon to 5pm; admission is free.

A Moving Museum

The superannuated streetcars of the **Electrische Museumtramlijn Amsterdam (Amsterdam Electric Tramline Museum),** Amstelveenseweg 264 (© **020/673-7538;** www.museumtramline.org; tram: 16), shake, rattle, and roll back and forth between Amsterdam's old Haarlemmermeer rail station (near the Olympic Stadium) and suburban Amstelveen. Most of the trams are at least 50 years old, and come from Amsterdam, The Hague, Berlin, Vienna, Prague, and other cities. If you feel like a walk in the woods, get out along the way in the Amsterdamse Bos (see "Green Amsterdam," below). Trams run July to October, on Sundays from 11am to 5pm (Aug also Wed 1–5pm). Round-trip tickets are 4€ for adults, 2€ for seniors and children ages 4 to 11, and free for children 3 and under.

GREEN AMSTERDAM

Amsterdam is not a notably green city, particularly in the Old Center, where the canal water is the most obvious and visible encroachment of the natural world. Still, the city has around 30 parks.

Vondelpark ★★

The famous Vondelpark is named after Amsterdam poet and playwright Joost van den Vondel (1587–1689), who's honored with a sculpture in the park. This mosaic of lakes, meadows, and woodland contains 120 tree varieties that include catalpa, chestnut, cypress, oak, and poplar. Vondelpark (tram: 1, 2, 3, 5, or 12) lies generally southwest of Leidseplein, and has entrances dotted all around; the busiest is on Stadhouderskade, adjacent to Leidseplein, where a sculpture of the *Maid of Amsterdam,* a symbol of the city, sits over the gate.

Some days, there's so much pot smoke on the air here that the trees likely are quite a bit higher than they seem. Otherwise, Vondelpark is a fairly standard park, the site of skateboarding, Frisbee-flipping, in-line skating, model-boat sailing, pickup soccer, softball, and basketball, smooching in the undergrowth, parties, picnics, and arts-and-crafts markets. Topless sunbathing has gone out of fashion, however. Best of all, it's free, or as the Dutch say, *gratis.* Also free are the many concerts, theater and dance performances, and all kinds of other events, including plenty for children, at the **Vondelpark Openluchttheater (Open-Air Theater).** These run from June to mid-August.

Rent in-line skates from **De Vondeltuin Rent A Skate,** Amstelveenseweg entrance ((C) **06/2157-5885;** www.skatedokter.nl). Including protective gear, it's 5€ for the first hour and 2.50€ for each subsequent hour, or 10€ for a full day (11am–11pm; but it closes earlier if the weather is bad), for both adults and children. Bring ID and leave 20€ as a refundable guarantee.

Should toting along a picnic bag not be your thing, quiet hunger at the casual and superb **Vertigo** (p. 131) on the edge of the park. Or, visit the even more casual **Het Blauwe Theehuis,** Vondelpark 5 ((C) **020/662-0254**), at the park's center. This functionalist-style circular cafe on two levels, with a park-level terrace and an upstairs balcony terrace, is good at any time of day and a fine place for indulging in a continental breakfast of coffee and croissant. At night, there's dancing and live music.

Amsterdamse Bos (Amsterdam Wood) ★

To enjoy fresh air and wide expanses of scenery, head out to this giant park in the southern suburb of Amstelveen. This is nature on the city's doorstep, and covers some 10 sq. km (4 sq. miles). The park was laid out during the Depression years as a public works project. By now, the woodlands, grasslands, moors, and marshes, along with their birds, insects, and small animals (and a herd of Highland cattle to keep the moors in shape), are firmly established. The best way to get to the Amsterdamse Bos from the city center is to take bus no. 170 or 172 from outside Centraal Station. The Amsterdamse Bos is open 24 hours; admission is free.

At the entrance on Amstelveenseweg, stop by the **Bezoekerscentrum (Visitor Center),** Bosbaanweg 5 ((C) **020/545-6100;** www.amsterdamsebos.nl), where you can trace the park's history, learn about its wildlife, and pick up a park map. The center is open daily (except Dec 25–26) from noon to 5pm, and admission is free.

Across the way is a bicycle rental shop (© **020/644-5473**; www.amsterdamsebos fietsverhuur.nl), open April through October, with fees starting at 10€ per day.

Then follow the path to a long stretch of water called the **Bosbaan,** a 2km (1¼-mile) competition-rowing course. Overlooking the finishing line, and with a great terrace beside the water, is the fine **Grand-Café De Bosbaan** (© **020/404-4869;** www. debosbaan.nl). Beyond the course's western end is **Boerderij Meerzicht** (© **020/679-2744;** www.boerderijmeerzicht.nl), a restaurant that sells great Dutch pancakes. It also has peacocks wandering around freely and a playground for kids. South of the course is a big pond, the **Grote Vijver,** where you can rent rowboats and pedal-boats, and the **Openluchttheater (Open-Air Theater),** where performances are presented on many summer evenings. The Japan Women's Club donated the 400 cherry trees of the **Kersenbloesempark (Cherry Blossom Park)** in 2000 to mark 400 years of cultural ties between the Netherlands and Japan.

Horseback riding through the Amsterdamse Bos is available from **De Amsterdamse Manege,** Nieuwe Kalfjeslaan 25 (© **020/643-1342;** www.deamsterdam semanege.nl).

More Parks

After Vondelpark, the city's other parks are fairly tame, but the following still make pleasant escapes on a warm summer day: **Sarphatipark,** 2 blocks behind the Albert Cuyp Markt in South Amsterdam; **Beatrixpark,** adjacent to the RAI Convention and Exhibition Center; **Rembrandtpark** and **Erasmuspark** in the west city; **Martin Luther Kingpark,** beside the Amstel River; **Oosterpark;** and East Amsterdam's **Flevopark,** which has two swimming pools.

A Colorful Garden

Hortus Botanicus (Botanical Garden) ★   The Botanical Garden, established here in 1682 (having been founded in 1638 in another location as an apothecaries' garden), is a medley of color and scent, with some 250,000 flowers and 115,000 plants and trees of 8,000 different varieties. It owes its origins to the treasure-trove of tropical plants the Dutch found in their exotic colonies, and its contemporary popularity to the Dutch love affair with flowers. Highlights include the Semicircle, which reconstructs part of the original 1682 design; the Mexico–California Desert House; the Palm House, home to one of the world's oldest palm trees; and the Tri-Climate House, which displays tropical, subtropical, and desert plants.

Plantage Middenlaan 2A (near Artis Zoo). © **020/625-9021.** www.dehortus.nl. Admission 7.50€ adults, 3.50€ seniors and children 5–14, free for children 4 and under. Feb–June and Sept–Nov Mon–Fri 9am–5pm, Sat–Sun and holidays 10am–5pm; July–Aug Mon–Fri 9am–9pm, Sat–Sun and holidays

---

📷 **Market Makers**

Amsterdam has more than 50 outdoor markets every week. Some are permanent or semipermanent, and others just pass through. For details, see "Street Markets," in chapter 9, but three you shouldn't miss are the floating **Bloemenmarkt (Flower Market)** on Singel, the **Waterloopleinmarkt Flea Market** on Waterlooplein, and the **Albert Cuypmarkt,** on Albert Cuypstraat.

10am–9pm; Dec–Jan Mon–Fri 9am–4pm, Sat–Sun and holidays 10am–4pm. Closed Jan 1 and Dec 25. Tram: 9 or 14 to Plantage Middenlaan.

OFFBEAT & ALTERNATIVE AMSTERDAM

Amsterdam's streets constitute an offbeat and alternative spectacle all by themselves. But you can also explore sex in the city, bizarre museums, and creations so ugly they could be modern-art masterpieces.

Erotic Museum   As its name suggests, this museum presents an allegedly artistic vision of eroticism; it focuses on prints and drawings, including some by John Lennon. There's a replica of a Red Light District alley, and an extensively equipped S&M playroom, both of which are rather antiseptic and serious. The only humorous note is an X-rated cartoon depicting some of the things Snow White apparently got up to with the Seven Dwarfs that Walt never told us about. Considering all this, it's ironic that the legend on the building's 1685 gable stone reads: *God is myn burgh* (God is my citadel).

Oudezijds Achterburgwal 54 (Red Light District). ✆ **020/624-7303.** www.janot.com. Admission 7€. Sun–Thurs 11am–1am; Fri–Sat 11am–2am. Tram: 4, 9, 14, 16, 24, 25, or 26 to the Dam.

Hash Marihuana & Hemp Museum ★   Well, it wouldn't really be Amsterdam, would it, without its fascination with intoxicating weeds? This museum will teach you everything you ever wanted to know, and much you didn't, about hash, marijuana, and related products. The museum does not promote drug use but aims to make you better informed before deciding whether to light up and, of course, whether to inhale. One way it does so is by having a cannabis garden in the joint . . . sorry, on the premises. Plants at various stages of development fill the air with an unmistakable, heady, resinous fragrance. And hemp, not plastic, could be the future if the exhibit on the plant's multifarious uses through the ages is anything to go by. Some exhibits shed light on cannabis's medicinal use, while others focus on hemp's use as a natural fiber. Among several notable artworks in the museum's collection is one from which the museum takes a proprietary satisfaction: David Teniers the Younger's painting, *Hemp-Smoking Peasants in a Smoke House* (1660).

Oudezijds Achterburgwal 148 (Red Light District). ✆ **020/624-8926.** www.hashmuseum.com. Admission 9€ adults, free for children 12 and under. Daily 10am–11pm. Closed Jan 1, Apr 30, and Dec 25. Tram: 4, 9, 14, 16, 24, or 25 to the Dam.

Sexmuseum Amsterdam   Behind its faux-marble facade, this museum isn't as sleazy as you might expect, apart from one room covered with straight-up pornography. Otherwise, presentation tends toward the tongue-in-cheek, and the place seems to be fine with its half-million annual visitors. Exhibits include erotic prints and drawings, and trinkets like tobacco boxes decorated with naughty pictures. Teenage visitors seem to find the whole place vastly amusing, judging by the giggling fits at the showcases. Spare a thought for the models of early erotic photography—slow film speeds in those days made for uncomfortably long posing times!

Damrak 18 (near Centraal Station). ✆ **020/622-8376.** www.sexmuseumamsterdam.com. Admission 4€ from age 16 only. Daily 9:30am–11:30pm. Tram: 1, 2, 4, 5, 9, 13, 16, 17, 24, 25, or 26 to Centraal Station.

Torture Museum   You enter through a gloomy tunnel, and emerge with a new appreciation of why the framers of the U.S. Constitution outlawed cruel and unusual punishment. Yet one suspects the motives of the Torture Museum—and its visitors?—are not purely educational. There's a terrible fascination with devices such as the Inquisition chair, the guillotine, and assorted grotesque implements of torture, punishment, and "redemption" favored by civil and ecclesiastic authorities in times not-so-far gone, if gone at all.

Singel 449 (at the Flower Market). ℂ **020/320-6642.** www.torturemuseum.com. Admission 7.50€ adults, 4€ children 11 and under. Daily 10am–11pm. Tram: 1, 2, or 5 to Koningsplein.

CONTEMPORARY GALLERIES

Visit the **Stedelijk Museum** (p. 148) for the mother of all Amsterdam modern art collections. But the Stedelijk's mission has been modified to focus more on exhibiting existing works by big names in the genre. The art galleries reviewed below aim to give new talent space to develop and be seen.

De Appel   Named after Amsterdam Cobra artist Karel Appel, this center for contemporary art provides cutting-edge artists, both known and unknown, with space for exhibits, projects, and research. Six yearly presentations of solo or group work are backed up by interaction with the artists through lectures, discussions, and video presentations.

Nieuwe Spiegelstraat 10 (off Keizersgracht). ℂ **020/625-5651.** www.deappel.nl. Admission 7€ adults, free for visitors 18 and under. Tues–Sun 11am–6pm. Closed Apr 30, Dec 25 and 26. Tram: 16, 24, or 25 to Keizersgracht.

Huis Marseille ★   The city's top international photography venue is in a monumental canal-house mansion, the Huis Marseille. Vast display rooms on four floors, renovated and restored to their 17th-century glory, showcase work by international talents. Shows change quarterly, at the beginning of March, June, September, and December. Even if you're not a shutterbug fan, the house alone is worth the visit. French merchant Isaac Focquier built it in 1665 with proceeds from a fortune-making cargo he sailed from Marseilles to Amsterdam. Of note are its period interior, a facade graced by a classical neck gable, and a stone relief of Marseilles with the city's name inscribed in gold letters below.

Keizersgracht 401 (at Leidsegracht). ℂ **020/531-8989.** www.huismarseille.nl. Admission 5€ adults, 3€ students, free for children 17 and under. Tues–Sun 11am–6pm. Closed Jan 1, Apr 30, and Dec 25. Tram: 1, 2, or 5 to Keizersgracht.

SMBA   An initiative by the modern-art Stedelijk Museum, this gallery was described in a Dutch newspaper as a "hatchery for young artistic talent," particularly from Amsterdam. Exhibits change constantly, but the works are always by promising young artists who embrace painting, sculpture, video, installations, or performance art.

Rozenstraat 59 (off Prinsengracht). ℂ **020/422-0471.** www.smba.nl. Free admission. Tues–Sun 11am–5pm. Closed Jan 1, Apr 30, and Dec 25. Tram: 13, 14, or 17 to Westermarkt.

ESPECIALLY FOR KIDS

Kids may get bored in Amsterdam's art museums, but they're likely to be interested in the **Anne Frankhuis** (see "The Big Three," earlier in this chapter). At **Tropenmuseum Junior,** Linnaeusstraat 2 (ℂ **020/568-8233;** www.tropenmuseum.nl; tram: 9, 10, or 14), a section of the **Tropenmuseum** (p. 148), kids learn about exotic tropical countries and their people through stories, songs, dances, games, and paintings. The

Science Center NEMO (p. 163) does a good job of appealing to the inner nerd. **Madame Tussauds** (p. 151) is always fun for kids, though if they're too young, they could be frightened by the wax statues.

Children can be amateur farmers for a while at **Geitenboerderij Ridammerhoeve,** Nieuwe Meerlaan 4 (© 020/645-5034; www.geitenboerderij.nl; bus: 167 or 170), inside the Amsterdamse Bos (p. 167). They get to feed 150 goats and lambs (along with chickens, a calf or two, and a few potbelly hogs); clean coops and pens; milk a goat; bottle-feed baby animals; and maybe even, between the months of January and April, be lucky enough to see kid goats being born. On Saturdays, they can watch goat's milk being turned into cheese. The farm is open Wednesday to Monday from 10am to 5pm; admission is free.

Before taking the kids back to the hotel for a nap, take them out to the tiny **Kinderboerderij De Dierencapel,** Bickersgracht 207 (© 020/420-6855; bus: 18, 21, or 22), an urban petting zoo in the Western Islands neighborhood, west of Centraal Station. Endearing piglets, kids (of the goat species), lambs, chickens, ducks, and rabbits nibble, root, and peck along the banks of the Bickersgracht canal; there's a play area too. It's not a bad place to bring a picnic when the weather's fine. The petting zoo is open Tuesday to Sunday from 9am to 5pm; admission is free.

Equally entertaining is **Kinderboerderij De Pijp,** Lizzy Ansinghstraat 82 (© 020/ 664-8303; www.kinderboerderijdepijp.nl; tram: 12 or 25), a children's farm off Ferdinand Bolstraat in the down-at-the-heels De Pijp (the Pipe) urban district south of the center. Here, in addition to the animals mentioned above, kids can get close to donkeys, ponies, peacocks, and turkeys. The farm is open Monday to Friday from 11am to 5pm, and Saturday to Sunday from 1 to 5pm; admission is free.

A Great Zoo

Artis Zoo ★★ ☺ If you're at a loss for what to do with the kids, Artis is a safe bet—more than a million visitors a year agree. Established in 1838, the oldest zoo in the Netherlands houses more than 6,000 animals of 1,400 species. Of course, you'll find the usual tigers, lions, giraffes, wolves, leopards, elephants, camels, monkeys, penguins, and peacocks no self-respecting zoo can do without. The African residents even stroll around on a miniature savanna. Yet there's also much more, for no extra charge. There's the excellent Planetarium (closed Mon mornings), a Geological and Zoological Museum, an Insectarium, and a Butterfly Garden. The Aquarium, built in 1882 and renovated in the late 1990s, is superbly presented, particularly the sections about the Amazon River, coral reefs, and Amsterdam's own canals. Finally, there's a children's farm, where kids can help tend to the needs of resident Dutch species, including moorland sheep, long-haired Veluwe goats, and tufted ducks. To rest for a while, dine at Artis Restaurant.

Plantage Kerklaan 38-40 (at Plantage Middenlaan). © **020/523-3400.** www.amsterdamzoo.nl. Admission 19€ adults, 17€ seniors, 15€ children 3-9, free for children 2 and under. Apr-Oct daily 9am-6pm (Sat June-Aug to sunset); Nov-Mar daily 9am-5pm. Tram: 9 or 14 to Plantage Kerklaan.

ORGANIZED TOURS

A convincing case could be made for the proposition that "disorganized tours"—making it up as you go along—are a better way of getting to the inner core of the Amsterdam experience. But there's no lack of choice or ingenuity among off-the-peg offerings.

Canal-Boat Cruise ★★

Amsterdam's 17th-century Golden Age becomes a vivid reality as you glide through the waterways that were largely responsible for those years of prosperity. You view the canal houses from canal level, just as they were meant to be seen. This is also the best way to see Amsterdam's large and busy harbor. Yes, you have to smile inanely for your boarding picture and sit through a thumbnail-sketch history in several different languages. No matter. The canals are Amsterdam's best starting point. Amsterdammers might scoff as they watch fleets of glass-topped boats prowling around, but secretly, they're proud of everything you will see. "I live here," you can almost hear them thinking. "All this belongs to me."

A typical canal tour-boat itinerary includes Centraal Station, the Haarlemmersluis floodgates (used in the nightly canal flushings), the Cat Boat (a houseboat with a permanent population of some 100 wayward felines), and the city's narrowest building, as well as one of the largest houses still in private hands. You'll also see the official residence of the *burgemeester* (mayor), at Herengracht 502, on the "Golden Bend" (traditionally the best address in the city), many picturesque bridges, including the famous Magere Brug (Skinny Bridge) over the Amstel, and the harbor. While on the canal-boat tour, take note of attractions you'd like to see up close later.

Trips last about an hour and depart at regular intervals from *rondvaart* (excursion) piers in key locations around town. The majority of launches are docked along Damrak and Prins Hendrikkade near Centraal Station, on Rokin near Muntplein, and at Leidseplein. Tours leave every 15 to 30 minutes during summer (9am–9pm), and every 45 to 60 minutes in winter (10am–5pm). Prices vary from company to company, but a basic 1-hour tour is around 10€ to 13€ for adults, 5€ to 7€ for children ages 4 to 12, and free for children 3 and under.

The canal tour-boat lines are **Amsterdam Canal Cruises** (☎ 020/626-5636; www.amsterdamcanalcruises.nl); **Canal Company** (☎ 0900/333-4442; www.canal. nl); **Holland International** (☎ 020/625-3035; www.hir.nl); **Gray Line** (☎ 020/ 623-4208; www.graylineamsterdam.com); **Rederij Boekel** (☎ 020/612-9905; www.rederijkooij.nl); **Rederij Hof van Holland** (☎ 020/623-7122; www.rederij kooij.nl); **Rederij Lovers** (☎ 020/530-5412; www.lovers.nl); **Reederij P. Kooij** (☎ 020/623-3810; www.rederijkooij.nl); **Rederij Plas** (☎ 020/624-5606; www. rederijplas.nl); and **Blue Boat Company** (☎ 020/679-1370; www.blueboat.nl).

Some lines offer specialized tours and services. These include the **Hop On Hop Off Museum Line** and the **Canal Bus** (see "On the Water" under "Getting Around," in chapter 3), the **Artis Zoo Express** (which plies a regular furrow between Centraal Station and the Artis Zoo), cruises amid the Eastern Islands' modern architecture, Red Light District cruises, dinner cruises, jazz cruises, candlelight cruises with wine and cheese, night cruises, and more. See "A Dinner Cruise," in chapter 6, and "More Evening Entertainment," in chapter 10, for information on after-dark tours.

Water Bikes ★

A water bike is a boat you pedal with your feet. These craft seat two or four people and are rentable from **Canal Bike** (☎ 0900/333-4442; www.canal.nl). Amsterdammers look down their tolerant noses at water bikes. On the other hand, tourists love the things. No prizes for guessing who has more fun. Your water bike, also known as a *pedalo,* comes with a detailed map. It's great fun in sunny weather, and still doable

BIKING ON THE water

A suggested tour by water bike: Start at the Canal Bike mooring on Prinsengracht (at Westermarkt). Pedal south along Prinsengracht, past Lauriergracht, Looiersgracht, and Passeerdersgracht, perhaps diverting into one or more of these quiet side canals if you fancy a closer look at their leafy linings. At Leidsegracht, go straight ahead under the Leidsestraat bridge until you come to Spiegelgracht, where you turn right. Continue to the end, then turn left under the bridge into Lijnbaansgracht.

Turn right at the first corner into a narrow connecting canal that merges with Singelgracht in front of the Rijksmuseum. Go right along this canal, which is bordered by overhanging trees and the back gardens of waterside villas. You pass the Holland Casino Amsterdam, Leidseplein, and the American Hotel.

Keep going, past the Bellevue Theater, and then turn right into Leidsegracht, which brings you back to Prinsengracht and the long home stretch back to Westermarkt.

when it rains; boats can be covered with a rain shield. But they don't go very fast and it can get tiring. In summer, rent a water bike for evening rambles, when the canals are illuminated and your bike is kitted out with its own Chinese lantern.

Moorings are on Prinsengracht, beside the Anne Frankhuis (tram: 13, 14, or 17); on Singelgracht, a few steps from Leidseplein (tram: 1, 2, 5, 7, or 10) and next to the Rijksmuseum (tram: 7 or 10); and on Keizersgracht at Leidsestraat (tram: 1, 2, or 5). You can rent a water bike at one mooring and leave it at another. The canals get busy with tour boats and other small vessels, so proceed carefully, particularly when going under bridges. Bikes can be rented daily from 10am to 10pm in summer, and to 7pm during other seasons. The cost is 8€ per person hourly for one or two people and 7€ per person hourly for three or four people. You need to leave a deposit of 50€. See "Biking on the Water," below, for a suggested tour.

By Vintage Boat

Using antique IJ passenger ferryboats from 1927, the **Historic Ferry** (© **0900/423-1100;** www.museum-ijveren-amsterdam.nl) takes a 2-hour trip through the eastern harbor and along the IJ channel, with stops at several places where you can disembark (and pick up a later boat if you want). The ferry departs from dock 14 behind Centraal Station. It operates Easter to October, on Sundays and some other days, with departures at 11:30am, 1:30pm, and 3:30pm. Tickets are 5€ for adults, 3€ children ages 4 to 11, and free for children 3 and under. On Saturday, there's a longer cruise (1½ hr. each way) to Fort Pampus, and one that's 2 hours each way to allow time to tour this old coastal fortification on the IJsselmeer.

By Bicycle ★

You'll look pretty conspicuous taking one of the guided tours offered by **Yellow Bike,** Nieuwezijds Kolk 29, off Nieuwezijds Voorburgwal (© **020/620-6940;** www.yellow bike.nl; tram: 1, 2, 5, 13, or 17). Why? Because you'll be cycling on a yellow bike along with a dozen other people also on yellow bikes. But you get a close encounter with Amsterdam or its nearby countryside. There are multiple tour options, with the shortest (2 hr.) costing 19€.

Mike's Bike Tours, Kerkstraat 123 (© **020/622-7970;** www.mikesbiketours amsterdam.com), offers tours of 2½–3 hours around the canals in town, plus a ride outside the city to see windmills, a cheese farm, and a clog factory. The cost is 18€ for adults, and 16€ for seniors and students; there's a reduction of 5€ if you bring your own bike. March to November, meet daily at 4pm near the reflecting pool behind the Rijksmuseum (tram: 2 or 5); December to February, you need to book in advance (minimum three people).

By Bus

A quick bus tour is a good way to get going on sightseeing in a strange city, and though a boat tour on Amsterdam's canals is a pertinent alternative, you might want to get your bearings on land as well. A basic 2½-hour bus tour is around 20€; on most tours, children ages 4 to 13 are charged half-fare, and children 3 and under go free. Itineraries vary from line to line, but a typical one might include the Royal Palace, the Mint Tower, the flower market, the old Jewish Quarter, the Waterlooplein flea market, the Museum Quarter, the Jordaan, the Westerkerk, the harbor, the Red Light District, a windmill, a visit to a diamond factory, and shopping and entertainment areas. Good sightseeing lines are **Keytours,** Paulus Potterstraat 8 (© **020/305-5333;** www.keytours.nl), and **Lindbergh,** Damrak 26 (© **020/622-2766;** www.lindbergh.nl).

These and other lines provide a variety of half-day and full-day tours into surrounding areas, particularly between April and October, and special excursions at tulip time and at the height of the summer season. Rates vary by company and tour, but typical half-day tours begin around 22€; full-day tours cost around 48€; children ages 4 to 13 are generally charged half-fare, and children 3 and under go free.

On Foot

Though you could see most of Amsterdam's important sights in one long walking tour, it's best to break the city into shorter walks. Luckily, the **VVV Amsterdam** tourist office has done that for you. For 3€, buy a brochure outlining one of three walking tours: City Center, Jewish Amsterdam, and the Jordaan. A fourth brochure, which costs 1€, covers the Pijp district.

Many companies offer specialized walking tours. **Let's Go** (© **036/545-0080;** www.letsgo-amsterdam.com) offers a range of 90-minute guided walks that cost around 15€ per head..

By Horse & Carriage

These romantic, kid-friendly vehicles run by **Karos** (© **020/691-3478;** www.karos. nl) depart from just outside the Royal Palace on the Dam for traipses through the Old City, along the canals, and into the Jordaan. Tours operate April to October, daily from 11am to 6pm (to 7pm in July–Aug), and on a limited schedule in winter. Rides are 35€ for 20 minutes, 45€ for 30 minutes, and 65€ for 45 minutes.

Diamond Tours

Visitors to Amsterdam during the 1950s and 1960s, when the diamond business was booming, were able to go to Amsterdam's diamond-cutting factories and take tours through their workrooms. Now you'll be lucky to see one lone polisher working at a small wheel set up in the back of a jewelry store or in the lobby of a factory building.

Never mind, you still can get an idea of how a diamond is cut and polished. You need no special directions or instructions to find this sightseeing activity; signs all over town direct you to diamond-cutting demonstrations.

Amsterdam's major diamond factories and showrooms are **Amsterdam Diamond Center,** Rokin 1, just off the Dam (✆ **020/624-5787;** www.amsterdamdiamond center.nl; tram: 4, 9, 14, 16, 24, or 25), **Coster Diamonds,** Paulus Potterstraat 2–8, near the Rijksmuseum (✆ **020/676-2222;** www.costerdiamonds.com; tram: 2 or 5), and **Gassan Diamonds,** Nieuwe Uilenburgerstraat 173–175 (✆ **020/622-5333;** www.gassandiamonds.com; Metro: Waterlooplein).

STAYING ACTIVE

Should a steady diet of Indonesian *rijsttafels,* brown-cafe beers and *jenevers,* and exotic smokes in "coffeeshops" begin to take its toll, don't despair. Amsterdam has ways of making you work up some healthy sweat—or at least of watching other people sweat. See also "Green Amsterdam," earlier in this chapter.

Sports & Outdoor Pursuits

BICYCLING
South of the city is **Amsterdamse Bos,** where you can rent bikes (✆ **020/644-5473;** www.amsterdamsebos.nl; bus: 166, 170, or 172) for touring the woodland's paths. Of course, you can always do as Amsterdammers do and explore all those city bridges and canals by bicycle (for rental information, see "By Bicycle" under "Getting Around," in chapter 3).

BOWLING
If you find you just have to knock down a few pins, head to **Knijn Bowling,** Scheldeplein 3 (✆ **020/664-2211;** www.knijnbowling.nl; tram: 12 or 25).

FISHING
Anglers should try the **Bosbaan** artificial lake (it's actually an Olympic rowing course) in **Amsterdamse Bos** (see "Green Amsterdam," earlier in this chapter), south of the city. You can get a license from **AHV,** Beethovenstraat 178 (✆ **020/626-4988;** www.ahv.nl; tram: 5), open Monday to Thursday from 9am to 1pm, and Friday from 1 to 5pm.

FITNESS CENTERS
If you don't want to neglect your exercise routine, there are many available centers. Good ones belong to the minichain **Splash** (www.splashhealthclubs.nl), with branches at Looiersgracht 26–30 (✆ **020/624-8404;** tram: 7, 10, or 17) and Lijnbaansgracht 241 (✆ **020/422-0280;** tram: 7 or 10).

GOLF
There are public golf courses in or near Amsterdam at 9-hole **Golfbaan Sloten,** Sloterweg 1045 (✆ **020/614-2402;** www.golfbaansloten.nl; bus: 145); 18-hole **Waterlandse Golf Club,** Buikslotermeerdijk 141 (✆ **020/636-1010;** www.waterlandse golfclub.nl; bus: 31, 33, or 38); and **Golfbaan Spaarnwoude,** Het Hoge Land 2, Spaarnwoude (✆ **020/538-5599;** www.golfbaanspaarnwoude.nl; bus: 82). Call ahead for greens fees and tee times.

HORSEBACK RIDING

From the comfort of its upper-floor cafe, watch horses being put through their paces in a sawdust-strewn arena at the regal **De Hollandsche Manege,** Vondelstraat 140 (© **020/618-0942;** www.dehollandschemanege.nl; tram: 1). Opened in 1882, this fusion of plaster, marble, and gilded mirrors was designed by **Concertgebouw** architect Adolf Leonard van Gendt and inspired by Vienna's Spanish Riding School. In addition to being a spectator, you can ride. Trot along to edge-of-town **Hippisch Centrum Sonnenburgh,** Nieuwe Kalfjeslaan 25 (© **020/643-1342;** bus: 142, 166, 170, 171, or 172); or to nearby **Manege Nieuw Amstelland,** Jan Tooropplantsoen 17 (© **020/643-2468;** www.nieuwamstelland.nl; bus: 142, 166, 170, 171, or 172).

ICE-SKATING

All those Dutch paintings of people skating and sledding—not to mention the story of Hans Brinker and his silver skates—will surely get you thinking about skating on Amsterdam's ponds and canals (see "Blades on Ice," below). However, doing this won't be easy unless you're willing to shell out for a new pair of skates, since very few places rent them. One that does is **Jaap Eden IJsbanen,** Radioweg 64 (© **0900/724-2287;** www.jaapeden.nl; tram: 9), from November to February, and they even allow you to take skates out of their marvelous outdoor rink, which is popular in wintertime. Unless you're highly competent, watch out for the long lines of speed skaters practicing for the next Eleven Cities Race in Friesland.

IN-LINE SKATING

De Vondeltuin Rent A Skate has a rent shop for in-line skates in Vondelpark, at the Amstelveenseweg entrance (© **06/2157-2885;** www.skatedokter.nl; tram: 2).

JOGGING

The two main jogging areas are **Vondelpark** in the Center and **Amsterdamse Bos** on the city's southern edge. You can also run along the Amstel River. If you choose to run along the canals, as many do, watch out for uneven cobbles, loose paving stones, and dog poop.

SAILING & BOATING

Sailboats, kayaks, and canoes can be rented on the Sloterplas Lake from **Watersportcentrum De Duikelaar,** Noordzijde 41 (© **020/613-8855;** www.deduikelaar.nl; tram: 7, 13, or 14). From March 15 to October 15, you can go to the Loosdrecht lakes, southeast of Amsterdam, to rent sailing equipment from **Ottenhome,** Zuwe 20,

Blades on Ice

In winter, when the temperature drops low enough for long enough, Amsterdam's canals become sparkling highways through the city. Skating to the strains of classical music is a memorable experience. Little kiosks are set up on the ice to dispense heart-warming liqueurs. Go cautiously when skating under bridges, where the ice is usually thinner, and don't go anywhere the Dutch don't. Few sounds generate more adrenaline than a sudden crackling of ice below, but the Dutch seem to know instinctively if it's just the natural rhythm of things or time to light the afterburners and be gone.

Kortenhoef (© **035/582-3331;** www. ottenhome.nl; bus: 106 from Weesp). Canoes can be rented in **Amsterdamse Bos** (see above), south of the city, for use in the park lakes only.

SNOOKER & POOL

Locals guzzle beer and get snookered at *carambole,* a devilishly complicated game played on pool tables without pockets. Billiards-type games are an obsession among the brown-cafe contingent; it's as easy to pick up a game as a flea. Try your hand at *carambole,* and delve deep into billiards, snooker, and pool at the **Pool Centrum Boven 't IJ,** Buikslotermeerplein 145 (© **020/634-1792;** www. boventij.com; bus: 30, 36, 37, 38, or 46), across the IJ waterway in Amsterdam-Noord. Sharps bring their own cues and call ahead to reserve a table. For pickup games, you'd better be good. It's open daily from 10am to 1am (Fri–Sat until 3am).

SQUASH

Squash courts and far more are at chic **Squash City,** Ketelmakerstraat 6 (© **020/626-7883;** www.squashcity.nl; bus: 18, 21, or 22), west of Centraal Station.

SWIMMING

Amsterdam's state-of-the-art swimming facility is centrally located **Het Marnix,** Marnixplein 1 (© **020/524-6000;** www.hetmarnix.nl; tram: 3 or 10). It has two heated pools along with a fitness center and spa, and a cafe-restaurant. The **Zuiderbad,** Hobbemastraat 26 (© **020/252-1390;** tram: 2 or 5), a handsome, refurbished place dating from 1911 near the Rijksmuseum, sets time aside for those who like to swim in their birthday suits. **De Mirandabad,** De Mirandalaan 9 (© **020/546-4444;** tram: 25), in Amsterdam-Zuid features an indoor pool with wave machines, slides, and other amusements, and an outdoor pool that's open May to September. Other decent public pools are the **Floraparkbad,** Sneeuwbalweg 5 (© **020/636-8121;** bus: 38), in Amsterdam-Noord, and the **Sloterparkbad,** President Allendelaan 3 (© **020/506-3506;** tram: 7 or 14), in Amsterdam-West. In 2010 and for the first time in the Netherlands, a floating pool opened in Amsterdam. Currently moored by the Karte Ouderkerkerdijk, it will remain open during summertimes until autumn 2013.

TENNIS

Find indoor courts at **Frans Otten Stadion,** IJsbaanpad 43 (© **020/662-8767;** www. fransottenstadion.nl; tram: 16), close to the Olympic Stadium. For indoor *and* outdoor courts, try **Sportcentrum Amstelpark,** Koenenkade 8, Amsterdamse Bos (© **020/301-0700;** www.amstelpark.nl; bus: 166, 170, 171, or 172), which has 36 courts.

Wellness Activities

The **Body Tuning Clinic,** Jan Luijkenstraat 40 (© **020/662-0909;** www.body tuningclinic.nl; tram: 2 or 5), will take excellent care of the outer you. At **Sauna Deco,** Herengracht 115 (© **020/623-8215;** www.saunadeco.nl; tram: 1, 2, 5, 13, or 17), in Dutch style, you sweat together in mixed facilities. Soothe away a hard day's stress at **Koan Float,** Herengracht 321 (© **020/555-0333;** www.koanfloat.nl; tram:

1, 2, or 5), while floating in warm saline water in a soundproof fiberglass capsule with light switches, ambient music, and a two-way intercom.

Spectator Sports

BASEBALL

Honk if you like baseball (the game is called *honkbal* in Holland). The **Amsterdam Pirates** (www.amsterdampirates.nl) may not be the greatest practitioners of the art, but they have their moments, as you can see at the **Sportpark Ookmeer,** Herman Bonpad 5 (© **020/616-2151;** bus: 19 or 192).

BASKETBALL

ABC Amsterdam (www.amsterdambasketball.nl) play their home games at **Sporthallen Zuid,** Burgerweeshuispad 54 (© **020/423-1818;** tram: 16 or 24), close to the Olympic Stadium.

ICE HOCKEY

The Dutch are known for their skill on ice, as local hotshots the **Amstel Tijgers** (www.amsteltijgerspro.nl) demonstrate at the **Jaap Edenhal,** Radioweg 64 (© **020/694-9652;** www.jaapeden.nl; tram: 9).

SOCCER

Soccer (known as *football* in Europe, and *voetbal* in Dutch) is absolutely the biggest game in Holland. **Ajax Amsterdam** is invariably the best team in the land, and often is among the best in Europe. Ajax plays home matches at a fabulous modern stadium with a retractable roof, the **Amsterdam ArenA,** ArenA Boulevard 1, Amsterdam Zuidoost (© **020/311-1444;** www.amsterdamarena.nl; Metro: Strandvliet/ArenA). There's even an on-site Ajax Museum.

STROLLING & BICYCLING IN AMSTERDAM

The best way to discover Amsterdam is on foot. The first tour described here takes you to the essential cultural and architectural sights along the city's 17th-century Golden Age canals. Tours 2, 3, and 4 focus, respectively, on the Old Center, the Jordaan district, and the city's fast developing Waterfront along the channel known as Het IJ.

Our fifth tour is no leisurely stroll, but a taste of that quintessential Amsterdam experience: Cycling. Bicycles are a key part of the mechanism that makes Holland tick, and no trip to Amsterdam is complete without some time in the saddle. This tour pedals you out from the Center, along the Amstel River, to breathe fresh country air at the old riverside village of **Ouderkerk aan de Amstel.**

Part of Amsterdam's enchantment comes from making your own discoveries. On each of my proposed itineraries, you'll come across points of interest I haven't written up for lack of space. It could be an unusually shaped gable, an offbeat boutique, a gaily painted bike, a sunken canal boat, whatever. And here's something to keep your eyes open for: Before house numbers were introduced on canal houses during Napoleon's occupation, engraved gable stones indicating the resident's trade or profession served for identification purposes; you'll still see many of these today.

WALKING TOUR 1: THE GOLDEN AGE CANALS

START:	**Herenmarkt (off Brouwersgracht).**
FINISH:	**Amstel River.**
TIME:	**3 hours to all day, depending on how long you linger along the way.**

BEST TIMES:	**First thing in the morning from spring through fall, so you can watch as city life along the canals wakes up and gets going. If you're not an early riser, then any hour (yes, even after dark) is fine.**
WORST TIMES:	**Mondays, when most museums are closed.**

The three 17th-century canals you explore on this tour—**Herengracht (Gentlemen's Canal), Keizersgracht (Emperor's Canal)**, and **Prinsengracht (Princes' Canal)**—are the very heart of Golden Age Amsterdam, emblems of the city's wealth and pride in its heyday. Each deserves at least a morning or afternoon to itself. Time being limited, we're going to combine them into one monumental effort. If you're not so pressed, by all means slice the tour up into segments for a more leisurely experience.

You'll stroll along miles of tree-lined canals, crisscrossed by smaller canals, and you'll pass innumerable 17th-century canal houses with gables in various styles (bell, step, clock, neck, and variations), classical facades, warehouses converted to apartments, houseboats moored along the banks, bridges, museums, cafes, restaurants, boutiques, offbeat stores, and battered bikes secured to lampposts. I'm going to mention only the most special sights and point out some insider tips along the way. This should leave you with plenty of space for making your own discoveries.

Take tram 1, 2, 5, 13, or 17 to Martelaarsgracht, or the Stop/Go bus (see "Stop & Go" under "Getting Around," in chapter 3) direct to the starting point, on Herenmarkt, just off Brouwersgracht:

1 West-Indisch Huis

The 17th-century Dutch West India Company's headquarters handled trade—including slave trade—between Holland, the Americas, and Africa. It later became the offices of a social-welfare organization and a Lutheran orphanage, and now houses a U.S.-linked educational institute (see "Historical Buildings & Monuments," in chapter 7).

Walk along tranquil:

2 Brouwersgracht

Humpback bridges, moored houseboats, and 17th- and 18th-century brewery pakhuizen (warehouses) that have been turned into chic, expensive apartments combine to make the Brewers' Canal one of Amsterdam's most photogenic corners. Worth special attention are nos. 204 and 206, Het Kleine Groene Hert (the Little Green Deer) and Het Groote Groene Hert (the Big Green Deer). Each has a gable crowned with a green-painted deer sculpture. Take note for possible future reference of two fine 17th-century "brown cafes": Tabac at Brouwersgracht 101 and Papeneiland at Prinsengracht 2–4. In the 17th century, Prinsengracht was home to storekeepers and craftsmen.

Along Prinsengracht, your first stop is:

3 Noordermarkt

Saturdays from 9am to 5pm, this old market square hosts a farmers' market for "bio" (organic) products. A popular flea market takes over Mondays from 8am to 2pm, at which clothes fashionable a decade or more ago are highly esteemed, and dealers peddle everything from Golden Age antiques to today's junk. Pause

Walking Tour 1: The Golden Age Canals

1 West-Indisch Huis
2 Brouwersgracht
3 Noordermarkt
4 Zon's Hofje
5 Groenland Pakhuizen
6 Huis met de Hoofden
7 Herengracht 168 &
   the Bartolottihuis

8 Anne Frankhuis
9 De Prins
10 Westerkerk
11 Felix Meritis
12 Berenstraat to Runstraat
13 Bijbels Museum
14 Nienhuys Mansion
15 Walem

16 Golden Bend
17 Museum Van Loon
18 Museum Willet-Holthuysen
19 Amstel River
20 Café Schiller

for a moment to admire the elaborate gables of the houses at nos. 15–22, each one decorated with an agricultural image—a cow, a sheep, a chicken—from the time when a livestock market was held here. No. 16 has a Louis XIV neck gable and a gable stone from 1726 depicting the goddess Fortuna and advertising the textile store that once occupied the building.

The **Noorderkerk (North Church)**—the last masterpiece by architect Hendrick de Keyser, who was the guiding hand behind many of Amsterdam's historic churches—dominates the square (see "Sights of Religious Significance," in chapter 7). It's something of a rarity in nominally Calvinist Amsterdam, since it has a large and active Calvinist congregation. On the facade, a plaque recalls the February 1941 strike protesting Nazi deportation of the city's Jews. A group of sculptures outside recalls the dead and wounded from the 1934 *Jordaanoproer* (Jordaan Insurrection) street riots protesting poverty; the army suppressed these. If you're lucky, you'll hear the church's carillon playing as you go by.

Continue along Prinsengracht to the bridge at Prinsenstraat, and cross over. A few steps back along the canal on this side is:

4 Zon's Hofje

At Prinsengracht 159–171, a hidden almshouse surrounds a courtyard garden at the end of a long passageway. People live here, but from 10am to 5pm the outer door is open and you can walk discreetly through the passageway to the courtyard, which belonged to the city's Mennonites. They worshiped at a clandestine church, **De Zon (the Sun)**—demolished in 1755—and held meetings in the courtyard, which they called De Kleine Zon (the Little Sun). Above the lintel of nos. 163–165, a carved plaque shows animals piling two by two into Noah's Ark (referencing the fact that in 1720 the church's name was changed to De Arke Noach).

Farther back along the canal, at nos. 85–133, is another former almshouse, built for the sick, elderly, and indigent: The carefully restored and immensely restful **Van Brienen's Hofje,** dating from 1804 (and also known as **De Star** after the De Star Brewery foundation that took over the site in 1841). A wealthy merchant named Jan van Brienen supposedly had it built in gratitude for his escape from a vault in which he'd accidentally been locked. It has a lovely garden with benches, but if you don't want to have to backtrack too far, and aren't much of a *hofje* (almshouse) enthusiast, you can let it alone.

Head down Prinsenstraat to Keizersgracht. A short detour to the left brings you to the:

5 Groenland Pakhuizen

Built in 1621 to store whale oil, the Greenland Warehouses are now chic apartments (nos. 40–44).

Cross the bridge over Keizersgracht. Note the houseboats moored on the canal. Ahead of you is Herenstraat, and at the far end of this short street, if you want to jog for a look, is Amsterdam's shortest canal, Blauburgwal, all 68m (74 yd.) of it. To stay on route, go right before Herenstraat on Keizersgracht, to the:

6 Huis met de Hoofden (House with the Heads)

At no. 123, the heads on the 1622 facade by Hendrick de Keyser represent, from left to right, Apollo, Ceres, Mars, Athena, Bacchus, and Diana.

Turn left along Leliegracht, then right on Herengracht, to the:

7 Herengracht 168 & the Bartolottihuis

Herengracht was the ultimate address for flourishing 17th-century bankers and merchants. The graceful house at no. 168, known as Het Witte Huijs (the White House) for its neoclassical facade made from gray-white German sandstone, was designed by Philips Vingboons in 1638 for Michiel Reyniersz Pauw, who established a short-lived trading colony in America at Hoboken, facing Nieuw Amsterdam (New York), and named it Pavonia after his august self. Note the classical neck gable, the city's first of its style. Dazzling interior ornamentation from around 1730 includes a spiral staircase, intricate stuccowork, and painted ceilings by Jacob de Wit.

Next door at no. 170–172, the flamboyant Bartolotti House, dating from 1618 and designed by Hendrick and Pieter de Keyser, was built for Guillielmo Bartolotti, who began life as homey old Willem van den Heuvel; he switched to the fancy moniker after making a bundle in brewing and banking. The house has an ornate redbrick gable and Dutch Renaissance facade. Its illuminated ceilings and other interior decoration also are by Jacob de Wit.

Backtrack to Leliegracht, and cross over Keizersgracht on the bridge. Note at Keizersgracht 176 a rare Amsterdam Art Nouveau house (1905), designed by architect Gerrit van Arkel. Continue up Leliegracht and take a left on Prinsengracht to the:

8 Anne Frankhuis

This house at no. 263 is where the young Jewish girl Anne Frank (1929–45) hid from the Nazis and wrote her imperishable diary. The earlier you get here the better, because the line to get in grows as the day progresses (see "The Big Three," in chapter 7).

You might be tempted by a *pedalo* tour from the Canal Bikes dock outside the Anne Frankhuis. But if you're more in need of lunch, cross over Prinsengracht by the canal bridge and pop into:

9 De Prins 🍴

Cafe-restaurant De Prins, Prinsengracht 124 (☎ 020/624-9382), which is my Best Value restaurant recommendation, and a great spot for a leisurely meal (see "The Canal Belt," in chapter 6).

Along this bank, at no. 170, Galleria d'Arte Rinascimento sells both old and new hand-painted Delftware from Koninklijke Porceleyne Fles (see "Shopping A to Z," in chapter 9). Continue to Rozengracht and turn left (east) to Westermarkt and its:

10 Westerkerk

The Dutch Renaissance church, begun by Hendrick de Keyser in 1620, became his son Pieter's project after Hendrick died. The church opened in 1631 (see "Sights of Religious Significance," in chapter 7).

In 1635, French philosopher René Descartes lived in the house at Westermarkt 6; this is where he wrote *Treatise on the Passions of the Soul*. Descartes evidently thought he was in need of some more down-to-earth passion—therefore he was—and had an affair with his maid, which produced a child whose reality could scarcely be doubted. Also on Westermarkt: A somber bronze sculpture of Anne Frank, and the **Homomonument**'s pink marble triangles, dedicated to persecuted gays and lesbians.

Cross over Westermarkt to Rozengracht, which once was a canal. Continue along Prinsengracht to Reestraat, where you turn left. At Keizersgracht go right, across Berenstraat, to Keizersgracht 324:

11 Felix Meritis

Jacob Otten Husly built this structure in 1788 as the headquarters of a Calvinist philosophical society. The name (which was the group's motto) means "happiness through merit," and they invited such luminaries as Czar Alexander I and Napoleon to this Palladian setting, with Corinthian columns and triangular pediment, to experience this philosophy's consolations. The building later housed the Dutch Communist Party, and now hosts avant-garde theater, music, and dance performances (see "Other Venues," in chapter 10).

The next stretch of Keizersgracht goes from:

12 Berenstraat to Runstraat

On this stretch of Keizersgracht, instead of standing directly in front of buildings of interest, craning your neck skyward, walk along near the canal's bank (on the side with even numbers) and look across the water to the other side, so you can view things in panorama. In summer, though, elm trees screen some facades, and you might prefer to cross over for a closer look.

The third building along from Wolvenstraat (no. 313), an office block from 1914, is almost modern in Keizersgracht-time. Two houses farther down (no. 317) is the stately canalside home that belonged to Christoffel Brants, who counted Peter the Great among his acquaintances. A story goes that Peter sailed into Amsterdam in 1716, planning to stay a night here. The Czar of All the Russias got royally drunk, kept the mayor waiting at a reception in his honor, then retreated to the Russian ambassador's residence (at Herengracht 527) to sleep off his hangover.

Next door (no. 319) is a work by architect Philips Vingboons from 1639, as you can easily tell from the inscribed Roman numerals MDCXXXIX. It's interesting to compare this ornate neoclassical facade with its graceful neck gable to the Theatermuseum building, by the same architect, at Herengracht 168 (p. 225).

Note the narrow facade of the seventh building before Huidenstraat (no. 345A), and run your eyes over the trio of graceful neck gables on the last three houses (nos. 353–357).

At Runstraat, cross over to Huidenstraat and go along to Herengracht. Turn right to Herengracht 366-368, for the:

13 Bijbels Museum (Biblical Museum)

Comprised of two of a group of four 1660s' houses (nos. 364–370) with delicate neck gables, this museum was designed by architect Philips Vingboons for timber merchant Jacob Cromhout. The four structures are known both as the Cromhuithuizen and as the "Father, Mother, and Twins." The museum features Bibles and things biblical, but its canal-house setting and illuminated ceilings by Jacob de Wit are at least as interesting (see "More Top Museums & Galleries," in chapter 7).

Continue a few doors farther along Herengracht, to nos. 380-382, the:

14 Nienhuys Mansion

This princely residence was constructed in 1889 for Dutch tobacco tycoon Jacob Nienhuys. Polite society was amused that the coach-house entrance was too narrow for coaches to make the turn in one go. The mansion now houses the **Netherlands Institute for War Documentation** and the **Center for Holocaust and Genocide Studies.** Across the canal, on Herengracht 395's facade (hard to see unless you cross over for a close-up look), a stone cat stalks a carved mouse that's on the facade of the neighboring house, no. 397.

Cross elegant Leidsegracht (dug in 1664 for barge traffic to and from Leiden) to busy Leidsestraat. Go along Leidsestraat to its junction with Keizersgracht, and turn right into:

15 Walem 🍴

Keizersgracht 449 (📞 020/625-3544). A cafe that's just about hung on to its once-undisputed trendy rep, and that (more importantly) still serves great food (see "The Canal Belt," in chapter 6).

Retrace your steps to Herengracht, and turn right to the:

16 Golden Bend

You can trace the development of rich folks' wealth and tastes as you progress up the house numbers on the section of the Herengracht canal between Leidsestraat and Vijzelstraat. Built with old money around the 1670s, in the Golden Age's fading afterglow, when French-influenced neoclassicism was all the rage, the opulent mansions here are mostly built of sandstone (rather than brick) on double lots with central entrances. Compare these sober baroque facades to the exuberant gabled houses from a half-century earlier, back along the canal. Look across the water to no. 475 for a particularly fine example of the later style.

Turn right on Nieuwe Spiegelstraat, a street lined with antiques stores, and go along it to Keizersgracht. A short detour to your right brings you to No. 529, which in 1781–82 was the residence of John Adams, the then U.S. ambassador to the Netherlands, and later the second U.S. president. The canalside house was in effect the first-ever embassy of the United States, and a plaque placed there in 2005 by Amsterdam's John Adams Institute records the fact. Turn around and cross over on the bridge at Nieuwe Spiegelstraat to the far bank of Keizersgracht, for the:

17 Museum Van Loon

This museum (at no. 672) gives a rare glimpse beyond a patrician post–Golden Age house's gables (see "More Top Museums & Galleries," in chapter 7).

Cross Reguliersgracht and return to Herengracht—from the bridge over Reguliersgracht at Herengracht, you can see no fewer than 15 bridges (including the one you're standing on). Skim the edge of neat little Thorbeckeplein, and go right along the canal across Utrechtsestraat, a cornucopia of good restaurants and variegated stores, to the:

18 Museum Willet-Holthuysen

At Herengracht 605, this patrician canal house dating from 1687 is richly decorated in Louis XIV style. A table, under a big chandelier in the dining salon, is set for a meal being served more than 300 years late (see "More Top Museums & Galleries," in chapter 7).

Stroll to the end of Herengracht and finish at the:

19 Amstel River

At this point, the river should be thick with houseboats and canal barges. To your left is the refurbished **Blauwbrug (Blue Bridge),** built in 1884 (p. 155); to your right is the famous **Magere Brug (Skinny Bridge),** a double draw-bridge (p. 155). Step out onto either of these for great views of the comings and goings on the water.

Walking the short distance along the river to Waterlooplein, or backtracking to Utre-chtsestraat, puts you on the tram net. If you're footsore and hungry, hobble the short distance to:

20 Café Schiller 🍺

Rembrandtplein 36 (📞 020/624-9846). Take the weight off your feet amid Art Deco surroundings, or on the glassed-in terrace next to the square (see "The Bar Scene," in chapter 10).

WALKING TOUR 2: **THE OLD CENTER**

START:	**The Dam.**
FINISH:	**Prins Hendrikkade, close to Centraal Station.**
TIME:	**2½ to 4 hours or more, depending on how long you spend in museums, attractions, cafes, and stores (and perusing the windows in the Red Light District).**
BEST TIMES:	**If you want to visit one or more of the museums or other attractions, most of them open at 10am (some are closed Mon). Morning is a good time to do the Red Light District, because by then most of its bizarre night owls—and raptors—have crashed for the day.**
WORST TIMES:	**Daylight hours are bad for perusing the Red Light District if you want to be there when business is humming. Then again, after-dark hours are bad for perusing the Red Light District if you don't want to be there when business is humming. It's a free country; the choice is yours.**

This tour takes you past some of the main city-center points of interest in the Nieuwe Zijde (New Side). It then goes into the Oude Zijde (Old Side), the oldest part of town, the first part of which is a place of tranquil canals; then it weaves through the bawdy Red Light District, a sex-for-sale zone which actually occupies a handsome area of 16th-century canals and gabled houses. "Ordinary" people still live in this area and go on with their daily lives, as you'll observe if you take your eyes for a moment off the barely clad women behind red-lit windows. I don't recommend you do the Red Light section after dark; the district is seedier and more sinister then, and while it's fascinat-ing, it no longer falls under the category of a casual stroll through town.

The starting point, reached by tram 1, 2, 4, 5, 9, 13, 14, 16, 17, 24, or 25, is the:

1 The Dam

It can be one hot Dam at times, especially in summer, when the city's main monumental square becomes a hangout for young and old, visitors and natives (see "The Dam," in chapter 7). Don't waste your time looking for a dam on the

Walking Tour 2: The Old Center

1 The Dam
2 Koninklijk Paleis
3 Nieuwe Kerk
4 De Drie Fleschjes
5 De Bijenkorf
6 Nationaal Monument
7 Madame Tussauds
8 Amsterdams Historisch
  Museum
9 Begijnhof

10 Spui
11 Café Luxembourg ☕
12 Gebed Zonder End
13 Huis aan de Drie
   Grachten
14 Agnietenkapel
15 Oudemanhuispoort
16 Poppenhuis
17 Trippenhuis
18 Oost-Indisch Huis

19 Amsterdams Brouwhuis
   Maximiliaan
20 De Waag
21 Oude Kerk
22 Ons' Lieve Heer op Solder
23 Sint-Olofskapel
24 Sint-Nicolaaskerk
25 Hudsons ☕

Dam, though; there hasn't been one here for centuries. Let's make a clockwise circuit of the square.

Dominating the western side is the neoclassical:

2 Koninklijk Paleis (Royal Palace)

Constructed between 1648 and 1655 as the Stadhuis (Town Hall), this was later chosen to be the royal family's official residence (see "The Dam," in chapter 7).

Cross over Mozes en Aäronstraat to the:

3 Nieuwe Kerk

Since 1814, all the kings and queens of the Netherlands have been inaugurated at the New Church (Dutch monarchs are not uppity enough to actually be crowned). Built between the late 15th and mid-17th centuries in elaborate late-Gothic style, the Nieuwe Kerk often hosts temporary exhibits expensive enough to maybe make you think twice (see "The Dam," in chapter 7).

Outside the church, take narrow Eggertstraat at the side of the Nieuwe Kerk's cafe, 't Nieuwe Kafé. On adjoining Gravenstraat, at no. 18, is:

4 De Drie Fleschjes

A character-rich *proeflokaal* (tasting house) dating from 1650, where merchants sampled liqueurs and spirits, it now specializes in *jenever* (Dutch gin). Among a warren of tiny alleyways around here, Blaeustraat, behind a locked gate next to De Drie Fleschjes, recalls the store at nearby Damrak 46 where the 17th-century mapmaker Johannes Blaeu sold his superb world atlases.

Return to the north side of the Dam and glance upward at the painted 15th-century wall sculpture of Sinter Claes (St. Nicholas), the city's patron saint, and Santa Claus's forerunner, on the building just before the corner at Damrak.

Cross over busy Damrak to Amsterdam's answer to Bloomingdale's:

5 De Bijenkorf

"The Beehive" department store dates from 1915 (see "Shopping A to Z," in chapter 9). In front is the **NH Grand Hotel Krasnapolsky** (p. 81). A short stroll along Damstraat at the side of the hotel would bring you right into the Red Light District, but we're not going there—not yet!

Cross over to the:

6 Nationaal Monument

Holland's obelisk-shaped World War II memorial was erected in 1956 (see "The Dam," in chapter 7).

From here, cross over to the Amsterdam Diamond Center on the corner of Rokin, then cross over busy Rokin to:

7 Madame Tussauds

Amsterdam's Madame Tussauds contains well-known characters, many of them sporting a peculiarly Dutch waxen stare (see "The Dam," in chapter 7).

Continue to Kalverstraat, and go left on this bustling, pedestrians-only shopping street lined with department stores and cheap, cheerful boutiques. Turn right on Sint-Luciënsteeg to the:

8 Amsterdams Historisch Museum

A porch from 1592 that used to be the city orphanage's entrance is now the museum entrance. The outer courtyard was for boys (to the left are cupboards where they stored their tools), and the inner courtyard was for girls (see "More Top Museums & Galleries," in chapter 7). Exit the museum through the **Schuttersgalerij,** a covered arcade lined with group portraits of 16th- and 17th-century militia companies (p. 143).

On the right side of narrow Gedempte Begijnensloot is the entrance to the:

9 Begijnhof

Devout women lived in this cloister from the 14th century onward. The house at no. 34, Amsterdam's oldest, was built in 1425 and is one of only two timber houses remaining in the city (see p. 152 in chapter 7).

Pass between nos. 37 and 38, to:

10 Spui

An elegant and animated square, Spui has at its west end a statue of a small boy, *Het Lieverdje* **(the Little Darling),** meant to represent a typical Amsterdam kid. Across the street, at no. 21, is the **Maagdenhuis,** the University of Amsterdam's main downtown building.

Go up on Spuistraat, to:

11 Café Luxembourg 🍺

Spuistraat 24 (📞 020/620-6264), which the *New York Times* considers "one of the world's great cafes," for drinks, snacks, or one of their renowned sandwiches (see "The Old Center," in chapter 6).

Walk to the end of Spui and cross over Rokin, past a statue of Queen Wilhelmina, a canal tour-boat dock, and the Allard-Pierson Museum (see "More Top Museums & Galleries," in chapter 7). Go straight ahead on Lange Brugsteeg to Grimburgwal, in the district known as De Wallen (the Walls). The first street on the left, Nes, is lined with alternative theaters. Keep straight ahead, though, to:

12 Gebed Zonder End

This alleyway's odd name, which means "Prayer Without End," comes from the convents that used to be here. It's said that the murmur of prayers from behind the walls could always be heard.

Stay on Grimburgwal across Oudezijds Voorburgwal and Oudezijds Achterburgwal. Between these two canals and the adjacent Grimburgwal canal is the:

13 Huis aan de Drie Grachten

At Oudezijds Voorburgwal 249, the House on the Three Canals (1609) is a handsome redbrick, step-gabled, Dutch Renaissance house.

Go a short way along Oudezijds Voorburgwal to the:

14 Agnietenkapel

You'll easily recognize the building at no. 231 by its elaborate ornamental gateway from 1571. This was St. Agnes Convent's chapel until the Protestants took Amsterdam over. The Agnietenkapel later formed part of the **Athenaeum**

Illustre, the city's first university, and now houses the university museum (which isn't very interesting unless there's a special exhibit).

Return to the House on the Three Canals and cross the bridge to Oudezijds Achterburgwal's far side, where you pass the **Gasthuis,** once a hospital and now part of the University of Amsterdam.

Turn right into the:

15 Oudemanhuispoort

A second-hand book market (Mon–Sat 10:30am–6pm) popular with students occupies this dimly lit arcade. Midway along, on the left, a doorway leads to a courtyard garden with a statue of Minerva. At the far end of the arcade, above the exterior doorway, is *The Liberality,* a sculpture of a seated female figure with three objects: A cornucopia symbolizing abundance, a book symbolizing wisdom, and an oil lamp symbolizing enlightenment. An old man and woman represent old age and poverty. City sculptor Antonie Ziesenis created these statues in 1785.

Turn right on Kloveniersburgwal, cross over the canal at the next bridge, and go left on the far bank of the canal to Kloveniersburgwal 95, the:

16 Poppenhuis

Architect Philips Vingboons designed this classical mansion in 1642 for Joan Poppen, a dissolute grandson of a rich German merchant and heir to his fortune. The youth hostel next door at no. 97 was originally a home for retired sea captains.

Continue on Kloveniersburgwal—behind the buildings to your right front as you cross Raamstraat, you'll see the tip of the Zuiderkerk (South Church) spire—to Kloveniersburgwal 29, the:

17 Trippenhuis

The Trip brothers commissioned Philips Vingboons to create their ideal mansion (1664). They were arms dealers, which accounts for the martial images and emblems about the house. Originally, there were two houses behind a single classical facade, but the two have since been joined. It now houses the **Royal Netherlands Academy of Science.**

Backtrack to the canal bridge and cross over to Oude Hoogstraat and the:

18 Oost-Indisch Huis

Enter the East India House (1606) via a courtyard on the left side of the street, at no. 24. Once the headquarters of the V.O.C., the Vereenigde Oostindische Compagnie (United East India Company), it now belongs to the University of Amsterdam (see "Historical Buildings & Monuments," in chapter 7). Next door, at Oude Hoogstraat 22, is Amsterdam's narrowest house, just 2.02m (6⅔ ft.) wide.

Back on Kloveniersburgwal, go left. At no. 26 is the Klein Trippenhuis, the narrow house of the Trip brothers' coachman (see "The Smallest Houses," in chapter 7), which now houses a fetishist fashion store called Webers. Note a few doors along, at nos. 10–12, the drugstore Jacob Hooy & Co., which has dispensed medicinal relief since 1743. A little farther along, at nos. 6–8, is the:

19 Amsterdams Brouwhuis Maximiliaan

The city's smallest brewery, in a surviving portion of the 16th-century **Bethaniënklooster (Bethanien Convent),** produces 10 different beers and serves them from copper vats. The nuns who once brewed beer here have long since departed, but this brewery maintains their beer-making tradition. It's got a rustic-chic, wood-floored bar and a restaurant attached. A part of the old convent, which belonged to the Sisters of St. Mary Magdalen of Bethanien, has been restored and is now used as a concert hall for chamber music recitals.

In the center of Nieuwmarkt, the large, open square dead ahead, is:

20 De Waag

This massive edifice was once one of the city's medieval gates, and later the Weigh House and guild offices (see "Historical Buildings & Monuments," in chapter 7). It now houses a specialized educational and cultural institute (rarely open to the public), and a fashionable cafe-restaurant, **In de Waag** (see "The Old Center," in chapter 6).

Take a turn around bustling **Nieuwmarkt,** the center of Amsterdam's diminutive **Chinatown** and site of a summertime Sunday antiques market, from May through October.

Now we're going to head into the **Red Light District.** If you don't want to come along, go instead along Zeedijk at the northwest corner of Nieuwmarkt and I'll pick you up again farther along that street (go straight to no. 23 on this tour). In compensation, you'll surely notice—you can't easily miss it—the Buddhist **Fo Guang Shan He Hua Temple** at Zeedijk 106–116, on the left, about midway along the street. It's open Monday to Saturday from noon to 5pm, and Sunday from 10am to 5pm. Admission's free, but donations are welcomed.

If, on the other hand, you have no objection to viewing the Red Light District in all its scuzzy glory, take Monnickenstraat to Oudezijds Achterburgwal and turn right to the next bridge, going past windows that frame prostitutes waiting for customers or that have closed curtains to signify that a deal is being consummated. Then go through Oude Kennissteeg (or take a neighboring street if this narrow alleyway is closed) directly ahead to Oudezijds Voorburgwal. Should you require proof that you can do more here than ogle the "views" through the multitudes of red-lit windows, turn right to no. 57, a 1615 baroque Renaissance canal house by architect Hendrick de Keyser, dubbed **De Gecroonde Raep (the Crowned Turnip)** for its facade's motif. Take in its graceful accolade arches, double pilasters, and window cartouches.

Cross over the canal by the nearest bridge, to the:

21 Oude Kerk

Rembrandt's wife Saskia is interred within the Old Church, the city's first great Gothic church (see "Sights of Religious Significance," in chapter 7). Nowadays, the pretty little gabled almshouses around the church have red-fringed windows in which you can see scantily clad hookers.

Go north on Oudezijds Voorburgwal to no. 40:

22 Ons' Lieve Heer op Solder

Visit Our Lord in the Attic, a hidden Catholic church in a superb example of a 17th-century patrician canal house (see "Sights of Religious Significance," in chapter 7).

A couple of blocks north, at Oudezijds Voorburgwal 14, on the corner of Oudezijds Armsteeg, you'll notice a step-gabled, redbrick building that leans out to a crazy angle —be careful not to trip over its projecting basement. It's called **Het Wapen van Riga (the Arms of Riga),** and it was built in 1605 in Dutch Renaissance style by a merchant from the Baltic city of Riga. It now houses a Leger des Heils (Salvation Army) hostel.

At the end of Oudezijds Voorburgwal, turn right on Sint-Olofssteeg to Zeedijk, one of the city's oldest streets. (Welcome back to anyone who forewent the Red Light District.) Go left now, to:

23 Sint-Olofskapel

The fishermen's dog that, according to some city legends, marked the spot where Amsterdam began by throwing up, is said to have done the deed on the site of St. Olaf's Chapel, at Zeedijk 2A. Supposedly, fishermen founded the chapel in gratitude for their escape from the sea. But discrepancies exist: The chapel was built around 1425 and Amsterdam dates from the end of the 12th century. Sometimes you can enter the church—which was over-restored in the 1990s and reopened as a congress center—via a tunnel under Zeedijk from the NH Barbizon Palace Hotel (see below); at such times you'll be able to view its spacious columned interior.

From here, continue past two great Amsterdam taverns: **Het Elfde Gebod** at Zeedijk 5, which stocks 50 different kinds of beer, and the traditional bar **In 't Aepjen** at Zeedijk 1, in one of Amsterdam's two surviving timber houses (the other is in the Begijnhof, see above), which dates from 1550.

Emerge on Prins Hendrikkade and go right to:

24 Sint-Nicolaaskerk

The city's main Catholic church (since Protestants took over most of the others during the Reformation), St. Nicholas's dates from 1887 and was originally the harbor church—primarily, but not exclusively, for seamen (see "Sights of Religious Significance," in chapter 7).

From here, you can get to Centraal Station by just crossing over busy Prins Hendrikkade. But before doing so, take a break next door at:

25 Hudsons 🍺

Prins Hendrikkade 59–72 (☎ 020/556-4564). A tiny place in the NH Barbizon Palace that serves light food and drinks (see "The Waterfront," in chapter 5).

WALKING TOUR 3: THE JORDAAN

START:	**Brouwersgracht.**
FINISH:	**Noordermarkt.**
TIME:	**Allow between 2 and 2½ hours.**
BEST TIMES:	**Anytime, but if you want to visit one of the Jordaan's lively markets, go on Monday morning or on Saturday. On Monday there's a flea market on Noordermarkt, and a textiles market on Westerstraat where you'll find, among other items, fabrics and second-hand clothing. On Saturday, Noordermarkt hosts a bird market and a farmers' market with organic produce, and Lindengracht has a general street market.**

Walking Tour 3: The Jordaan

1 Brouwersgracht	7 Egelantiersgracht
2 Palmgracht	8 't Smalle ☕
3 Lindengracht	9 Claes Claeszhofje
4 Karthuizersplantsoen	10 Westerstraat
5 Egelantiersgracht	11 Winkel ☕
6 Bloemgracht	

If you hate street markets, you won't want to go plowing through them on the days mentioned above. Don't visit the *hofjes* (almshouses) on the route too early or too late—people live in them and don't enjoy the disturbance.

It's easy to get lost in the character-rich maze of the Jordaan—not that getting lost is a bad thing. It affords you an opportunity to make your own discoveries, which is the key to appreciating the Jordaan. Among the district's sights are several of the delightful, centuries-old almshouses known as *hofjes*. Students, seniors, and people requiring supervised accommodations live in these small houses. If you enter their courtyards, be sure to tread softly.

To avoid an overly long walk, I've restricted this tour to the northern—and more interesting—half of the Jordaan, from Brouwersgracht down to Rozengracht. That leaves the southern half, from Rozengracht down to Leidsegracht, for your own perusal.

Take tram 1, 2, 5, 13, or 17 to Martelaarsgracht, or the Stop/Go bus (see "Stop & Go" under "Getting Around," in chapter 3) direct to the starting point, on:

1 Brouwersgracht

A walk northwest along this venerable houseboat-lined canal (see stop 2 in Walking Tour 1), takes you across Lindengracht, past a 1979 bronze sculpture of writer Theo Thijssen (1879–1943) with one of his popular fictional characters, the Jordaan schoolchild Kees de Jongen. Farther along, across Willemstraat, look across the water to the modern De Blauwe Burgt apartment block for an idea of how the new complements (or degrades) the old.

Go left on tree-shaded:

2 Palmgracht

This street was once a canal. The house at 28–38 hides a small cobblestone courtyard garden behind an orange door that's the entrance to the **Raepenhofje,** an almshouse dating from 1648. The turnip on the gable stone is a pun on the original owner's name, Pieter Adriaenszoon Raep (*raep* means "turnip" in Dutch). Across the courtyard, at nos. 20–26, is the **Bosschehofje,** which Arent Dirkszoon Bossch built in 1648.

Go left on Palmdwarsstraat and cross over Willemstraat (which used to be a canal called Goudsbloemgracht), onto Tweede Goudsbloemdwarsstraat. Cross over Goudsbloemdwarsstraat to:

3 Lindengracht

Like Palmgracht, Lindengracht was once a canal, and is now the scene of a lively Saturday street market. Continue along to the **Suyckerhoff Hofje,** at nos. 149–163. The 15 small houses (originally there were 19) of this pretty *hofje* were built in 1670 by order of Pieter Janszoon Suyckerhoff's 1667 testament, which aimed to provide refuge for Protestant widows and women of good moral standing and "tranquil character," who'd been abandoned by their husbands. The door may appear to be locked, but you can usually open it during daylight hours and walk along the narrow entrance corridor to a flower-filled courtyard garden.

Farther up, at Lindengracht 171, you pass an Old Jordaan–style coffeehouse in a building from 1884. **Koffiehuis Oor** (☎ **020/626-5077**) isn't a dope-dealing "coffeeshop" but a genuine coffee-brewing little gem.

Take the first street on the left, Tweede Lindendwarsstraat, to:

4 Karthuizersplantsoen

Nothing's left of the Carthusian monastery built in 1394. It stretched from here to Lijnbaansgracht before being demolished in the 1570s during Amsterdam's transition from Catholicism to Protestantism. A children's playground is now where the monastery's cemetery once was. There are still sights to see here, however: At Karthuizersstraat 11–19 is a row of neck-gabled houses from 1737, named after the four seasons (Lente, Zomer, Herfst, and Winter). Next-door (forgive the illogical numbering) at nos. 69–191, is the 1650 **Huyszitten-Weduwenhof,** a large interior courtyard surrounded by houses that were once poor widows' homes—they now board students.

Go left on Tichelstraat, cross Westerstraat, once a broad canal, and continue along a string of *dwarsstraten* (side streets)—Tweede Anjeliersdwarsstraat, Tweede Tuind-warsstraat, and Tweede Egelantiersdwarsstraat—it may take you longer to pronounce the names of these lively little cafe-lined streets than to walk through them—to:

5 Egelantiersgracht

On the way you'll notice the Westerkerk's tall spire, called the Westertoren, which has a carillon that breaks into song at every opportunity (see "Sights of Religious Significance," in chapter 7). Genuine Jordaaners, it is said, are born within earshot of the bells.

Named for the eglantine rose, or sweetbriar, Egelantiersgracht is one of the city's most elegant and tranquil small canals. Its many interesting 17th- and 18th-century houses afford a tantalizing insight into the kinds of modestly elegant living quarters successful Amsterdam artisans could aspire to.

On the gable stone of a trio of simple bell gables at nos. 61–65 is a carved falcon.

If the door's open, peek into the **Andrieshofje** at nos. 107–145. Cattle farmer Ivo Gerrittszoon provided funds in his will to build these 36 alms-houses; they were completed in 1617 and remodeled in 1884. A corridor deco-rated with Delft blue tiles leads up to a small courtyard with a leafy garden. An old water pump stands here, as does a stone bearing the inscription: *Vrede Sy Met U* (Peace be with you).

Retrace your steps to turn right on Tweede Leliedwarsstraat (from 1637 to 1696, the famous Blaeu family of cartographers lived at no. 76) and continue to:

6 Bloemgracht

The grandest of the Jordaan canals was originally home to workers who produced dyes and paints. Architect Hendrick de Keyser built the three step-gabled houses at nos. 87–91 in 1642—they're gems, and now house a foundation established to preserve the architect's works. Their carved gable stones represent a townsman, a countryman, and a seaman.

Nos. 77 and 81 are former sugar refineries from 1752 and 1763, respectively. Their gable stones, De Saayer (the Sower) and De Jonge Saayer (the Young Sower), are of recent origin.

Walk east toward Prinsengracht, where you can see the Westertoren again. Go left on Prinsengracht to:

7 Egelantiersgracht

You visited this canal earlier at a point farther west. A hardware store at nos. 2–6, at the corner of Prinsengracht, is a fine example of Amsterdam School architecture from 1917, with its intricate brickwork and cast-iron, Art Nouveau–influenced ornaments. To the store's left, at no. 8, a 1649 step-gabled house is decorated with sandstone ornaments and gable stones that depict St. Willibrord and a brewer.

On Egelantiersgracht is a particularly good place to:

8 't Smalle 🍺

Though there are plenty of cafes in the Jordaan at which you can rest your legs and quench your walker's thirst, the best terrace is along the waterside at 't Smalle, Egelantiersgracht 12 (℡ 020/623-9617). This cafe serves snacks like *bitterballen* and homemade soups (see "The Bar Scene," in chapter 10).

When you've finished your break, turn right off Egelantiersgracht to another sequence of side streets—Eerste Egelantiersdwarsstraat, Eerste Tuindwarsstraat, and Eerste Anjeliersdwarsstraat. On the way, at Eerste Egelantiersdwarsstraat 1–3, is a passage leading to the:

9 Claes Claeszhofje

Claes Claesz Anslo, a cloth merchant, founded this (now handsomely restored) almshouse in 1616. It's also known as the **Anslohofje**—a plaque on the neighboring entrance bears Anslo's coat of arms. Also note the "writing hand" gable stone at no. 52. Tiny apartments surround two equally minuscule courtyards.

Continue through those three side streets to:

10 Westerstraat

This broad street, formerly a canal known as Anjeliersgracht, hosts a Monday street market. At Westerstraat 109, at the corner of Eerste Anjeliersdwarsstraat, you pass a characteristic Jordaan bar, **Café Nol.** Across the street is the **Pianola Museum,** Westerstraat 106 (see "Minor Museums," in chapter 7).

11 Winkel 🍺

A cafe that's a contender for serving the best *appelgebak met slagroom* (apple pie with cream) in town, Winkel, Noordermarkt 43 (℡ 020/623-0223), also does a fair breakfast and snacks. It's a little gloomy (okay, *atmospheric*) inside, but has a great outdoor terrace on Westerstraat and a sliver of patio on Noordermarkt.

Continue east on Westerstraat to Noordermarkt (see stop 3 in Walking Tour 1).

TOUR 4: THE WATERFRONT

START:	**Centraal Station.**
FINISH:	**Centraal Station.**
TIME:	**Between 4 hours—not including a museum visit, rest stops, and an optional tram ride— and all day, should you find there's enough to hold your interest.**

| BEST TIMES: | **Morning or afternoon, it makes no difference—but see "Worst Times," below.** |
| WORST TIMES: | **During the morning and evening rush hours (8–9am and 5–6pm), Monday to Friday.** |

Amsterdam's waterfront, the narrow channel known as Het IJ (the IJ) that separates the main city on the south bank from Amsterdam-Noord (North), has been gaining ground as a visitor attraction in recent years. This changing circumstance is a by-product of the city opening up the old harbor to redevelopment. There's more to see and do than there used to be, both on the water and along the shore, and this tour is designed to bring you close to it all without you ever getting your feet wet. You'll get around with a mixture of walking and by riding buses, trams, and harbor ferries. This is a good tour to do with kids, because walking comprises only a part of it. There's much that should be of interest to them along the way; and going by ferry should be fun. Since the IJ will be a big feature on the tour, you should know that the word is pronounced more or less like "eye."

Most city trams and Metro lines, along with many bus lines (and trains, of course) end up at Amsterdam's main rail station:

1 Centraal Station

The hub of Amsterdam's transit network is an attraction in its own right. But you'll have more opportunities on this tour to sample its delights, so for now let's get started on the itinerary.

Cross over the bridge in front of Centraal Station, and from the bus stops to your front right, take bus 18, 21, or 22 westbound. It's just three stops to the Buiten Oranjestraat bus stop on Harlemmer Houttuinen, where you get out. Cross over the street and go under the railway arches in front of you. This brings you to the:

2 Westelijke Eilanden

The three artificial islands of the Western Islands, connected by drawbridges in this artmospheric old district are **Bickerseiland, Prinseneiland,** and **Realeneiland.** For all that they are only a short distance from the city center, they form a village-like community that seems set apart from the rest of Amsterdam. Centuries-old harbor warehouses converted to desirable apartments and artists' studios, along with some modern apartment blocks, line the connecting waterways. Berthed at the wharves are houseboats, barges, sailboats, cabin cruisers, motorboats, and all kinds of small boats.

The first thing you'll see after you pass under the railway arches and enter tree-shaded Hendrik Jonkerplein is the great Dutch *eetcafé* **'t Blaauwhooft** (see "The Waterfront," in chapter 6). It's early on the tour for taking a break (and besides the place doesn't open until 3pm), but it's worth noting for future reference. Go left to the canal, and then north along Bickersgracht. About midway along is a bridge that leads to Prinseneiland. Staying on Bickersgracht, you pass by a tiny petting zoo, **Kinderboerderij De Dierencapel** (see "Especially for Kids," in chapter 7).

Cross over the drawbridge onto Realenisland, and go north on Zandhoek, keeping the water to your right. Looking across the Westerdok in that direction,

Tour 4: The Waterfront

Greenpeace Ship
Sirius

NDSM-
Werf
3

4

Pannenkoekenboot
(Pancake Boat)

Amstel
Botel
(floating
hotel)

Russian
submarine

Coru. Douwes-
kanaal-Oost

Zijkanaal I

Klaprozenweg

Floraweg

Wingerdweg

Papaverkanaal

Kamperfoelieweg

Klaprozenweg

Ridderspoorweg

Papaverweg

Ribesstraat

Johan van Hasselt-

Kanaal-West

Houthavenveer

Distelweg

Distelweg-veer

Het IJ

Oude
Houthaven

Van Diemenstraat

ZEEHELDENBUURT

Barentszstr.

Louikeesgracht

REALEN-
EILAND

Houtmankade

Westerkanaal

Kinderboerderij
De Dierencapel

PRINSEN-
EILAND

BICKERS-
EILAND

Westerdok

Westerdoksdijk

Hendrik Jonker-
plein

WESTERDOKS-
EILAND

Haarlemmer Houttuinen

Haarlemmerdijk

Vinkenstraat

Westerdokskade

Nieuwe Westerdoksstr.

De Ruijterkade

2

Graszweg

Tollhuiskanaal

Asterweg

NDSM-werfveer

Ranonkelkade

Buiksloterkanaal

Graszweg

Mos-
plein

Johan van
Mosveld

Distelweg

Hagedoornweg

NOORD

Van der Pekstraat

Badhuiskade

6

Buiksloterweg

Noordhollandsch kanaal

Meeuwenlaan

St. haven

17

Buiksloterweg-
veer

IJpleinveer

Het IJ

Waterplein
West

**start
here** ★

1 **5** **7** **8**

16

Centraal Station

De Ruijterkade

Prins Hendrik-

kade

Nieuwendijk

Centraal
Station

OOSTERDOKS-
EILAND

Oosterdoks-

Ooster-

Eerste Marnix-
plantsoen

Palmgracht

Palmstraat

Willemsstraat

Goudsbloemstraat

Lindengracht

Nassaukade

Singelgracht

Lijnbaansgracht

Marnixstraat

JORDAAN

Westerstraat

Aniëliersstraat

Tuinstraat

Egelantiersstraat

Brouwersgracht

Haarlemmerstraat

Noorderkerk

Prinsengracht

Prinsen-
straat

Heren-
straat

Keizersgracht

Herengracht

Singel

Spuistraat

Voorburgwal

Nieuwendijk

Warmoes-

Damrak

Damrak

Singel

CENTRUM

Oude
Kerk

Nieuwe
Kerk

RED LIGHT
DISTRICT

Zeedijk

Geldersekade

Nieuw-
markt

Prins Hendrik-

Wijde
straat

Kromme Waal

Eilandsgracht

Oude Waal

Nieuwmarkt

Leliegracht

Egelantiersgracht

1 Centraal Station
2 Westelijke Eilanden
3 NDSM-Werf
4 IJ-Kantine ☕
5 Centraal Station
6 Amsterdam-Noord
7 Centraal Station
8 Grand Café-Restaurant 1e Klas ☕
9 Science Center NEMO
10 Scheepvaartmuseum
11 Muziekgebouw aan 't IJ/Bimhuis
12 Passenger Terminal Amsterdam
13 KNSM-Eiland
14 Kanis en Meiland ☕
15 IJburg
16 Centraal Station
17 IJplein
18 Wilhelmina Dok ☕

Legend:
ⓘ Information
Ⓜ Metro station
····· Ferry route
🚌 Ferry dock
🚌 Bus stop
🚊 Tram stop

0 — 1/4 mi
0 — 0.25 km

FLORA-PARK
VOLEWIJKS-PARK
W.H. VLIEGENBOS
Noordhollandsch Kanaal
Wingerdweg
Leeuwarderweg
Wadden-weg
Nieuwe-weg
Meeuwenlaan
Nieuwendammerdijk
Zamenhofstraat
Hasseltweg
Adelaars-weg
Johan van Hasseltweg
Havikslaan
Meeuwenlaan
Pont-haven
Gedempte Insteekhaven
Noordwal
Motorkanaal

Het IJ

KNSM-EILAND
Azartplein
Surinamekade
KNSM-laan
Sumatrakade
JAVA-EILAND
Javakade
Levantkade
Verbindingsdam
13
14

18 ★ finish here

Jan Schaefer Brug
IJhaven
IJ-Tunnel
11 **12**
Veem-kade
Piet Heinkade
OOSTELIJKE HANDELSKADE
Veemkade
Oostelijke Handelskade
Piet Heinkade
RIETLANDEN
Piet Hein-tunnel
15 →
Dijksgracht
Panamalaan
MARINE ETABLISSEMENT (NAVAL COMPLEX)
kade
dok
9
10
Kattenburgerstraat
Grote Wittenburgerstraat
Wittenburgervaart
Valkenburgerstr
kade
Kattenburger-gracht
Wittenburger-gracht
Oostenburgergracht
Nieuwe Vaart
Cruquiuskade
Nieuwe-vaart
Lozings-kanaal
Zeeburgerdijk

you'll see the modern apartments and offices that line narrow **Westerdok-seiland** (Western Docks Island). Farther along Zandhoek, at the corner of Zoutkeetsgracht, is the fine French bistro **De Gouden Reael.** Go left on Zoutkeetsgracht, then right on Houtmankade.

From the intersection of Tasmanstraat and Houtmankade, walk north on Tasmanstraat for 300m (330 yds.) to the ferry dock at the end of the street. Take the free passengers-and-bikes Houthavenveer (Houthaven Ferry)—not the Distelwegveer (Distelweg Ferry) that departs from the same dock—for the 6-minute ride across the IJ to the north shore to the:

3 NDSM-Werf

The former facility of the Nederlandsche Dok en Scheepsbouw Maatschappij (Netherlands Dock and Shipyard Corporation) was used for shipbuilding, dry-docking, and ship repair. Now in the process of large-scale redevelopment, it's an expanding star on the city's cultural scene, providing a home for performance venues, and art and design studios.

Here, too is the **Amstel Botel** (see "The Waterfront," in chapter 5), the city's only floating hotel. Within easy torpedo range of this waterborne lodging, a rusting, 1950s-vintage ex-Soviet Navy Zulu class **attack submarine** is tied up at an off-shore wharf. Greenpeace International's environmental warrior of the seas, *Sirius,* is based across the dock from the Amstel Botel. The **Pannekoekenboot (Pancake Boat; ℂ 020/636-8817;** www.pannenkoekenboot.nl) sorties from here to prowl the harbor laden with pancake-munching kids and shanghaied parents.

4 IJ-Kantine ☕

MT Ondinaweg 15–17 (ℂ 020/633-7162). Even if "IJ Canteen" doesn't immediately grab as an alluring name, the reality behind the handle is far superior. This large and multi-faceted cafe, brasserie, and restaurant on the NDSM Wharf waterfront does indeed occupy the former shipyard's cafeteria—restored to a squared-away shine, and sporting a grand dockside terrace.

Board the free passengers-and-bikes NDSM-Werfveer (NDSM Wharf Ferry)—not the Houthavenveer (Houthaven Ferry)—to:

5 Centraal Station

The 14-minute ferry ride is your best chance to take in much of the city's harbor in a single gulp. Along the way you'll likely notice the distinctive green-and-blue Fast Flying Ferry passenger hydrofoils (see "Hot Jets," in chapter 11), outbound to or inbound from the Nordzeekanaal (North Sea Canal). You'll pass the modern architecture on the long, narrow redeveloped **Westerdokseiland (Western Docks Island)** jutting out from the IJ's south shore.

At the end of your minicruise, you arrive at the Waterplein-West dock behind Centraal Station. Explore the station and its immediate surroundings (see "By Train" under "Getting to Amsterdam," in chapter 3, and "Historical Buildings & Monuments," in chapter 7).

Oosterdokseiland (Eastern Docks Island), just east of Centraal Station, is the latest piece in the rapidly-filling jigsaw of harbor redevelopment. The city's giant new **Centrale Bibliotheek (Central Library)** opened here in 2008; it has an excellent English department, for anyone who wants to spend a rainy day browsing the bookshelves. Nearby is the shiny new **Conservatorium van**

Amsterdam, the city's music school, where you can take in concerts staged by the students in their fine new concert hall.

From Waterplein-West, take the free passengers-and-bikes Buiksloterwegveer (Buiksloterweg Ferry)—not the IJplein-veer (IJplein Ferry) that departs from the same dock—for the 5-minute ride across the IJ to:

6 Amsterdam-Noord

There's not a lot you can get to see in this northern district of Amsterdam without a bicycle, nor time enough to shuttle around by bus (there's no tram or Metro service in Noord). I suggest you just kick around on the north shore for a short time. If the weather is bad, you can retreat to the more-than-decent **Café-Restaurant De Pont,** Buiksloterweg 3–5 (✆ **020/636-3388**), at the ferry dock.

Take the ferry—one departs every 5 to 10 minutes—back to:

7 Centraal Station

See waypoint 5, above.

8 Grand Café-Restaurant 1e Klas 🍽

Spoor 2B, Centraal Station (✆ 020/625-0131). Head to platform 2, for that surely rare phenomenon—a station restaurant that's just about worth missing your train for. An alternative that keeps you right at the water's edge is Pier 10, De Ruyterkade, Steiger 10 (✆ 020/427-2310; www.pier10.nl), an atmospheric small place for lunch or dinner, right behind Centraal Station. See "The Waterfront," in chapter 6, for both restaurants.

At this point, if you have no interest in visiting either one of the two museums (don't try to do both) covered in waypoints 9 and 10, below, stay put at Centraal Station, and pick up the itinerary again at waypoint 11. Otherwise, remember to choose between waypoints 7A and 7B, and follow the getting-there instructions for the one you select.

Take bus 22, 42, or 43 from outside Centraal Station (no. 22 departs from the stops to your front right as you exit the station, and nos. 42 and 43 from the stops to your front left), for two stops, to the IJ-Tunnel bus stop, and then walk the short distance north to:

9 Science Center NEMO

This hands-on science and technology attraction (see "Multimedia Attractions," in chapter 7) should have a strong appeal to kids, of all ages. Its striking design by celeb Italian architect Renzo Piano gives it something of the look of an ocean liner. In fine weather, the rooftop terrace of NEMO's **Café DEK5** (✆ **020/531-3533;** www.e-nemo.nl) affords grand views over Amsterdam's harbor.

Take bus 22, 42, or 43 from outside Centraal Station (no. 22 departs from the stops to your front right as you exit the station, and nos. 42 and 43 from the stops to your front left), for three stops, to the Kadijksplein bus stop, and then walk the short distance to the:

10 Scheepvaartmuseum

The **Maritime Museum,** Oosterdok 2 (✆ **020/523-2222;** www.scheepvaart museum.nl), where a thousand years of Holland's history as a seafaring power is recorded, makes a good alternative to NEMO (see above), and on a tour of the city's harbor it's even more fitting. There's just one catch. The museum, housed in the 17th-century Amsterdam Admiralty Arsenal, is closed until the summer of 2011 for a much-needed modernization. Call ahead or check the museum's website for the latest state of play. In the meantime, one of the museum's star attractions, a full-size replica of an 18th-century sailing ship, the *Amsterdam* (see "Sail Ahoy," in chapter 7), is moored to a dock just across the water at Science Center NEMO, and is currently open to visitors.

If you passed on the museum visits associated with options 9 and 10, you can now leave Centraal Station from behind the station, and walk east on Piet Heinkade, keeping the waters of the IJ on your left, before descending to waterside Oostelijke Handelskade, and the series of large modern buildings along this waterfront street, the first of which is the combined:

11 Muziekgebouw aan 't IJ/Bimhuis

These two ultra-modern concert halls—the Muziekgebouw aan 't IJ for contemporary, electronic, and world music, and Bimhuis for jazz—opened in 2005 (see "The Performing Arts," in chapter 10). The Muziekgebouw aan 't IJ has a hip cafe-restaurant, the **Star Ferry** (© **020/788-2090**), with big picture windows looking out on the harbor, and a great, if on occasion breezy, outdoor terrace at the western end of the wharf. The neighboring concert hall's **Bimhuiscafé** (© **020/788-2158**) is equally trendy and boasts just as fine views.

Continue east on Oostelijke Handelskade, past the Mövenpick Hotel Amsterdam City Center, to the:

12 Passenger Terminal Amsterdam

The PTA should usually be easy to recognize—it will often have a large and colorful ocean cruise liner "parked" right outside, one of around 100 that dock here every year. Like the Muziekgebouw aan 't IJ, Bimhuis, the Mövenpick Hotel, and the Passenger Terminal Amsterdam, all the buildings stretching east from here along the water are either the latest thing in cutting-edge modern architecture, or are converted old harbor warehouses.

Either walk east on waterfront Veemkade for the harbor views—past Jamie Olivers's cool restaurant Fifteen Amsterdam (see "The Waterfont," in chapter 6). Or, spare your feet by boarding tram 26 at the Kattenburgerstraat stop and going east for one stop, to the Rietlandpark stop. From here, either transfer to tram 10 going north for three stops to the Azartplein terminus, or walk north across the Verbindingsdam bridge to:

13 KNSM-Eiland

The long, artificial KNSM Island—its name comes from the initials of the old Koninklijke Nederlandse Stoomboot-Maatschappij (Royal Dutch Steamship Company)—was once thickly strewn with harbor warehouses and other port installations. Now it's a shiny modern residential zone. You might easily be trampled by hordes of visiting architects and city planners, both professionals and students, in town to get a handle on where cities are headed in the 21st century. The best thing you can do here is to stroll up and down the island, and in and out of the vast apartment complexes, until your interest or energy, or both, run out. Then, make for the island's south bank, to:

14 Kanis en Meiland 🍺

Levantkade 127 (📞 020/418-2439), is both a Dutch play on words with the island's name, and a decent bar and eatery (see "The Bar Scene," in chapter 10).

Re-cross the Verbindingsdam bridge, onboard tram 10 or on foot, to the Rietlandpark tram stop. From here you can take an optional ride east on tram 26 to the end of the line, at:

15 IJburg

This new Amsterdam residential district has a population of more than 10,000 and counting, living on artificial islands on the Buiten IJ (Outer IJ), a southern bay of the IJsselmeer lake (formerly the Zuiderzee, or Southern Sea). You should maybe only do this side trip if you are interested to see how Amsterdam is providing homes for a fast-expanding population in a country where what little land there is to spare has to be reclaimed from the sea, lakes, and wetlands.

If you passed on the side trip to IJburg, board tram 26 (if you're returning from IJburg, you'll already be on the tram, of course), for the ride west back to:

16 Centraal Station

See waypoints 5 and 7, above.

Take the free passengers-and-bikes IJplein-veer (IJplein Ferry) from the Waterplein-West dock behind Centraal Station—not the Buiksloterwegveer (Buiksloterweg Ferry), which departs from the same dock—for the 5-minute ride across the harbor to:

17 IJplein

From the ferry dock and the nearby sea dike, you get fine views of the central harbor zone.

Go east along the dike for around 300m (330 yds.), to:

18 Wilhelmina Dok 🍺

Noordwal 1 (📞 020/632-3701), an orange-painted waterfront cafe-restaurant (see "The Waterfront," in chapter 6). You'll get great views of passing ships from here. Maybe too good—a few years back a canal barge strayed from the ship channel and rammed the restaurant!

Walk back along the dike to the ferry dock and take the IJplein-veer (IJplein Ferry) back to Centraal Station. Note that the last ferry from here departs at 11:50pm. If you miss it, you'll have to hoof it around to the Buiksloterwegveer (Buiksloterweg Ferry) dock farther west; this ferry runs all night.

BIKE TOUR: **ALONG THE AMSTEL RIVER**

START:	**Waterlooplein.**
FINISH:	**Amstel Station.**
TIME:	**Allow between 3 and 4 hours, not including rest stops.**
BEST TIMES:	**May to September, outside of rush hour (rush hour is around 8–10am and 5–7pm).**

This biking route begins in the city center and follows a scenic, relatively quiet way through the city, emerging into the countryside alongside the Amstel River for a short but glorious hop out to the pretty village of **Ouderkerk aan de Amstel.**

Also see "Bicycling in Amsterdam," in chapter 3.

The starting point is Waterlooplein and the:

1 Amstel River

The Amstel is likely to be fairly busy with waterborne traffic, and has house-boats moored along both banks.

Continue to the:

2 Magere Brug

Known as the Amstel's "Skinny Bridge," the Magere Brug is actually an 18th-century replacement for the original 17th-century bridge. Cross over to the west (left) bank and cycle south along the Amstel. On the river's other side, you can see the **Koninklijk Theater Carré** (see "The Performing Arts," in chapter 10). Continue over Sarphatistraat, which you'll easily recognize by its tram lines.

Detour around a break in the road, cross busy Stadhouderskade, and get back to the river at:

3 Amsteldijk

Keep pedaling south on this road, enjoying the riverside views, until you reach the Berlagebrug (Berlage Bridge), where you need to be careful, as the traffic gets noticeably busier at this point.

Stay on Amsteldijk until you arrive at:

4 Martin Luther Kingpark

Most of the road traffic swings away to the right on President Kennedylaan at this park, but stay on Amsteldijk, which gradually becomes almost rural, though with houseboats alongside the road in place of country cottages. Up ahead, you'll hear a noise like a substantial storm; it means you're getting closer to the highway bridge that carries the city's A10 ring road (beltway) across the river.

Go under the bridge and finally you're out in the country, passing:

5 Amstelpark

The riverside stays tranquil and scenic from now on. Continue past the statue of Rembrandt and a windmill at the park's end. Around this characteristic old Dutch scene, there'll likely be busloads of tourists photographing Rembrandt, the windmill, themselves, and everything in sight, probably including you as you pedal past.

Bike Tour: Along the Amstel River

1 Amstel
2 Magere Brug
3 Amsteldijk
4 Martin Luther Kingpark
5 Amstelpark
6 Klein Kalfje
7 Ouderkerk aan de Amstel
8 Ouderkerkerdijk
9 Utrechtsebrug

Beyond this is:

6 Klein Kalfje ☕

Amsteldijk 355 (℗ 020/644-5338), a small atmospheric Dutch cafe with a riverside terrace and canal barges moored alongside. A road separates the terrace from the cafe. There used to be an unofficial traffic sign here that indicated CAUTION: WAITER CROSSING.

You pass cottages and villas all the way to:

7 Ouderkerk aan de Amstel

The idyllically sited village has an abundance of cafes and restaurants with riverside or outdoor terraces. If you've still got energy, explore the village before settling down at one of the terraces for something restorative.

To return, switch to the right bank of the river, on:

8 Ouderkerkerdijk

Narrower than Amsteldijk, this road has almost no traffic. Along the way, you'll pass a windmill and several tiny hamlets.

Recross the Amstel at the:

9 Utrechtsebrug

Now you return to Amsteldijk and busy city streets. At Berlagebrug, recross the river and pedal the short distance to Amstel Station, where you, your bike, and your weary legs can board a Metro train back to Waterlooplein. Or you can bike back along either bank.

SHOPPING IN AMSTERDAM

As a city with a long history of trading, Amsterdam is loaded with tempting wares, at premium prices, from all over the world, and homegrown products both traditional and contemporary. The best Dutch porcelain comes from nearby Delft, or from Makkum in Friesland. Much ado is made of mock-antique pewter wares and grandfather clocks, but the less said about these the better (unless you're into high kitsch).

The Dutch flower and plant industry is a booming business indeed, but foreign visitors can take home only certain certified bulbs. Nonetheless, there are plenty of creative ways to spend your euros.

Adding a contemporary dimension to this tradition-laden scene are the funky boutiques scattered around Amsterdam, and adding sparkle are the diamond cutters. The city has a full range of shopping options, from small and highly individualistic—perhaps eccentric—boutiques showcasing a growing number of highly regarded local designers to chains, department stores, and malls.

THE SHOPPING SCENE

Shopping can be an interesting extension to your Amsterdam experience, because the city center is small enough that stores and attractions are often right beside each other. Rather than going on dedicated shopping expeditions, it may make more sense to simply drop into close-by stores while you're touring.

OPENING HOURS Regular store hours are Monday, Tuesday, Wednesday, and Friday from 9 or 10am to 6pm (some stores don't open until as late as 1pm on Mon), Thursday from 9 or 10am to 9pm, and Saturday from 9 or 10am to 5pm. Many city stores open on Sunday too, usually from noon to 5pm.

PRICES All applicable taxes are included in amounts shown on tags. End-of-season and other special sales occur occasionally throughout the year.

Tax Return

If you live outside the European Union (E.U.), you're entitled to a refund of |part of the value-added tax *(BTW/omzetbelasting)* on goods purchased in the Netherlands for personal use, and totaling 50€ or more per shop in a day. Savings of up to 18% of the purchase price can be garnered. Your purchases need to be made at a store that subscribes to the refund system, identified by a TAX FREE sticker, and exported in your hand baggage or checked baggage. To obtain the refund, ask the store for a **refund check.** When you leave the E.U., present this check along with your purchases and receipts to Customs. They'll stamp the check, and you can get the refund in cash or paid to your credit card at a **refund office.** Schiphol Airport has two such locations: **Global Refund** in Departures Lounge 3, and **ABN-AMRO** in Departures Lounge 2.

A Europe-wide list of refund offices, and more information on tax-free shopping, are available from **Global Refund** (✆ 421-232/111-111; www.globalrefund.com). Local toll-free phone numbers and an e-mail address for inquiries can be found on the website. For a cut of your savings, **VATfree.nl** (✆ 084/836-7640; www.vatfree.nl) will handle the bureaucratic details.

DUTY-FREE ITEMS If you are traveling from one E.U. country to another, you can't buy duty-free goods at airports, on ferries, or at border crossings; you can make duty-free purchases only when traveling to or from the E.U. from a nonmember country. Schiphol Airport's duty-free shopping center offers reduced prices for intra-E.U. travelers.

Best Buys

ANTIQUES There are hundreds of reputable dealers, and you're sure to find something worth shipping or carrying home. Antiques—maps, prints, old-fashioned clocks, Chinese urns, silver boxes, books, furniture, old pewter, porcelain, crystal, and jewelry—are a major attraction here.

ART Contemporary art is a vibrant activity in this city of young artists. Galleries abound, particularly in the canal area near the Rijksmuseum. Posters and reproductions of famous artworks are other excellent items to buy in Amsterdam. The Dutch are known for their high-quality printing and color-reproduction work, and one of their favorite subjects is Holland's rich artistic treasure-trove.

CHEESE Gouda (*khow*-duh) and Edam (*ay*-dam) are the two most familiar Dutch cheeses, among dozens of varieties. You have the choice between factory cheese, made from pasteurized milk, or *boerenkaas*, farm cheese produced the old way with fresh, unpasteurized milk straight from the cow. *Boerenkaas* is more expensive, but has more taste. Another choice is between young (*jonge*) and old (*oude*) cheese. Young cheese is sweeter, moister, and has that melt-in-your-mouth quality, while old cheese has a sharper, drier taste, and a crumbly texture.

CHOCOLATE Droste, Verkade, and van Houten are three of the best names to look for. Or seek out small specialty stores that still hand-fill bonbon boxes (see "Food & Drink," later in this chapter).

CRYSTAL & PEWTER　If you recall classic Dutch still-life paintings portraying scenes of 17th-century family life, you'll know that crystal and pewter objects are part of Holland's heritage. Crystal has long been associated with the towns of Leerdam and Maastricht (to spot the genuine article, look for the four triangles of the **Royal Leerdam** label), and pewter with Tiel. *Note:* The Dutch government bans the use of lead as a hardening agent, but this assurance only protects you from toxicity in new pewter, so don't buy any antiques for use with food or drink.

DELFTWARE & MAKKUMWARE　Porcelain from the royal factories at Delft and Makkum can be wonderful. None of it is cheap. With a lowercase *d,* delftware is an umbrella name for all Dutch hand-painted earthenware pottery resembling ancient Chinese porcelain, whether it is blue and white, red and white, or polychrome, and regardless of the Dutch city in which it was produced. Delftware, or Delft Blue (with a capital *D*) refers to the predominantly, but not exclusively, blue-and-white products of the Delft-based firms **De Koninklijke Porceleyne Fles** and **De Delftse Pauw.** Similarly, *makkumware* is synonymous with polychrome pottery, whereas Makkumware is the hand-painted polychrome earthenware produced only in Makkum, a town in Friesland province, by the family-owned firm **Koninklijke Tichelaars,** which was founded in 1594.

Genuine Delftware and Makkumware are for sale in specialized stores (De Delftse Pauw sells its pottery only from its factory and by mail order), but it is far more interesting to go to the workshops in the towns and see how they are made. Little has changed over the centuries, and all the decorating is still done by hand. This makes it quite pricey, but each piece is a unique product, made by craftsmen. Some of the numerous copies of De Porceleyne Fles and Tichelaars products are nearly equal in quality, while others miss by miles the delicacy of the brush stroke, the richness of color, or the sheen of the secret glazes that make the items produced by these firms so highly prized.

To be sure that you're looking at a *real* Delft vase from De Koninklijke Porceleyne Fles, look on the bottom for the distinctive three-part hallmark: An outline of a small pot, above an initial *J* crossed with a short stroke, above the scripted word *Delft;* for De Delftse Pauw, look for three blue stars separated by a drafting compass, above the scripted text *D.P. Delft.* To distinguish Koninklijke Tichelaars's Makkumware products, look for two scripted *T*s overlapped like crossed swords.

Blue Days

Only a few remain of the more than 30 potteries in Delft that in the 17th century worked overtime to meet the newly affluent Dutch's clamoring demand for Chinese-style vases, urns, wall tiles, and knickknacks. Originally, pottery made in Delft was white, to imitate tin-glazed products from Italy and Spain. During the 16th century, superior-quality Chinese porcelain, decorated in blue, was imported to Holland. Delftware factories refined their products accordingly, using a white tin glaze to cover the red clay, then decorating it in blue. This Delft Blue became famous the world over; it was less expensive than Chinese porcelain, and skillfully made. Polychrome decorations were also used, on both white and black backgrounds.

SAY IT WITH flowers

Holland has long had a close relationship with flowers, and it's not merely that the tulip fields south of Haarlem are a spring-time blaze of color that attracts world-wide admirers. Flowers have deeper roots in this land of flat, green polders. Amsterdam's floating flower market is only the best-known example of a sales network that makes a flower store a vital service in Dutch towns and villages.

Maybe because so many people live side by side in such a small, well-ordered country, flowers provide a breath of fresh air, a touch of the natural world when much of the environment is artificial. A Dutch house without flowers would be like Edam without the cheese. Gardens, balconies, rooftop terraces, window boxes, and vases, are all pressed into ser-vice. Additionally, no visit to a dinner party would be complete without an accompanying bunch of flowers for the host. And Dutch men don't share the macho hang-up of some nationalities at being seen carrying flowers in public.

DIAMONDS   Since the 15th century, Amsterdam has been a major diamond-cutting center. Diamonds are a big industry, and prices are competitive, but make sure you take your time to decide on a purchase. Diamond-cutting houses generally give you a brisk tour, deposit you in the salesroom, and wait for the pressure to build.

DRINKS   Inexpensive products primarily or exclusively for immediate consump-tion include Dutch beer, gin (*jenever*), and white wine (yes, it does exist, from vineyards in the southern province of Limburg, but not in quantity).

FASHIONS   Paris may set the styles, but young Dutch women—and some of their mothers—often know better than the French how to make them work. Whatever the current European fashion rage is, you can expect to see it in store windows all over Amsterdam, and in all price ranges. It's fun to ferret out the new, young crop of Dutch designers who regularly open stores in unpredictable locations all over town.

FLOWER BULBS   Nothing is more Dutch than a tulip—even though the flow-er's natural home is on the high plains of Turkey and Iran. You may have a problem making your choices, however, since there's an incredible array of colors and shapes among the hundreds of varieties of tulip bulbs available. Some tulip bulbs are named after famous people—Sophia Loren, President Kennedy, Queen Juliana, even Cyrano de Bergerac. Not all bulbs are certified for entry into other countries, so look for the numbered phyto-sanitary certificate attached to the label—these allow you to import bulbs. Among other popular flower bulbs are those for daffodils, narcissi, hyacinths, and crocuses.

TOBACCO   Some of the world's best cigars and pipe tobacco are available in Amsterdam. Serious smokers know that Dutch cigars are different, and drier, than Cuban or other traditional cigars. It's partly because of the Indonesian tobacco and partly because of how the cigar is made.

TRADITIONAL CLOCKS   Two types of handcrafted clocks have retained popu-larity through the centuries. One is the Zaandam clock, or *Zaanseklok,* identified by its ornately carved oak or walnut case, brass panels, tiny windows on the dial face, and the motto *Nu Eick Syn Sin* ("To each his own"). The other is the Frisian clock, or *Friese Stoelklok,* which is even more heavily decorated, customarily with hand-painted scenes of the Dutch countryside, a smiling moon face, or ships at sea that may bob back and forth in time with the ticks.

Great Shopping Areas

A few shopping streets are pedestrians-only, some are busy thoroughfares, and others are peaceful canalside esplanades or fashionable promenades. Yet others are in suburban malls, or opening up in new waterfront development zones. Each segment in this ever-growing network has developed its own identity or predominant selection of goods as a specialty. To plan your own shopping trails, here are brief descriptions of the major shopping areas and what you can expect to find in each of them:

AMSTELVEEN This new town built around an old village south of Amsterdam offers up clean, efficient living in a garden city. The shopping center has many of the nonspecialist types of outlets—department stores, boutiques, toy stores, and the like—that you'll find throughout Amsterdam. Here, however, they're in an enclosed mall and you can visit them all a lot quicker. So if you don't like shopping but can just about tolerate it if you get through it quickly, this may be the place for you. Take the no. 5 tram from Centraal Station to the terminus, which is right beside the Amstelveen mall; the ride takes around 25 minutes.

THE JORDAAN The entire Jordaan district, a nest of streets beyond Westermarkt to the west of central Amsterdam, is a junk-and-oddity-lover's paradise, and is a good place to seek out Amsterdam's up-and-coming funky boutiques.

KALVERSTRAAT At one end of this long, pedestrians-only shopping street is the Dam; at the other is the Muntplein traffic hub. In between is a hodgepodge of shopping

---

NINE GREAT little streets

If your idea of a good shopping day includes browsing through fashion boutiques and funky specialty stores, garnished with cool little cafes, salons, and galleries, cut a west-to-east path through the northern *Grachtengordel* (Canal Belt). Begin at Westermarkt and crisscross Herengracht, Keizersgracht, and Prinsengracht. By doing so, you'll pass through the *Negen Straatjes* (Nine Streets, though since *straatjes* is the diminutive of *straten,* which means streets, the Nine Little Streets), 17th-century side streets that connect the stately big canals in this part of town.

The streets are grouped in three lines of three, on the canal stretches that lie between Westermarkt and Raadhuisstraat in the north, and Leidsegracht and Beulingstraat in the south. From north to south, they are: Reestraat, Hartenstraat, and Gasthuismolensteeg; Berenstraat, Wolvenstraat, and Oude Spiegelstraat; and Runstraat, Huidenstraat, and Wijde Heisteeg.

Nine Streets stores featured in this chapter are: **Antonia by Yvette** (see p. 226); **BLGK Edelsmeden** (see p. 224); **Cortina Papier** (see p. 217); **De Kaaskamer** (see p. 222); **E. Kramer Candle Shop** (see p. 227); **Gerda's Bloemen & Planten** (see p. 222); **H.J. van de Kerkhof** (see p. 224); **McLennan's** (see p. 221); **Miauw** (see p. 221); and **Patisserie Pompadour** (see p. 223).

For more information about the Nine Streets, visit **www.theninestreets.com** and **www.de9straatjes.nl**.

possibilities—trendy boutiques, mass-market clothes, athletic-gear emporiums, tacky gift stuff, stores selling dowdy raincoats and conservative business suits, bookstores, fur salons, maternity and baby stores, record stores, and more. A clutch of department stores—high-brow, mid-brow, and low-brow—are to be found in this area. If you're looking for jewelry, trendy clothing, or athletic gear, these department stores have it all. The shopping parade that begins on Kalverstraat continues around the corner on Heiligeweg, across Koningsplein and along Leidsestraat, all the way to Leidseplein.

PIETER CORNELISZ HOOFTSTRAAT & VAN BAERLESTRAAT Dozens of international and Dutch designer boutiques, plus antiques and porcelain dealers, are on elegant Pieter Cornelisz Hooftstraat and adjoining streets near the Museum District. Known to insiders as "P.C. Hooftstraat" (www.pchooftstraat.nl), or just "the P.C. Hooft" (pronounced pay-say-*hooft*), this street is where well-dressed, well-coiffed Amsterdammers buy everything from lingerie to light bulbs. Along its 3 short blocks, stores sell furniture, antiques, toys, shoes, chocolates, Persian rugs, designer clothes, fresh-baked bread, fresh-caught fish, china, books, furs, perfume, leather goods, office supplies, flowers, and jewelry. Around the corner on Van Baerlestraat are more boutiques, shoe stores, and enough branches of major banks to guarantee that you can continue to buy as long as your plastic holds out. If you're feeling rich or simply want to feast your eyes on lovely things (fashion, antiques, and art), begin at the Concertgebouw and walk along Van Baerlestraat toward Vondelpark. Nearby, Cornelis Schuytstraat has upmarket stores selling fashion, food, flowers, and collectibles.

ROKIN Parallel to Kalverstraat and also running from the Dam to Muntplein is Rokin. Along here, you'll find art galleries, antiques stores, elegant fashion boutiques, and tobacco.

SPIEGELKWARTIER (SPIEGEL QUARTER) Spiegelgracht, a small and quiet bit of canal east of Leidseplein, is the gateway to one of Europe's finest antiques-hunting grounds: The best antiques-store street in Amsterdam, Nieuwe Spiegelstraat, contains nearly 100 stores. All those tankards, pipes, cabinets, clocks, kettles, vases, and other bric-a-brac you see in old Dutch paintings still show up among stores' treasures here. This antiques esplanade covers only a short 4-block stretch between the Rijksmuseum and Herengracht's Golden Bend, where Amsterdam's wealthiest burghers once lived. Among the items you might see are dolls with china heads, rare editions of early children's books, Indonesian puppets, Persian tapestries, landscape paintings, art prints and reproductions, brass Bible stands, candlesticks, copper kettles, music boxes, and old Dutch clocks. Nearby, dozens of antiquarian bookstores can be found between central Spui and the Royal Palace, on Spuistraat, Singel, and Nieuwezijds Voorburgwal. For more antiques stores, look along Prinsengracht between Leidsestraat and Westermarkt.

> **Impressions**
>
> *I challenge you to find anything open 24 hours a day in this supposedly world-class city. Indeed, most shops close by 6pm—precisely when people leaving work might actually want to patronize them.*
> —Russell Shorto, director of Amsterdam's John Adams Institute, *The Times Magazine*, 2009

SHOPPING A TO Z

Here is a selection of interesting Amsterdam stores, some of which you might not otherwise have found. Use this list to save you time and trouble with your shopping list, or simply to locate interesting stores.

Antiques

Antiquariaat Brinkman ★ A leading light in Amsterdam's flourishing antique book trade, and a haunt of bibliophiles, historians, collectors, and researchers, this atmospheric store was one of just a handful of booksellers when it opened in the 1950s. Singel 319 (at Raamsteeg). ✆ **020/623-8353.** www.antiquariaatbrinkman.nl. Tram: 1, 2, or 5 to Spui.

Mathieu Hart ★★ If you're interested in an artistic view of Amsterdam or the Dutch countryside, this discreet store, which has been in business as a fine antiquarian since 1878, stocks color etchings of Dutch cities alongside rare old prints, 18th-century Delftware, and grandfather clocks. Rokin 122 (at Spui). ✆ **020/623-1658.** www.hartantiques.com. Tram: 4, 9, 14, 16, 24, or 25 to Spui.

Premsela & Hamburger ★ Opposite the Allard Pierson Museum (p. 141), this jewelry and antique silver establishment—purveyors to the Dutch royal court—opened in 1823. Inside their brocaded display cases and richly carved cabinets is a variety of exquisite, distinctive items. Poise and polish are the operative words, with authentic silver baubles ranging from 19th-century English saltcellars to 18th-century tea strainers and Art Deco silverware. Open Monday to Friday from 9:30am to 6pm. Rokin 98 (at Spui). ✆ **020/624-9688.** www.premsela.com. Tram: 4, 9, 14, 16, 24, or 25 to Spui.

Art

Galerie Carla Koch ★ For ceramics and glassware, this waterfront gallery employs some of the raciest design talent in Holland; their products are always different and interesting, if inevitably not to everyone's taste. Open Thursday to Saturday from noon to 6pm, and the first Sunday of the month from 2 to 6pm. Detroit Building (6th Floor), Veemkade 500 (at Piet Heinkade). ✆ **020/673-7310.** www.carlakoch.nl. Tram: 26 to Kattenburgerstraat.

Italiaander Galleries Art from around the world (particularly Africa and Asia), and all sorts of ethnic jewelry, are displayed here. Open Wednesday to Saturday from noon to 5:30pm. Prinsengracht 526 (at Spiegelgracht). ✆ **020/625-0942.** Tram: 1, 2, or 5 to Prinsengracht.

Museum Het Rembrandthuis You can purchase high-quality reproduction Rembrandt etchings in the museum store, done by hand in the traditional manner. Jodenbreestraat 4 (at Waterlooplein). ✆ **020/520-0040.** www.rembrandthuis.nl. Tram: 9 or 14 to Waterlooplein.

Rijksmuseum ★ Holland's finest museum might itself be a shrunken treasure while the main building is closed for refurbishment, but its gift store has a nice line in repro Rembrandts and Vermeers, framed or unframed. Jan Luijkenstraat 1B (at Museumplein). ✆ **020/647-7000.** www.rijksmuseum.nl. Tram: 2 or 5 to Hobbemastraat.

Torch ★ The occasional international name makes this hip Jordaan gallery a prime venue for progressive contemporary art, the place to hobnob with the young, beautiful, and creative. It's open Thursday to Saturday 2 to 6pm. Lauriergracht 94 (at Lijnbaansgracht). ✆ **020/626-0284.** www.torchgallery.com. Tram: 13, 14, or 17 to Westermarkt.

Central Amsterdam Shopping

9

SHOPPING IN AMSTERDAM | Shopping A to Z

Italiaander Galleries **3**
Jacob Hooy **79**
Jan Jansen **38**
Jorrit Heinen **5, 13**
Keet in Huis **72**
Kitsch Kitchen
 Supermercado **59**
Kunst & Antiekcentrum
 De Looier **26**
Kunstmarkt **20**
La Savonnerie **30**
Lindengracht Market **68**
Lush **37**
Magic Mushroom Gallery **11**
Magna Plaza **47**
Mathieu Hart **17**
McLennan's **50**
Mechanisch Speelgoed **66**
Megazino **56**
Metz&Co. **7**
Miauw **51**
Mister B **75**
Modern Art Market **88**
Museum Het
 Rembrandthuis **82**
Nieuws Innovations **58**

Patisserie Pompadour **22**
Peek & Cloppenburg **43**
P.G.C. Hajenius **36**
Pol's Potten **72**
Postzegelmarkt **41**
Premsela & Hamburger **35**
Puccini Bomboni **62, 86**
Shoebaloo **8, 10**
Simon Levelt **60**
Smokiana **4**
Spr Specials **40**
Sprmrkt **55**
't Curiosa Winkeltje **54**
Tinkerbell Fun &
 Discovery Shop **2**
Torch **29**
Van Ravenstein **23**
Victoria Gifts **71**
Vroom & Dreesmann
 (V&D) **14**
Waterlooplein
 Flea Market **87**
Waterstone's **18**
Webers Holland **80**
Westermarkt **67**
WonderWood **84**

Museum District & Amsterdam South Shopping

9

SHOPPING IN AMSTERDAM | Shopping A to Z

Albert Cuypmarkt **14**	Coster Diamonds **13**	Shoebaloo **3, 11**
Azzurro Due **8**	De Waterkinkel **4**	Sprmrkt Sth **2**
Brandmeester's **7**	Edgar Vos **9**	Van Gogh Museum **5**
Cartier **10**	Louis Vuitton **12**	
Charly Ensuite **1**	Rijksmuseum **6**	

Van Gogh Museum ★★ If you can't afford a genuine van Gogh, shop at the museum gift store here for everything from imitations of Vincent's classics to mugs painted with his famous sunflowers, plus a good selection of art books. Paulus Potterstraat 7 (at Museumplein). ✆ **020/570-5200.** www.vangoghmuseum.nl. Tram: 2, 3, 5, or 12 to Van Baerlestraat.

Books

American Book Center ★ Laying claim to be the biggest U.S.-style bookstore in Europe, the ABC stocks magazines and hardcover books, hot off the presses. Prices are higher than back in the States, but the selection beats any airport or hotel gift store. The range of categories includes ancient civilizations, astrology, baby care, science, science fiction, and war. Students and teachers get 10% off simply by showing a school ID. Spui 12. © **020/625-5537.** www.abc.nl. Tram: 1, 2, or 5 to Spui.

Athenaeum Boekhandel & Nieuwscentrum   A place that's always crowded with book lovers, students, and scholars, the Art Nouveau Athenaeum is best known for its nonfiction collection and has books in a number of languages. Magazine stands are on the sidewalk. Spui 14–16. © **020/514-1460.** www.athenaeum.nl. Tram: 1, 2, or 5 to Spui.

De Slegte   You won't find too many English-language books here—most are in Dutch or other languages—but there are a few. If you collect books as a hobby, you might come across a real gem. Kalverstraat 48–52 (at Gapersteeg). © **020/622-5933.** www. deslegte.com. Tram: 4, 9, 14, 16, 24, or 25 to the Dam.

English Bookshop   On the edge of the Jordaan, this small bookstore has a wonderful selection of books in English, mainly fiction and biography, and a small selection of British magazines. Occasionally, you can find a great book at a discount. It's open Tuesday to Friday from 1 to 6pm and Saturday from 11am to 5pm. Lauriergracht 71 (at Hazenstraat). © **020/626-4230.** www.englishbookshop.nl. Tram: 7, 10, or 17 to Elandsgracht.

Evenaar   Since you're traveling, you may be in the mood for travel literature. This store has a wide range, including large-format photo books about travel and anthropology, and second-hand and antique travel books. It's open Monday to Friday from noon to 6pm, Saturday from 11am to 5pm. Singel 348 (at Oude Spiegelstraat). © **020/624-6289.** www.evenaar.net. Tram: 1, 2, or 5 to Spui.

Waterstone's ★   This branch of a British chain has a large stock of fiction and nonfiction titles. You'll probably be able to find almost any in-print book you're looking for on one of its three floors. Kalverstraat 152 (at Spui). © **020/638-3821.** www.waterstones.com. Tram: 1, 2, 4, 5, 14, 16, 24, or 25 to Spui.

Crafts & Gifts

Blue Gold Fish 👔   "Dive into the pool of fantasy," say the owners of this colorful store and gallery. There's no real rhyme or reason to the items for sale. Still, there's unity in diversity in the more-or-less fantastic design sensibility that goes into each piece. It's open Monday to Saturday from 11:30am to 6:30pm. Rozengracht 17 (at Westermarkt). © **020/623-3134.** Tram: 13, 14, or 17 to Westermarkt.

Cortina Papier   If you'd like the kind of personal journal that makes your recollections look good, this is your place. Cortina showcases fancy notebooks, agenda and address books, writing paper, envelopes, and other fine stationery. Reestraat 22 (btw. Prinsengracht and Keizersgracht). © **020/623-6676.** www.cortinapapier.nl. Tram: 13, 14, or 17 to Westermarkt.

E. Kramer Candle Shop   Illuminate everything from a romantic candlelit dinner to a wake. Some of the candles are little melting works of art while others are outrageously kitschy. The store also sells scented oils and incense. Reestraat 20 (btw. Prinsengracht and Keizersgracht). © **020/626-5274.** http://sites.google.com/site/pontifexkramer. Tram: 13, 14, or 17 to Westermarkt.

La Savonnerie   In the kind of clean-living store that a raffish place like Amsterdam can't use enough of, you can purchase artisanal soap in all shapes and sizes, including personalized soap, and even make your own. How about a soap chess set, soap alphabet blocks, or soap animals? Prinsengracht 294 (at Elandsgracht). © **020/428-1139.** www.savonnerie.nl. Tram: 7, 10, or 17 to Elandsgracht.

Lush A British chain store that sells fragrant and fresh handmade soaps in all scents and sizes, is a fun place even for just a quick browse (and a sniff), and the attractive gift-packaging makes for great souvenir shopping. Kalverstraat 98 (2 blocks east of the Begijnhof). © **020/330-6376.** www.lush.nl. Tram: 4, 9, 14, 16, 24, or 25 to Spui.

Nieuws Innovations Shop here for all kinds of offbeat souvenirs, such as pens in the shape of fish, washcloths in the form of hand-glove puppets; spherical dice; and many other hard-to-define but colorful little bits and pieces. Prinsengracht 297 (at Westermarkt). © **020/627-9540.** Tram: 13, 14, or 17 to Westermarkt.

't Curiosa Winkeltje This place sells knickknacks such as colored bottles and glasses, modern versions of old tin cars and other children's toys from the 1950s and earlier, big plastic butterflies, banana-shaped lamps, and many other such useful things. Prinsengracht 228 (at Laurierstraat). © **020/625-1352.** Tram: 13, 14, or 17 to Westermarkt.

Victoria Gifts Dutch clockmakers turn out timepieces with soft-toned chimes in Old Dutch–style handcrafted cases covered with tiny figures and mottoes, hand-painted Dutch scenes, and decorated porcelain insets. This small store has some of these treasures along with Delftware, embroidered flags, chocolates, and other gifts at reasonable prices. Prins Hendrikkade 47 (opposite Centraal Station). © **020/427-2051.** www.victoriagifts.nl. Tram: 1, 2, 4, 5, 9, 13, 16, 17, 24, or 25 to Centraal Station.

Delftware

Galleria d'Arte Rinascimento This well-stocked emporium sells hand-painted Delftware of every conceivable type from De Porceleyne Fles, and Makkumware from Koninklijke Tichelaars (see "Delftware & Makkumware," earlier in this chapter). You can pick up the knockoffs and the real thing, too. Both come in elegant as well as sublimely ridiculous shapes: Ceramic clogs, Christmas ornaments, contorted vases, and the like. Prinsengracht 170 (facing the Anne Frankhuis). © **020/622-7509.** www.delft-art-gallery.com. Tram: 13, 14, or 17 to Westermarkt.

Jorrit Heinen ★★ Two upscale stores offer a good selection of quality porcelain from De Porceleyne Fles (Delft), Tichelaars (Makkum), Heinen, and more. The Munt-plein store has the additional attraction of being inside the medieval Munttoren (Mint Tower). Prinsengracht 440 (at Leidsestraat). © **020/627-8299.** www.jorritheinen.com. Tram: 1, 2, or 5 to Prinsengracht. Muntplein 12 (at Singel). © **020/623-2271.** Tram: 4, 9, 14, 16, 24, or 25 to Muntplein.

Department Stores

De Bijenkorf ★★ Amsterdam's best-known department store is the one with the best variety of goods. The ground floor has ranks of cosmetic counters, plus a men's department and odds and ends such as socks and stockings, purses and belts, costume jewelry, and stationery. And umbrellas—plenty of umbrellas! On upper floors, there's everything from ladies' fashions to down comforters, plus a bookstore, several eating spots, and a luggage section at which you can pick up an extra suitcase or bag to tote home your purchases. Records, TVs, books, shoes, clothing, personal effects, appliances—it's all here. Several worthwhile eateries include **La Ruche ★**, a classy Rietveld-style cafeteria on the second floor (its big windows afford a fine view of the Dam), and the more intimate fourth-floor **Literair Café,** where you can have sushi, sandwiches, and light snacks. Dam 1. © **0900/0919.** www.bijenkorf.nl. Tram: 4, 9, 14, 16, 24, or 25 to the Dam.

HEMA If you can't figure out where to find something, a good bet is to check out this cheap 'n' cheerful department store (or one of HEMA's dozen other stores around town), selling things like socks, toothbrushes, stationery, clothes, kids' stuff, chocolate, cookies, and cheese. Kalvertoren, Kalverstraat 212 (close to Muntplein). ℃ **020/422-8988.** www.hema.nl. Tram: 4, 9, 14, 16, 24, or 25 to Muntplein.

Metz&Co. ★★ Constructed in 1891 for a company founded in 1740, the store of choice for Amsterdam's power shoppers sells modern furniture, fabrics, kitchenware, and other home-based items. The in-store rooftop **M'Café,** designed by De Stijl architect Gerrit Rietveld in 1933, has a section in the cupola for special events and affords a spectacular panoramic view across Amsterdam's rooftops. Leidsestraat 34–36 (at Keizersgracht). ℃ **020/520-7020.** www.metzandco.eu. Tram: 1, 2, or 5 to Keizersgracht.

Peek & Cloppenburg Occupying an unbeatable central location just off the Dam, this moderately upmarket department store focuses on each of its floors on clothes and fashion, for both men and women. The wide-ranging stock goes all the way from street wear to black-tie and evening-gown wear, and takes in a sporty, outdoors look along the way. Dam 20. ℃ **020/623-2837.** www.peek-cloppenburg.nl. Tram: 4, 9, 14, 16, 24, or 25 to the Dam.

Sprmrkt ★ An Aladdin's cave filled with wonderful things, this rambling but stylish lifestyle store with no vowels in its name stocks everything from vintage furniture to books, CDs, and the latest designer fashions and accessories—look for names like Maison Martin Margiela, Damir Doma, and Acne. In addition, there's **Spr Specials,** a sister outlet close to the Royal Palace, and **Sprmrkt Sth,** an upmarket branch in the tony southern Oud Zuid district. Sprmrkt: Rozengracht 191–193 (at Lijnbaansgracht). ℃ **020/330-5601.** www.sprmrkt.nl. Tram: 10, 13, 14, or 17 to Rozengracht-Marnixstraat. Spr Specials: Nieuwezijds Voorburgwal 262 (at Wijdesteeg). ℃ **020/627-7690.** Tram: 1, 2, 5, 13, 14, or 17 to the Dam. Sprmrkt Sth: Willemsparkweg 168 (at Cornelis Schuytstraat). ℃ **020/470-2558.** Tram: 2 to Cornelis Schuytstraat.

Vroom & Dreesmann (V&D) Less polished and pretentious than Metz&Co. (see above), this is the Amsterdam branch of a department-store chain that pops up in key shopping locations all over Holland. V&D is a no-nonsense sort of store with a wide range of middle-of-the-road goods, and prices and service to match. Its vast multilevel **La Place** food depot has something for everyone. Kalverstraat 203 (at Muntplein; there's also an entrance on Rokin). ℃ **0900/235-8363.** www.vd.nl. Tram: 4, 9, 14, 16, 24, or 25 to Muntplein.

Design Stores

Droog ★★ Loading up your luggage with the kind of preternaturally cool chairs, tables, and other furniture from this stable of innovative Dutch designers likely isn't a viable proposition, but it might seem like it should be after a visit to the design studio's outlet close to Waterlooplein. Besides, you can always ship your purchase, or settle for accessories that embrace the same design sensibility. Staalstraat 7B (at Kloveniersburgwal). ℃ **020/523-5050.** www.droog.com. Tram: 4, 9, 14, 16, 24, or 25 to Muntplein.

Frozen Fountain ★ At this stylish canalside showroom, plenty of contemporary designer furniture and other clever objects by young Dutch fashioners of the gorgeous-but-impractical-yet-irresistible draw the media crowd and beautiful people from surrounding canal houses and converted warehouses. Prinsengracht 645 (at Leidsegracht). ℃ **020/622-9375.** www.frozenfountain.nl. Tram: 1, 2, or 5 to Prinsengracht.

From Ships to Shops

KNSM-Eiland (KNSM Island), in the redeveloping Eastern Harbor area, has a streetload of interior design stores. The island is named after the Dutch initials of the old Royal Dutch Steamship Line that was based there—the Koninklijke Nederlandse Stoomboot Maatschappij. Shops here include the bizarrely named

Pol's Potten, KNSM-laan 39 (© 020/419-3541; www.polspotten.nl), for furnishings, accessories, kitchen stuff, and knickknacks by hip young designers; and **Keet in Huis,** KNSM-laan 297 (© 020/419-5958; www.keetinhuis.nl), for children's lifestyles. Tram: 10.

WonderWood Plywood chairs, tables, and other genuine vintage and classic (1930s–1970s), and modern retro-repro furniture and fittings don't appear to exactly fly off the shelves and sales floor of this part gallery and part store in the Oudezijds, the oldest part of town. Yet they do attract aficionados of the minimalist, formed-wood genre. Rusland 3 (at Oudezijds Achtwerburgwal). © **020/625-3738.** www.wonderwood.nl. Open Wed–Sat noon–6pm. Tram: 4, 9, 14, 16, 24, or 25 to Spui.

Diamonds

Amsterdam Diamond Center This serious gem complex on the Dam was created after the war by several families, one of which spent 8 months cutting the world's biggest diamond—a 3,106-carat rough—into nine gems, including the famed Cullinan I (530 carats) and Cullinan II (317 carats). Free guided diamond-cutting and polishing tours are available. Rokin 1-5 (at the Dam). © **020/624-5787.** www.amsterdam diamondcenter.nl. Tram: 4, 9, 14, 16, 24, or 25.

Cartier If you must have the best, you've come to the right place. You'll find intricately designed jewelry, watches, pens, and other accessories at this quintessential French shop found on the swankiest city block. Pieter Cornelisz Hooftstraat 132-134. © **020/670-3434.** www.cartier.com. Tram: 2, 3, 5, or 12 to Van Baerlestraat.

Coster Diamonds Across the street from the Rijksmuseum, one of the biggest, glitziest diamond operations in town won renown in the 1930s by restyling the 186-carat Koh-i-Noor ("Mountain of Light") into the 108-carat centerpiece of the British royal crown (now in the Tower of London). Free guided diamond-cutting and polishing tours are available. Paulus Potterstraat 2-8 (at Museumplein). © **020/305-5555.** www. costerdiamonds.com. Tram: 2 or 5.

Gassan Diamonds ★ In addition to being one of the city's top diamond-polishing houses and dealers, Gassan has a Royal Delftware painting workshop and boutique at its factory—a stunning Amsterdam School–style building—on a canal-fringed island. Free guided diamond-cutting and polishing tours are available. Nieuwe Uilenburgerstraat 173-175 (at Oudeschans, 3 blocks north of Waterlooplein). © **020/622-5333.** www.gassandiamonds. com. Metro: Waterlooplein.

Drugs

Magic Mushroom Gallery How to define this place that treads a thin line? It sells "natural drugs" and "psychoactive mushrooms" that are much better for you, so they say, than illegal narcotics. Improve your sex life with Yohimbe Rush and Horn E, boost your energy with Space Liquid and Herbal Booster, grow your own Mexican mushrooms, then unwind with After Glow and Rapture. Singel 524 (at the Flower Market). ℂ **020/422-7845.** www.magicmushroom.com. Tram: 4, 9, 14, 16, 24, or 25 to Muntplein.

Fashions

Azzurro Due ★   The ultimate address for finding a pair of designer jeans or that elusive Prada accessory for both men and women. Very chic, very trendy. Pieter Cornelisz Hooftstraat 138 (Azzurro Kids is some doors down at no. 122). ℂ **020/671-9708.** www.azzurro fashiongroup.nl. Tram: 2, 3, 5, or 12 to Van Baerlestraat.

Charly Ensuite ★★   A perfect fit for the posh Museum District, this boutique specializes in designer clothing for women. Expect the latest fashions from the likes of Alexander McQueen, Diane von Fürstenberg, Giambattista Valli, Dusan, and Yigal Azrouël. Cross over to an annex at no. 45, and pick up casual apparel and accessories by Rosemunde, Barong Barong, Fabrizio Giannone, MVN, Tritoni, and more. Cornelis Schuytstraat 48 (at Johannes Verhulststraat). ℂ **020/670-1370.** www.charlyensuite. nl. Tram: 2 to Cornelis Schuytstraat.

Edgar Vos   Stylish staff members listen and advise while customers don the kind of pricey classic creations favored by rich Amsterdam businesswomen, socialites, and country-clubbers. Pieter Cornelisz Hooftstraat 136 (at Van Baerlestraat). ℂ **020/671-2748.** www.edgarvos.nl. Tram: 2, 3, 5, or 12 to Van Baerlestraat.

Episode   Jackets, dresses, scarves, belts, funky brooches, boots—you'll find all these and more at this unisex vintage shop. Specialties include flamboyant evening gowns and leather jackets, all in pretty good shape and reasonably priced. Waterlooplein 1. ℂ **020/320-3000.** www.episode.eu. Tram: 9 or 14 to Waterlooplein.

Louis Vuitton   Of course, you'll find the usual upmarket suitcases and purses here that Vuitton is famous for, but you'll also find a good selection of shoes, jewelry, belts, and ties. Pieter Cornelisz Hooftstraat 65-67. ℂ **020/575-5775.** www.louisvuitton.com. Tram: 2, 3, 5, or 12 to Van Baerlestraat.

McLennan's   If silk is what turns you on, the pure silk sold here by the meter or snipped into kimonos, ties, scarves, and other accessories, artfully displayed in a chic silk-only Nine Streets boutique, are for you. Hartenstraat 22 (at Herengracht). ℂ **020/ 622-7693.** www.puresilk.nl. Tram: 13, 14, or 17 to Westermarkt.

Megazino   Large for Amsterdam, this designer outlet store in the Jordaan sells everything from Armani, Gucci, and Prada to Calvin Klein and Dolce & Gabbana— all at 30% to 50% off the original price. It's a great place to burn some plastic without breaking the bank. Rozengracht 207-213 (at Lijnbaansgracht). ℂ **020/330-1031.** www.megazino. nl. Tram: 13, 14, or 17 to Westermarkt.

Miauw ★   This two-room store is owned by one of Amsterdam's renowned designers, Analik. One room is filled with small pieces of clothing for young and skinny women, the other with funky purses and other accessories designed by local Dutch artists. Hartenstraat 36 (at Keizersgracht). ℂ **020/422-0561.** www.analik.com. Tram: 13, 14, or 17 to Westermarkt.

Van Ravenstein ★★   You're likely to bump into media stars, gallery owners, and the moneyed creative crowd of both sexes at this small boutique, buying the latest creations by Dutch and Belgian designers; Victor and Rolf, Martin Margiela, Dirk

Bikkembergs, Dries van Noten, and Bernhard Willhelm are stock in trade. In the basement, a collection of last season's discards is on sale. Keizersgracht 359 (at Huidenstraat). © **020/639-0067.** www.van-ravenstein.nl. Tram: 1, 2, or 5 to Keizersgracht.

Webers Holland ★   The venerable 17th-century **Klein Trippenhuis** (p. 155), a protected historical monument, is the counterintuitive setting for this avant-garde, sexy, humorous—and, to a degree, in-your-face—store for women. The designer fashions here are mainly by co-proprietor Désirée Webers, but other Dutch and international designers are represented. It's open Sunday and Monday from 1 to 7pm, and Tuesday to Saturday from 11am to 7pm. Kloveniersburgwal 26 (at Nieuwmarkt). © **020/638-1777.** www.webersholland.nl. Metro: Nieuwmarkt.

Flowers

Bloomings-Amsterdam   This friendly florist sells expertly arranged flowers and exquisite vases of all shapes and sizes. Elandsgracht 134 (at Lijnbaansgracht). © **06/2421-3723.** www.bloomings-amsterdam.nl. Tram: 7, 10, or 17 to Elandsgracht.

Gerda's Bloemen & Planten ★   One of the most elegant florists in the city boasts a fantastic selection of exotic flowers and unusual plants artfully arranged and presented at its Canal Belt store. Runstraat 16 (at Keizersgracht). © **020/624-2912.** www.theninestreets.com. Tram: 1, 2, or 5 to Spui.

Food & Drink

Brandmeester's   Hard-edged decor rounds out a sleek, ultra-modern coffee-roasting store and tasting bar. Van Baerlestraat 13 (at Pieter Cornelisz Hooftstraat). © **020/572-0811.** www.brandmeesters.nl. Tram: 2, 3, 5, or 12 to Van Baerlestraat.

De Kaaskamer ★   Possibly Amsterdam's best cheese store, with deli delights to boot. You may have a hard time choosing from the 300 different cheeses for sale, including rows and rows of authentic wheels of aged Gouda stamped with their farm of origin, and cumin-flavored *komijnenkaas*. They will vacuum-pack and courier cheese anywhere for travelers. Runstraat 7 (at Keizersgracht). © **020/623-3483.** www.kaaskamer.nl. Tram: 1, 2, or 5 to Spui.

De Ware Jacob   Since 1970 this small but charming Canal Belt wine shop has carried the finest wines from boutique wineries around the world. Herenstraat 41 (at Keizersgracht). © **020/623-9877.** Tram: 13, 14, or 17 to Westermarkt.

De Waterwinkel   Quality and purity are the watchwords at the tastefully designed Water Shop. More than 100 varieties of mineral water from around the planet, ranging from ordinary to designer, are for sale here. Some bottles are miniature works of art. Roelof Hartstraat 10 (at Roelof Hartplein). © **020/675-5932.** www.dewaterwinkel.nl. Tram: 3, 5, 12, or 24 to Roelof Hartplein.

Geels & Co. ★   Devotees of the legal drug from Colombia and other coffee-producing nations will be tempted by the smell of fresh-roasted coffee beans at this coffee-roasting and tea-importing establishment in a 17th-century building. Geels & Co. has been going strong since 1864, and goes a long way toward raising the tone of shabby Warmoesstraat on the Red Light District's edge. Offerings (besides coffee, of course) include beverage accessories, tastings by appointment, old-fashioned fudges and toffees, and a coffee-and-tea museum on the second floor. Warmoesstraat 67 (at Oude Brugsteeg). © **020/624-0683.** www.geels.nl. Tram: 4, 9, 14, 16, 24, or 25 to the Dam.

Night Owls

A local *avondwinkel* (evening store) is a resource not to be ignored for keeping you stocked with after-hours munchies. Suppose you feel like an evening in your hotel, and you either don't fancy the room-service menu or your hotel doesn't provide one. Not to worry: There's bound to be an evening store close to the hotel (ask the front desk). Many can prepare takeout meals to about the same standard as you would find in a typical Dutch *eetcafé*, for 10% to 20% less than restaurant prices. Hours are usually from 5 to 11pm or midnight.

H.P. de Vreng en Zonen 📷 This traditional distillery, founded in 1710, creates Dutch liqueurs and gins according to old-fashioned methods, *sans* additives. Try the Old Amsterdam *jenever* or some of the more flamboyantly colored liquids, like the bright-green plum liqueur *Pruimpje prik in;* some supposedly have aphrodisiac power. A chance to see the collection of 15,000 miniature bottles alone makes a visit worthwhile. Nieuwendijk 75 (at Martelaarsgracht). ℂ **020/624-4581.** www.oudamsterdam.nl. Tram: 1, 2, 5, 13, or 17 to Martelaarsgracht.

Jacob Hooy 🏢 You'll feel like you've stepped back into history when you visit this store, which opened in 1743. For the past 130 years, the Oldenboom family has operated this wonderland of fragrant smells from more than 600 different herbs and spices, and 30 different teas, all sold loose by weight. Wooden drawers and barrels hand-scripted in gold lettering store everything. Across the counter are fishbowl jars in racks containing some 30 types of licorice and other *dropjes* (drops or lozenges) that range in taste from sweet to sour to salty. Health foods, homeopathic products, and natural cosmetics are also available here. Kloveniersburgwal 10–12 (at Nieuwmarkt). ℂ **020/624-3041.** www.jacobhooy.nl. Metro: Nieuwmarkt.

Patisserie Pompadour The counter display here is amazing. It groans under the weight of some 50 kinds of luscious pastries and tarts, complemented by endless dollops of whipped cream. Enjoy these genuine Dutch treats in the exquisite Louis XVI tearoom or wrapped to go. A second branch is across town on Kerkstraat. It's open Tuesday to Friday from 9am to 6pm, and Saturday from 9am to 5pm. Huidenstraat 12 (at Herengracht). ℂ **020/623-9554.** Tram: 1, 2, or 5 to Spui. Kerkstraat 148 (at Nieuwe Spiegelstraat). ℂ **020/330-0981.** Tram: 16, 24, or 25 to Keizersgracht.

Puccini Bomboni ★ A long, open table supports fresh, handmade pralines in a plethora of shapes and styles—pure, milk, white—at each of Puccini Bomboni's two branches. Peruse the multifarious merchandise and breathe in its sultry scents to the strains of soft classical music. There are at least six liqueur-filled varieties and more than 20 with non-alcoholic, often exotic, fillings—you can try these little chocolate heavens with flavors like Drambuie, Calvados, cognac, rum, marzipan, ginger, nutmeg, cinnamon, fig, lemon grass, thyme, and many more. Singel 184 (at Oude Leliestraat). ℂ **020/427-8341.** www.puccinibomboni.com. Tram: 1, 2, 5, 13, or 17 to the Dam. Staalstraat 17 (at Waterlooplein). ℂ **020/626-5474.** Tram: 9 or 14 to Waterlooplein.

Simon Levelt Founded in 1839 as H. Keijzer, this tea-and-coffee store now belongs to a Dutch chain founded in 1817. Consider taking home several 100-gram (3½ oz.) tea packets from different parts of the globe: Ceylon Melange (or Delmar

9

SHOPPING IN AMSTERDAM

Shopping A to Z

Melange), an English-style blend from Sri Lanka; Darjeeling First Flush, from India; Yunnan, from China; and Java O. P. (Orange Pekoe), from Indonesia. To come away with a delightful gift, select from an assortment of tea boxes. Prinsengracht 180 (at Westermarkt). ✆ **020/624-0823.** www.simonlevelt.nl. Tram: 13, 14, or 17 to Westermarkt.

Gay & Lesbian

Boekhandel Vrolijk ★   The city's main bookstore for gays and lesbians stocks a wide range of books, many of them in English. It's invariably cheaper to buy here than at the gay sections of general bookstores, but is still likely to be more expensive than at home. Paleisstraat 135 (at the Dam). ✆ **020/623-5142.** www.vrolijk.nu. Tram: 1, 2, 4, 5, 9, 13, 14, 16, 17, 24, or 25 to Centraal Station.

Intermale   In addition to books, magazines, and greeting cards in English, this large bookstore stocks Dutch and German periodicals. It claims to have the largest collection of books of interest to gay men in Europe. Spuistraat 251 (at Spui). ✆ **020/625-0009.** www.intermale.nl. Tram: 1, 2, or 5 to Spui.

Mister B   This no-holds-barred store is known for its high-quality leather goods, from basic trousers and chaps to more revealing fetish wear. The store's window often displays erotic art, S&M accessories, and a selection of piercing jewelry—it ensures many a gaping tourist. Visiting tattoo and piercing artists from around the world make guest appearances. Racy postcards are available. Warmoesstraat 89 (edge of the Red Light District). ✆ **020/788-3060.** www.misterb.com. Tram: 1, 2, 4, 5, 9, 13, 14, 16, 17, 24, or 25 to Centraal Station.

Haberdashery

H.J. van de Kerkhof   This store's walls are lined with spools of ribbon and cord, and its notebooks filled with examples of patches and appliqués. Key tassels and tiebacks come in all sizes, including very large. Wolvenstraat 9-11 (at Herengracht). Closed Fri–Sun. ✆ **020/623-4666.** Tram: 1, 2, or 5 to Spui.

Household

Kitsch Kitchen Supermercado ★   The name just about says it all. You'll want to put on your shades before entering this world of glaringly bright colors. Kitsch Kitchen's utensils and household fittings—not just for kitchens—come in plastic, enamel, and papier-mâché. A separate department caters to culinary-oriented kids. Rozengracht 8–12 (at Westermarkt). ✆ **020/429-4969.** www.kitschkitchen.nl. Tram: 13, 14, or 17 to Westermarkt.

Jewelry

BLGK Edelsmeden   Run by a group of jewelry designers, this store sells affordable jewelry with character. Each designer has a unique slant: Some pieces represent a new and fresh spin on classic forms, while others are more innovative and imaginative. Hartenstraat 28 (at Herengracht). ✆ **020/624-8154.** www.blgk.nl. Tram: 13, 14, or 17 to Westermarkt.

Galerie Ra   Marvelous contemporary designs and materials turn jewelry into an art form here. Owner Paul Derrez specializes in stunning modern jewelry in gold and silver, and goes a bit further, turning feathers, rubber, foam, and other materials into pieces he describes as "playful." Vijzelstraat 80 (at Prinsengracht). ✆ **020/626-5100.** www.galerie-ra.nl. Tram: 16, 24, or 25 to Keizersgracht.

Gort ★   This beautiful little shop specializes in unique and innovative jewelry design. If you like modern, minimalist designs, then this could be the place for you. Herenstraat 11 (at Herengracht). ✆ **020/620-6240.** www.juweliergort.nl. Tram: 13, 14, or 17 to Westermarkt.

Kids

Some museum gift stores are good sources for toys and other children's knickknacks. Try the stores at the **Theatermuseum,** Herengracht 168 (✆ **020/551-3300;** tram: 13, 14, or 17), for masks, costumes, and minitheaters; **Science Center NEMO,** Oosterdokskade 2 (✆ **0900/919-1100;** bus: 22), for scientific and educational toys and gadgets; and both the **Tropenmuseum,** Linnaeusstraat 2 (✆ **020/568-8469;** tram: 9, 10, or 14), and **Artis Zoo,** Plantage Kerklaan 38–40 (✆ **020/523-3400;** tram: 9 or 14), for model animals and eco-stuff. In addition, look for the "Kids" icon ☺ attached to some of the other reviews in this chapter.

Gone With the Wind   The countless sculptural mobiles, plus many kinds of traditional toys, in this colorful wonderland of a store are sure to lift your darling's heart. Vijzelstraat 22 (at Herengracht). ✆ **020/423-0230.** www.gonewind-mobiles.com. Tram: 16, 24, or 25 to Herengracht.

Mechanisch Speelgoed ★ 🎁 ☺   Your grandparents, when they were children, surely would have appreciated this old-fashioned toy store in the Jordaan. And plenty of today's kids seem equally attracted by this tiny shop's trove of traditional games, wooden houses, and other delights like tin drums, rag dolls, teddy bears, masks, and costumes. Tin toys are upstairs and other toys are downstairs. It's open Monday, Tuesday, and Thursday to Saturday from 10am to 6pm. Westerstraat 67 (at Violettenstraat). ✆ **020/638-1680.** Tram: 3 or 10 to Marnixplein.

Tinkerbell Fun & Discovery Shop ☺   This is the place to find treasures for kids. The toys here don't blink, bleep, or run out of batteries—many are actually made from wood. But none of this is old-fashioned—this is real up-to-the-minute gear. Spiegelgracht 10–12 (at Prinsengracht). ✆ **020/625-8830.** www.tinkerbelltoys.nl. Tram: 7 or 10 to Spiegelgracht.

Malls

Magna Plaza ★   Located amid the extravagant neo-Gothic architecture of the former central Post Office, which dates from 1908, the Plaza's four elegant, column-lined floors are decked with around 50 specialist stores of all kinds. Yet it's small enough to function almost like a department store. Nieuwezijds Voorburgwal 182 (behind the Royal Palace). www.magnaplaza.nl. Tram: 1, 2, 5, 13, 14, or 17 to the Dam.

Music

Free Record Shop   No, the records here aren't free, sadly, but this store holds an incredible number of cassettes, CDs, and videos at competitive prices. Kalverstraat 230 (at Muntplein). ✆ **020/625-3034.** www.freerecordshop.nl. Tram: 4, 9, 14, 16, 24, or 25 to Muntplein.

Sex

Amsterdam's free and easy—you could even say laid-back—attitude to the mysteries of the flesh has spawned a vast range of stores devoted to satisfying customers' needs, whether real or pure fantasy. Many of these are down-and-dirty, sleazeball kinds of places, but not all. Here are some with a sense of style.

Absolute Danny   Owner Danny Linden, a graduate of Amsterdam's Fashion Academy and the Academy of Fine Arts, brings her artistic sensibilities to bear on the erotic lifestyle her store supports. You'll find everything from sexy tableware (if you can imagine such a thing) to S&M clothing and accessories in leather and latex to sexy lingerie. It's open Monday to Saturday from 11am to 9pm, and Sunday from noon to 9pm. Oudezijds Achterburgwal 78 (close to Nieuwmarkt). *©* **020/421-0915.** www.absolute danny.com. Metro: Nieuwmarkt.

Condomerie Het Gulden Vlies ★ 👜   This shop, named "The Golden Fleece," is located on the edge of the Red Light District and claims to be the world's first specialized condom store—the start of a whole new protection racket. It stocks a vast range of these singular items, in all shapes, sizes, and flavors, from common brands to flashy designer fittings, all but guaranteeing your apparel of choice. It's open Monday to Wednesday, Friday, and Saturday from noon to 6pm, and Thursday from noon to 8pm. Warmoesstraat 141 (behind De Bijenkorf). *©* **020/627-4174.** www.condomerie. com. Tram: 4, 9, 14, 16, 24, or 25 to the Dam.

Female & Partners   Here, you'll find all sorts of lingerie and female-oriented sex articles, like dildos and other imaginative toys. This chic store caters to women who like women, women who like men, and those who like both, and is close to the Royal Palace (p. 149). Not that the queen has anything to do with it, so far as I know. If the vibrator display makes you hesitant to enter, you can order the goods by phone, mail, or Internet. It's open Tuesday to Saturday 11am to 6pm, and Sunday and Monday 1 to 6pm. Spuistraat 100 (at Nieuwe Sparpotsteeg). *©* **020/620-9152.** www.femaleand partners.nl. Tram: 1, 2, 5, 13, 14, or 17 to the Dam.

Shoes

Antonia by Yvette   When it comes to fanciful footwear, trendies hotfoot to this Canal Belt boutique for hip Dutch designer shoes by the likes of Hester Vlamings. Gasthuismolensteeg 18 (at Singel). *©* **020/320-9443.** www.antoniabyyvette.nl. Tram: 1, 2, 5, 13, 14, or 17 to the Dam.

Betsy Palmer ★   There are no classic shoes here, but there's an incredible collection of trendy women's footwear, with obscure but fun brands like Sexy Chic, Sunloving Babe, and Serious Partying. Rokin 9-15 (at the Dam). *©* **020/422-1040.** www. betsypalmer.com. Tram: 4, 9, 14, 16, 24, or 25 to the Dam.

Jan Jansen ★★   Award-winning Dutch shoe designer Jan Jansen sells his men's and women's footwear in this chic store. Well-heeled customers can choose each piece of leather to make up exclusive shoes. You can special-order colors and sizes if you can't find yours—it takes about 3 weeks and they will mail your shoes to you. Rokin 42 (btw. the Dam and Spui). *©* **020/625-1350.** www.janjansenshoes.com. Tram: 4, 9, 14, 16, 24, or 25 to the Dam or Spui.

Shoebaloo ★   Four chic boutiques, selling women's footwear that's not as outrageous as you'd expect from the decor by celebrated Czech designer Borek Sipek. Leidsestraat 10 (at Herengracht). *©* **020/330-9147.** www.shoebaloo.nl. Tram: 1, 2, or 5 to Keizersgracht. Koningsplein 7 (at Herengracht). *©* **020/626-7993.** Tram: 1, 2, or 5 to Koningsplein. Pieter Cornelisz Hooftstraat 80 (at Honthorststraat). *©* **020/671-2210.** Tram: 2, 3, 5, or 12 to Van Baerlestraat. Cornelis Schuytstraat 9 (at Willemsparkweg). *©* **020/662-5779.** Tram: 2 to Cornelis Schuytstraat.

Smoking Articles

P.G.C. Hajenius ★ Amsterdam's leading purveyor of cigars and smoking articles has been in business since 1826, first with a store on the Dam and then (since 1915) in its present elegant Art Deco headquarters. Cigars are the house specialty; there's a room full of Havanas, and Hajenius also sells cigars from Sumatra, Brazil, and more. One good gift idea is the long, handmade clay pipes you see in old paintings—they're uniquely Dutch. Other good gifts include the ceramic pipes, some painted in the blue-and-white Chinese-inspired patterns of Delftware. You can also find lighters, cigarette holders, clippers, and flasks. Rokin 92-96 (at Spui). ℭ **020/623-7494.** www. hajenius.com. Tram: 4, 9, 14, 16, 24, or 25 to Spui.

Smokiana This is where to buy that unique pipe into which tobacco can be tamped with an air of deliberate insouciance, and the resulting fug flaunted in the faces of nonsmokers everywhere. Smokiana stocks a vast range of pipes from the antique to the exotic to the downright weird. While you're here, be sure to step into the **Pijpenkabinet (Pipe Cabinet),** an in-store museum (p. 166). It's open Wednesday to Saturday from 11am to 6pm. Prinsengracht 488 (at Leidsestraat). ℭ **020/421-1779.** www.pipeshop.nl. Tram: 1, 2, or 5 to Prinsengracht.

STREET MARKETS

Amsterdammers are traders to the tips of their fingers, as you'll quickly find if you visit a street market, but they won't bargain with you—they have much less interest in haggling, or margin in their prices, than their counterparts in countries farther south. They're simply too practical to quote a ridiculous price in the expectation that it'll be cut in half or that you'll be fool enough to pay it. No, Dutch street merchants exhibit their enthusiasm for trade in a more stolid way—simply by being permanent. Many of Amsterdam's open-air salesmen are at the stalls, vans, tents, and barges of the city's markets 6 days a week, 52 weeks a year. In all, Amsterdam and its outlying neighborhoods have more than 50 outdoor markets every week, on any given day, except Sunday, when you have a choice of several.

Finding a bargain-basement souvenir is easy at the **Waterlooplein Flea Market** ★, on Waterlooplein (tram: 9 or 14). All kinds of stuff is here, not all of it junk, and a constant press of people with good buys on their minds. This is Amsterdam's classic market: It's often said that in its glory days before World War II, when it was a fixture of the city's Jewish community, you could find amazing antiques amid the lesser goods—possibly even a dusty old Rembrandt. Today, however, your luck is more apt to run in the opposite direction. Most merchants work out of tents, and some sell *patates frites met mayonnaise* (french fries eaten Dutch style, with mayonnaise) from vans that are a long way from the pushcarts of yesteryear; but among old CDs and leather jackets, you'll still find cooking pots, mariners' telescopes, coal scuttles, bargain watches, nuts and bolts, and decent prints of Dutch cities. The market is open Monday to Saturday from 10am to 5pm.

At the **Bloemenmarkt (Flower Market)** ★, Singel (tram: 4, 9, 14, 16, 24, or 25), at Muntplein, awnings stretch to cover some 15 stalls of brightly colored blossoms, bulbs, and potted plants. This row of permanently moored barges is one of Amsterdam's stellar spots, though you might find it overrated, especially since it doesn't look like it's actually floating—and indeed, most of it isn't. Still, this is probably the most atmospheric place to buy fresh-cut flowers, bright and healthy plants, ready-to-travel packets of tulip bulbs, and any necessary home-gardening accessory. A stroll down that fragrant line is surely one of Amsterdam's most heart-lifting experiences. An added plus is that tulips here cost a few cents less than at the flower stands around town. The market is open daily from 8am to 8pm.

Borrowed Blooms

Berliner Klaus-Günter Neumann wrote the classic "Dutch" song *Tulips from Amsterdam*—in German.

At the colorful, kilometer-long **Albert Cuypmarkt** (www.albert cuypmarkt.com), Albert Cuypstraat (tram: 16, 24, or 25), you find just about anything your imagination can conjure: 350 stalls sell different types of food, clothing, flowers, plants, and textiles. Cheesemongers slice wedges from Frisbee-shaped disks of Edam. The market is open Monday to Saturday from 9am to 6pm.

The Friday **Boekenmarkt (Book Market)** on Spui (tram: 1, 2, or 5) has around 25 booths with second-hand books. You can often find some great deals (even for books in English), and perhaps even a rare book or two. Just about any subject is available, both fiction and nonfiction. The market is open Friday from 10am to 6pm.

Local artists mount outdoor exhibits at the **Kunstmarkt (Art Market)** on Spui, April to November, Sunday from 10am to 6pm.

Kunst & Antiekcentrum De Looier ★, Elandsgracht 109 (© 020/624-9038; www.looier.nl; tram: 7, 10, or 17), is a big indoor antiques market spread through several old warehouses in the Jordaan. Individual dealers rent small stalls and corners to showcase their best wares. The old armoires and other heavy pieces of traditional Dutch furniture are likely too large to consider buying, but many dealers offer antique jewelry, prints and engravings, old porcelain table settings, bathroom fixtures, 19th-century tin toys, Delft tiles, furniture, Dutch knickknacks, and much more. De Looier is open Saturday to Thursday from 11am to 5pm.

Local artists come to show off their wares at the **Modern Art Market,** Thorbeckeplein (© 0527/201-559; www.modernartmarket.nl; tram: 4, 9, or 14). Picking your way through the tables, you'll find sculptures, ceramics, paintings, jewelry, and mixed-media pieces. The market runs from April to October, Sunday from 11am to 6pm.

The **Boerenmarkt** (**Farmers' Market;** www.boerenmarktamsterdam.nl) at Noordermarkt (tram: 3 or 10), also known as the **Biologische Markt (Organic Market),** caters to Amsterdam's infatuation with health foods and natural products, sold by green-living enthusiasts who know and love what they do. Popular items include fruit and vegetables, homemade bread, colorful Dutch cheeses, and natural soap. It takes place on Saturday from 9am to 5pm. A similar **Boerenmarkt (Farmers' Market)** at Nieuwmarkt (Metro: Nieuwmarkt) operates on the same day and hours. Bargains may be thin on the ground but quality is pretty much assured. The crowd browsing here is invariably large.

Other notable street markets are the **Westermarkt,** which sells textiles and clothes on Westerstraat, at Noordermarkt, Monday from 9am to 1pm; the **Lindengracht** general market, on the long Jordaan street of the same name, Saturday from 9am to 5pm; the **Bloemen en Planten Markt (Flower and Plant Market),** at Amstelveld, on Prinsengracht, Easter to Christmas, Monday from 9am to 6pm; the

Curiosamarkt (Collectors' Market), at the same Amstelveld location, from 9am to 6pm on the last Friday in June, July, and August; the **Postzegelmarkt (Stamp Market),** around Nieuwezijds Voorburgwal 276, on Wednesday and Saturday from 1 to 4pm; and the **Antiek en Curiosamarkt (Antiques and Collectors' Market),** Nieuwmarkt (Metro: Nieuwmarkt), for antiques and curios, May to October, Sunday from 9am to 6pm.

AMSTERDAM AFTER DARK

Nightlife in Amsterdam, like an Indonesian *rijsttafel,* is a bit of this and a bit of that. The cultural calendar is full, but not jammed. There's a strong jazz scene, good music clubs, and enjoyable English-language shows at the little cabarets and theaters along the canals.

The club and bar scene can be entertaining if not outrageous; the dance clubs may indeed seem quiet and small to anyone used to the flash of clubs in New York City, Los Angeles, or London. However, the brown cafes—the typical Amsterdam pubs—have never been better. And there are always the movies: You can watch first-run U.S. blockbuster hits with their English soundtracks intact.

Hot and cool at the same time, Leidseplein is the center of Amsterdam's nightlife, with some of the city's most popular restaurants, bars, and nightspots all within dancing distance of each other around the square. Leidseplein never really closes, so you can greet the dawn and start again. Rembrandtplein is a brash and brassy square that really comes alive at night, when it's awash with neon. Although it has a more downscale reputation than Leidseplein, this area often seems even more intent on having fun, and there are enough hip, sophisticated places to go around. These two areas are connected by Reguliersdwarsstraat, which has some good cafes, including a few gay ones, and also several fine clubs and restaurants. The Rosse Buurt (Red Light District) serves up its own unique brand of nightlife, and adjoining this is Nieuwmarkt, which has become a popular alternative hangout.

> ## Impressions
>
> *It often seems to me that the night is much more alive and richly colored than the day.*
> —Vincent van Gogh, September 8, 1888

Information

Your best source of information in English for nightlife and cultural events is the monthly magazine *Time Out Amsterdam,* which costs 2.95€. It provides a complete cultural guide to Amsterdam, with listings for concerts and recitals, theater, cabaret, opera, dance performances, rock

No Smoking

Second-hand smoke no longer gets in your eyes and up your nose as much as formerly, in this city where rolling one's own cigarettes from foul-smelling loose tobacco known as *shag* is in the way of being a traditional craft. Smoking is banned in restaurants, bars, cafes, clubs, and other places, and in public spaces in hotels. There are exemptions only for separate enclosed spaces where smokers are kept (and taken care of) by themselves. In a typically Dutch compromise, the tobacco ban applies to drug-selling "smoking coffeeshops," where patrons are still permitted to puff joints, but not cigarettes, cigars, or pipes. This applies even if you are merely mixing tobacco with marijuana to form a joint: If you choose to mix the two, puff it outside.

concerts, art films, film festivals, special museum and art gallery exhibitions, and lots more. There's also the free monthly listings magazine *De Uitkrant* from the Amsterdams Uitburo (see below), which you can pick up at many performance venues; it's in Dutch, but it isn't difficult to understand the listings information.

Tickets

If you want to attend any of Amsterdam's theatrical or musical events (including rock concerts), make it your first task on arrival to get tickets. The **Amsterdams Uitburo (AUB) Ticketshop,** Leidseplein 26 (© **0900/0191** or 31-20/621-1288 from outside the Netherlands; www.uitburo.nl; tram: 1, 2, 5, 7, or 10), can reserve tickets online, in person, or by phone, for almost every venue in town, for a reservations charge of 2€–4.65€ per ticket. Discounted last-minute tickets may be available. Using this service instead of chasing down tickets on your own can save you precious hours. The office is open Monday to Saturday from 10am to 7:30pm, and Sunday from noon to 6pm.

THE PERFORMING ARTS

Amsterdam's top orchestra is the famed **Koninklijk Concertgebouworkest (Royal Concertgebouw Orchestra)** (© **02/305-1010;** www.concertgebouworkest.nl), which performs mainly in the **Concertgebouw,** and gives occasional open-air concerts in the **Vondelpark.** The Concertgebouw Orchestra, under Latvian lead conductor Mariss Jansons, can produce any of the great classical works at the tap of a baton, yet is also willing to go out on a limb from time to time with modern and experimental pieces.

The city's other full orchestra, the **Nederlands Philharmonisch Orkest (Netherlands Philharmonic Orchestra)** (© **02/521-7500;** www.orkest.nl), fondly known as the NedPhO, isn't far behind its illustrious cousin, if behind at all. The NedPhO has found its niche in an adventurous repertoire, which includes opera collaborations. Its main Amsterdam concert venue is also the Concertgebouw, though it is based at the **Beurs van Berlage,** and it shows up regularly for opera in the **Muziektheater.**

Holland's other top orchestras, such as The Hague's **Residentie Orchestra** and the **Rotterdam Philharmonic,** as well as visiting orchestras from abroad, also appear regularly at Amsterdam venues.

Central Amsterdam After Dark

Lux **12**
Maloe Melo **29**
Melkweg **13**
The Movies **42**
Mulligans Irish Music
    Bar **74**
Muziekgebouw
    aan 't IJ **50**
Muziektheater **75**
Nieuwe Kerk **34**
Odeon **20**
Oude Kerk **61**
Panama **53**
Paradiso **1**
Paradox **36**
The Rookies **7**
Saarein2 **28**
Seymour Likely **32**
Sheeba **60**
Spijker **18**
Stadsschouwburg **9**
Theater Bellevue **11**
Theater Tuschinski **72**
Three Sisters **14**
't Loosje **63**
Tonight **82**
't Smalle **38**
Vive-la-Vie **77**
Vlaams Cultuurhuis
    De Brakke Grond **67**
Waalse Kerk **69**
Web **49**
WesterUnie **43**
Wynand Fockink **65**

AMSTERDAM AFTER DARK | The Performing Arts

Museum District & Amsterdam South After Dark

Amsterdam ArenA **13**	Heineken Music Hall **13**	Smart Cinema **4**
Café Kale de Derde **8**	Helden **9**	Twenty Third **12**
Chocolate Bar **10**	O'Donnell's **7**	VakZuid **1**
Concertgebouw **6**	OCCII **2**	Vondelpark
EYE **5**	Rialto **11**	Openluchttheater **3**

When it comes to chamber music, the **Nederlands Kamerorkest (Nether-lands Chamber Orchestra)** (© 02/521-7500; www.orkest.nl), the **Amsterdam Baroque Orchestra** (© 035/692-6006; www.tonkoopman.nl), and the **Orkest van de Achttiende Eeuw (Orchestra of the Eighteenth Century)** (© 020/626-8236; www.orchestra18c.com) provide plenty of possibilities, often playing with authentic period instruments and ably supported by the **Nederlands Kamerkoor (Netherlands Chamber Choir)** (© 020/578-7978; www.nederlandskamerkoor. nl). You often hear these outfits in the Concertgebouw's Recital Hall, at the Beurs van Berlage, or in one of Amsterdam's historic churches. For information on some of these venues, see "Major Concert Halls & Theaters," below.

Opera

Productions by **De Nederlandse Opera (Netherlands Opera)** (✆ 020/551-8922; www.dno.nl), under Pierre Audi's artistic direction, dominate the **Muziektheater**'s schedule, and attract a devoted following.

Dance

The Dutch take pride in the international prestige of their major dance companies. **Het Nationale Ballet (National Ballet)** (✆ 020/551-8225; www.het-nationale-ballet.nl), based at the **Muziektheater,** has a repertoire of both classical and modern works, many by choreographers George Balanchine and Hans van Manen. The **Nederlands Dans Theater (Netherlands Dance Theater)** (✆ 070/880-0100; www.ndt.nl), choreographed by artistic director Jiří Kylián, is based in The Hague but frequently comes to the Muziektheater. Both companies are usually accompanied by the specialized ballet and opera orchestra **Holland Symfonia** (✆ 088/796-3600; www.hollandsymfonia.com).

Theater

Amsterdammers speak English so well that Broadway and London roadshows and English-language touring companies sometimes make Amsterdam a stop on their European itineraries. However, many of Amsterdam's best theatergoing opportunities are more experimental and avant-garde, and most of these are in Dutch.

Major Concert Halls & Theaters

Some tickets for the **Muziektheater** and the **Concertgebouw** are eminently affordable. Experiencing the Netherlands Opera, National Ballet, or Royal Concertgebouw Orchestra is well worth a bit of financial trimming in other departments.

Beurs van Berlage ★   The former home of the Amsterdam Stock Exchange now houses the **Netherlands Philharmonic Orchestra** and the **Netherlands Chamber Orchestra.** What was once the exchange's trading floor, built in 1903 by Amsterdam School architect Hendrik Petrus Berlage, has since 1988 been a concert venue with two halls: The 665-seat Yakult Zaal and the 200-seat AGA Zaal. Holland's **Concertzender** classical radio station is based here. Damrak 213 (at Beursplein). ✆ 020/521-7575. www.beursvanberlage.nl. Tickets 15€–75€. Box office Tues–Fri 12:30–6pm, Sat 12:30–5pm, and 1¼ hr. before performances begin. Tram: 4, 9, 14, 16, 24, or 25 to the Dam.

Concertgebouw ★★★   The Concertgebouw (Concert Building), home base of the **Royal Concertgebouw Orchestra,** opened its doors in 1888 and is said to be one of the world's most acoustically perfect concert halls. Musical performances have a distinctive richness of tone that is as much a pleasure for the performer as for the audience. During the musical season (Sept–Mar) and the annual **Holland Festival** (p. 31), the world's greatest orchestras, ensembles, conductors, and soloists perform here. Concerts and recitals happen every day and often there's a choice of two programs at the same time on the same evening: One in the Grote Zaal (Great Hall), the other in the smaller Kleine Zaal (Little Hall). Don't worry about your location—every seat in the Grote Zaal has a clear view. It's even possible to sit on stage behind the performers; tonal quality is altered there, however, so those seats are actually cheaper.

Vondelpark Open-Air Theater

From June to August, in the midst of peaceful, green Vondelpark, the open-air stage of the **Vondelpark Openlucht-theater** (✆ 020/428-3360; www.openluchttheater.nl) comes to life for theater, all kinds of music (including concerts by the Royal Concertgebouw Orchestra), dance, operetta, and more. The events are free, but reserving a seat costs 2.50€ per person. Bring a picnic and enjoy an enchanting evening under the stars.

The main concert season is from September to mid-June, but during July and August there's the Robeco Summer Series, world-class but with seats priced from 10€ to 35€. There are **free lunchtime rehearsal concerts** at 12:30pm on Wednesdays during the October to June concert season. These may feature chamber music, symphonic performances, or abbreviated previews of a full concert to be played that same evening. Concertgebouwplein 2-6. ✆ **0900/671-8345** (daily 10am–5pm). www.concertgebouw.nl. Tickets 17€–100€; summer concerts (Aug) 35€. Box office daily 9:30am–7pm, until 8pm for same-day tickets. Tram: 3, 5, 12, 16, or 24 to Museumplein.

Koninklijk Theater Carré The big, plush Royal Carré Theater, on the banks of the Amstel River, opened in 1887 and used to be a full-time circus arena. These days, clowns and animals are infrequent visitors, though spectacles such as the Flying Karamazov Brothers fill the gap. In addition to opera, modern dance, and ballet, look for lavish Dutch-language productions of top Broadway and London musicals. On occasion, a visiting show is in English. Top rockers and pop stars have performed here, but the biggest names now strut their stuff at Amsterdam ArenA (see p. 239). Get tickets as far in advance as possible—the hottest shows always sell out quickly. Amstel 115-125. ✆ **0900/252-5255.** www.theatercarre.nl. Tickets 15€–125€. Box office daily 9am–9pm. Tram: 7 or 10 to Weesperplein.

Muziekgebouw aan 't IJ ★★ Opened in 2005 in a spectacular piece of modern architecture, an ocean of glass on the IJ waterfront, this is the city's home of avant-garde and experimental music. The main hall seats around 750 and a smaller foyer hall has space for 125. Performances here feature contemporary, jazz, electronic, and non-Western music, along with small-scale musical theater, opera, and dance. Visit the concert hall's in-house cafe-restaurant, the **Star Ferry;** it became one of Amsterdam's hit eateries the moment it opened. In fine weather, you can dine outside on its waterfront terrace. From Centraal Station, it's a short walk or tram ride to here. Piet Heinkade 1 (IJ waterfront, just east of Centraal Station). ✆ **020/788-2000.** www.muziekgebouw.nl. Tickets 10€–65€. Box office Mon–Sat noon–7pm. Tram: 25 or 26 to Muziekgebouw.

Muziektheater ★★★ In the 1980s, construction of this superbly equipped 1,600-seat auditorium sparked street riots that sent teargas drifting across what is now the stage. Today, it's the performances that cause a stir. The Muziektheater is one of the city's stellar venues and home base of the highly regarded **Netherlands Opera** and **National Ballet.** As at the Concertgebouw, there are free "musical lunches" from October to June—these half-hour concerts are on Tuesdays at 12:30pm (doors open

10

The Performing Arts

AMSTERDAM AFTER DARK

236

at 12:15pm). Waterlooplein 22 (at the Amstel River). ℂ **020/625-5455.** www.het-muziektheater.nl. Tickets 10€–110€. Box office Mon–Sat 10am–6pm, Sun 11:30am–6pm. Tram: 9 or 14 to Waterlooplein.

Stadsschouwburg   The plushly upholstered, 950-seat Municipal Theater (1894) is Amsterdam's principal venue for mainstream Dutch theater. Dutch (and, occasionally, English) productions of international plays, both classic and modern, are presented here, as are opera and ballet performances. Leidseplein 26. ℂ **020/624-2311.** www.stadsschouwburgamsterdam.nl. Tickets 10€–50€. Tram: 1, 2, 5, 7, or 10 to Leidseplein.

OTHER VENUES

In addition to the major ones, there are plenty of other venues in Amsterdam. No fewer than 42 of the city's churches are equipped with organs, some of them historic works of art in their own right. Four churches in particular—the **Engelse Kerk,** Begijnhof 48 (ℂ **020/624-9665;** www.ercadam.nl; tram: 1, 2, 4, 5, 9, 14, 16, 24, or 25); **Nieuwe Kerk,** the Dam (ℂ **020/626-8168;** www.nieuwekerk.nl; tram: 1, 2, 4, 5, 9, 13, 14, 16, 17, 24, or 25); **Oude Kerk,** Oudekerksplein 23 (ℂ **020/625-8284;** www.oudekerk.nl; Metro: Nieuwmarkt); and **Waalse Kerk,** Walenpleintje 157 (ℂ **020/623-2074;** www.waalsekerk-amsterdam.nl; tram: 4, 9, 14, 16, 24, or 25)— are regularly in use for baroque chamber music and organ recitals.

A place worth checking out for potential new talent is the city's music school, the **Conservatorium van Amsterdam,** Oosterdokskade 151 (ℂ **020/527-7550;** www. conservatoriumvanamsterdam.nl; Metro: Centraal Station), which moved to a shiny new home on redeveloped Oosterdokseiland, just east of Centraal Station, in 2008.

Theaters, some of which occasionally feature performances in English, include **De Balie,** Kleine Gartmanplantsoen 10 (ℂ **020/553-5100;** www.debalie.nl; tram: 1, 2, 5, 7, or 10); **Theater Bellevue,** Leidsekade 90 (ℂ **020/530-5301;** www.theater bellevue.nl; tram: 1, 2, 5, 7, or 10), which also hosts modern dance; **Vlaams Cultuurhuis De Brakke Grond,** Nes 43 (ℂ **020/626-6866;** www.brakkegrond.nl; tram: 4, 9, 14, 16, 24, or 25), which has mostly Flemish theater; **Felix Meritis,** Keizersgracht 324 (ℂ **020/626-1311;** www.felixmeritis.nl; tram: 1, 2, or 5); **Frascati,** Nes 63 (ℂ **020/626-6866;** www.theater frascati.nl; tram: 4, 9, 14, 16, 24, or 25), which focuses on modern theater; **DeLaMar,** Johannes Vermeerstraat 20 (ℂ **0900/335-2627;** www.delamar. nl; tram: 1, 2, 5, 7, or 10); and the **Cultuurpark Westergasfabriek,** Haarlemmerweg 8–10 (ℂ **020/586-0710;** www.westergasfabriek.com; tram: 10), a multipurpose arts complex in an old gas-works building.

There's no language barrier at **Het Veem,** Van Diemenstraat 410 (ℂ **020/626-9291;** hetveemtheater. nl; tram: 3), at Houtmankade. This converted warehouse way beyond Westerdok and the Western Islands hosts experimental dance, movement, and mime theater. It's great if you're keen on these, but the uninitiated may feel lost.

> ### What to Wear
>
> If you intend to go to the opera, a classical music concert, or the theater, don't worry about what to wear, since Amsterdam has a very informal dress code—no code at all, really. Of course, you might want to dress up, and in fact many people do, but you're unlikely to be turned away for being improperly dressed.

10

AMSTERDAM AFTER DARK

The Performing Arts

THE CLUB & MUSIC SCENE

Visiting a jazz club or music bar is always a good way to round off your day.

Jazz & Blues

Jazz, Dixieland, and blues may be American musical forms, but Europeans—and certainly the Dutch—have adopted them with gusto. July is the best month for jazz lovers in Europe: Three major festivals are scheduled almost back-to-back in France, Switzerland, and Holland, including the 3-day **North Sea Jazz Festival** (www. northseajazz.com), held at Rotterdam's **Ahoy** (✆ **010/293-3300;** www.ahoy.nl). The festival convenes the international jazz world's biggest names with more than 100 concerts involving more than 600 artists (p. 280).

Described below are some of the jazz hangouts that dot Amsterdam's cityscape.

Bimhuis ★   Since 2005, a shiny metal box with windows has been home to the city's premier jazz, blues, and improvisational club. It's an extension of the new **Muziekgebouw aan 't IJ.** This venue represents a big change from its previous tatty premises amid the old warehouses of the Oude Schans canal, but the "Bim," as locals affectionately call it, has handled the move well—and, in truth, the new purpose-built venue is a big improvement acoustically and in other respects, even if it's lost some street cred along the way. Top local and international musicians regularly perform here. Piet Heinkade 3 (IJ waterfront, just east of Centraal Station). ✆ **020/788-2188.** www.bimhuis.nl. Cover 10€–30€. Tram: 25 or 26 to Muziekgebouw.

Bourbon Street ★★   This intimate little cafe hosts local blues, jazz, soul, and funk talent from the States and elsewhere. There's a cover charge for well-known groups or musicians, but the music plays well into the night. Leidsekruisstraat 6–8 (off Leidseplein). ✆ **020/623-3440.** www.bourbonstreet.nl. No cover, except for special acts. Tram: 1, 2, 5, 7, or 10 to Leidseplein.

Jazz Café Alto   A regular quartet plays jazz nightly to a diverse crowd in this small, comfortable cafe. There are also guest combos and occasional blues as well—the music is always top-notch. On Wednesday evening, noted saxophonist Hans Dulfer plays, sometimes accompanied by his equally noted daughter, Candy. Korte Leidsedwarsstraat 115 (off Leidseplein). ✆ **020/626-3249.** www.jazz-cafe-alto.nl. No cover. Tram: 1, 2, 5, 7, or 10 to Leidseplein.

Maloe Melo ★   This small club isn't the Mississippi Delta, but Amsterdam's "home of the blues" features live blues most nights, though some evenings feature jazz and country. Tuesday and Thursday nights are for jams, which pack the place. Music quality varies from sounds lovingly created by capable amateurs to, occasionally, those cooked up by a big name. A pleasantly intimate setting and eager audiences always make for a good time. Lijnbaansgracht 163. ✆ **020/420-4592.** www.maloemelo. nl. Cover 5€. Tram: 7, 10, or 17 to Elandsgracht.

Rock & Pop

Nothing changes faster in Holland—or exhibits more variety—than the pop music scene, whether the latest craze is rock, reggae, new wave, or whatever. Performers en route to world-class stardom always seem to turn up in Amsterdam, and few of their shows have difficulty selling out. Big stars and large-scale productions are occasionally featured at **Koninklijk Theater Carré** (see "Major Concert Halls &

Theaters," above). Rock stars strut their stuff at the giant **Amsterdam ArenA,** ArenA Boulevard, Amsterdam Zuidoost (☎ **020/311-1313;** www.amsterdamarena. nl; Metro: Bijlmer/ArenA), the Ajax soccer club's stadium in the southeastern suburbs, which has a sliding roof to keep out the ubiquitous Dutch rain.

Near Amsterdam ArenA, the smaller **Heineken Music Hall** ★, ArenA Boulevard 590 (☎ **0900/687-4242;** www.heineken-music-hall.nl; Metro: Bijlmer/ArenA), hosts more intimate concerts by well-known international performers.

For ticket info, go to **Mojo Concerts** (☎ **015/212-1980;** www.mojo.nl), and (online only) to **Livenation** (www.livenation.nl).

Dance Clubs

For local residents, the Amsterdam club scene is generally a members-only situation. But as a tourist, you can simply show up and, so long as your attire and behavior suit management's sensibilities, you shouldn't have problems getting past the bouncer. Drinks can be expensive—a beer or Coke averages 5€, and a whiskey or cocktail 8€—but you can nurse just one drink while you dance the night away, or down a quick beer and move on if the crowd or the music mix isn't your style. The places listed below are some of the most popular at press time, and, in Amsterdam, the nightclub hierarchy doesn't change very quickly. But don't hesitate to ask around for new places once you get here.

Akhnaton Jazz, African, and salsa music are regular features at this spot that caters to a youthful, multiethnic, hash-smoking crowd of joyful dancers. Nieuwezijds Kolk 25 (near Centraal Station). ☎ **020/624-3396.** www.akhnaton.nl. Cover 4€–8€. Tram: 1, 2, 5, 13, or 17 to Martelaarsgracht.

Escape ★★ Three dance floors, a great sound system, and a healthy mix of local and international DJs make this one of the prime choices for the young and trendy. The multifloor setting puts on some of the city's hottest club and party nights, hosted by top local and European DJs. Rembrandtplein 11. ☎ **020/622-1111.** www.escape.nl. Cover 10€–25€. Tram: 4, 9, or 14 to Rembrandtplein.

Home This ultra-trendy place tends to attract Dutch celebs (and wannabes) and offers a variety of music on its three floors, depending on the night—but the main deal here is house. Wagenstraat 3-7 (off Rembrandtplein). ☎ **020/620-1375.** www.clubhome.nl. Cover 10€–12€. Tram: 4, 9, or 14 to Rembrandtplein.

Jimmy Woo ★ A Hong Kong–style club, Jimmy Woo attracts a slow-burning crowd, but the music gets hotter and the vibes begin to smolder the later it gets. Guest-list entry only on some nights makes this luxe spot occasionally hard to get into. Korte Leidsedwarsstraat 18 (off Leidseplein). ☎ **020/626-3150.** www.jimmywoo.com. Cover 10€–20€. Tram: 1, 2, 5, 7, or 10 to Leidseplein.

Panama ★★ A waterfront building from 1899 that used to be a power station houses this hip club. The attractive bar/restaurant in the lobby opens up into the cavernous club, which hosts big-name DJs and special events, depending on the day and seasons. This is a see-and-be-seen place for 30- to 40-something professionals. So dress to impress and bring some attitude. Oostelijke Handelskade 4. ☎ **020/311-8689.** www.panama.nl. Cover 10€–25€. Tram: 10 or 26 to Rietlandpark.

Paradiso ★ This old church has been transformed into a space that presents an eclectic variety of music, both live and canned. A dark and somewhat forbidding

The Club & Music Scene

exterior belies the bright inside. The majestic interior has lofty ceilings and a high balcony encircling the room, which affords great views of the central dance floor. The club revels in name DJs and has popular theme nights, ranging from jazz to disco to raves. The Friday-night VIP Club is stylish. Weteringschans 6-8 (near Leidseplein). © **020/626-4521.** www.paradiso.nl. Cover 8€–18€. Tram: 1, 2, 5, 7, or 10 to Leidseplein.

Tonight ★★ A former 17th-century orphanage chapel with frescoed walls is the atmospheric, if unlikely, setting for one of Amsterdam's hottest clubs. DJs rustle up music from the '60s to the '90s, drawing a surprisingly youthful crowd to the Timezone club nights, where funk, soul, and New York disco reign. 's Gravesandestraat 51 (near the Tropenmuseum). © **020/850-2400.** www.hotelarena.nl. Cover 6€–10€. Tram: 7 or 10 to Korte 's Gravesandestraat.

WesterUnie Step on the gas for hip-hop and Latin dance at this cavernous place, in the unlikely setting of the Cultuurpark Westergasfabriek, a decommissioned gas plant in the Westerpark district west of Centraal Station. It's now a cultural center, restaurant, and bar (open longer hours than the dance club) with an outdoor terrace. It's often crowded and hard to get in. Klönneplein 4-6 (at Haarlemmerweg, west of Centraal Station). © **020/684-8496.** www.westerunie.nl. No cover. Tram: 10 to Van Hallstraat.

Multidimensional Venues

Melkweg ★★ 🏛 A one-time hippie haven in an old dairy factory, the Melkweg (Milky Way) constantly reinvents its multimedia persona. It houses a reasonably priced international restaurant (**Eat@Jo's**), coffeeshop, bar, art center, dance floor, cinema, theater, concert hall, photo gallery, and exhibition space. You need to get a temporary membership before they'll let you in, but it's worth it. International big-name groups perform here, and DJs spin a musical mix ranging from ska to house. Melkweg's organizers have always embraced liberalism and experimentalism, and its theater showcases new groups, both international and local, and performances ranging from comedy to multicultural and gay- and lesbian-oriented. Lijnbaansgracht 234A (near Leidseplein). © **020/531-8181.** www.melkweg.nl. Cover 5€–10€ plus 3.50€ monthly club membership. Box office Mon–Fri 1–5pm, Sat–Sun 4–6pm. Tram: 1, 2, 5, 7, or 10 to Leidseplein.

OCCII A laid-back fringe spot beyond Vondelpark, OCCII is a bar, club, and performance venue where young Amsterdammers belt out unclassifiable music and fling themselves into off-the-wall cabaret or stand-up comedy acts. Amstelveenseweg 134 (at Vondelpark). © **020/671-7778.** www.occii.org. Cover varies. Tram: 1 to Overtoomsesluis; 2 to Zeilstraat/Amstelveenseweg.

Leather & Lash

When it comes to getting past the "doorbitch" into Amsterdam's twice-yearly **Wasteland** (www.wasteland.nl) fetish-glam rave—a monster bash attended by thousands of fetishistas from around the world—be sure to suit up with outlandish leather or kinky latex, uniforms, plastic, rubber, and metal. What larks! Bring your S&M toys. No less an authority than *Penthouse* called the extravaganza "Probably the wildest party on earth." Check the website for location details and dates. Cover is around 50€.

Odeon ★   Your feet might not know what to do at first amid the graceful surroundings of this reconverted old canalside building (1663). The period ceiling paintings and stucco decor seem more suited to minuets than disco moves. A mix of '50s–'80s music is played. In addition to dance at the Odeon Club, there's a chic restaurant, the Cocktailbrasserie; a laid-back cellar cafe/brasserie, the Café Odeon; the funky Odeon Bar; and a performance hall that's used for music concerts, from classical to jazz and rock, as well as theater, lectures, and other events (until it gets made over to dance-club mode in the late evening). Singel 460 (near Muntplein). ✆ 020/521-8555. www.odeonamsterdam. nl. Cover 5€–15€. Odeon Club: Fri–Sat 11pm–5am. Tram: 1, 2, or 5 to Koningsplein.

Comedy Theater

Boom Chicago ★ 🏠👤   Since 1993, Boom Chicago has been successfully importing American and British brands of comedy to Amsterdam. *Time* magazine compared them to Chicago's famous Second City comedy troupe, and the *Chicago Tribune*'s critic reported back to the Windy City that "big talents turn in a very funny show." The partly scripted, partly improvised humor takes aim at life in Amsterdam, the Dutch, tourists, and any other convenient target. Dutch audiences don't have much problem with the English sketches, and often seem to get the joke ahead of the native English speakers in attendance. Spectators sit around candlelit tables for eight and can dine on what *The Wall Street Journal* called "surprisingly good food" and a drink while enjoying the show. The restaurant opens at 7pm (it closes when the theater closes), and meals cost 30€ to 35€ per person. Leidseplein Theater, Leidseplein 12. ✆ 020/423-0101. www.boomchicago.nl. Cover 15€–35€ (not including dinner). Box office daily noon–8:30pm. Tram: 1, 2, 5, 7, or 10 to Leidseplein.

Comedy Café Amsterdam   Most of the standup and improvmeisters here are Dutch, with an occasional American, Brit, or other English speaker; Sunday is an all-English day. They serve up a mixed bag of chuckles, guffaws, and groans, washed down by suds and, if you're daring, accompanied by delicacies such as meat pastries or turkey tournedos swimming in mustard-dill sauce. Max Euweplein 43-45 (at Leidseplein). ✆ 020/638-3971. www.comedycafe.nl. Cover from 16€ (not including dinner). Tram 1, 2, 5, 7, or 10 to Leidseplein.

THE BAR SCENE

Amsterdam's more than 1,400 cafes and bars are a hard act to follow. A lot of Amsterdammers still start their day at their favorite cafe (usually a so-called brown cafe), have lunch there, return for drinks before dinner, and then go back for a bit of socializing, a game of snooker, and some live (or canned) music and a singalong. Since everyone goes to cafes, they are the ultimate democratic institutions. You, the street sweeper, drink with the CEOs and politicos and speak your mind about everything from croquettes to geopolitics. The average price for a beer in Amsterdam is 1.50€ to 3€—clubs and hotel bars will charge more.

Brown Cafes

You haven't really tasted Dutch beer until you've tasted it in Holland, served Dutch-style in a real *bruine kroeg* (brown cafe). These traditional Dutch bars are unpretentious, unpolished institutions filled with camaraderie, like a British pub or an American neighborhood bar. In a brown cafe, pouring another beer is much more important than dusting off the back bottles on the bar; the ritual is to draw a beer to get as much foam as possible, then to use a wet knife to shave off the head between a series of final fill-ups.

Even if you're not a beer lover, venturing into a brown cafe in Amsterdam will give you a peek into the city's everyday life. In old neighborhoods, brown cafes are on almost every corner—you can't miss them. Most have lacy curtains on the bottom half of the window, and perhaps a cat sleeping on the ledge. In winter (and sometimes into spring), their front doors are hung with a thick drape to keep out drafts. Once inside, you'll find the smoky, mustard brownness that's unique to an Amsterdam brown cafe, the result of years—no, centuries—of thick smoke and warm conversation.

There may be booths or little tables sprinkled around, but the only spots of color and light will be the shining metal of the beer tap and, perhaps, a touch of red still showing in the Persian rugs thrown across the tables (a practice that's typically Dutch, if you recall the old paintings). You'll feel the eons of conviviality the minute you walk into a really old, really *brown* brown cafe. Some have been on their corners since Rembrandt's time, haunted by the ghosts of drinkers past. The best of them are on the Prinsengracht, below Westermarkt, at the Dam, at Leidseplein, on Spui, or with a bit of searching, on tiny streets between canals.

Café Chris ★ Amsterdam's oldest remaining drinking den opened in 1624 and has been going strong ever since. It's said to be where the builders of Westerkerk (p. 162) were paid every week or two. There are a lot of curious old features at this bar that keep drawing people year after year, including the quirky toilet in the bathroom, which, oddly, flushes from outside the door and inside the bar! On Sunday nights, loud opera music engulfs the bar, attracting a cultured bohemian crowd. Bloemstraat 42 (near Westermarkt). ℂ **020/624-5942.** www.cafechris.nl. Tram: 13, 14, or 17 to Westermarkt.

De Druif This is one of those places that not many visitors know about, though it's the third-oldest tavern in town. "The Grape" is on the waterfront and mainly frequented by a friendly local crowd. The bar's mythology has it that the Dutch naval hero, Piet Hein, was a frequent patron (he lived nearby). However, as happens often when good beer is at hand, this is a tall tale told from wishful thinking—the bar opened in 1631 and Heyn died in 1629. Rapenburgerplein 83 (behind the Eastern Dock). ℂ **020/624-4530.** Bus: 22 to Kadijksplein.

De Karpershoek Opened in 1629, this bar—the city's second-oldest—was once a favorite hangout of sailors and seamen. Nowadays, given its prime location across the street from Centraal Station, the clientele is a mix of Dutch regulars, commuters popping in for a quick drink, and tourists, some of whom seem to settle in nicely while others look out of place, as if they've wandered in by mistake. The floor is covered with sand, just like it was in the 17th century. Martelaarsgracht 2 (facing Centraal Station). ℂ **020/624-7886.** Tram: 1, 2, 5, 13, or 17 to Martelaarsgracht.

> ### A Lost Art?
>
> Today's Amsterdammers are no more than a pale shadow of their esteemed ancestors when it comes to quaffing beer. In 1613, Amsterdam's 518 taverns assured one for every 200 inhabitants. Today, the ratio has slipped to one per 725. The 17th century, clearly, was a Golden Age in more senses than one.

De Vergulde Gaper This place is a double delight: In bad weather, you can retreat into the warm, cozy interior, decorated with vintage posters and old medicine bottles (it used to be a pharmacy). In good weather, you can sit on a terrace beside the Prinsengracht—if you can get a seat. There's an unseemly dash whenever a table is vacated. Prinsenstraat 30 (at Prinsengracht). ☎ **020/624-8975.** www.goodfoodgroup.nl. Tram: 1, 2, 5, 13, or 17 to Martelaarsgracht.

Gollem More than 200 kinds of beer are for sale in this ever-popular brown cafe near Spui. Many of them are imported, many of them favorites from Belgium, but do look for some weird-and-wonderful brews from other parts of the world. Raamsteeg 4 (off Spui). ☎ **06/5378-0273.** www.cafegollem.nl. Tram: 1, 2, or 5 to Spui.

Hoppe ★ Standing room only is often the space situation here, and the crowds sometimes overflow onto the sidewalk. It seems that, quite by accident, Hoppe has become a tourist attraction. Locals love this spot, which dates from 1670. Trendy young professionals often pass through for a drink on their way home, mingling with hardened drinkers who pass through at any time and rarely leave. A convivial, smoky atmosphere and authentic decor make it a great place to while away an afternoon. It's worth stopping by just to see. Spui 18–20. ☎ **020/420-4420.** www.cafe-hoppe.nl. Tram: 1, 2, or 5 to Spui.

In de Wildeman Tucked away in a medieval alley, this wood-paneled *bier-proeflokaal* (beer-tasting house) dates from 1690. The tiled floor and rows of bottles and jars behind the counters are remnants of earlier days, when it functioned as a distillery. Today, it serves 17 draft and 200 bottled beers from around the world. It's a laid-back atmosphere, with mostly hard-drinking but very friendly locals ranging from 30- to 50-something. There's a separate room for nonsmokers. Kolksteeg 3 (off Nieuwezijds Voorburgwal). ☎ **020/638-2348.** www.indewildeman.nl. Tram: 1, 2, 5, 13, or 17 to Nieuwezijds Kolk.

't Loosje This is a friendly place in the up-and-coming Nieuwmarkt area, popular with students, artists—and guidebook writers. It was built around 1900 and was originally used as a waiting room for the horse-drawn tram. The walls are still ornamented with tiles from that period and a painting of the South Holland Beer Brewery. There are lots of beers on tap. Nieuwmarkt 32–34. ☎ **020/627-2635.** Metro: Nieuwmarkt.

't Smalle ★ For an authentic brown-cafe experience—though it opened only in 1978—stop by this place which, in 1786, Pieter Hoppe used as a warehouse and distillery for his Hoppe *jenever* and as a *proeflokaal* (tasting house). The air is invariably thick with cigar smoke, *jenever* vapor, and animated conversation. You're unlikely to find a free seat, but you can escape the crush out on the canalside terrace, a perfect place to watch bikes and boats going by. Egelantiersgracht 12 (at Prinsengracht). ☎ **020/623-9617.** www.t-smalle.nl. Tram: 13, 14, or 17 to Westermarkt.

Tasting Houses

There are only three differences between a brown cafe and a *proeflokaal*, or tasting house: What you drink, how you drink it, and who owns the place. A *proeflokaal*'s decor will still be basically brown and typically Old Dutch—and its age may be even more impressive than that of its beer-swilling neighbors—but in a tasting house, you traditionally order *jenever* (Dutch gin, taken "neat," without ice) or another product of the distillery that owns the place. Then, to drink your libation, custom decrees that you lean over the bar with your hands behind your back to take the first sip from your full-to-the-brim *borreltje* (small drinking glass).

MESSAGE IN THE bottle

You can smooth the process of conversing with locals in a bar if you can bandy about some Dutch drinking terminology. The most common word for a glass of *jenever* (Dutch gin) is a *borrel* (*bo*-rel) or the diminutive *borreltje* (*bo*-rel-che), though you'll also hear it called a *vaderlandje* (*fader*-lant-che), meaning "little fatherland," and other terms such as *hassebassie* (*hass*-uh-bassie), *keiltje* (*kyle*-che), *piketanussie* (*pik*-et-an-oossee), *recht op neer* (*rekht op near*), and *slokkie* (*slok*-ee). Avant-garde imbibers may ask for an "uppercut" to prove their international credentials. A glass of *jenever* filled to the rim, as tradition requires, is called a *kamelenrug* (cam-*ay*-len-rookh), meaning "camel's back," or an *over Het IJ-kijkertje* (*over het eye kyk*-erche), meaning "view over the IJ" (an Amsterdam water channel). *Jenever* is often ordered with a beer chaser. The barkeep will place the *kopstoot* (*cop*-stoat), meaning "knock on the head," of a *stelletje* (*stel*-etche), meaning "couple," on the bar. Beer or *pils* (*pilss*) in a small glass is called a *colaatje pils* (co-la-che *pilss*); a *kabouter pils* (ka-*bou*-ter *pilss*), meaning "dwarf beer"; or a *lampie licht* (*lam*-pee *likht*), meaning "little lamp." Ale in a large glass is known as a *bakkie* (*bak*-ee) or a *vaas*, which means jar or vase. If it's served in a half-liter (1-pint) glass, it's known locally as an *amsterdammertje* (little Amsterdammer).

So if you breeze into a brown cafe, park yourself at the bar, and call the bartender over for a *"Recht op neer borrel,"* then ask him to "make sure it's a proper *over Het IJ-kijkertje,* put a *kopstoot* with it, a *colaatje* if you please, and set up a *bakkie* for later," you should get on swimmingly (of course, they might also send for the men in white coats).

Brouwerij 't IJ ★★ In addition to the usual features, this slightly down-at-the-heels *proeflokaal* has a small brewery and a fascinating location—it's in the De Gooyer windmill in the city's old harbor area. You can take guided tours of the beer-making facilities (Fri at 4pm), then taste the brewery's Pilzen or Mug Bitter brews, or the slightly stronger Pasij or Zatte brews. Columbus, a hearty wheat beer that's reddish, flavorful, and fierce (almost 10% alcohol by volume), is the new brew of choice among many Amsterdam barflies. Funenkade 7 (at Sarphatistraat). ✆ **020/320-1768.** www.brouwerijhetij.nl. Tram: 10 to Hoogte Kadijk.

De Admiraal This tasting house has a small and pleasant outdoor cafe patio. Inside, sofas and big cozy armchairs make things comfortable, as do 15 different *jenevers* and 55 liqueurs, plus a fair Dutch dinner-and-snacks menu. Herengracht 319 (along the canal near Oude Spiegelstraat). ✆ **020/625-4334.** www.proeflokaaldeadmiraal.nl. Tram: 1, 2, or 5 to Spui.

De Dokter This antiques-filled tasting house is near Spui, the student quarter's main square. Ask to sample the homemade *boeren jongens* and *boeren meisjes*, the brandied fruits—raisins and apricots—that serve as the traditional introduction to "spirits" for Dutch *jongen* and *meisjes*—boys and girls. Rozenboomsteeg 4 (off Spui). ✆ **020/626-4427.** www.cafe-de-dokter.nl. Tram: 1, 2, 4, 5, 9, 14, 16, 24, or 25 to Spui.

De Drie Fleschjes Not much has changed in this tidy tasting house ("The Three Little Bottles") since its 1650 opening, except that in 1816, Heindrik Bootz liqueurs took over. Fifty-two wooden casks along the wall face the bar. It's open Monday to

Saturday from noon to 8:30pm, Sunday from 3 to 8pm. Gravenstraat 18 (off the Dam, behind the Nieuwe Kerk). © **020/624-8443.** Tram: 1, 2, 4, 9, 14, 16, 24, or 25 to the Dam.

De Ooievaar   This tiny place, Holland's smallest *proeflokaal*, dispenses *jenevers* and Oudhollandse liqueurs. It's a pleasant place, with a bright bar area to offset the brown walls and wooden casks. Sint Olofspoort 1 (at Zeedijk). © **020/420-8004.** www. proeflokaaldeooievaar.nl. Tram: 1, 2, 4, 5, 9, 13, 16, 17, 24, 25, or 26 to Centraal Station.

In 't Aepjen   An old sailor's tavern near the waterfront, this small traditional Dutch bar is housed in one of Amsterdam's two surviving timber buildings, which dates from 1550. The "ape" of the name refers to images of monkeys in the tap room. Zeedijk 1 (at Prins Hendrikkade). © **020/626-8401.** Tram: 1, 2, 4, 5, 9, 13, 16, 17, 24, 25, or 26 to Centraal Station.

Wynand Fockink ★ 🍸   Don't waste your breath—regulars here know all about the English pronunciation bomb hidden in the Dutch name. This popular old-world *proeflokaal*, tucked away in a quiet alleyway off brash Damstraat, dates from 1679. Aficionados of the 50 varieties of Dutch *jenever* and 70 traditional liqueurs on hand often have to maneuver for elbow-room to raise their glasses. One of the wow-worthy attractions here is the collection of liqueur bottles on which are painted portraits of every Amsterdam mayor since 1591. It's open daily from 3 to 9pm. The attached *lunchlokaal* is, as its name implies, open for lunch. Pijlsteeg 31 (off the Dam). © **020/639-2695.** www.wynand-fockink.nl. Tram: 4, 9, 14, 16, 24, or 25 to the Dam.

Modern Cafes

Amsterdam has many contemporary cafes that are neither brown cafes nor friendly watering holes (though many examples in both categories are acceptably trendy). You may hear some contemporary cafes described as "white cafes," as distinct from brown cafes. You may also hear talk of the "coke-trail circuit," though that's a bit passé nowadays. Besides the trendy cafes listed below, you might want to check out some of Amsterdam's "Grand Cafes" reviewed in chapter 6: **De Jaren, Café Luxembourg, Grand Café De Balie,** and **Grand Café l'Opera.**

GREAT DUTCH drinks

The Dutch are famous for their gin, or *jenever,* and their beer. The former is a fiery, colorless liquid served ice-cold and drunk "neat"—it's not a mixer. You can get flavored *jenever*—from berry to lemon—and, just as with Dutch cheese, you can get *oude* or *jonge* (old or young) *jenever*—every bar has a wide selection on its shelves. But while cheese gets harder and sharper with age, *jenever* grows smooth and soft; *jonge* is less sweet and creamy than *oude.* All are known for their delayed-action effectiveness, so beware if you don't feel it right away.

As for **beer,** you can get regular **Heineken, Grolsch,** or **Amstel**—called *pils* in Amsterdam—or you can try something different as you make the rounds. I happen to like the *witte* (white) beer, which is sweeter than *pils:* Belgian **Hoegaarden** is a good example. On the opposite end of the spectrum are the Belgian dark beers, like **De Koninck** or **Duvel.** Belgian beers are quite popular in Holland and are, in general, better made and more artisanal than the native brews.

bubbles&wines This fancy champagne and wine bar (think subdued lighting, dark wood surfaces, and red tones) serves an extensive roster of champagne and wine labels, along with light snacks. It's just a few minutes' walk from the Dam. Nes 37 (at Pieter Jacob-szstraat). ℂ **020/422-3318.** www.bubblesandwines.com. Tram: 4, 9, 14, 16, 24, or 25 to the Dam.

Café Kale de Derde ★★ Soft chairs, long banquettes, and chandeliers draw a hip, youthful crowd to this place in the Pijp district, to sip mojitos and other cocktails, graze on plates of tempura, and dance to DJs on Friday and Saturday nights. Ferdinand Bolstraat 18–20 (at Marie Heinekenplein). ℂ **020/470-0651.** www.18twintig.nl. Tram: 16, 24, or 25 to Stadhouderskade.

Café Schiller ★ A bright glassed-in terrace on the square and a finely carved Art Deco interior make a nice backdrop for the friendly, laid-back atmosphere, good food, and lively crowd of artistic and literary types on offer here. Rembrandtplein 36. ℂ **020/624-9846.** www.cafeschiller.nl. Tram: 4, 9, or 14 to Rembrandtplein.

Chocolate Bar ★ The hippest bar in the Pijp also serves up delicious light meals. DJs spin great music on the weekends, and there's a terrace for when the weather's fine. Eerste Van der Helststraat 62A (at Govert Flinckstraat). ℂ **020/675-7672.** www.chocolate-bar. nl. Tram: 16 or 24 to Albert Cuypstraat.

SMOKING coffeeshops

Amsterdam's reputation as a wild party town is in part a result of its tolerance toward cannabis. Yet the practice is technically illegal and only just tolerated. Local producers are allowed to operate so long as they don't go in for large-scale production. Individuals are allowed to be in possession of up to 30 grams (about 1 oz.) for personal use, but can only purchase 5 grams (about ⅙ oz.) at a time. "Coffeeshops" in Amsterdam are places where a customer can purchase marijuana or hashish. They are licensed and controlled and provide a place where patrons can sit and smoke all day if they so choose; they are not allowed to sell alcohol, and only some serve food (usually light snacks)—but the coffee is not bad. Warmoesstraat, on the edge of the Red Light District, is lined with coffeeshops, making it a prime spot for coffeeshop crawls by bands of young tourists (they're usually dazed by the end of the evening, as you can imagine, so things are quite mellow). Like the John Travolta character Vincent Vega in *Pulp Fiction*, you'll find it's mostly fellow tourists you'll be gazing at through the fug of bitter-smelling smoke in these places.

Some notable coffeeshops: **The Rookies,** Korte Leidsedwarsstraat 145 (ℂ **020/ 428-3125;** www.rookies.nl; tram: 1, 2, 5, 7, or 10); **Sheeba,** Warmoesstraat 73 (ℂ no phone; Metro: Centraal Station); and the brash **Bulldog,** Leidseplein 17 (ℂ **020/ 624-8248;** www.thebulldogshops.com; tram: 1, 2, 5, 7, or 10). Two places with more of a neighborhood atmosphere (even if a thick one) are relaxed, clean smoking **Kadinsky,** Rosmarijnsteeg 9 (ℂ **020/624-7023;** tram: 1, 2, or 5), at Spuistraat; and friendly **Paradox,** Eerste Bloemdwarsstraat 2 (ℂ **020/623-5639;** www.paradoxcoffeeshop.com; tram: 13, 14, or 17), off Bloemgracht, in the Jordaan.

Toker's tip: Don't buy on the street. You stand a fair chance of being ripped off, the quality will be questionable, and there may be unpleasant additives.

Frascati   Frascati belongs to a category similar to Schiller's (see above), except that, in this case, the cafe's good looks have a theatrical bent. The surrounding neighborhood is rife with alternative theater, and Frascati is a major player in this scene. Nes 59 (behind Rokin). © **020/624-1324.** www.theaterfrascati.nl. Tram: 4, 9, 14, 16, 24, or 25 to Spui.

Helden ★   A young, well-heeled crowd sinks into the sofas and sips martinis and mojitos over soft music at this trendy place in the Pijp district. The food's good, too, and there's a pleasant summer terrace where you can lounge alfresco. Eerste Van der Helststraat 42 (at Quellijnstraat). © **020/673-3332.** www.helden.nu. Tram: 16 or 24 to Stadhouderskade.

Kanis en Meiland   On a redeveloped island named KNSM Eiland in the old Eastern Docks Area, this cafe takes its moniker from a clever play on the islet's name. Equally inventive is a time-warp design that has you stepping from 1990s' functional urban architecture on the outside into a traditional brown cafe interior. The illusion is genuine enough that K&M has become a near-classic on the city's cafe roster and a legend in its own lunchtime for freshly made snacks. Levantkade 127. © **020/418-2439.** www.kanisenmeiland.nl. Tram: 10 to Azartplein.

Lux   Although the Leidseplein area is quite touristy, laid-back Lux draws in a healthy dose of locals with its chic attitude. Sit on the upper level to enjoy a sweeping view of the place. Marnixstraat 403 (at Leidseplein). © **020/422-1412.** www.hotelweber.nl. Tram: 1, 2, 5, 7, or 10 to Leidseplein.

Seymour Likely   Woe unto you if you enter here wearing out-of-date duds. And it's no use wailing that they were the latest and hippest thing only yesterday—that's the whole point. The lips of all those beautiful young things inside that aren't on a glass, or each other, will curl into a sneer. Nieuwezijds Voorburgwal 250 (near Amsterdam Historical Museum). © **020/627-1427.** Tram: 1, 2, 5, 13, or 17 to Nieuwezijds Voorburgwal.

VakZuid ★   Located inside the Olympic Stadium used for the 1928 Games, this chic cocktail bar/lounge/restaurant/club evokes the interior design of that period in an updated form, and has a large canalside terrace. Olympisch Stadion 35 (at Stadionplein in Amsterdam-Zuid). © **020/570-8400.** www.vakzuid.nl. Tram: 16 or 24 to Stadionplein.

English & Irish Pubs

Mulligans Irish Music Bar   Both the Irish music and the *craic* (pronounced "crack," and meaning fast wit and good conversation, not that other stuff) at Mulligans are lively. Bring an instrument and you may be allowed to play. Amstel 100 (off Rembrandtplein). © **020/622-1330.** www.mulligans.nl. Tram: 4, 9, or 14 to Rembrandtplein.

O'Donnell's   A happy, boisterous place where the Guinness is good and the bartenders are Irish and friendly, this neighborhood Irish pub pulls in many of the young, up-and-coming professionals who live in the Pijp, not least for its down-to-earth food—Guinness stew, fish and chips, grilled lamb chops—and busy sidewalk terrace. Ferdinand Bolstraat 5 (at Marie Heinekenplein). © **020/676-7786.** www.odonnellsirishpub.com. Tram: 16 or 24 to Stadhouderskade.

Three Sisters   There's an English-style pub on the first floor, with lots of snug corners for conversation about Shakespeare or Manchester United over pints of warm ale (they have cold beers too), and a New York steakhouse upstairs. Leidseplein 2. ✆ **020/428-0428.** Tram: 1, 2, 5, 7, or 10 to Leidseplein.

Jordaan Cafes

The Jordaan is Amsterdam's iconoclastic blue-collar district. It has suffered from the depredations of gentrifiers, demolition experts, and cleaner-uppers, but still retains its distinctive style and preoccupation with itself. Cafes here are old-style and colorful. You might even take in a singsong of schmaltzy Dutch songs about stolen kisses behind the windmill.

Café Nol   Younger and cooler than your typical Jordaan cafe, but not by much, this place is decked out with crystal chandeliers, mirrors, a red carpet, and hanging potted plants. It caters to a mix of young, cool Jordaaners and old-timers who have lived in the neighborhood for ages. Young folks love to sing here. Westerstraat 109 (near Noordermarkt). ✆ **020/624-5380.** www.cafenolamsterdam.nl. Tram: 3 or 10 to Marnixplein.

Café Rooie Nelis   The kitsch decor here has to be seen to be believed—and even then you might not. The same family has owned this place for generations; it's real down-home Jordaan. Laurierstraat 101 (off Prinsengracht). ✆ **020/624-4167.** Tram: 13, 14, or 17 to Westermarkt.

De Twee Zwaantjes   The two swans of the cafe's name would find it hard to spread their wings here. But the little place's intimacy means you're brought face-to-face with the Jordaanese in all their glory. On some evenings, they'll break into traditional Dutch song. Prinsengracht 114 (at Egelantiersgracht). ✆ 020/625-2729. www.detweezwaantjes.nl. Tram: 13, 14, or 17 to Westermarkt.

> ### 💬 A Sobering Thought
>
> The Dutch from the southern Netherlands, whose spiritual capital is the city of Maastricht, lump Amsterdammers together with other "coldblooded" northerners, as people too straitlaced to know how to have a good time.

Cocktails with a View

Twenty Third   Even a low-rise city like Amsterdam has a high-rise hotel with a rooftop cocktail lounge. This one is located on the 23rd floor. The drink prices are a little higher than what you'd find at ground level, but the view is worth the cost. From a comfortable vantage point in Amsterdam South, the big picture windows provide a sweeping panorama of the city. In the Hotel Okura Amsterdam, Ferdinand Bolstraat 333. ✆ **020/678-7111.** www.okura.nl. Tram: 25 to Ferdinand Bolstraat.

THE GAY & LESBIAN SCENE

Amsterdam's gay scene is strong, and there is no lack of gay bars and nightspots. Below are listings of some of the most popular spots for gay men. For lesbians, the scene is a little more difficult to uncover. Places that are hot now might not be later, so contact **COC,** Rozenstraat 14 (✆ **020/626-3087;** www.cocamsterdam. nl; tram: 13, 14, or 17), the Organization of Homosexuals in the Netherlands. The office and telephone lines operate daily from 10am to 5pm. More information is available from the **Gay and Lesbian Switchboard** (✆ **020/623-6565**). *Gay*

Those Closure Blues

The chic end of Amsterdam's gay community experienced an attack of the vapors in 2010, when a prominent local business went bust, taking down a bunch of the city's trendiest gay watering holes. Particularly hard hit was the Reguliersdwarsstraat strip, which went almost overnight from a vital scene to a virtual desert. Distraught ex-patrons were left wondering where, if anywhere, was left for them to go at night. Given time, new bars and dance venues will no doubt replace those that were lost. To keep up with developments on Reguliersdwarsstraat, turn to **www.reguliers.net.**

News, a monthly newspaper in English, is available for free in gay establishments throughout Amsterdam.

Most of the city's gay bars and other venues are in well-defined areas. For frivolous, old-style camp, look along the Amstel near **Muntplein** and on **Halvemaansteeg.** The trendier places are along **Reguliersdwarsstraat.** Casual locals head for **Kerkstraat,** on both sides of Leidsestraat. Lesbian bars are more thinly spread. There are few of them, but there are no neighborhoods or streets that specialize in lesbian bars. Amstel and Amstelstraat at Rembrandtplein, the Jordaan, and to a limited extent the edge of the Red Light District are the likeliest zones to check out.

Bars & Cafes

Amstel FiftyFour   One of Amsterdam's most venerable gay bars, on gay-friendly Amstel, has had a makeover, changing it from a cozily old-fashioned place to one which, if not exactly hip, has a definite sense of style. It remains engagingly convivial, and the regulars will occasionally break into song. Amstel 54 (behind Rembrandtplein). 𝄞 **020/623-4254.** www.amstelfiftyfour.nl. Tram: 4, 9, or 14 to Rembrandtplein.

Arc ★★   Arc, one of the most attractive and trendy bars in the city, pulls in both gays and straights. The friendly, 20- and 30-something mixed crowd is very hip. Many opt to lounge the night away here and indulge in the delicious appetizer platters. Reguliersdwarsstraat 44 (a block behind the Flower Market). 𝄞 **020/689-7070.** www.bararc.eu. Tram: 1, 2, or 5 to Koningsplein.

Getto   This bar and restaurant attracts an equal mix of males and females with its hip interior and such events as "Club Fu" karaoke (first Mon of each month) and bingo (every Thurs). An eclectic dinner menu offers food from around the world, whether vegetarian or Cajun crocodile steak, and the kitchen stays open until 11pm. Open Wednesday, Thursday, and Sunday from 5pm to 1am, Friday and Saturday from 5pm to 2am. Warmoesstraat 51 (Red Light District). 𝄞 **020/421-5151.** www.getto.nl. Tram: 1, 2, 4, 5, 9, 13, 14, 16, 17, 24, or 25 to Centraal Station.

Saarein2   Once a female-only enclave with a feisty atmosphere, this bar is now open to both genders and has livened up a bit. Attractions include pool, darts, and pinball. The change in atmosphere has included the addition of food, with a well-priced Continental dinner menu served from 6 to 9:30pm. Open Sunday to Thursday from 5pm to 1am, Friday and Saturday from 5pm to 2am. Elandsstraat 119 (Jordaan). 𝄞 **020/623-4901.** http://cafesaarein.hyves.nl. Tram: 7, 10, or 17 to Marnixstraat.

Spijker This long-standing neighborhood bar attracts a casual crowd that extends a friendly welcome to visitors. The pinball machine and pool table are social focal points, and side-by-side video screens broadcast an amusing juxtaposition of cartoons and erotica. Lively staffers keep the atmosphere relaxed with a varied selection of music and stiff drinks. Happy "hour" draws crowds in daily from 5 to 7pm. Open Sunday to Thursday from 4pm to 1am, Friday and Saturday from 4pm to 3am. Kerkstraat 4 (corner with Leidsegracht). ☎ 020/620-5919. www.spijkerbar.nl. Tram: 1, 2, or 5 to Prinsengracht.

Vive-la-Vie This lesbian bar celebrated its 20th anniversary in 2000. It attracts a young, lively crowd before club-hopping time, and lipstick isn't forbidden. The sidewalk terrace offers great summertime relaxation and a fine view of the flocks of tourists in neighboring Rembrandtplein. Open Sunday to Thursday from 2:30pm to 1am, Friday and Saturday from 3pm to 3am. Amstelstraat 7 (off Rembrandtplein). ☎ 020/624-0114. www.vivelavie.net. Tram: 4, 9, or 14 to Rembrandtplein.

Web Behind its corrugated metal facade, this popular after-work drinks venue has a raunchy atmosphere and plenty of space to walk. Tuesday is "beer bust" (an intense beer-drinking session) and Wednesday is prize-draw night. On Sunday evening at 7pm, line up for the food buffet. Open Sunday to Thursday from 2pm to 1am, Friday and Saturday from 2pm to 2am. Sint-Jacobsstraat 6 (at Nieuwendijk). ☎ 020/623-6758. Tram: 1, 2, 5, 13, or 17 to Nieuwezijds Kolk.

Clubs

Club COC Amsterdam's main advocacy organization for gays, lesbians, bisexuals, and transgender individuals (see "Gay & Lesbian Travelers," in chapter 3) organizes occasional club and dance events at their Jordaan headquarters. These are favored by clean-cut locals—so don't expect hardcore fun and games—and some of them are women-only. Look for details on the COC website, since there is no fixed program. Rozenstraat 14 (at Prinsengracht). ☎ 020/626-3087. www.cocamsterdam.nl. Tram: 13, 14, or 17 to Westermarkt. Hours vary, and generally there's no cover.

Cockring This none-too-subtly named gay disco is the most popular in town. On the dance floor, DJs lay down no-nonsense, hard-core, high-decibel dance and techno music. More relaxed beats in the sociable upstairs bar make for a welcome break. Live shows with male strippers keep things hot. Warmoesstraat 96 (Red Light District). ☎ 020/623-9604. www.clubcockring.com. Cover 6€–12€. Tram: 4, 9, 14, 16, 24, or 25 to the Dam.

THE RED LIGHT DISTRICT

Prostitution is legal in the Netherlands, and in Amsterdam most of it is concentrated in the Red Light District. Even if you don't want to play, this is a place you may want to see at night, when the red lights reflect from the canals' inky surfaces. Lots of visitors come here out of curiosity or just for fun. There's no problem with wandering around, and you don't need to worry much about crime as long as you stick to busier streets—and keep an eye out for pickpockets. Visiting women going around in groups of two or more won't be noticed any more than anyone else, but a single female might be subject to misrepresentation. See also "Offbeat & Alternative Amsterdam," in chapter 7, and "Walking Tour 2: The Old Center," in chapter 8, both of which have sections that cover the Red Light District as a daytime attraction.

The Red Light District, known in Dutch as *Rosse Buurt,* isn't very big. The easiest way in is on **Damstraat,** beside the Krasnapolsky Hotel on the Dam. Then stick to the main drag on **Oudezijds Voorburgwal,** as far north as the **Oude Kerk,** the venerable Old Church, which stands watch over this passable representation of Sodom and Gomorrah. If you don't mind the weird-looking, sad-sack males and the heroin whores hanging around on the bridges, you can go farther in to the parallel canal, **Oudezijds Achterburgwal,** and to **Nieuwmarkt**'s cluster of good bars and Chinese restaurants.

In recent years, as part of a continuing effort to clean up the "unsavory" side of Amsterdam, the mayor forced the closure of a third of the red-light windows and bought up properties to be rented as fashion boutiques and other upscale small businesses. Some of the more raucous sex clubs may also be shuttered.

Despite this effort, "ladies of ill repute" still populate the many red-fringed window parlors; they're minimally dressed, and tap (or pound) on the windows as potential customers go by. Then there are peep-show joints with private cabins, dark and noisy bars, "theaters" mounting (ouch!) a popular form of performance art, bookstores filled with the illustrated works of specialists in a wide range of interpersonal relationships, video libraries, and dedicated apparel and appliance stores.

For safety's sake, stick to the main streets and the crowds. It's asking for trouble to go off on your own at night down some of those narrow, dark side streets and connecting lanes between the canals—some are so narrow you literally have to squeeze past other people, and on slow days, hookers come out from behind their windows to turn some of that squeezing into a marketing move. The main streets are usually busy and brightly lit (what with all those red lights and neon signs) and most clubs have security, since they have a vested interest in not having their customers bothered. Remember, though, that the industries active here attract less savory types, including muggers, pickpockets, drug dealers, junkies, street prostitutes, pimps, and weird folks in general. But there are also plenty of tour groups who seem to be having a whale of a time, judging by all the laughing they do as they go around.

Without going into detail about the services on offer in the Red Light District, here are a couple of places that have shown an enduring popularity with visitors.

Bananenbar   Scantily clad females and gyrating bananas are the essential ingredients of the nightly drama here, and audience participation is encouraged. Needless to say, the show is mainly of interest to young red-blooded males on temporary vegetarian diets. Let your sense of taste be your guide. Oudezijds Achterburgwal 37. ✆ **020/627-8954.** www.janot.com. Tram: 1, 2, 4, 5, 9, 13, 16, 17, 24, or 25 to Centraal Station.

Casa Rosso   In its own words, Casa Rosso puts on "one of the most superior erotic shows in the world, with a tremendous choreography and a high-level cast." Not everyone would describe it in those exact words, perhaps, but this is the local market leader in live shows. Oudezijds Achterburgwal 106–108. ✆ **020/627-8954.** www.janot. com. Tram: 4, 9, 14, 16, 24, or 25 to the Dam.

MORE EVENING ENTERTAINMENT
Evening Canal-Boat tours

Even if you took a daytime canal-boat tour, come back after dark for a cruise on the inky waters. Special evening jaunts are available from all of the city's canal tour-boat lines (see "Organized Tours," in chapter 7, for a list of these companies and their contact details). Drinks, snacks, dinners, and music are served as you glide through the canal district, which is quiet and calm at night. It's a leisurely, convivial, and romantic way to spend an Amsterdam evening. The price of these special evening cruises varies from company to company, and depends on the particular offering.

10 Movies

In Amsterdam, you'll find a dozen or more first-run features, most of them Hollywood's finest, in English with Dutch subtitles. You can find showtimes in various publications available free from movie theaters—in Dutch, a movie theater is called a *bioscoop*—as well as hotels and cafes. Most of the information is in Dutch, but the movie titles and screening times are hard to get wrong. Admission prices are around 9€, depending on the day, time, and movie, and you can reserve advance tickets for a small charge. A string of commercials and trailers always precedes the main feature (except at art-house cinemas).

   Note: If all of a sudden there's a break in the movie, which happens at some movie theaters, don't fret; this is a *pauze* and it lasts about 15 minutes. It can be incredibly annoying, especially as it seems always to come during an arresting on-screen moment, but at least it gives you time to visit the toilet, buy an ice cream, or grab a smoke.

   Multiplexes are to be found around Leidseplein, on Kleine-Gartmanplantsoen, Marnixstraat, and Lijnbaansgracht; around Rembrandtplein, on Vijzelstraat and Reguliersbreestraat; and in Amsterdam-Zuidoost on ArenA Boulevard.

Through a Glass, Clearly

One of the city's simplest, and cheapest, evening activities is walking along the canals and looking into the houses as you pass. You may think I'm making the shocking suggestion that you window-peep, but in Amsterdam, it's not peeping. The Dutch take great pride in their homes and keep their curtains open in the evening because they want you to see how tidy and *gezellig* (cozy, homey, warm, and inviting) their living quarters are. This doesn't mean you should linger on the sidewalk gawking, but a leisurely peek inside at the decor is okay.

MOVIE THEATERS OF NOTE

De Balie This all-purpose cultural center has an eclectic calendar of workshops, lectures, and film festivals. You can view controversial and award-winning features and documentaries, and lots of interesting movies from around the world that don't make it to mainstream theaters. Kleine-Gartmanplantsoen 10 (at Leidseplein). *℗* **020/553-5151.** www.debalie.nl. Tram: 1, 2, 5, 7, or 10 to Leidseplein.

EYE ★ The Film Instituut Nederland's striking venue inside the Vondelpark has two theaters (one of them with an Art Deco interior) that schedule interesting retrospectives and film festivals. ***Note:*** At the end of 2011 (or possibly later), EYE is due to move to a brand-new facility in Amsterdam-Noord, on the north shore of the IJ waterway. Vondelpark 3 (at Vondelstraat). *℗* **020/589-1400.** www.eyefilm.nl. Tram: 1 to Eerste Constantijn Huygensstraat; 3 or 12 to Overtoom.

> **Impressions**
>
> *A nearby movie house sells not popcorn but demitasses of espresso and glasses of Dutch gin from behind a wood-paneled bar, which somehow makes you feel sane and adult and enfolded in civilization.*
> —Russell Shorto, director of Amsterdam's John Adams Institute, *The Times Magazine,* 2009

Theater Tuschinski ★★ This theater is well worth a visit for its extravagant, Art Deco style from 1921. On its upper balconies, you'll sit on plush chairs and can sip champagne during the flick. An organ from silent-movie days is used for occasional concerts and to accompany silent films. Reguliersbreestraat 26–34. (*℗* **0900/1458.** www.pathe.nl/tuschinski. Tram: 4, 9, or 14 to Rembrandtplein.

ART-HOUSE & ALTERNATIVE MOVIE THEATERS

Lesser-known movies are often screened at **De Uitkijk,** Prinsengracht 452 (*℗* **020/623-7460;** www.uitkijk.nl; tram: 1, 2, or 5); **Het Ketelhuis,** Pazzanistraat 4, Cultuurpark Westergasfabriek (*℗* **020/684-0090;** www.ketelhuis.nl; tram: 10); **Kriterion,** Roetersstraat 170 (*℗* **020/623-1708;** www.kriterion.nl; tram: 7 or 10); **Melkweg Cinema,** Lijnbaansgracht 234A (*℗* **020/531-8181;** www.melkweg.nl; tram: 1, 2, 5, 7, or 10); **Rialto,** Ceintuurbaan 338 (*℗* **020/676-8700;** www.rialto film.nl; tram: 3); **Smart Cinema,** Arie Biemondstraat 101–111 (*℗* **020/427-5951;** www.smartprojectspace.net; tram: 7 or 17); and **The Movies,** Haarlemmerdijk 161–163 (*℗* **020/638-6016;** www.themovies.nl; tram: 3).

Amsterdam's Casino

Holland Casino Amsterdam, in the Lido, Max Euweplein 62 (*℗* **020/521-1111;** www.hollandcasino.com; tram: 1, 2, 5, 7, or 10), at Leidseplein, is the only legal casino in town. This place deals in European gambling, with an emphasis on roulette, baccarat, punto banco, blackjack, and others, though there are also abundant one-armed bandits, which the Dutch call "fruit machines." You need correct attire to get in (jacket and tie or turtleneck for men), and you also need to bring your passport to register at the door. The minimum age is 18. The casino is open daily (except May 4 and Dec 31) from 12:30pm to 3am. Admission is 5€. Wednesday is "ladies day," and admission is free for all visitors.

SIDE TRIPS FROM AMSTERDAM

msterdam is the brightest star in a galaxy of cities and towns that together form what the Dutch call the **Randstad (Rim City),** a budding megalopolis that stretches from Amsterdam to Rotterdam and contains two-thirds of the country's 16 million inhabitants.

Both **Noord-Holland (North Holland)** province, to which Amsterdam belongs, and neighboring **Zuid-Holland (South Holland)** province afford a variety of options for a day outside the city. It won't be a day in the outback, exactly, but you don't have to go far from Amsterdam to see the flat in the *polder* (the Dutch word for land reclaimed from water) landscape, with its tulips, windmills, rivers, and dikes, where Rembrandt strolled, sketchbook in hand. You can climb tall towers, visit cheese markets and multifarious museums, ride a steam train, tour the world's largest harbor, and see giant locks and tiny canals.

On your first day of touring, I suggest you travel from Amsterdam to **Haarlem,** and maybe squeeze into the same day a visit to the North Sea coast at nearby **Zandvoort,** which has a fine beach and a casino. On your second day of touring, head to **Hoorn** on the IJsselmeer. If you're driving, take in **Volendam** and **Marken** along the way. From Hoorn, continue along the lakeshore to **Enkhuizen** and the **Afsluitdijk (Enclosing Dike).**

With more time, you can alternate days spent in Amsterdam with visits to, for instance, the **Bulb Fields** and **Keukenhof Gardens** when it's tulip time; **Zaanse Schans** for its windmills; **Leiden** for the Pilgrim Fathers; **Delft** for Holland's historical royal city; **The Hague** for the government seat and home-base for the royal family; and **Rotterdam** for Europe's largest and the world's second-busiest port (after Shanghai).

HAARLEM ★★

18km (11 miles) W of Amsterdam

If you have only a day to travel beyond Amsterdam, spend it in the small city of Haarlem (pop. 150,000)—it's traditionally considered the capital's little sister city, though since it was likely founded in the 10th century,

Side Trips: The Randstad

Side Trips: The Randstad

📎 **Getting There**

Travel times from Amsterdam by public transportation to the places covered in this chapter are short. Rotterdam, the most distant destination, is just 40 minutes away by Fyra high-speed train. **NS (Netherlands Railways)** (📞 0900/9292; www.ns.nl) trains run frequently throughout the day from Amsterdam Centraal Station and other stations around the city to many, but not all, destinations. A bus service, by **Connexxion** (📞 0900/266-6399; www.connexxion.nl) and **Arriva** (📞 0900/202-2022; www.arriva.nl), covers the places the rails don't reach. In addition, chapter and verse on getting around in the Netherlands is available from a single, all-knowing source: **OV** (📞 0900/9292; www.9292ov.nl).

it's actually older than Amsterdam. Granted municipal status by Count Willem II of Holland in 1245, it's where Frans Hals, Jacob van Ruisdael, and Pieter Saenredam lived and painted their famous portraits, landscapes, and church interiors during the same years that Rembrandt lived and worked in Amsterdam.

Some visitors even prefer to "commute" to Amsterdam from here, since Haarlem has a similar 17th-century look, but by being thoroughly provincial, prosperous, and conservative (meaning there's only a tiny red-light district here), it gets along nicely without the many hassles that accompany the capital's eccentric lifestyle. You can easily get around this quaint, quiet city of music and art on foot, and Haarlem is home to the **Frans Hals Museum** (see below), one of Holland's premier art museums. In addition, it's close to the North Sea beaches and to the bulb fields, in the heart of an area dotted with elegant manors and picturesque villages.

Essentials

GETTING THERE   Trains depart from Amsterdam Centraal Station for Haarlem at intervals ranging from 4 minutes to 15 minutes; the ride takes 15 minutes. A round-trip ticket is 7€ in second class or 12€ in first class. By car from Amsterdam, take N200/A200 west.

VISITOR INFORMATION   The **City Marketing Haarlem/VVV Informatiecentrum,** Verwulft 11, 2011 GJ Haarlem (📞 0900/616-1600; fax 023/534-0537; www.vvvhaarlem.nl), is in the center of town, at the intersection of Grote Houtstraat and Gedempte Oude Gracht. The office is open Monday to Friday from 9:30am to 5:30pm, Saturday from 10am to 5pm, and Sunday from noon to 4pm.

What To See & Do

The historic center is a 5- to 10-minute walk from the graceful 1908 Art Nouveau rail station (with decorative painted tiles and a fine restaurant), most of it on pedestrian-only shopping streets. First-time visitors generally head straight to the **Grote Markt ★★**, the central market square. Most points of interest in Haarlem are within easy walking distance of the Grote Markt. The monumental buildings, dating from the 15th to the 19th centuries, around the tree-lined square are a visual minicourse in the development of Dutch architecture. Here stands Haarlem's

14th-century **Stadhuis (Town Hall),** a former hunting lodge which Holland's counts rebuilt in the 17th century. It contains a magnificent 1629 tapestry, *Crusades,* by Josef Thienpont of Oudenaarde.

Adjacent to the Grote Markt, the splendid **Sint-Bavokerk (St. Bavo's Church)** ★, Oude Groenmarkt 23 (© **023/553-2040;** www.bavo.nl), also known as the Grote Kerk (Great Church), soars skyward. Finished in 1520 after a relatively short building period, it has a rare unity of structure and proportion. The interior is light and airy, with whitewashed walls and sandstone pillars. Look for painter **Frans Hals's tombstone** and for a **cannonball** that's been embedded in the wall ever since it came flying

257

through a window during the Spanish siege in 1572 to 1573. The elegant wooden tower is covered with lead sheets and adorned with gilt spheres.

Mozart (at just 10 years old), Handel, Mendelssohn, Schubert, and Liszt all visited Haarlem to play the church's magnificent, soaring **Christian Müller Organ** (1738). It has 5,068 pipes and is nearly 30m (98 ft.) tall, and when it's going, it can blow your socks off. Jan van Logteren crafted its woodwork. Enjoy the organ in a free recital Tuesday at 8:15pm from May to October; in July and August there's an additional free recital on Thursday at 3pm. From May to October, church services using the organ take place Sunday at 10am; from June to October there's an additional 7pm Vespers and Cantata service. St. Bavo's is open Monday to Saturday from 10am to 4pm, and (June–Sept) Sunday from 10am to 7pm. Admission is 2€ for adults, and 1.25€ for children ages 12 to 16, and free for children 11 and under.

Haarlem's finest attraction is the **Frans Hals Museum ★★**, Groot Heiligland 62 (**© 023/511-5775;** www.franshalsmuseum.nl), housed in galleries that were the rooms of handsome gabled cottages of the Oudemannenhuis (1608), an almshouse for retired gentlemen, arranged around a courtyard garden. The famous paintings by Antwerp-born Frans Hals (ca. 1580–1686) and other Haarlem School masters hang in settings that look like the 17th-century houses they were intended to adorn. Hals, who died here, earned his bread and butter by painting members of the local Schutters (Musketeers) Guild. Typified by his *Officers of the Militia Company of St. George* (ca. 1627), five other such works hang in the museum, along with six more Hals paintings. Other exhibits include fine collections of antique silver, porcelain, clocks, and a superb dollhouse-like piece from around 1750 that's actually an exquisitely detailed miniature replica of an Amsterdam merchant's canal house. The museum is open Tuesday to Saturday from 11am to 5pm, and Sunday and holidays from noon to 5pm; it's closed January 1 and December 25. Admission is 7.50€ for adults ages 25 and over, 3.75€ for visitors ages 19 to 24, and free for visitors 18 and under.

From St. Bavo's, it's a short walk to Holland's oldest and perhaps most unusual museum, the **Teylers Museum,** Spaarne 16 (**© 023/531-9010;** www.teylers museum.eu). Its diverse collection encompasses drawings by Michelangelo, Raphael, and Rembrandt; fossils, minerals, and skeletons; physics instruments; and an odd assortment of inventions, including the world's largest electrostatic generator (1784) and a 19th-century radarscope. The museum is open Tuesday to Saturday from 10am to 5pm, and Sunday and holidays from noon to 5pm; it's closed January 1 and December 25. Admission is 9€ for adults, 2€ for children ages 6 to 17, and free for children 5 and under.

Organized Tours

An ideal way to view Haarlem is by canal tour-boat. Tours are operated by **Post Verkade Cruises** (**© 023/535-7723;** www.postverkadecruises.nl), from the Spaarne River dock next to the Gravenstenenbrug, a handsome lift bridge. April to October, Tuesday to Sunday, boats depart hourly from noon to 4pm on a 45-minute cruise. Tickets are 9.50€, 4.50€ for children ages 3 to 12, and free for children 2 and under. In addition, there are longer cruises that go outside of town, candlelight cruises, and more.

Where to Dine

Dijkers INTERNATIONAL Near the start of a short but chic shopping street a block south of the Grote Markt, this tiny restaurant, popular with locals, serves an unlikely mix of Italian and Asian dishes, from Thai green curry to lighter fare such as club and toasted sandwiches—the mozzarella and prosciutto club sandwich is an excellent choice for a quick bite at lunch. A bright, orange-toned designer-ish setting with transparent plastic chairs meshes nicely with the breezy service. On warm sunny days, a few tables are set out on the sidewalk.

Warmoesstraat 5-7 (off Oude Groenmarkt). © 023/551-1564. www.restaurantdijkers.nl. Main courses 14€–23€; *dagschotel* 12€. AE, MC, V. Wed–Mon 10am–10pm.

Jacobus Pieck ★ DUTCH/INTERNATIONAL   This popular cafe-restaurant has a lovely shaded terrace in the garden for fine-weather days; inside, it's bustling and stylish. Outside or in, you get excellent food for reasonable prices and friendly, efficient service. Lunchtime features generous sandwiches and burgers, and salads that are particularly good. Main dinner courses range from pastas and Middle Eastern or Asian dishes to wholesome Dutch standards.

Warmoesstraat 18 (off Oude Groenmarkt). © **023/532-6144.** www.jacobuspieck.nl. Main courses 13€–18€; *dagschotel* 12€. AE, MC, V. Mon 11am–4pm; Tues–Sat 11am–4pm and 5:30–10pm.

ZANDVOORT

24km (15 miles) W of Amsterdam; 7km (4½ miles) W of Haarlem

If you feel like drawing a breath of fresh sea air and you don't have much time for it, do what most Amsterdammers do: Head for Zandvoort. On the North Sea coast just west of Haarlem and on the same rail line from Amsterdam, the resort is brash in summer, though it often looks forlorn in the off season.

Essentials

GETTING THERE   Trains depart every half hour from Amsterdam Centraal Station for Zandvoort (the station's name is Zandvoort aan Zee). Transfer at Haarlem, where the Zandvoort train usually waits on the adjacent platform. During summer months, extra trains go direct from Centraal Station. In either case, the ride takes around 30 minutes, and a round-trip ticket is 9.20€ in second class or 16€ in first class. By car, go via Haarlem, on N200/A200/N200, but be ready for long traffic lines in summer.

VISITOR INFORMATION   VVV Zandvoort, Bakkerstraat 2B (at Kerkstraat), 2042 HK Zandvoort (© **023/571-7947;** fax 023/571-7003; www.vvvzk.nl), is in the center of town. The office is open Monday to Friday from 9am to 5pm, Saturday from 10am to 5pm, and Sunday from 11am to 4pm.

What To See & Do

There isn't much more to Zandvoort than its **beach,** but what a beach! In summer, this seemingly endless stretch of smooth sand is lined with dozens of temporary beach cafe-restaurants. Besides the mainstream sections, there are gay and naturist zones where the shocking sight of a clothed individual can generate considerable moral outrage. **Windsurfing** is pretty good, and Zandvoort hosts international competitions in this sport, and in **catamaran racing.** The sea—a soup of suspended sand, jellyfish, and seaweed—doesn't look inviting, but the Dutch swim in it anyway (in summer).

   The Dutch Formula One Grand Prix motor race used to happen at **Circuit Park Zandvoort,** Burg van Alphenstraat 63 (© **023/574-0740;** www.cpz.nl), in the north of the town. Now, the circuit hosts only smaller events. If you come on a summer weekend, you might find a Formula Three training session or a Porsche meeting underway.

Hot Jets

How about a jetfoil ride to the seacoast? **Fast Flying Ferry** (🕻 **0900/266-6399; www.fff.nl**) runs a scheduled service on the Noordzeekanaal between Amsterdam and Velsen-Zuid. At the nearby seaport of IJmuiden (connected with the Velsen-Zuid jetfoil dock by frequent bus service), you can view the three great locks of the **North Sea Canal,** and visit the **fish auctions** at Halkade 4, held Monday to Friday from 7 to 11am. Jetfoils depart from a dock behind Amsterdam Centraal Station, Monday to Friday every half-hour from 7am to 10pm, and Saturday and Sunday from 7am to 6:30pm; the ride takes 30 minutes. Round-trip tickets are 9.40€ at peak times and 8€ at off-peak times for adults, 6.20€ for seniors and children ages 4 to 11, and free for children 3 and under.

Equally racy, and far less noisy, is **Holland Casino Zandvoort,** Badhuisplein 7 (🕻 **023/574-0574;** www.hollandcasino.com), behind the seafront promenade. You'll find roulette, blackjack, punto banco, slot machines, and more. The dress code is "correct" (collar and tie for men), and the minimum age is 18. You need your passport to get in. The casino is open daily (except May 4 and Dec 31) from 12:30pm to 3am. Admission is 5€; Wednesday is "ladies day," and admission is free for all visitors.

Find solitude amid nature by walking some of the 2,500 hectares (6,200 acres) of sand dunes, deciduous and pine forest, grassland, and small lakes in the **Nationaal Park Zuid-Kennemerland** (🕻 **023/541-1123;** www.npzk.nl), north of town. Reinforced by native vegetation, these dunes play an important part in the defenses against the sea and are designated nature reserves. Stroll along pathways once used by fishermen's wives bringing their husbands' catch from the coast to market, through the woods on the landward side and westward across the dunes toward the sea. A variety of plants, some of them rare, occupy this relatively small area, and you can spot up to 230 species of birds, including rare crossbills and sea eagles. The beach is never far away.

Even in winter, it's an Amsterdam tradition to take the train to Zandvoort, stroll up and down the shore for an hour or so, then repair to one of the town's cafes, such as **Wapen van Zandvoort,** Gasthuisplein 10 (🕻 **023/822-3780;** www.wapenvanzandvoort.nl), or **Café Alex,** Gasthuisplein 9A (🕻 **023/571-9205**), a few blocks back from the seafront, in the heart of town.

THE IJSSELMEER ★★

Some of Holland's most popular places—**Hoorn, Edam,** and **Marken** among them—lie along this great lake's western shore. Painterly light washes through clouds, and luminous mists seem to merge water and sky. Cyclists test both speed and endurance, zipping round the 400km (250-mile) circumference in bright Lycra blurs, or plodding along on the lonesome dike-top. The IJsselmeer (pronounced *Eye*-sselmeer) hosts fleets of traditional Dutch *boter* and *skûtsje* sailing ships, fishing smacks, modern sailboats, powerboats, and canoes. Its waters are an important feeding ground for migrating and resident birds.

Volendam, Marken ★ & Monnickendam

18km (11 miles), 16km (10 miles), and 14km (9 miles) NE of Amsterdam

Volendam and Marken are combined on bus-tour itineraries from Amsterdam as a kind of packaged-Holland-to-go. Nonetheless, it's possible to have a delightful full day in the bracing air of these two lakeside communities, where a few residents (fewer all the time) may be seen going about their daily business in traditional dress. Monnickendam lies between them.

ESSENTIALS

GETTING THERE   **Arriva** buses depart every 15 to 30 minutes from outside Amsterdam Centraal Station. Nos. 110, 112, 116, and 118 go to Volendam; nos. 111 and 115 go to Monnickendam; and no. 111 goes on to Marken. The ride to Volendam is 35 minutes; to Monnickendam 30 minutes; and to Marken 45 minutes. The round-trip fare is 7.50€.

By car, go north on N247. Driving to Marken, which was once an island, you cross over a 3km (2-mile)-long causeway from Monnickendam. You then need to leave your car in a parking lot outside the village before walking through the narrow streets to the harbor.

VISITOR INFORMATION   **VVV Volendam,** Zeestraat 37, 1131 ZD Volendam (© **0299/363-747;** fax 0299/368-484; www.vvv-volendam.nl), is just off Julianaweg

BY THE SIDE OF THE zuiderzee

Only in Holland could you say, "This used to be a sea." The IJsselmeer actually was once a sea, until the Dutch decided they didn't want it to be one anymore—it was always threatening to flood Amsterdam and other towns and villages along its low-lying coastline.

For centuries, the Dutch have been protecting themselves from encroaching seas and snatching more land to accommodate their expanding population. One of their most formidable opponents was the Zuiderzee (Southern Sea), an incursion of the North Sea that washed over Frisian dunes to flood vast inland areas between A.D. 200 and 300. Over the centuries, the Zuiderzee continued to expand, and in the 1200s, a series of storms drove its waters far inland.

Despite the sea's reputation as a graveyard of ships, the sleepy, picturesque villages that today line the IJsselmeer's shores presented quite a different picture when their harbors were alive with great ships that sailed for the Dutch West and East India Companies. North Sea fishermen added to the maritime traffic as they returned to Zuiderzee home ports, and Amsterdam flourished as ships from around the world sailed to its front door.

Still, as early as the 1600s, there was talk of driving back the sea and reclaiming the land it covered. Parliament got around to authorizing the project in 1918, and in the 1920s, work was begun. In 1932, in an unparalleled engineering feat, the North Sea was sealed off, from Noord-Holland to Friesland, by the 30km (19-mile) Afsluitdijk (Enclosing Dike), and the saltwater Zuiderzee became, in time, the freshwater IJsselmeer lake.

in the heart of town. The office is open mid-March to September, Monday to Saturday from 10am to 5pm, and Sunday from 11am to 4pm; October, Monday to Saturday from 10am to 5pm; and November to mid-March, Monday to Saturday from 10am to 3pm.

WHAT TO SEE & DO

A small Catholic town on the mainland, **Volendam** lost most of its fishing industry to the enclosure of the Zuiderzee. It's geared now to tourism in a big way and has souvenir shops, boutiques, cafes, and restaurants. Lots of people come to town to pig out on the town's near-legendary *gerookte paling* (smoked eel), and to visit such attractions as the **fish auction,** the **diamond cutter,** the **clog maker,** and the **old house** with a room entirely wallpapered in cigar bands. Still, Volendam's boat-filled harbor, tiny streets, and traditional houses maintain an undeniable enchantment. If you must have a snapshot of yourself in traditional Dutch costume—local women wear white caps with wings—this is a good place to do it.

Volendam's historic rival, **Marken,** is Protestant and was an island until a narrow causeway connected it to the mainland. It remains insular. Smaller and less rambunctious than Volendam, it is rural, with clusters of farmhouses dotted around on the polders. A white-painted **lighthouse** stands on the IJsselmeer shore. One half of Marken village, **Havenbuurt,** consists of stilted green-and-white–painted houses grouped around a tiny harbor. A clog maker works in summer in the village parking lot. Four old smokehouses in the other half of the village, **Kerkbuurt,** serve as the **Museum Marken,** Kerkbuurt 44–47 (✆ **0299/601-904;** www.markermuseum.nl), which covers traditional furnishings, costumes, and more. The museum is open April to September, Monday to Saturday from 10am to 5pm, and Sunday from noon to 4pm; and October Monday to Saturday from 11am to 4pm, and Sunday from noon to 4pm. Admission is 2.50€, 1.25€ for children ages 5 to 12, and free for children 4 and under.

Marken doesn't go all gushy for tourists—though a tax levied on every tour goes directly into village coffers. The village merely feeds and waters its visitors, and allows them to wander around its pretty streets gawking at locals going about their daily routines of hanging out laundry, washing windows, and shopping for groceries. Some residents occasionally wear traditional dress—for women, caps with ribbons and black aprons over striped petticoats—but as much to preserve the custom as for the tourists.

From April to October, a passenger-and-bike ferry, the *Marken Express* (✆ **0299/363-331;** www.markenexpress.nl), sails every hour or so from 11am to 6pm between Volendam and Marken. The boat ride takes 30 minutes, and fares are 7.50€ round-trip and 5€ one-way, 4.50€ round-trip and 4€ one-way for children ages 4 to 11, and free for children under 4; bicycles are carried for an additional 1€ one-way.

By way of contrast to its two neighbors, **Monnickendam** doesn't pay much attention to tourists at all, but gets on with its own life as a boating and fishing center, as you can see in its busy **harbor.** Take a walk through streets lined with gabled houses and stop to admire the 15th-century late Gothic **Sint-Nicolaaskerk (St. Nicholas's Church),** at Zarken 2. Be sure to visit the **Stadhuis (Town Hall),** at Noordeinde 5, which began life as a private residence in 1746 and has an elaborately decorated ceiling. Across the street, a 15th-century tower, the **Speeltoren,** has a carillon that chimes every hour, accompanied by a parade of mechanical knights. Inside is the town museum, **Museum de Speeltoren,** Noordeinde 4 (✆ **0299/652-203;** www.despeeltoren.nl), open mid-April to mid-May and mid-September to mid-October, Saturday from 11am to 4:30pm, and Sunday from 1 to 4:30pm; and mid-May to mid-September, Tuesday to Saturday from 11am to 4:30pm, and Sunday from 1 to 4:40pm. Admission is 1.50€, .50€ for children ages 5 to 12, and free for children 4 and under.

WHERE TO STAY

Best Western Hotel Spaander ★   This old-fashioned hotel has real harbor flavor to go with its lakeside setting. The public spaces have an Old Dutch interior look, appropriate to a lodging that started out in 1881, and the entire space is a kind of art gallery, speckled with a thousand 19th-century paintings. Its guest rooms, however, are modern, brightly furnished, comfortable, and attractive. The hotel's two dining rooms, an old-style inn and an elegant sun lounge, serve local IJsselmeer and other Dutch specialties, like smoked eel. The outside terrace cafe is great when the weather is fine.

Haven 15–19 (north end of the harbor), 1131 EP Volendam. © **0299/363-595.** Fax 0299/369-615. www.spaander.com. 79 rooms. 95€–169€ double; 169€ suite. Rates include continental breakfast. AE, DC, MC, V. Parking 5€. **Amenities:** 2 restaurants; 2 bars; small heated indoor pool; health club; sauna; smoke-free rooms. *In room:* TV, hair dryer, Wi-Fi (free).

WHERE TO DINE

De Taanderij ★ DUTCH/FRENCH   Lunch at this little *eethuis* at the harbor's end (yes, seafood is served). For dessert, try the traditional Dutch treat of *koffie en appelgebak met slagroom* (coffee with apple pie and cream) or *poffertjes* (small fried pancake puffs coated with confectioners' sugar and filled with syrup or liqueur). The interior is an elegant and cozy interpretation of old Marken style. When the weather's good, a terrace spreads onto the harborside, where you can absorb the sunshine, the tranquil view over the IJsselmeer, and, of course, the menu's luscious goodies.

Havenbuurt 1, Marken. © **0299/602-206.** Main courses 15€–19€; snacks 4€–13€. AE, DC, MC, V. Apr–Sept daily 10am–10pm; Oct–Mar Tues–Sun 11am–7pm.

Perchance to Dream

To overnight in traditional style in Volendam and Monnickendam, ask at their VVV offices (p. 261) about sleeping aboard one of the old wooden IJsselmeer *boters* and *skûtsjes* (sailing ships) moored in the harbor (this option isn't available in Marken). It's a romantic, if somewhat cramped, way to spend the night.

Edam ★

18km (11 miles) NE of Amsterdam; 2km (1 mile) N of Volendam

A little way inland from the IJsselmeer, Edam (pronounced *ay*-dam) gives its name to one of Holland's most famous cheeses. Don't expect to find it in the familiar red skin, though—that's for export. In Holland, the skin is yellow. This pretty little town (pop. 7,000), a whaling port during Holland's 17th-century Golden Age, is centered around canals you cross by way of drawbridges that offer views of canal houses, gardens, and teahouses.

ESSENTIALS

GETTING THERE   There is a frequent bus service by **Arriva.** Bus nos. 110, 112, 113, 116, and 118 depart from outside Amsterdam Centraal Station for the 35-minute ride; the round-trip fare is 7.50€. By car, go north on N247, via Monnickendam and Volendam (see "The IJsselmeer," p. 260).

VISITOR INFORMATION   VVV Edam, Stadhuis (Town Hall), Damplein 1, 1135 BK Edam (© **0299/315-125;** fax 0299/374-236; www.vvv-edam.nl), is in the town center. The office is open mid-March to June and September to October, Monday to Saturday from 10am to 5pm; July to August, Monday to Saturday from 10am to 5pm, and Sunday from 11am to 3:30pm; and November to mid-March, Monday to Saturday from 10am to 3pm.

WHAT TO SEE & DO

Edam was once a port of some prominence, and a visit to the modest **Edams Museum,** Damplein 8 (© **0299/372-644;** www.edamsmuseum.nl), opposite the former Town Hall, gives you a peek not only at its history but also at some of its most illustrious citizens over the centuries. Look for the portrait of Pieter Dirckz, a one-time mayor and proud possessor of what is probably the longest beard on record anywhere: It was 2.5m (8 ft.) long! An intriguing feature of this merchant's house (ca. 1530) is the cellar, which is actually a box floating on water, constructed that way so changing water levels wouldn't upset the house's foundations. The museum is open April to late October, Tuesday to Saturday from 10am to 4:30pm, and Sunday from 1 to 4:30pm. Admission is 3€ for adults, 2€ for seniors, 1€ for children ages 13 to 17, and free for children 12 and under.

Take a look at the lovely wedding room in the **Stadhuis (Town Hall),** and if you visit during summer months, don't miss the cheese-making display at the **Kaaswaag (Weigh House).** The **Speeltoren (Carillon Tower)** from 1561 tilts a bit and was very nearly lost when the church to which it belonged was destroyed.

Hoorn ★★

32km (20 miles) NE of Amsterdam; 17km (11 miles) N of Edam

Historically, Hoorn (pronounced *Hoarn*) is one of the great names in Dutch seafaring. Even now, with the open sea no longer on its doorstep, it remains water-oriented and is a busy IJsselmeer sailing center. On a tour of the graceful Golden Age town, be sure to visit the old harbor, the **Binnenhaven.** Hoorn (pop. 69,000) is the home-town of Willem Cornelisz Schouten, who in 1616 rounded South America's south-ernmost tip, which he named Kap Hoorn (Cape Horn) in his hometown's honor.

GETTING THERE   Trains depart at least every hour from Amsterdam Centraal Station to Hoorn; the ride takes from 33 to 45 minutes, and a round-trip ticket is 14€ in second class or 24€ in first class. **Arriva** bus nos. 114 and 117 depart between two and four times hourly from outside Amsterdam Centraal Station for the 1-hour ride; the round-trip fare is 11€. By car from Amsterdam, take A7/E22 north.

VISITOR INFORMATION   VVV Hoorn, Veemarkt 44, 1621 JC Hoorn (© **072/ 511-4284;** fax 0229/215-023; www.vvvhoorn.nl), is close to the rail station. The office is open May to August Monday from 1 to 6pm, Tuesday, Wednesday, Friday, and Saturday from 9:30am to 5:30pm, and Thursday from 9:30am to 9pm; and September to April, Monday from 1 to 5pm, and Tuesday to Saturday from 10am to 5pm.

WHAT TO SEE & DO

Visit the **Westfries Museum,** Rode Steen 1 (© **0229/280-022;** www.westfries museum.nl), housed in a 1632 building containing a wide-ranging historical collection that includes armor, weapons, paper cuttings, costumes, toys, naive paintings (which embody a deliberately childlike style), coins, medals, jewels, paintings of civic guards, and porcelain. A second-floor exhibit details the town's maritime history, with an emphasis on ships and voyages of the United East India Company

(V.O.C.). There are fine tapestries and 17th- and 18th-century period rooms. A basement exhibit showcases a collection of Bronze Age relics. The museum is open Monday to Friday from 11am to 5pm, Saturday and Sunday from 1 to 5pm; it's closed January 1, April 30, and December 25. Admission is 5€ for adults, 3.50€ for seniors and children ages 5 to 16, and free for children 4 and under.

During summer, an antique steam tram, the **Museumstoomtram Hoorn-Medemblik** (℡ 0229/214-862; www.museumstoomtram.nl) transports tourists from Hoorn to nearby **Medemblik** (p. 266). Round-trip tickets are 19€, 14€ for children ages 4 to 12, and free for children 3 and under.

WHERE TO DINE

De Hoofdtoren ★ DUTCH   Boat lovers will want to linger on this cafe-restaurant's terrace on the edge of Hoorn's busy harbor, surrounded by traditional IJsselmeer sailing ships and pleasure boats large and small. The restaurant is housed in an old defense tower that dates from 1532—its one-time purpose was to protect the harbor entrance; its interior retains many antique features. Traditional Dutch fare and grilled meat and fish specialties are served at dinner. During the day, there's a lunch-and-snacks menu.

Hoofd 2. ℡ **0229/215-487.** www.hoofdtoren.nl. Main courses 17€–25€. AE, DC, MC, V. Daily 10am–10pm.

De Waag CONTINENTAL   This grand cafe in the monumental Weigh House (from 1609) on the town's main square is open all day, for breakfast, lunch, and dinner. It is located on one of the country's squares, surrounded by 17th-century buildings from the town's heyday. You can still see antique weighing scales in the wood-beamed interior.

Rode Steen 8. ℡ **0229/215-195.** www.dewaaghoorn.nl. Main courses 13€–24€. AE, DC, MC, V. Mon-Thurs 11am–midnight, Fri-Sun 11am–1am.

Enkhuizen ★

44km (27 miles) NE of Amsterdam; 15km (9 miles) NE of Hoorn

A 400-boat herring fleet once sailed out of Enkhuizen. Then in 1932 came the Enclosing Dike (see below), closing off the North Sea. Today, the town looks to pleasure boating, tourism, and bulb-growing for its livelihood, and boasts one of the country's most fascinating open-air museums (see below).

ESSENTIALS

GETTING THERE   Trains depart every half hour from Amsterdam Centraal Station, going via Hoorn. The ride takes just under 1 hour; a round-trip ticket is 19€ in second class or 32€ in first class. By car from Amsterdam, drive to Hoorn, and then take N302 or N506 northeast.

VISITOR INFORMATION   VVV Enkhuizen, Tussen Twee Havens 1, 1601 EM Enkhuizen (℡ **0228/313-164;** fax 0228/315-531; www.vvvenkhuizen.nl), is at the harbor. The office is open mid-April to October, daily from 9am to 5pm.

WHAT TO SEE & DO

From a dock in Veerhaven next to Enkhuizen rail station, or from another next to the dike road from Enkhuizen to Lelystad, take a boat over to one of Holland's finest museums, the **Zuiderzeemuseum** ★★, Wierdijk 12–22 (℡ **0228/351-111;** www.zuiderzeemuseum.nl), dedicated to re-creating the historic way of life on the shores of the old Zuiderzee. Its two sections, the indoor **Binnenmuseum** and the outdoor **Museumpark** feature many exhibits, of which the most dramatic are 130 complete old buildings. Farmhouses, public buildings, stores, and a church have been moved here from lakeside villages, and from elsewhere in Holland, brought together to form a cobblestone-street village. There are, too, examples of the fishing boats that provided the incomes on which villagers depended. The Zuiderzeemuseum is open daily from 10am to 5pm (the Museumpark is fully operational from April to October); closed January 1 and December 25. Admission is 14€, 8.40€ for children ages 4 to 12, free for children 3 and under, and 35€ for families.

Medemblik

46km (29 miles) NE of Amsterdam; 14km (9 miles) NW of Enkhuizen

Medemblik is a small IJsselmeer town with busy twin harbors. Founded in the 7th century, it later joined the powerful Hanseatic League trading federation.

There are two great ways to get to Medemblik in the summer. One is onboard the 1956 passenger-and-bike ferry *Friesland* from Enkhuizen (see above). Tickets are 16€ round-trip and 9.30€ one-way, 12€ round-trip and 7€ one-way for children ages 4 to 12, and free for children 3 and under. An equally atmospheric way is from Hoorn (see above) by **antique steam tram.** Tickets are 20€ round-trip and 15€ one-way for adults, 11€ round-trip and 8.30€ one-way for children ages 4 to 12, and free for children 3 and under. Both the boat and the tram are operated by **Stoomtram Hoorn–Medemblik** (✆ **0229/214-862;** www.museumstoomtram.nl).

Medemblik tourist information is available from **VVV Medemblik,** Kaasmarkt 1, 1671 BH Medemblik (✆ **072/511-4284;** fax 072/511-7513; www.vvvmedemblik.nl).

Adjacent to Medemblik's **Oosterhaven (East Harbor)**—twin to the **Westerhaven (West Harbor)**—is the moated **Kasteel Radboud,** Oudevaartsgat 8 (✆ **0227/541-960;** www.kasteelradboud.nl), an 8th-century castle refortified by the Count of Holland in 1289 against a possible rebellion by the troublesome Frisians. The remaining section has been restored to its 13th-century state and is well worth a visit. The castle is open May to mid-September, Monday to Saturday from 11am to 5pm, and Sunday from 2 to 5pm; and mid-September to April, Sunday from 2 to 5pm (and during school vacations 11am–5pm). Admission is 5€ for adults, 3€ for seniors and children ages 5 to 13, and free for children 4 and under.

Afsluitdijk (Enclosing Dike) ★

62km (38 miles) N of Amsterdam; 30km (19 miles) NW of Enkhuizen

It's hard to grasp what a monumental work the great barrier that separates the salty Waddenzee from the freshwater IJsselmeer is until you drive its 30-km (19-mile) length. The Afsluitdijk connects the provinces of **Noord-Holland** and **Friesland.** Dr. Cornelis Lely came up with the plans in 1891, but construction was delayed for 25 years while he tried to convince the government to allocate funding.

Massive effort went into building the dike, which is 100m (330 ft.) wide and 7m (23 ft.) above mean water level. Many communities around the shores of what used to be the saltwater Zuiderzee lost their livelihood when access to the open sea was shut off. Some of the fishing boats that now sail the IJsselmeer hoist dark-brown sails as a sign of mourning for their lost sea fishing industry.

BY bicycle TO HOORN

For a great day trip from Amsterdam, go by bike along the IJsselmeer shore to Hoorn, and return by train (with your bike). (Do this on a halfway decent bike, not a decrepit old Amsterdam bike.) Riding along between the polders and the lake is a perfect Dutch experience—but you need to be ready for some vigorous pedaling. You can't get lost if you stay on the road that runs along the IJsselmeer and keep the lake to your immediate right.

Board the IJ ferry at the pier behind Centraal Station and cross to Amsterdam North. Take Durgerdammerdijk, a road leading east alongside the IJsselmeer shore to Durgerdam, a lakeside village huddled below water level behind a protective dike, with its roofs sticking up over the top. Ride either next to the houses and the polders or up on the dike-top path, immersed in wind, rain, and shine—and with fine lake views.

Beyond Uitdam, either go left on the lakeside road through Monnickendam to Volendam, or right on the causeway to Marken. The first option cuts overall distance because Marken is a dead end and you need to come back across the causeway again. But in summer, you can take the *Marken Express* passenger boat (see above). One way or the other, you'll arrive in Volendam.

Go inland a short way along a canal that runs from the lakeside dike to Edam, famed for its cheese. Cross over the canal on the bridge at Damplein in Edam's center, and go back along the far bank to regain the IJsselmeer shore. Up ahead is a straight run north to Hoorn through the pastoral villages of Warder, Etersheim, Schardam, and Scharwoude.

After exploring Hoorn—or flopping down exhausted in a cafe—follow the green-painted signs pointing the way to the station for the train ride back to Amsterdam.

Midway along the dike's length, at the point where it was completed in 1932, stands a **monument** to the men who put their backs to the task, and a memorial to Dr. Lely. Stop for a snack at **Afsluitdijk Café** in the monument's base and pick up an illustrated booklet that explains the dike's construction. For those crossing over by bike or on foot, there's a bike path as well as a pedestrian path.

ZAANSE SCHANS ★★

16km (10 miles) NW of Amsterdam

Nestled like a pearl at the heart of the Zaanstreek district is **Zaanse Schans** (www. zaanseschans.nl), a replica village of houses, workshops, and windmills moved to this site when industrialization leveled their original locations. Though most of the distinctive green-painted timber houses are inhabited by those who can afford and appreciate their historic timbers (and have the patience for the pedestrian traffic from the tour buses), a few can be visited as museums.

Trains depart every 15 minutes or so from Amsterdam Centraal Station via Zaandam to Koog-Zaandijk station, from where it's a 1km (⅔-mile) walk to Zaanse Schans. The train ride takes 17 minutes, and a round-trip ticket is 5.20€ in second class or 8.80€ in first class. Or, take **Connexxion** bus no. 91 from outside Amsterdam Centraal Station for the 40-minute ride direct. By car from Amsterdam, take the A8 north, then switch to the A7/E22 north to exit 2, from where you follow the signs to Zaanse Schans.

To the pleasure of just walking through Zaanse Schans, add a visit to one or more of the five working **windmills** (out of a total of eight) on the site: a sawmill (the wind-powered sawmill was invented in the Zaan district in 1592), and mills that specialized in producing paint, vegetable oil (two mills), and the renowned Zaanse mustard; three smaller mills are speckled around. At one time the Zaanstreek had more than 1,000 windmills. Only 15 have survived, including these eight. A short tour shows you just how these wind machines worked. Stop, too, at an 18th-century **grocery store,** an old-style **bakery,** and a **clog workshop** to see how the wooden shoes called *klompen* are made.

> ### 📎 Get Your Clogs On
>
> Wood clogs are still a fixture in many farming areas, where they're much more effective against wet and cold than leather shoes or boots. If you plan to buy a pair, Zaanse Schans is a good place to do it. Traditionally, clogs with pointed toes are for women and rounded toes are for men. They must be worn with heavy socks, so when buying, add the width of one finger when measuring for size.

Most of these and other attractions are open March to October, daily from 10am to 5 or 6pm, and November to February, Saturday and Sunday from around 11am to 4pm; open hours for some sites are more restricted. Admission (where it's not free) is 1€ to 2.50€, .50€ to 1€ for children ages 5 to 12, and free for children 4 and under.

Tour the **Zaans Museum,** Schansend 7 (✆ **075/681-0000;** www.zaans museum.nl), at the site, where this fascinating district's history is told. The architecturally novel museum is open daily from 9am to 5pm (closed Jan 1 and Dec 25). Admission is 7.50€ for adults, 6€ for seniors, 4€ for children ages 4 to 17, and free for children 3 and under.

For a view from a different perspective, take a 45-minute **cruise** on the **Zaan River** aboard a **Rederij De Schans** tour boat (✆ **075/614-6762;** www.rederijde schans.nl). Boats depart from a river dock next to the **De Huisman windmill,** April to September, daily every hour from 10am to 4pm. Cruises are 6€, 3€ for children ages 3 to 12, and free for children 2 and under.

Where to Dine

De Hoop Op d'Swarte Walvis ★ FRENCH/CONTINENTAL   A stellar restaurant with a mouthful of a name borrowed from a 19th-century local whaling ship, the "Hope for the Black Whale" occupies a refined brick building that now stands amid Zaanse Schans's green-painted houses, having been originally constructed as an orphanage in nearby Westzaan. Its glass pavilion and memorable outdoor terrace overlook the Zaan River and the waterside villas on the far bank. Gastronomes can expect an unforgettable treat from the hands of master chef Marco Krispijn, with subtle mixtures of superior produce prepared to perfection.

Kalverringdijk 15, Zaanse Schans. ✆ **075/616-5629.** www.dewalvis.nl. Main courses 24€–29€; 4-course menu du chef 49€. AE, DC, MC, V. Sun–Fri noon–10pm; Sat 6–10pm.

TULIPS & CHEESE

The place to see flowers in their full glory is **Keukenhof,** where vast numbers of tulips and other flowers create dazzling mosaics of color. Combine your visit with a trip through the **bulb fields.** And if all of the above isn't Dutch enough for you, there's always the incomparable **Alkmaar cheese market.**

Keukenhof ★★

26km (16 miles) SW of Amsterdam

In **Keukenhof,** Stationsweg 166A, Lisse (© **0252/465-555;** www.keukenhof.nl), gardens and flowers at their peak have short seasons, but if you're here in the spring, you'll never forget a visit. This park's meandering 32 hectares (79 acres) of wooded green are in the heart of the bulb-producing region, planted each fall by the major Dutch growers (each plants his own plot or establishes his own greenhouse display). Come spring, the bulbs burst forth and produce not hundreds, or even thousands, but *millions* (more than 7 million at last count) of tulips of hundreds of varieties, narcissi, daffodils, hyacinths, bluebells, crocuses, lilies, amaryllis, and many others. The color blaze is everywhere in the park; it's also in the greenhouses, next to the brooks and shady ponds, along the paths and in the neighboring fields, in neat little plots and helter-skelter on the lawns, and alongside the inevitable windmill. Keukenhof claims to be the world's greatest flower show, and around 800,000 visitors show up to evaluate this claim. Count on spending an entire morning or afternoon here, and grab a quick bite at one of several on-site cafes so that you don't have to go looking for a place to eat when you'd rather be enjoying the flowers. The park is open from around March 20 to around May 20, daily from 8am to 7:30pm. Admission is 15€, 7€ for children ages 4 to 11, and free for children 3 and under. Special train/bus connections run via Haarlem and Leiden.

The Bulb Fields ★

The largest bulb growers are in the southern part of Noord-Holland province and the northern corner of Zuid-Holland, with the heaviest concentration lying between Haarlem and Leiden. Each year from mid-March until late April, the bulb fields cover a strip of land 16km (10 miles) long and 6km (4 miles) wide with tulips, crocuses, daffodils, narcissi, hyacinths, lilies, and more. A signposted **Bollenstreek (Bulb District)** route that covers about 60km (38 miles) makes viewing the flowers easy (VVV tourist information offices provide a detailed "Bulb Route" brochure). Roadside stalls sell flower garlands—do as the natives do and buy one for yourself and another for the car.

To tour the bulb fields from Amsterdam, either drive first to Haarlem, then south on the N206 through De Zilk and Noordwijkerhout, or on the N208, through Hillegom, Lisse, and Sassenheim. Alternatively, go south from Amsterdam on the A4/E19, past Schiphol Airport, to exit 4 (Nieuw-Vennep), and then northwest on the N207 for 8km (5 miles) until you hit the N208.

Aalsmeer

18km (11 miles) SW of Amsterdam

Selling flowers and plants nets around 1.5€ billion a year at the **Bloemenveiling (Flower Auction)** ★, Legmeerdijk 313 (*©* **0297/393-939;** www.floraholland.com), in the lakeside community of Aalsmeer close to Schiphol Airport. Every day, the auction vends 19 million cut flowers and 2 million plants, in 12,000 varieties, from 7,000 nurseries, representing 30% of the worldwide trade. So vast is the auction house that 120 soccer fields would fit inside.

Get here early to see the biggest array of flowers in the distribution rooms, and to have as much time as possible to watch the computerized auction. Buyers sit in rows in five auditorium-style auction halls; they have microphones to ask questions and buttons to electronically register their bids. As the bunches of tulips or daffodils go by the stand on carts, they're auctioned in a matter of seconds. A mammoth timer, which starts at 100 and counts clockwise to 1, determines the bidding: The winning, and only, bid is placed by the person who stops the clock. It's like a gigantic game of chicken. Press too early and you pay more than necessary; wait too long and someone else already has the lot.

> ### Impressions
>
> *Aalsmeer is an auction house in the sense that Shanghai is a city or Everest a mountain.*
> —*National Geographic* (Apr 2001)

The auction is held Monday to Friday from 7 to 11am (there's little point in arriving after 9:30am). Admission is 5€, 3€ for children ages 6 to 11, and free for children 5 and under. To get there from Amsterdam, take the train to Schiphol Station, and then **Connexxion** bus no. 198 from outside Schiphol Plaza to the auction entrance; the journey takes around an hour. By car, take the A4/E19 south to the Hoofddorp junction, then go southeast on the N201.

Alkmaar

30km (19 miles) N of Amsterdam

Every Friday morning during the long Dutch summer season, a steady parade of tourists arrives to visit the famous cheese market in this handsome, canal-lined town (pop. 94,000), founded in the 10th century. It's quite a show they're on their way to see. For another town with a cheesy disposition, see also the sections on Edam in "The IJsselmeer," earlier in this chapter.

GETTING THERE   Trains depart every 15 minutes or so from Amsterdam Centraal Station to Alkmaar; the ride takes around 35 minutes. A round-trip ticket is 13€ in second class or 22€ in first class. By car from Amsterdam, take the A8, N246, N203, and A9 north.

VISITOR INFORMATION   **VVV Alkmaar,** Waagplein 2, 1811 JP Alkmaar (*©* **072/511-4284;** fax 072/511-7513; www.vvvalkmaar.nl), is in the center. The office is open April to September, Monday to Thursday and Saturday from 10am to 5pm, and Friday from 9am to 5pm; and October to March, Monday from 1am to 5pm, and Tuesday to Saturday from 10am to 5pm.

WHAT TO SEE & DO

At the Friday morning **Kaasmarkt (Cheese Market)** ★ in Waagplein, yellow-skinned Edam, Gouda, and Leidse (Leiden) cheeses are piled high on the cobblestone square. The carillon in the 16th-century **Waaggebouw (Weigh House)** tower hourly showers the streets with tinkling Dutch folk music, accompanying a jousting performance of mechanical knights. The square is filled with sightseers, barrel organs, souvenir stalls, and tangible excitement. White-clad *kaasdragers* (cheese porters) dart around wearing colored lacquered-straw hats in red, blue, yellow, or green as a sign of which more-than-400-year-old guild they belong to. Porters, who aren't permitted to smoke, drink, or curse while on duty, are so proud of their standards that every week they post on a "shame board" the name of any carrier who indulged in profanity or showed up late at the auction.

Bidding is carried on in the traditional Dutch manner of hand clapping to bid the price up or down; a good, solid hand clap seals the deal. Once a buyer has accumulated his lot of cheeses, teams of porters move in with shiny, shallow barrows, and, using slings that hang from their shoulders, carry the golden wheels and balls of cheese to the scales in the Weigh House for the final tally. The market is held from the first Friday of April to the first Friday of September, from 10am to 12:30pm.

DEN HELDER & TEXEL

The harbor town and navy base of Den Helder, at the tip of Noord-Holland province, is the gateway to the island of Texel.

Den Helder

67km (42 miles) N of Amsterdam; 31km (19 miles) NW of Medemblik

Den Helder has Holland's most important navy base and hosts the annual Navy Days national fleet festival, in July.

ESSENTIALS

GETTING THERE   Trains depart every half hour from Amsterdam Centraal Station for Den Helder; the ride takes around 75 minutes. A round-trip ticket is 24€ in second class or 41€ in first class. By car from Amsterdam, take the A8, A9, and N9 north.

VISITOR INFORMATION   VVV Den Helder, Bernhardplein 14, 1781 HH Den Helder (© 0223/625-544; fax 0223/614-888; www.vvvkopvannoordholland.nl), is next to the rail station. The office is open Monday from 10:30am to 5:30pm, Tuesday to Friday from 9:30am to 5:30pm, and Saturday from 9:30am to 5pm.

WHAT TO SEE & DO

For an insight into the Royal Netherlands Navy's illustrious past, by way of models, marine paintings, weapons and equipment, and some real warships, visit the **Marinemuseum (Navy Museum),** Hoofdgracht 3 (© 0223/657-534; www.marinemuseum.nl), just 200m (660 ft.) west of the Texel ferry dock. Several retired combatants on display include the steam-and-sail ram *De Schorpioen,* built in 1868. Now tied to a dock, the *Scorpion* was once a vessel with a sting in its bow, from which a below-the-water ram could deal fatal blows to enemy ships—not that it ever did. The steam engine still works, and you can visit the captain's cabin and crew's quarters. Equally fascinating is the dry-landed submarine *Tonijn (Tunny)*, which has a torpedo emerging from its front tube—go aboard to experience a submariner's claustrophobic quarters. The museum is open May to October, Monday to Friday from 10am to 5pm, and Saturday, Sunday, and holidays from noon to 5pm; November to April, Tuesday to Friday from 10am to 5pm, and Saturday, Sunday, and holidays from noon to 5pm; it's closed January 1 and December 25. Admission is 6€ for adults, 3€ for children ages 5 to 15, free for children 4 and under, and 15€ for families.

While you're in naval mode, visit the **Nationaal Reddingmuseum Dorus Rijkers (Dorus Rijkers National Lifeboat Museum),** Oude Rijkswerf, Willemsoord 60G (© **0223/618-320;** www.reddingmuseum.nl), which chronicles the Lifeboat Service's history. The museum is open April to October and Christmas school vacation, Monday to Friday from 10am to 5pm, and Saturday and Sunday from noon to 5pm; November to mid-December, Sunday from noon to 5pm; closed January 1 and December 25. Admission is 6€ for adults, 5€ for children ages 4 to 17, free for children 3 and under, and 18€ for families.

The Bulb District between Leiden and Haarlem (p. 269) may be better known, but around Den Helder is Holland's largest area of **bulb fields;** the serried ranks of spring tulips look every bit as colorful here as there.

Texel ★

69km (43 miles) N of Amsterdam

A short ferry trip from Den Helder, family-orientated Texel (pronounced *Tess*-uhl) is the largest and most populated of the Wadden Islands archipelago. With just 14,000 permanent inhabitants, that's not saying much. Texel, 24km (15 miles) long and 9km (6 miles) wide, has a varied landscape of tidal gullies, sand dunes, and rolling meadows. Its entire North Sea shoreline is just one long beach. It has some of the serenity intrinsic to islands, even allowing for the many visitors who pour in during summer months.

ESSENTIALS

GETTING THERE The **TESO** line (© **0222/369-600;** www.teso.nl) operates a car-ferry service from Den Helder across the Marsdiep strait to 't Horntje on Texel—a 20-minute trip. In Den Helder, **Connexxion** bus no. 33 shuttles between the rail station and the ferry dock (a 10-minute ride). Ferries depart hourly at peak times and reservations are not accepted. Round-trip fares for cars, including two passengers, are Friday to Monday 18€, and Tuesday to Thursday 12€; for passengers alone, round-trip fares are 2.50€, and free for children 3 and under. Bicycles and mopeds cost 2.50€ in addition to the passenger's fare.

VISITOR INFORMATION **VVV Texel,** Emmalaan 66, 1791 AV Den Burg (© **0222/314-741;** fax 0222/310-054; www.texel.net), is just off the main road from the ferry dock into the island's main town. The office is open Monday to Friday from 9am to 5:30pm, and Saturday from 9am to 5pm.

GETTING AROUND Cars are permitted on Texel and buses connect the villages and the main beaches, but the best way to get around and to respect the island's environment is to go by bike. Bring yours over for free on the ferry, or rent one from dozens of outlets around the island.

EXPLORING TEXEL

Beaches, sailing, biking, hiking, and bird-watching are Texel's big attractions, but eating, drinking, and partying certainly have a place too. The main village, **Den Burg,** is a bustling settlement near the center of the island. To gain an insight into Texel's centuries-long relationship with the sea, head to nearby Oudeschild on the island's east coast, to visit the **Maritiem & Jutters Museum,** Barentszstraat 21 (*②* **0222/314-956;** www.texelsmaritiem.nl), at the small town's harbor. The museum is open July to August, Tuesday to Saturday from 10am to 5pm, and Sunday from noon to 5pm; and September to June, Monday to Saturday from 10am to 5pm, and Sunday from noon to 5pm. Admission is 6.25€, 4.75€ for children ages 5 to 14, and free for children 4 and under.

You're allowed to freely visit the dune and forest area belonging to the **Staatsbos-beheer (State Forest Authority),** so long as you stick to the marked trails. Wildlife biologists from **EcoMare,** Ruijslaan 92 (*②* **0222/317-741;** www.ecomare.nl), a Wadden Islands research center, conduct guided tours of some of these areas. Eco-Mare's visitor center, amid the sand dunes just south of a coastal village called **De Koog,** houses a small natural history museum featuring Texel's geology, plants, and its wildlife of land, sea, and air. The Wadden Sea is rich in seals, and EcoMare has a seal rehabilitation facility that cares for weak and injured seals until they are strong enough to be returned to the sea. Another of their rehabilitation projects cares for birds affected by pollution and other hazards. The center is open daily from 9am to 5pm. Admission is 9€, 6.25€ for children ages 4 to 13, and free for children 3 and under.

Some 300 bird species frequent Texel, of which around 100 breed on the island. Among the avian stars: Oyster-catchers, Bewicks swans, spoonbills, eider ducks, Brent geese, avocets, marsh harriers, snow buntings, ringed plovers, kestrels, short-eared owls, and bar-tailed godwits. Observe these and more in the **De Schorren, De Bol,** and **Dijkmanshuizen**—three protected nature reserves that you can only enter if you're on an EcoMare-conducted tour.

CASTLE COUNTRY

In earlier times, the territory southeast of Amsterdam was a place of strategic importance, as evidenced by the grand military constructions still standing today, such as the 13th-century Muiderslot moated castle in Muiden and the star-shaped fortifications of Naarden.

Muiden

13km (8 miles) SE of Amsterdam

A 14th-century, fairy-tale-princess castle, with a moat, turrets, and stout crenelated walls, **Muiderslot** ★, Herengracht 1 (*②* **0294/256-262;** www.muiderslot.nl), perches on the bank of the Vecht River just outside the small IJsselmeer harbor town of Muiden, a handsome place with gabled waterfront houses. Count Floris V of Holland, who in 1275 granted toll privileges to the vibrant new Aemstelledamme (Amsterdam) settlement, built the castle around 1280, and was murdered here by rival nobles in 1296.

The poet Pieter Cornelisz Hooft served here as castle steward and local bailiff for 40 years in the early 17th century, and the castle is furnished essentially as Hooft and his artistic circle of friends—known in Dutch literary history as the *Muiderkring* (Muiden Circle)—knew it. You'll find distinctly Dutch carved cupboard beds, heavy chests, fireside benches, and mantelpieces. The castle is open April to October, Monday to Friday from 10am to 5pm, Saturday, Sunday, and holidays from noon to 6pm; November to March, Saturday and Sunday from noon to 6pm. Admission is 11€, 6.25€ for children ages 4 to 11, and free for children 3 and under.

Connexxion bus 157 departs every 15 minutes or so from outside Amsterdam Amstel station for the 20-minute ride to Muiden; from there it's a walk of 1km (⅔ mile) north through Muiden to the castle. By car from Amsterdam, take the A1/E231 east.

Naarden

19km (12 miles) E of Amsterdam

This small town doesn't have too much to recommend in it, but it does have one of Holland's best-preserved rings of old military fortifications.

ESSENTIALS

GETTING THERE   Trains depart every 15 minutes or so from Amsterdam Centraal Station for Naarden-Bussum station; the trip takes around 25 minutes. A round-trip ticket is 8.10€ in second class or 14€ in first class. By car from Amsterdam, take the A1/E231 east.

VISITOR INFORMATION   VVV Naarden, Adriaan Dortsmanplein 1B, 1411 RC Naarden (🕿 035/694-2836; fax 035/694-3424; www.vvvhollandsmidden.nl), is located inside the old town's walls. The office is open May to mid-September, Tuesday to Friday from 10am to 3pm, and Saturday from 10am to 2pm; and mid-September to April, Saturday from 10am to 2pm.

WHAT TO SEE & DO

Much in the spirit of locking the barn door after the horse was gone, Naarden erected its star-shaped double fortifications after Don Fadrique Álvarez de Toledo and his Spanish troops brutally sacked the town in 1572. The fortifications were begun in 1580 and completed in 1730, and since the inner ring wasn't completed until 1685, the French were able to storm the works in 1673.

Beneath the **Turfpoort,** one of six bastions, visit the casemates (artillery vaults) which house the **Nederlands Vestingmuseum (Dutch Fortification Museum),** Westwalstraat 6 (🕿 035/694-5459; www.vestingmuseum.nl), filled with cannons, muskets, accoutrements, and documentation. The museum is open mid-March to October, Tuesday to Friday from 10:30am to 5pm, and Saturday, Sunday, and holidays from noon to 5pm; November to mid-March, Sunday, and Saturday before Christmas to Sunday after New Year, Tuesday to Friday from 10:30am to 5pm, and Sunday from noon to 5pm; it's closed January 1, and December 25 and 31. Admission is 5.50€, 4.50€ for seniors, 3€ for children 5 to 12, and free for children 4 and under.

Also take in the town's 15th-century late-Gothic **Grote Kerk (Great Church),** Marktstraat (🕿 035/694-9873), noted for its 45-m (148-ft.) tower, fine acoustics, and annual pre-Easter performances of Bach's *St. Matthew Passion.* The church is open June to September daily from 1 to 4pm. Admission is free.

THE HAGUE ★★★

50km (31 miles) SW of Amsterdam

Amsterdam may be the capital of the Netherlands, but The Hague (Den Haag, or the formal 's-Gravenhage, in Dutch) has always been the seat of government and Dutch monarchs' official residence. This tradition began in 1248, when Count Willem II of Holland was crowned king of the Romans in the German city of Aachen, but chose to live at the Binnenhof palace in what's now The Hague. Sophisticated, full of parks and elegant homes, the city has an 18th-century French look that suits its role as the Dutch nation's diplomatic center. Nowadays, as the seat of the International Court of Justice, the city's name is associated with international law.

Essentials

GETTING THERE The Hague is an easy day trip from Amsterdam. Up to six trains an hour depart from Amsterdam Centraal Station, on a ride of around 50 minutes to The Hague. A round-trip ticket is 19€ in second class or 33€ in first class. The city has two main rail stations, Den Haag Centraal Station and Den Haag HS; most sights are closer to Centraal Station, but some trains stop only at HS (in 2010, a complete refurbishment of this old station began and is due to be completed in 2011). By car from Amsterdam, take the A4/E19.

VISITOR INFORMATION VVV Den Haag, Hofweg 1 (mailing address: Postbus 85456, 2500 CD Den Haag; ✆ 070/361-8860; fax 070/361-7915; www.den haag.nl; tram: 1 or 16), faces the Binnenhof (Parliament) in the center of town. The office is open Monday to Friday from 9:30am to 6pm, Saturday from 9:30am to 5pm, and Sunday from 11am to 6pm.

What To See & Do

The Hague's most notable attraction is the impressive **Binnenhof (Inner Court),** Binnenhof 8A (✆ 070/364-6144; www.binnenhofbezoek.nl; tram: 1, 10, 16, or 17), a complex of Parliament buildings, in the center. Join a tour to visit the lofty medieval **Ridderzaal (Hall of the Knights);** this is where the queen delivers a speech from the throne each third Tuesday in September. If you're lucky enough to be in The Hague on that day, be sure to be here to see her arrive and depart in her golden coach—like Cinderella—drawn by high-stepping royal horses. Government business permitting, you can tour the two chambers of the **Staten-Generaal (States General),** the Dutch Parliament. Guided tours (the only way guests are permitted to visit) take place Monday to Saturday hourly from 10am to 4pm (closed holidays and during special events), and cost 4€ or 6€ for adults, depending on the tour. Reserve ahead of time by phone, and confirm that tours are happening on the day you intend to visit. Admission to the Parliament exhibit in the Hall of Knights reception room is free.

Adjacent to the Binnenhof is the neoclassical **Mauritshuis ★★**, Korte Vijverberg 8 (✆ 070/302-3456; www.mauritshuis.nl; tram: 1, 10, 16, or 17), built in 1637 as the residence of Count Johan Maurits van Nassau-Siegen, court dandy and cousin of the ruling Oranje-Nassaus (House of Orange). Today, it houses the **Koninklijk Kabinet van Schilderijen (Royal Cabinet of Paintings),** an impressive art collection that King Willem I gave to the nation in 1816. Highlights include

13 Rembrandts, three Frans Hals, and three Vermeers (including his famous *View of Delft* and *Girl With a Pearl Earring*), plus hundreds of other paintings by the likes of Bruegel, Rubens, Steen, and Holbein. The gallery is open April to September, Monday to Saturday from 10am to 5pm, and Sunday and holidays from 11am to 5pm; and October to March, Tuesday to Saturday from 10am to 5pm, and Sunday and holidays from 11am to 5pm; it's closed January 1 and December 25. Admission is 12€ for adults, and free for visitors 18 and under. *Note:* The Mauritshuis is due to close in mid-2012 for two years of reconstruction and refurbishment, during which it will be joined by way of an underground corridor to part of the Art Deco building across Korte Vijverberg, at Plein 26. During the period of closure, important works from the collection will be displayed at other venues around The Hague.

Venture beyond the center to visit the **Gemeentemuseum Den Haag (the Hague Municipal Museum)** ★, Stadhouderslaan 41 (© **070/338-1111;** www.gemeentemuseum.nl; tram: 17), from 1935. Designed by Hendrik Petrus Berlage, the museum possesses a world-famous collection of works by De Stijl artist Piet Mondrian (1872–1944), including his last work, *Victory Boogie Woogie* (1944). There's more art (from the 19th c. onward), decorative arts, musical instruments, and fashion. The museum is open Tuesday to Sunday and holidays from 11am to 5pm; it's closed January 1 and December 25. Admission is 10€ for adults, 6.50€ for students, and free for visitors 18 and under.

Andrew Carnegie donated the famous **Vredespaleis (Peace Palace),** Carnegieplein 2 (© **070/302-4242;** www.vredespaleis.nl; tram: 1 or 10) as a home for the **International Court of Justice** and the **Permanent Court of Arbitration.** The palace is open for guided tours only, Monday to Friday at 10 and 11am, and 2, 3, and 4pm (there isn't always a 4pm tour); these should be reserved at least 1 or 2 days ahead of time (© **070/302-4137;** fax 070/302-4234; guidedtours@carnegie-stichting.nl), though booking a week ahead would better guarantee securing a spot. Guides usually speak English, but it can't hurt to confirm this for your chosen time. Also note that you can only visit the Peace Palace's museum on the 11am and 3pm tours. Tours last 50 minutes without the museum visit and 1½ hours with. They're 5€, 3€ for children ages 5 to 13, and free for children 4 and under; add 3€ per person for the museum visit.

Not far away, in the **Scheveningse Bosjes (Scheveningen Woods),** is the enchanting **Madurodam** ★, George Maduroplein 1 (© **070/416-2400;** www.madurodam.nl; tram: 9), a miniature village in 1:25 scale. It presents many of the country's most historic buildings in miniature, with lights that work, bells that ring, and trains that run. It's open April to June, daily from 9am to 8pm; July to August, daily from 9am to 11pm; and September to March, daily from 9am to 6pm. Admission is 15€ for adults, 14€ for seniors, 11€ for children ages 3 to 11, and free for children 2 and under.

> **Rising Roses**
>
> In Westbroekpark's **Rosarium,** more than 20,000 roses of 300 varieties bloom each year between July and September. Its grounds are open daily from 9am to 1 hour before sunset.

If you don't have time to visit The Hague's seacoast resort of Scheveningen (see below), you can still hit the beach, kind of, at **Panorama Mesdag,** Zeestraat 65 (© **070/364-4544;** www.panorama-mesdag.com; tram: 1 or 10), a superb panoramic painting of the resort town as it was in 1880, done in the style of The Hague school—its perimeter is 119m (395 ft.).

The Hague & Scheveningen

ATTRACTIONS ●
Binnenhof/Ridderzaal **11**
Gemeentemuseum
  Den Haag **5**
Holland Casino
  Scheveningen **3**
Madurodam **6**

Mauritshuis/Koninklijk
  Kabinet van Schilderijen **12**
Panorama Mesdag **8**
Scheveningen Pier **1**
Sea Life Scheveningen **2**
Vredespaleis **7**

DINING ◆
The Harbour Club **4**
Le Bistroquet **9**
Stadsherberg 't Goude
  Hooft **10**

ⓘ Information
✉ Post office

View it Monday to Saturday from 10am to 5pm, Sunday and holidays from noon to 5pm; it's closed January 1 and December 25. Admission is 6.50€, 5.50€ for seniors and students, 3€ for children ages 3 to 12, and free for children 2 and under.

A Side-Trip to Scheveningen ★

5km (3 miles) NW of The Hague center

A chic beach resort with a notoriously hard-to-pronounce name, Scheveningen (try *Skhe*-ven-ing-en) is virtually a part of The Hague. It sports a cast of upscale restaurants with international cuisine, accommodations in all price ranges, international-name boutiques, and abundant nighttime entertainment. Until the early 19th century, this was a sleepy fishing village. You might still sight costumed fishermen's wives near the harbor—they dress up in traditional Dutch garb only for special events, like *Vlaggetjesdag* (Flag Day), around the first week of June (see "When to Go," in chapter 3), when the first of the new season's herring are landed.

To get there from The Hague, take tram no. 1 or 9 to the beach at Gevers Deynootplein in front of the Kurhaus Hotel; 11 to the beach between the Kurhaus and the fishing harbor; or 10 or 17 to the harbor area. Tourist information is available from VVV Den Haag's **Informatiepunt Scheveningen** on the Pier (tram: 1 or 9), open mid-May to August daily from 11am to 5pm. For mail, phone, fax, and website details, see "Visitor Information" for The Hague, p. 275.

In Scheveningen, you can stroll on dunes, go deep-sea fishing in the North Sea, and splash in the waves. The beach zone is called Scheveningen Bad—but it looks pretty good. A 3-km (2-mile) promenade borders the wide sand beach and has as its highlight the **Scheveningen Pier ★** (✆ 070/306-5500; www.pier.nl; tram: 1 or 9), jutting out onto the North Sea. There's plenty to do here, from a casino, cafe-restaurant, and 60-m-high (200-ft.) observation tower, to a "play island" for kids.

At **Sea Life Scheveningen,** Strandweg (aka the Boulevard) 13 (✆ 070/354-2100; www.sealife.nl; tram: 1), an aquarium, you can observe denizens of the deep, including sharks, swimming above your head in a walk-through underwater tunnel. The aquarium is open July to August, daily from 10am to 8pm; February to June and September to November, daily from 10am to 7pm; and December to January daily from 10am to 6pm; it's closed December 25. Admission is 15€ for adults, 13€ for seniors and visitors with disabilities, 9.50€ for children ages 3 to 11, and free for children 2 and under.

Tuxedoed croupiers serve up blackjack and roulette at **Holland Casino Scheveningen,** Kurhausweg 1 (✆ 070/306-7777; www.hollandcasino.com; tram: 1 or 9), across from the restored 19th-century Kurhaus Hotel. There's roulette, blackjack, punto banco, slot machines, and more. The dress code is "correct" (collar and tie for men), and the minimum age is 18. You need your passport to get in. The casino is open daily (except May 4 and Dec 31) from 12:30pm to 3am. Admission is 5€; Wednesday is "ladies day," and admission is free for all visitors.

Where to Dine

The Harbour Club ★ SEAFOOD   While some seafoodies mourned the passing of the traditional old restaurant Ducdalf from this spot on Scheveningen's yacht harbor, others liked the cut of its successor's jib. You dine amid a thoroughly modern *joie de vivre* in a trendily rambling interior of bare brick walls, or outside by the water's edge.

The kitchen can handle everything from sushi through *nouvelle*-style grilled North Sea fish, and oyster or mixed-shellfish platters, to surf-and-organic turf.

Dr. Lelykade 5-13, Scheveningen. ✆ **070/891-3224.** www.theharbourclub.nl. Main courses 20€-45€; fixed-price menus 25€-45€. AE, DC, MC, V. Daily 11am-1am. Tram: 11 to Dr. Lelykade.

Le Bistroquet ★ CONTINENTAL   This small, popular restaurant in the city center is one of The Hague's finest. Its quietly elegant dining room features lovely table settings. The menu, though short, is to the point, and covers lamb, fish, and poultry dishes. A fine choice is the three variations of Texel lamb with roasted garlic and a basil sauce. Seafood checks in with an excellent lemon-crusted halibut served with asparagus, scallop-stuffed cannelloni, and a parsley sauce.

Lange Voorhout 98. ✆ **070/360-1170.** www.bistroquet.nl. Reservations recommended on weekends. Main courses 25€-38€; fixed-price menus 39€-49€. AE, DC, MC, V. Mon-Fri noon-2pm and 6-10pm; Sat 6-10pm. Tram: 10, 16, or 17 to Kneuterdijk.

Stadsherberg 't Goude Hooft ★★ DUTCH/CONTINENTAL   There's an old Dutch flavor to this wonderful cafe-restaurant overlooking the city's market square. Its 1600s' exterior cloaks a 1939 interior installed after a fire. In fact, the establishment dates back to 1423, and was originally a tavern before being transformed in 1660 into a coffeehouse, and finally a cafe-restaurant in 1939. Wood beams, brass chandeliers, and rustic furnishings harmonize with stained-glass windows, medieval banners, and murals. An extensive menu covers everything from snacks to light lunches to full dinners. Look for dishes like Guinea fowl with thyme sauce, or red perch with saffron sauce. This also is a good place to drop by for a cocktail and snack, or just for a beer or coffee. There's a sidewalk terrace on Dagelijkse Groenmarkt.

Dagelijkse Groenmarkt 13 (at the Grote Kerk). ✆ **070/346-9713.** www.tgoudehooft.nl. Main courses 22€-30€. AE, DC, MC, V. Mon-Sat 8am-1am; Sun 10am-midnight. Tram: 17 to Gravenstraat.

ROTTERDAM ★★

58km (36 miles) SW of Amsterdam

For a change from the thick blanket of history in and around Amsterdam, consider a visit to this cutting-edge Dutch city. Here, instead of the usual Dutch web of little streets and alleyways, there's a spacious and elegant shopping mall; instead of Amsterdam's miles of winding canals, there's the world's busiest ocean harbor: Europoort.

Rotterdam is fascinating to see and experience, particularly considering that this city was a living monument to Holland's 17th-century Golden Age until it was bombed to rubble during World War II. At the war's end, rather than try to re-create the old, Rotterdammers looked on their misfortune as an opportunity and approached their city as a clean slate. They relished the chance to create an efficient, elegant, and workable modern city. The result won't be to everybody's taste, but does attest to their ability to find impressive solutions.

Essentials

GETTING THERE   Two **NS Hispeed** *Fyra* trains depart hourly from Amsterdam Centraal Station for Rotterdam Centraal Station; the ride takes 40 minutes. Ordinary Inter-City trains depart every 10 minutes or so, and take around 70 minutes for the ride. A round-trip ticket is 25€ in second class or 43€ in first class; a

> ### 💬 Working People
>
> **So hard-working are Rotterdam's citizens that they are said to be "born with their sleeves already rolled up."**

supplement is charged for the high-speed service, ranging from 11€ to 21€ in second class, or 17€–28€ in first class, depending on the ticket type purchased. By car from Amsterdam, take the A4/E19 to The Hague, then the A13/E19 to Rotterdam.

VISITOR INFORMATION ROTTERDAM.INFO, Coolsingel 195–197 (📞 **0900/403-4065;** fax 010/271-0128; www.vvvrotterdam.nl), close to the junction with Westblaak, is open Monday to Thursday and Saturday from 9:30am to 6pm, Friday from 9:30am to 9pm, and Sunday from 10am to 5pm. The **VVV Rotterdam Info Cafe** in the Grand Café-Restaurant Engels, Stationsplein 45 (Weena entrance), is open Monday to Saturday from 9am to 5:30pm, and Sunday from 10am to 5pm.

SPECIAL EVENTS Each year, for 3 days every July, jazz greats from around the world gather in Holland for the **North Sea Jazz Festival** (📞 **0900/1010-2020,** or 31-20/511-0070 from outside Holland; www.northseajazz.com). This non-stop extravaganza features star performances by internationally acclaimed musicians, in some 200 concerts of jazz, blues, bebop, and world music, at the giant Ahoy venue. For more information, see "Amsterdam Calendar of Events" in chapter 3.

What To See & Do

Another of Holland's fine-art treasure-troves is the **Museum Boijmans Van Beuningen** ★, Museumpark 18–20 (📞 **010/441-9400;** www.boijmans.rotterdam.nl; tram: 4 or 5). Dutch painters share wall space with an international contingent that includes Salvador Dalí and Man Ray, Titian and Tintoretto, Degas and Daumier. Fine collections of porcelain, silver, glass, and Delftware are also on display. The museum is open Tuesday to Sunday from 11am to 5pm; it's closed January 1, April 30, and December 25. Admission is 10€ for adults, 5€ for students, free for children 18 and under, and free for all visitors on Wednesday.

A city landmark near the Old Harbor is a geometric chaos of quirky, cube-shaped apartments balancing atop tall concrete stalks; the elevated, tree house–like yellow **Kubuswoningen (Cube Houses)** were designed by Dutch architect Piet Blom in the early 1970s. One of these quirky, lopsided little abodes, the **Kijk-Kubus (Show-Cube),** Overblaak 70 (📞 **010/414-2285;** www.kubuswoning.nl; Metro: Blaak), is open for visits daily from 11am to 5pm. Admission is 2.50€, 2€ for seniors and students, 1.50€ for children ages 4 to 12, and free for children 3 and under.

Not all of Rotterdam is spanking new. A neighborhood the German bombers missed is the tiny harbor area known as **Delfshaven (Delft Harbor),** where the Puritans known as Pilgrims embarked on the first leg of their trip to Massachusetts. This is a pleasant place to spend an afternoon. Wander into the 15th-century **Pelgrimvaderskerk (Pilgrim Fathers Church),** Aelbrechtskolk 20 (📞 **010/477-4156;** www.pilgrimfatherschurch.nl), in which the Pilgrims prayed before their departure. The church is open irregularly; admission is free. Then, peek into antiques stores and galleries, and check on the progress of this historic area's housing renovations.

Two interesting places to visit in Delfshaven are the **Zakkendragershuisje (Sack Carriers' Guild House),** Voorstraat 13–15, where artisans demonstrate the

Amsterdam

NETHERLANDS

Rotterdam

0   50 mi
0   50 km

Rotterdam
Centraal Station

Delftseplein
Delftsestraat
Hofplein
Pempenburg
Haagseveer

Conradstraat
*(i) Stations-
plein*
2

Weena

Weena

Kruisstr.
Kruiskade
Doelwater
Stadhuisstr.

Drievriendenstr.
Diergaardesingel
Kruisplein

Karel Doormanstraat
Stadhuisplein
Coolsingel
Meent
Westewagenstr.
Roderand
Keizerstraat

West-Kruiskade
Coolsestraat
Schouw-
burgplein
Lijn-
baan
Ghent
straat.
Hennekijnstraat
Beursplein
Korte Hoogstr.

Henegouwerlaan
Tiendplein
Aert van Nesstraat

Eerste
Middellandstr.
Kogelvangerstr.
Mauritsweg
Westersingel
Oldenbarneveltplts.
Binnenwegplein
Blaak

Adrianaplein
Bajonet-
str.
Van Speyk-
straat
Josephstraat
Gaffelstraat
Sint-Mariastr.
Gouvernestraat
Mauritsstr.
Karel Doormanstr.
(i)
Churchillplein

Schermlaan
's-Gravendijkwal
Adriana
Oude Binnenweg
Westblaak
Schilderstr.

Claes de Vrieselaan
Bellevoys-
straat
Schietbaanaan
Schietbaanstr.
Nieuwe Binnenweg
Breitnerstraat
Eendrachtsplein
Witte de Withstraat
Boomgaardsstr.
Eendrachtsstr.
Schiedamse Vest
Schiedamsedijk
Leuvehaven

Mathenesser-
laan
Jonge
Kindstr.
Museumpark
3
Eendrachtsweg
Eendrachtsweg
Boomgaardssingel
Schiebroekssessingel
Schildersstr.

Volmarijnstr.
Nieuwe Binnenweg
Zwaerdecroon-
str.
Saftleveltstr.
Ochterveltstr.
Rochussenstraat
Wytemaweg
Zimmerfrfahnreg

**Museum
Boijmans
Van Beuningen**

Museumpark
Vasteland

Snellinckstr.
Burgemeester
's Jacobplein
's-Gravendijkwal

**Natuurhistorisch Museum
Rotterdam**
🏛 **Kunsthal**

Rochussenstraat
**ERASMUS MC
(HOSPITAL)**
Van Vollenhovenstr.
Westmaaslaan
Zalmhaven

G.J. de Jonghweg
Westzeedijk
Westplein
Houtlaan
Zalmstr.
Westerstr.
Maasstr.
Willemsplein
Willemskade
4
5

Willem
Buytewechstraat
Puntegaalstraat
Droogleever
Fortuynplein
Parklaan
Parklaan
Klevitslaan
Veerkade
Veerhaven

1

Westzeedijk

HET
PARK
Nieuwe Maas

Parkhaven
Euromast ■
Maastunnel

0   1/5 mi
0   0.2 km

(i) Information
✉ Post office
🚢 Harbor cruises

ATTRACTIONS ●
Delfshaven **1**
Museum Boijmans Van Beuningen **3**
Museum De Dubbelde Palmboom **1**
Spido Harbor Tours **4**
Zakkendragershuisje **1**

DINING ◆
Café-Restaurant
Rotterdam **5**
Grand Café-Restaurant
Engels **2**

Grand Harbor

A dredged deepwater channel connects Rotterdam with the North Sea and forms a 32-km-long (20-mile) harbor known as **Europoort** (*"poort"* is pronounced like "port" in English). This handles more ships and more cargo every year than any other port in the world—20,000 ships and more than 300 million metric tons of cargo. You may think visiting a harbor is boring business on a vacation, but Rotterdam's is one of the most memorable sights in Holland.

art of pewter casting, and the adjoining warehouses that together make up the **Museum De Dubbelde Palmboom (Double Palm Tree Museum),** Voorhaven 12 (✆ **010/476-1533;** www.hmr.rotterdam.nl; Metro: Delfshaven), which displays objects unearthed during the excavations of Rotterdam. Both are open Tuesday to Sunday from 11am to 5pm (closed Jan 1, Apr 30, Dec 25). Admission is 5€ for adults, and free for children 17 and under.

HARBOR TOURS

An essential part of the Rotterdam experience is taking a **Spido Harbor Tour** (✆ **010/275-9988;** www.spido.nl; Metro: Leuvehaven). It's an unforgettable experience to board a boat that seems large in comparison to the canal launches of Amsterdam—two tiers of indoor seating and open decks—and then to feel dwarfed by the hulking oil tankers and container ships that glide like giant whales into their berths along the miles of docks. April to September, departures from a dock below the Erasmus Bridge are every 30 to 45 minutes from 9:30am to 5pm; and October to March, two to four times a day. The basic tour, offered year-round, is a 75-minute sail along the city's waterfront; between April and September, it's possible to take an extended (2¼-hr.) trip daily at 10am and 12:30pm; and on a limited schedule in July and August, you can make all-day excursions along Europoort's full length and to the Delta Works sluices. Tours start out at 9.50€, 5.80€ for children ages 4 to 11, and free for children 3 and under.

Where to Dine

Café-Restaurant Rotterdam ★★ INTERNATIONAL   A jewel in Rotterdam's crown, where royalty, dockworkers, and visitors can feel equally at home, this is a good choice at any time. The architecture of the light-flooded old cruise-ship terminal on Kop van Zuid peninsula, sporting views of low-lying barges gliding down the Nieuwe Maas waterway outside, and the potted olive trees, give its four floors a special atmosphere. The menu covers a lot of European ground, from pasta to shellfish, and mixes influences from around the world.

Wilhelminakade 699. ✆ **010/290-8442.** www.caferotterdam.nl. Main courses 23€–24€; fixed-price menus 28€–32€. AE, DC, MC, V. Mon–Thurs 11am–midnight; Fri–Sat 11am–1am; Sun 10am–midnight. Metro: Wilhelminaplein.

Grand Café-Restaurant Engels INTERNATIONAL   This eatery is actually a complex of four restaurants, each dedicated to a different international cuisine: Don Quijote (Spanish), Tokaj (Hungarian), the Beefeater (British), and Brasserie Engels (Dutch/Continental). Tokaj and Don Quijote offer live music. Each restaurant offers an a la carte menu (listing full dinners, light meals, sandwiches, omelets, and snacks) and vegetarian options.

Stationsplein 45 (next to Centraal Station, in the Groothandelsgebouw). © **010/411-9550.** www. engels.nl. Main courses 16€–20€; fixed-price menus and buffet 19€–24€. AE, DC, MC, V. Daily 8am–1am. Metro: Centraal Station.

DELFT★★

54km (33 miles) SW of Amsterdam

Yes, this is the home of the famous blue-and-white porcelain, and you can visit the factory where it's produced. But don't let Delftware be your only reason to visit. The small, handsome city was the cradle of the Dutch Republic, is the burial place of the royal family, and was the birthplace and inspiration of artist Jan Vermeer, the 17th-century master of light and subtle emotion. Quiet and intimate, Delft has linden trees bending over gracious canals.

Essentials

GETTING THERE There's hourly direct train service from Amsterdam Centraal Station, and an additional five or six trains on which you need to transfer at Rotterdam Centraal; either way, the ride takes around 1 hour. A round-trip ticket costs 22€ in second class or 37€ in first class. By car, Delft is just off the A13/E19, the Hague-Rotterdam expressway.

VISITOR INFORMATION Delft's **Touristen Informatie Punt (TIP),** Hippolytusbuurt 4, 2611 HN Delft (© **0900/515-1555** from inside Holland, 31-15/215-4051 from abroad; fax 015/215-4055; www.delft.nl), is in the center of town. The office is open April to September, Sunday and Monday from 10am to 4pm, Tuesday to Friday from 9am to 6pm, and Saturday from 10am to 5pm; October to March, Sunday from 10am to 3pm, Monday from 11am to 4pm, and Tuesday to Saturday from 10am to 4pm.

What to See & Do

Vermeer's house is long gone, as are his paintings. But you can visit the **Oude Kerk (Old Church),** Heilige Geestkerkhof (© 015/212-3015; www.oudekerk-delft.nl), where he's buried; it's noted for its 27 stained-glass windows by Joep Nicolas. You should also visit the **Nieuwe Kerk (New Church) ★,** Markt (© 015/212-3025; www.nieuwekerk-delft.nl), where Prince William of Orange and other members of the House of Oranje-Nassau are buried. Climb its tower, which is 109m (357 ft.) high. Both churches are open April to October, Monday to Saturday from 9am to 6pm; November to January, Monday to Friday from 11am to 4pm, and Saturday from 11am to 5pm; and February to March, Monday to Saturday from 10am to 5pm. Combined admission is 3.50€, 3€ for seniors, 1.50€ for children ages 6 to 12, and free for children 5 and under. Admission to the Nieuwe Kerk tower is 3€, 2.50€ for seniors, 1.50€ for children ages 6 to 12, and free for children 5 and under.

The **Stedelijk Museum Het Prinsenhof ★,** Sint-Agathaplein 1 (© 015/260-2358; www.prinsenhof-delft.nl), on the nearby Oude Delft canal, is where William I of Orange (William the Silent) lived and had his headquarters over the years during which he helped found the Dutch Republic. He was assassinated here in 1584 by

Delft

ATTRACTIONS ●
De Koninklijke
  Porceleyne Fles
  (Royal Delft) **7**
Museum Lambert
  van Meerten **1**
Nieuwe Kerk **4**
Oude Kerk **3**
Stedelijk Museum
  Het Prinsenhof **2**
DINING ◆
Spijshuis de Dis **5**
Stadsherberg
  De Mol **6**

Canal-boat
cruises
ⓘ Information
✉ Post office

Balthasar Gérard, a French Catholic, and you can see the bullet holes from the fusil-lade that felled him in the stairwell. Today, the Prinsenhof is a museum of paintings, tapestries, silverware, and pottery. The museum is open Tuesday to Sunday from 11am to 5pm; it's closed January 1, Easter Monday, April 30, and December 25. Admission is 7.50€ for adults, 4€ for students and children ages 12 to 16, and free for children 11 and under.

In the same neighborhood, view a fine collection of old Delft tiles displayed in the wood-paneled setting of a 19th-century mansion-museum called **Lambert van Meerten,** Oude Delft 199 (🕾 **015/260-2358;** www.lambertvanmeerten-delft.nl).

The museum is open Tuesday to Sunday from 11am to 5pm; it's closed January 1, Easter Monday, April 30, and December 25. Admission is 3.50€ for adults, 1.50€ for students and children ages 12 to 16, and free for children 11 and under.

To witness a demonstration of the traditional art of making and hand-painting Delftware, visit the factory and showroom at **De Koninklijke Porceleyne Fles (Royal Delft)** ★, Rotterdamseweg 196 (✆ **015/251-2030**; www.royaldelft.com; bus: 40, 63, 121, or 129 to Jaffalaan), founded in 1653. It's open from the third week in March to October, daily from 9am to 5pm; November to the third week in March, Monday to Saturday from 9am to 5pm; it's closed January 1, and December 25 and 26. Admission is 8€, and free for children 12 and under.

Where to Dine

Spijshuis de Dis ★ DUTCH   Some of Holland's best Dutch cooking is at this atmospheric restaurant east of the market. Traditional plates presented in modern variations include *bakke pot*—a served-in-the-pan stew made from three kinds of meat (beef, chicken, and rabbit) in beer sauce and VOC mussels (named after the Dutch initials for the United East India Company), with garlic, ginger, and curry. Steaks and lamb filet are other specialties. If you're feeling decadent, go for the luscious dessert of vanilla ice cream with hot cherries, whipped cream, and cherry brandy.

Beestenmarkt 36 (2 blocks from the Markt). ✆ **015/213-1782.** www.spijshuisdedis.com. Main courses 18€–23€; fixed-price menu 30€. AE, DC, MC, V. Thurs–Tues 5–9:30pm.

Stadsherberg De Mol TRADITIONAL DUTCH   Food is served here in the medieval manner, in a building that dates from 1563, in wooden bowls from which you eat with your hands. Prices are moderate and quantities copious. Live music and dancing add to the fun.

Molslaan 104 (off Beestenmarkt). ✆ **015/212-1343.** www.stadsherbergdemol.nl. Main courses 12€–18€. MC, V. Tues–Sun 6–11pm.

LEIDEN ★

36km (22 miles) SW of Amsterdam

Stately yet bustling, the old heart of Leiden is classic Dutch, and filled with handsome, gabled brick houses along canals spanned by graceful bridges. The Pilgrims lived here for 11 years before sailing to North America on the *Mayflower*. Leiden's proudest homegrown moment came in 1574, when it became the only Dutch town to withstand a Spanish siege. This is also the birthplace of the Dutch tulip trade—and of Rembrandt. The home of the oldest university in the Netherlands is here too, founded in 1575. With 14 museums, covering subjects ranging from antiquities, natural history, and anatomy to clay pipes and coins, Leiden seems perfectly justified in calling itself Holland's *Museumstad* (Museum City).

> ### 💬 Intelligence Test
>
> As a reward for their heroic resistance during the 1574 Spanish siege, Prince William of Orange offered the people of Leiden a choice—a tax break or a university. They chose the university.

Leiden

ATTRACTIONS ●
Hortus Botanicus **4**
Jean Pesijnshofje **6**
Leiden American
  Pilgrim Museum **7**
Pieterskerk **5**
Rijksmuseum van
  Oudheden **3**
Stedelijk Museum
  De Lakenhal **2**

DINING ◆
Annie's **8**
Stadscafé van
  der Werff **1**

Canal-boat cruises
(i) Information
✉ Post office

Essentials

GETTING THERE Up to eight trains per hour run from Amsterdam Centraal Station to Leiden Centraal Station. The ride takes around 35 minutes, and the round-trip fare is 15€ in second class or 26€ in first class. The center of Leiden is a walk of around 1.5km (1 mile) south from the station. By car, take the A4/E19.

VISITOR INFORMATION VVV Leiden, Stationsweg 2D, 2312 AV Leiden (© 071/516-6000; fax 071/516-6009; www.vvvleiden.nl), is just outside the train station. The office is open Monday to Friday from 8am to 6pm, Saturday from 10am to 4pm, and Sunday from 11am to 3pm.

What to See & Do

Among the spectacular antiquities at the **Rijksmuseum van Oudheden (National Museum of Antiquities)** ★★, Rapenburg 28 (© 071/516-3163; www.rmo.nl), is the 4.5m-high (15-ft.), 1st-century-A.D. Temple of Taffeh, which the Egyptian government gave to the Dutch nation for its assistance with saving monuments before the construction of the Aswan High Dam. The museum is open Tuesday to Sunday from 10am to 5pm; it's closed January 1, October 3, and December 25. Admission is 9€ for adults, 7.50€ for seniors, 5.50€ for children ages 13 to 17, free for children 12 and under, and 25€ for families.

The university's **Hortus Botanicus (Botanical Garden,** ca. 1587), Rapenburg 73 (✆ **071/527-7249;** www.hortus.leidenuniv.nl), is also noteworthy. In 1592, botanist Carolus Clusius (see the "Roots of a Love Affair" box, below) brought the first tulip bulbs to Holland and planted them here—but he never got to see them flower because rivals stole them. The garden is open April to October, daily from 10am to 6pm; and November to March Tuesday to Sunday from 10am to 4pm. It's closed January 1, the last week in December, and October 3. Admission is 6€, 3€ for children ages 4 to 12, and free for children 3 and under.

Visit the **Stedelijk Museum De Lakenhal,** Oude Singel 28–32 (✆ **071/516-5360;** www.lakenhal.nl), to view works by native sons Rembrandt and Jan Steen, plus period rooms from the 17th to 19th centuries, and temporary modern-art exhibits. Also on display is Leiden's pride and joy: A copper stewpot said to have been retrieved by a small boy who crawled through a chink in the city wall just minutes after the lifting of the Spanish siege. In the enemy's camp, he found this very pot full of boiling stew and brought it back to feed Leiden's starving inhabitants. Ever since, stew has been a national dish and is still traditionally prepared for the Leiden city holiday, October 3, the anniversary of its liberation. Every year on this day, *haring en witte brood* (herring and white bread) are distributed, just as they were in 1574. The museum is open Tuesday to Friday from 10am to 5pm, and Saturday, Sunday, and holidays from noon to 5pm; October 3 from 10am to noon; it's closed January 1 and December 25. Admission is 7.50€ for adults, 4.50€ for seniors, and free for children 17 and under.

LEIDEN & THE PILGRIMS

To touch base with the Pilgrims, who lived in Leiden between 1609 and 1620, pick up the VVV brochure *A Pilgrimage Through Leiden: A Walk in the Footsteps of the Pilgrim Fathers.* The walk starts at the **Lodewijkskerk (Louis Church),** which was used as a meeting place by the town's cloth guild. William Bradford, who later became the governor of New Plymouth (Plymouth, Massachusetts), was a member of this guild. The walk takes you past the site of the Groenehuis (Green House) on William Brewstersteeg, where in an attached printing shop, William Brewster's and Thomas Brewer's *Pilgrim Press* published the religious views that so

---

Roots of a Love Affair

In the spring of 1594, a respected yet perennially grouchy botanist, Carolus Clusius, strode into the Hortus Botanicus, the University of Leiden's research garden. He stopped beside an experiment begun the previous year, and cast a critical eye over some colorful flowers waving in the breeze. Clusius was no admirer of humanity, but flowers were something else, so we may suppose that his dyspeptic disposition softened for a moment as he admired the first tulips ever grown in Holland. A nation's love affair with a flower had begun.

angered King James and the Church of England. Plaques at the Late Gothic, brick **Pieterskerk (Peter's Church),** in a small square off Kloksteeg, memorialize the Pilgrims, who worshiped here and lived in its shadow.

Across the street from the church, at Kloksteeg 21, the **Jean Pesijnshofje,** an almshouse constructed in 1683, occupies the ground where earlier stood the Groene Poort (Green Close), a cluster of small houses in which Rev. John Robinson and 21 Pilgrim families had lived. Robinson was forced to stay behind because of illness and is buried in the Pieterskerk. The almshouse is named for Jean Pesijn, a Belgian Protestant who joined the Leiden community along with his wife, Marie de la Noye, and whose son Philip sailed for North America in 1621, where his surname would change to Delano. On July 21, 1620, the first group of 66 departing Pilgrims boarded barges at Rapenburg Quay for the trip by canal from Leiden to the harbor of Delft, now Delfshaven in Rotterdam. From there, they sailed on the *Speedwell* for England, where the *Mayflower* awaited them.

At the **Leiden American Pilgrim Museum,** Beschuitsteeg 9 (© **071/512-2413;** www.pilgrimhall.org), you'll hear a recorded commentary about the Pilgrims and see photocopies of documents relating to their 11-year residence in Leiden. The museum is open Wednesday to Saturday from 1 to 5pm. Admission is 3€, and free for children 5 and under.

LEIDEN & REMBRANDT

The great artist Rembrandt van Rijn was born in Leiden in 1606. He later moved to Amsterdam, where he won fame and fortune—and later suffered bankruptcy and obscurity. In his hometown, a **Rembrandt Walk** includes the site of the birthplace (since demolished), the Latin School he attended as a boy, and his first studio.

Where to Dine

Annie's DUTCH/CONTINENTAL   This lively restaurant at water level has vaulted cellars that are a favorite eating spot for students and locals, who spill out onto the waterfront terrace in fine weather. When the canals are frozen, the view of skaters practicing their turns is enchanting. The dinner menu is simple but wholesome and, during the day, you can enjoy sandwiches or tapas.

Hoogstraat 1A (at Oude Rijn). © **071/512-5737.** www.annies.nu. Main courses 13€–28€. MC, V. Sun-Mon noon–1am, Tues & Thurs-Fri 11am–1am; Wed & Sat 10am–1am.

Stadscafé van der Werff ★ CONTINENTAL   This relaxed cafe-restaurant in a grand 1930s' villa on the old town's edge is popular with the town's students and citizens. Even if you're not having dinner, enjoying dishes like an Indonesian satay, or the surf-and-turf *kalfsbiefstukje met gebakken gambas en een kreeftensaus* (beef-steak with fried shrimps in lobster sauce), you can still while away your evening just having a drink and reading a paper. The cafe is open until 1am.

Steenstraat 2 (off Beestenmarkt). © **071/513-0335.** www.stadscafevanderwerff.nl. Main courses 14€–20€. AE, DC, MC, V. Daily 9am–1am.

FAST FACTS: AMSTERDAM

Area Codes   See "Staying Connected" for info, p. 56.

Business Hours   **Banks** are open Monday to Friday from 9am to 4 or 5pm (on Thurs, some stay open until 7pm). **Offices** are generally open Monday to Friday from 9 or 10am to 4 or 5pm. Regular **shopping** hours are Monday from 10 or 11am to 6pm; Tuesday, Wednesday, and Friday from 9am to 6pm; Thursday from 9am to 9pm (Thurs is *koopavond*/late shopping evening); and Saturday from 9am to 5pm. Some stores are open Sunday from noon to 5pm.

Cellphones (Mobile Phones)   See "Staying Connected," p. 56.

Drinking & Drug Laws   There is no minimum legal drinking age in the Netherlands—but other laws may be used against a parent, guardian, or other third party who permits or causes a minor to abuse alcohol. For purchasing drinks that have less than 15% alcohol by volume, the minimum legal age is 16; for drinks with more than 15% alcohol by volume, the minimum legal age is 18. In both cases ID must be produced.

Using narcotic drugs is officially illegal in the Netherlands. Peddling drugs is a serious offense, and buying on the street is illegal. But in licensed premises, Amsterdam allows the sale of up to 5 grams (⅛ oz.), and possession of 30 grams (1 oz.) of hashish or marijuana for personal use (since you are allowed to buy only 5 grams/⅛ oz. at a time, you might conceivably face questions if you actually have 30 grams/1 oz. on you). Not every municipality in the Netherlands is as liberal-minded as Amsterdam when it comes to smoking pot—and even Amsterdam isn't so tolerant that you should just light up on the street, in cafes, or on trams and trains (though enough dopey people do). Possessing and using hard drugs like heroin, cocaine, and ecstasy is an offense, and the police have swept most of the downtown heroin-shooters away from the tourist centers. However, drug abusers are considered a medical and social problem here rather than merely a law-enforcement issue.

Driving Rules   See "Getting There & Getting Around," p. 35.

Electricity   As in most of Europe, the Netherlands uses 230 (220–240) volts AC (50 cycles), compared to 110–120 volts AC (60 cycles) in the United States and Canada. Upward converters that change 110–120 volts to 220–240 volts are difficult to find in Holland, so bring one with you.

Bring a **connection kit** of the right power and phone adapters, a spare phone cord, and a spare Ethernet network cable—or find out whether your hotel supplies them to guests.

Embassies & Consulates   Both the U.S. and the U.K. have consulates in Amsterdam, and both countries along with other English-speaking countries have embassies in The Hague (Den Haag).

The consulate of the **United Kingdom** is at Koningslaan 44, 1070 AL Amsterdam
(© 020/676-4343; www.britain.nl; tram: 2). The embassy of the **United Kingdom** is at
Lange Voorhout 10, 2514 ED Den Haag (© 070/427-0427; www.britain.nl).

The consulate of the **United States** is at Museumplein 19, 1071 DJ Amsterdam
(© 020/575-5300; http://amsterdam.usconsulate.gov; tram: 3, 5, 12, or 16). The embassy
of the **United States** is at Lange Voorhout 102, 2514 EJ Den Haag (© 070/310-2209;
http://thehague.usembassy.gov).

The embassy of **Australia** is at Carnegielaan 4, 2517 KH Den Haag (© 070/310-8200;
www.australian-embassy.nl).

The embassy of **Canada** is at Sophialaan 7, 2514 JP Den Haag (© 070/311-1600; www.
canada.nl).

The embassy of **Ireland** is at Scheveningseweg 112, 2584 AE Den Haag (© 070/363-
0993; www.irishembassy.nl).

The embassy of **New Zealand** is at Eisenhowerlaan 77N, 2517 KK Den Haag (© 070/
346-9324; www.nzembassy.com).

Emergencies For police assistance, an emergency doctor or an ambulance with
paramedics, and for the fire department, call © **112.**

Gasoline (Petrol) A gas (petrol) station is a *benzinestation,* a *pompstation,* or a
tankstation in Dutch. Gasoline is lead-free and sold in two varieties: Euro 95 or euro
98 (for its octane number). Diesel is sold in all stations; *autogas,* also known as LPG
(liquid petroleum gas), is sold in many. The Netherlands "boasts" some of the world's
highest gasoline prices. Taxes are already included in the printed price. One U.S. gallon
equals 3.8 liters, and 1 imperial gallon equals 4.4 liters.

Holidays See "Amsterdam Calendar of Events," in chapter 3.

Hospitals Two hospitals with an emergency service are the **Onze-Lieve-Vrouwe
Gasthuis,** Oosterpark 9 (© 020/599-9111; www.olvg.nl; tram: 3, 7, or 10), Amsterdam-
Oost; and the **Academisch Medisch Centrum (AMC),** Meibergdreef 9 (© 020/566-
9111; www.amc.uva.nl; Metro: Holendrecht), Amsterdam-Zuidoost.

Insurance For travel overseas, most U.S. health plans (including Medicare and Medic-
aid) do not provide coverage, and the ones that do often require you to pay for services
upfront and reimburse you only after you return home. As a safety net, you may want to
buy travel medical insurance.

Canadians should check with their provincial health plan offices or call **Health Canada**
(© 866/225-0709; www.hc-sc.gc.ca) to find out the extent of their coverage and what
documentation and receipts they must take home in case they are treated overseas.

Travelers from the U.K. and Ireland should carry their European Health Insurance Card
(EHIC), which replaced the E111 form as proof of entitlement to free/reduced cost medical
treatment abroad (© 0845/606-2030; www.ehic.org.uk). Note that the EHIC covers only
"necessary medical treatment."

For information on traveler's insurance, trip cancellation insurance, and medical
insurance while traveling, please visit www.frommers.com/tips.

Internet Access Many hotels, coffeehouses (note that this doesn't mean pot-
selling "coffeeshops"), and other businesses offer Internet access, either Wi-Fi or
with online computers. The dedicated Internet cafe business seems to be dying out.

Language Dutch people speak Dutch, of course, but English is the second language of the Netherlands and is taught in school from the early grades. The result is
that nearly everyone speaks English fluently—so you may speak English in Amsterdam
almost as freely as you do at home, particularly to anyone providing tourist services,

whether a hotel receptionist, waitperson, or store clerk (cabdrivers might be another story). See also "Useful Terms & Phrases," p. 295.

Legal Aid   The police are allowed to levy on-the-spot fines for traffic offenses, but they are obliged to provide a receipt. Aid may be provided in legal cases that cost more than 180€. If you are accused of a more serious offense, say and do nothing before consulting a lawyer. Here the burden is on the state to prove a person's guilt beyond a reasonable doubt, and everyone has the right to remain silent, whether he or she is suspected of a crime or actually arrested. Once arrested, a person can ask the police to make a telephone call to a lawyer, or in the case of international visitors, your embassy or consulate.

Mail   Most offices of the efficient and reliable **TNT Post** (🕾 076/527-2727; www.tnt post.nl) are open Monday to Friday from 9am to 5pm. The office at Singel 250, at the corner of Raadhuisstraat (tram: 13, 14, or 17), is open Monday to Friday from 7:30am to 6pm, and Saturday from 7:30 to 9:30am. Standard postage for a postcard or letter to the U.S., Canada, Australia, or New Zealand is .95€; to the U.K. and Ireland, it's .77€. To appear really conversant, address your letters home in Dutch: Verenigde Staten van Amerika, Canada, Groot-Britannië, Ierland, Australië, Nieuw-Zeeland.

Newspapers & Magazines   See "Staying Connected," p. 56.

Passports   See "Embassies & Consulates," above, for whom to contact if you lose your passport while traveling in the Netherlands. For other information, contact the following agencies:

For Residents of Australia   Contact the Australian Passport Information Service (🕾 **131-232;** www.passports.gov.au).

For Residents of Canada   Contact the central Passport Office, Department of Foreign Affairs and International Trade, Ottawa K1A 0G3 (🕾 **800/567-6868;** www.ppt.gc.ca).

For Residents of Ireland   Contact the Passport Office, Setanta Centre, Molesworth Street, Dublin 2 (🕾 **01/671-1633;** www.foreignaffairs.gov.ie).

For Residents of New Zealand   Contact the Passports Office, Department of Internal Affairs, 47 Boulcott Street, Wellington 6011 (🕾 **0800/225-050** or 04/474-8100; www. passports.govt.nz).

For Residents of the United Kingdom   Visit your nearest passport office, major post office, or travel agency or contact the **Identity and Passport Service (IPS),** 89 Eccleston Square, London SW1V 1PN (🕾 **0300/222-0000;** www.ips.gov.uk).

For Residents of the United States   To find your regional passport office, check the U.S. State Department website (travel.state.gov/passport) or call the **National Passport Information Center** (🕾 **877/487-2778**) for automated information.

Police   Holland's emergency phone number for the police *(politie)*—along with the fire department and the ambulance service—is 🕾 **112.** For routine matters, visit a district police office. A centrally located one is at Lijnbaansgracht 219 (🕾 **0900/ 8844;** tram: 1, 2, 5, 7, or 10), off Leidseplein; calling its number can also provide details about other district police offices.

Smoking   In a city where smoking hashish is an acceptable use of the public air, it used to be that there was no mercy shown to anyone who squirmed at the thought of mere tobacco. Since July 1, 2008, all that has changed. Smoking is now forbidden in restaurants, bars, cafes, hotel public areas, and most hotel rooms. Exceptions are in separate enclosed areas for smokers, in which staff are not allowed to provide drinks, meals, or other services. Smoking tobacco in "coffeeshops" is likewise forbidden, but smoking the marijuana that is their stock in trade is allowed—don't ask me to explain it! Trams, buses, and Metro trains are smoke-free.

Taxes   There's a value-added tax (BTW) in Holland of 6% on hotel and restaurant bills (19% on beer, wine, and liquor), and 6% or 19% (depending on the product) on purchases. This tax is always included in the price. Visitors coming from outside the European Union can shop tax-free in Amsterdam. Stores that offer tax-free shopping advertise with a HOLLAND TAX-FREE SHOPPING sign in the window, and provide the form you need to recover taxes when you leave the European Union. Refunds are available only when you spend more than 50€ in a participating store. See "The Shopping Scene" in chapter 9 for more details.

Telephones   See "Staying Connected" for info, p. 56.

Time   Amsterdam is on Central European Time (CET), which is Coordinated Universal Time (UTC), or Greenwich Mean Time (GMT), plus 1 hour. Clocks are moved ahead 1 hour for daylight-saving Central European Summer Time (CEST) between the last Sunday in March and the last Sunday in October. For example, when it's 6pm in Amsterdam, it's 9am in Los Angeles (PST), 7am in Honolulu (HST), 10am in Denver (MST), 11am in Chicago (CST), noon in New York City (EST), 5pm in London (GMT), and 2am the next day in Sydney.

For the exact local time from a "speaking clock," dial *℡* **0900/8002.**

Tipping   The Dutch government requires that all taxes and service charges be included in the published prices of hotels, restaurants, cafes, nightclubs, salons, and sightseeing companies. Even taxi fares include taxes and a standard 15% service charge. To be absolutely sure if a restaurant is including tax and service, look for the words *inclusief BTW en service* (BTW is the abbreviation for the Dutch words that mean value-added tax) on the bill, or ask the waitstaff.

Dutch waitstaff and hotel staff often "forget" that a service charge and a tip are in effect the same thing. If you query them, they'll likely tell you that the tip isn't included in the bill—slightly true, since it's not called a tip but a service charge. Customers pay a standard 15% whether they liked the service or not. The VVV tourist office's advice is: "Tips for extra service are always appreciated but not necessary."

To tip like the Dutch in a cafe or snack bar, leave some small change on the counter or table. In a restaurant, leave 1€ to 2€ per person, or to generously reward good service, 5€ per person or 10% of the tab. Since service can tend toward the lackadaisical, you may need to make due allowance for what constitutes "good." If another staffer took the payment, give the tip to your waitperson directly.

In a hotel, tip for a long stay or extra service, if you wish, but don't worry about not tipping—you're unlikely to be hassled by a bellboy who lights every lamp in your room until he hears the rattle of spare change.

Should you feel an irrational compulsion to tip taxi drivers, round up the fare by a euro or two, or splash out 5% to 10%.

Toilets   Maybe you better sit down for this one. The most important thing to remember about public toilets in Amsterdam—apart from calling them *toiletten* (twa-*lett*-en) or "WC" (*vay say*) and not restrooms—is not the usual male/female (*heren/dames*) distinction (important though that is), but to pay the person who sits at the entrance to many such places of relief. He or she has a saucer in which you're supposed to deposit your payment. If you don't, you may have a vexed visitor in the inner sanctum while you transact your business. It's tiresome, but toilets usually cost only about .40€, and the attendant makes sure they're clean.

If you have a toilet emergency in the Center, a good place to find relief is the NH Grand Hotel Krasnapolsky (see "The Old Center," in chapter 5). Just breeze in as if you own the "Kras," swing left past the front desk and along the corridor, past the Winter Garden restaurant, then up some steps. Another option: The restrooms at the University of Amsterdam's Atrium cafeteria (see "The Old Center," in chapter 6) are clean and open to all. Restrooms in department stores (see "Shopping A to Z," in chapter 9) are also useful. Try to avoid visiting a *urinoir* (or *pissoir*)—these malodorous, open-air, male-only "comfort stations" are a standing provocation to feminists.

Visas Citizens of the U.S., Canada, the European Union, Australia, and New Zealand need only a valid passport if visiting the Netherlands for fewer than 3 months. In the case of visitors who reside in most other E.U. countries, a valid identity card from that country is sufficient. Citizens of other countries should be sure to check travel regulations before leaving. You can get these in English from the website of the Ministry of Foreign Affairs in The Hague: **www.minbuza.nl**.

Visitor Information Before leaving for the Netherlands, obtain information on the country and its travel facilities by contacting the **Netherlands Board of Tourism & Conventions (NBTC),** which maintains offices around the world. Their Internet address is **www.holland.com**.

For the **U.S. and Canada,** they're at 215 Park Avenue South, Suite 2005, New York, NY 10003 (© **212/370-7360;** fax 212/370-9507). For **Great Britain** and **Ireland** (no walk-in service), the info is P.O. Box 30783, London WC2B 6DH (© **020/7539-7950;** fax 020/7539-7953).

Or contact the Dutch umbrella organization for the country's many local tourist information organizations (no walk-in service): **Netherlands Board of Tourism & Conventions,** Vlietweg 15, 2260 KA Leidschendam (© **070/370-5705;** fax 070/320-1654). In addition, for those flying into Amsterdam's Schiphol Airport, there's the **Holland Tourist Information** (www.holland.com).

Amsterdam's own tourist information organization (no walk-in service) is the **Amsterdam Tourism & Convention Board,** P.O. Box 3901, 1001 AS Amsterdam (© **0900/400-4040,** or 31-20/201-8800 from outside the Netherlands; fax 020/201-8850; www.iamsterdam.nl). The 0900 phone number costs .40€ per minute, which is tolerable if you get a fast response and not so good if you have to hold. Calls made from outside the Netherlands are at the usual international rate.

This organization operates two **Amsterdam Tourist Information** offices. Both offices are efficient and have multilingual attendants on duty. They can help you with almost any question about the city, and provide brochures and maps, and reserve last-minute hotel rooms.

One office is inside Centraal Station, on platform 2B, open Monday to Wednesday from 9am to 8pm, Thursday to Saturday from 8am to 8pm, and Sunday and holidays from 9am to 6pm. A second office is right in front of the station, at Stationsplein 10, open daily from 8am to 9pm (tram for both offices: 1, 2, 4, 5, 9, 13, 16, 17, 24, 25, or 26). Both offices are invariably extremely busy.

Be sure to pick up a copy of *Time Out Amsterdam,* for 2.95€. This monthly magazine in English is full of details about the month's art exhibits, concerts, and theater performances, and lists restaurants, bars, dance clubs, and more. Or get a free copy of the yellow *Visitors Guide,* which is a directory with a wealth of addresses and phone numbers, from any tourist office and some hotels.

The Times, also free, covers Amsterdam, The Hague, and Rotterdam and is available from select outlets like the American Book Center (see chapter 9 under "Books," p. 216).

One of the best virtual tours on the Net is **www.channels.nl**—the images are clear, you can direct your own tour, and you can chat with others about Amsterdam. Visitors provide their impressions of restaurants, hotels, museums, and hash houses. At **www.amsterdam hotspots.nl,** they really do mean "hot." Here are *the* places to fill your nights, from eating and drinking to where to toke, what the top gay bars are, and where to see those famous working girls on display behind picture windows. Good eating-out info is available from **www.dinnersite.nl**.

Buying a street map will make detailed navigation easier. The most cost-effective map is Amsterdam Tourism & Congress Bureau's **Amsterdam City Map,** available from VVV Amsterdam offices for 2€. It shows every street and canal, museums and churches, and tram routes and stops, extending as far as the ring road. For even more meticulous coverage of the city (and its suburbs), purchase the Falk **Easy City Amsterdam Professional Map** for 9.95€.

Water   Faucet water in Amsterdam is safe to drink—it's referred to locally as *gemeente pils* (municipal beer). Many people drink bottled mineral water, generically called *spa* even though it's not all from the Belgian Spa brand.

Wi-Fi   See "Staying Connected," p. 56.

AIRLINE WEBSITES

MAJOR AIRLINES

Aer Lingus
www.aerlingus.com

Aeroflot
www.aeroflot.com

Air France
www.airfrance.com

Alitalia
www.alitalia.com

Austrian Airlines
www.austrian.com

BMI
www.flybmi.com

British Airways
www.british-airways.com

China Airlines
www.china-airlines.com

Continental Airlines
www.continental.com

CSA Czech Airlines
www.czechairlines.nl

Delta
www.delta.com

EgyptAir
www.egyptair.com

El Al
www.elal.co.il

Emirates
www.emirates.com

Finnair
www.finnair.com

Iberia
www.iberia.com

Icelandair
www.icelandair.com

Japan Airlines
www.jal.co.jp

KLM
www.klm.com

Korean Air
www.koreanair.com

Lufthansa
www.lufthansa.com

SAS
www.flysas.com

Swiss International Air Lines
www.swiss.com

Turkish Airlines
www.thy.com

United
www.united.com

US Airways
www.usairways.com

BUDGET AIRLINES

airberlin
www.airberlin.com

bmibaby
www.bmibaby.com

easyJet
www.easyjet.com

flybe
www.flybe.com

USEFUL TERMS & PHRASES

The Dutch people you encounter will likely speak English every bit as well as you do—some of them, annoyingly, even better. That said, no Amsterdammer will fault you for having a go at Dutch. In fact, they'll hugely appreciate any effort you make in their tongue-twister of a *taal* (language). An occasional *alstublieft* (please) and *dank u wel* (thank you) can take you a long way.

These words and phrases should get you started—and help in the rare situation of dealing with people who don't speak English. Painless pronunciation practice is provided. If you can pronounce van Gogh (*vahn khokh*) correctly (see "Don't 'Go,'" in chapter 7), you should be able to handle the hard stuff, like Schiphol (*skhip*-ol), Scheveningen (*skheven*-ingen), and 's-Gravenhage (ss-*khraven*-hakhe; the full name of Den Haag/The Hague).

BASIC VOCABULARY

USEFUL ENGLISH & DUTCH PHRASES

English	Dutch	Pronunciation
Hello	**Dag/Hallo**	dakh/*ha*-loh
Good morning	**Goedemorgen**	*khoo*-yuh-*mor*-khun
Good afternoon/evening	**Goedenavond**	*khoo*-yuhn-*af*-ond
How are you?	**Hoe gaat het met u?**	hoo *khaht* et met oo?
Very well	**Uitstekend**	out-*stayk*-end
Thank you	**Dank u wel**	*dahnk* oo wel
Goodbye	**Dag/Tot ziens**	dakh/tot zeenss
Good night	**Goedenacht**	*khoo*-duh-nakht
See you later	**Tot straks**	Tot strahkss
Please	**Alstublieft**	*ahl*-stoo-bleeft
Yes	**Ja**	yah
No	**Nee**	Nay
Excuse me	**Pardon**	par-*dawn*
Sorry	**Sorry**	*so*-ree
Do you speak English?	**Spreekt u Engels?**	spraykt oo *eng*-els
Can you help me?	**Kunt u mij helpen?**	koont oo *may*-ee *hel*-pen?
Give me . . .	**Geeft u mij . . .**	*khayft* oo may . . .

English	Dutch	Pronunciation
Where is . . . ?	**Waar is . . . ?**	*vahr* iz . . . ?
the station	**het station**	het *stah*-ssyonh
the post office	**het postkantoor**	het *post*-kan-tohr
a bank	**een bank**	ayn bank
a hotel	**een hotel**	ayn *ho*-tel
a restaurant	**een restaurant**	ayn res-to-*rahng*
a drug store/pharmacy/chemist	**een apotheek**	ayn a-po-*tayk*
the toilet	**het toilet**	het *twah*-let
To the right	**Rechts**	rekhts
To the left	**Links**	links
Straight ahead	**Rechtdoor**	rekht-*doar*
I would like . . .	**Ik zou graag . . .**	ik zow khrakh . . .
to eat	**eten**	*ay*-ten
a room for 1 night	**een kamer voor een nacht willen**	ayn *kah*-mer voor ayn nakht *vi*-llen
How much is it?	**Hoeveel kost het?**	hoo fayl kawst het
The check	**De rekening**	duh *ray*-ken-ing
When?	**Wanneer?**	vah-*neer*
Yesterday	**Gisteren**	*khis*-ter-en
Today	**Vandaag**	van-*dahkh*
Tomorrow	**Morgen**	*mor*-khen
Breakfast	**Ontbijt**	*ohnt*-bayt
Lunch	**Lunch**	lunch
Dinner	**Diner**	dee-nay

NUMBERS

English	Dutch	Pronunciation
1	**een**	(ayn)
2	**twee**	(tway)
3	**drie**	(dree)
4	**vier**	(veer)
5	**vijf**	(vayf)
6	**zes**	(zes)
7	**zeven**	(*zay*-vun)
8	**acht**	(akht)
9	**negen**	(*nay*-khen)
10	**tien**	(teen)
11	**elf**	(elf)
12	**twaalf**	(tvahlf)
13	**dertien**	(*dayr*-teen)

English	Dutch	Pronunciation
14	**veertien**	(*vayr*-teen)
15	**vijftien**	(*vayf*-teen)
16	**zestien**	(*zes*-teen)
17	**zeventien**	(*zay*-vun-teen)
18	**achttien**	(*akh*-teen)
19	**negentien**	(*nay*-khun-teen)
20	**twintig**	(*twin*-tikh)
30	**dertig**	(*der*-tukh)
40	**veertig**	(*vayr*-tukh)
50	**vijftig**	(*vayf*-tukh)
60	**zestig**	(*zes*-tukh)
70	**zeventig**	(*zay*-vun-tukh)
80	**tachtig**	(*takh*-tukh)
90	**negentig**	(*nay*-khen-tukh)
100	**honderd**	(*hon*-dayrt)
1,000	**duizend**	(*douw*-zend)

DAYS OF THE WEEK

English	Dutch	Pronunciation
Monday	**Maandag**	(*mahn*-dakh)
Tuesday	**Dinsdag**	(*deens*-dakh)
Wednesday	**Woensdag**	(*voohns*-dakh)
Thursday	**Donderdag**	(*donder*-dakh)
Friday	**Vrijdag**	(*vray*-dakh)
Saturday	**Zaterdag**	(*zahter*-dakh)
Sunday	**Zondag**	(*zohn*-dakh)

MONTHS

English	Dutch	Pronunciation
January	**Januari**	(*yahn*-oo-aree)
February	**Februari**	(*fayhb*-roo-aree)
March	**Maart**	(mahrt)
April	**April**	(ah-*pril*)
May	**Mei**	(*meh*-eey)
June	**Juni**	(yoo-*nee*)
July	**Juli**	(yoo-*lee*)
August	**Augustus**	(awh-*khoost*-us)
September	**September**	(sep-*tem*-buhr)

English	Dutch	Pronunciation
October	**Oktober**	(oct-*oah*-buhr)
November	**November**	(noa-*vem*-buhr)
December	**December**	(day-*sem*-buhr)

SEASONS

English	Dutch	Pronunciation
Spring	**Lente**	(*len*-tuh)
Summer	**Zomer**	(*zoh*-muhr)
Fall/Autumn	**Herfst**	(herfsst)
Winter	**Winter**	(*vin*-tuhr)

SIGNS

Dutch	English
Doorgaand Verkeer	Through Traffic
Doorgaand Verkeer Gestremd	Road Closed
Geen Doorgaand Verkeer	No Through Traffic
Niet Parkeren	No Parking
Verboden Te Roken	No Smoking
Vrije Toegang	Admission Free/Allowed
Wegomlegging	Diversion

DUTCH MENU TERMS

BASICS

ontbijt   breakfast
lunch   lunch
diner   dinner
voorgerechten   starters/appetizers
hoofdgerechten   main courses
nagerechten   desserts
boter   butter
brood   bread
aardappelpuree   mashed potatoes
honing   honey
hutspot   mashed potatoes and carrots, with onions

jam   jam
kaas   cheese
mosterd   mustard
pannenkoeken   pancakes
peper   pepper
saus   sauce
stokbrood   French bread
suiker   sugar
zout   salt

SOUPS (SOEPEN)

bonensoep   bean soup
erwtensoep   pea soup (usually includes bacon or sausage)
groentesoep   vegetable soup

kippensoep   chicken soup
soep   soup
tomatensoep   tomato soup
uiensoep   onion soup

EGGS (EIEREN)

ei egg
hardgekookte eieren hard-boiled eggs
omelette omelet

roereieren scrambled eggs
spiegeleieren fried eggs
zachtgekookte eieren soft-boiled eggs

FISH (VIS) & SEAFOOD (ZEEBANKET)

forel trout
garnalen shrimps
gerookte zalm smoked salmon
haring herring
kabeljauw cod
kreeft lobster
makreel mackerel

mosselen mussels
oesters oysters
paling eel
sardientjes sardines
schelvis haddock
tong sole
zalm salmon

MEATS (VLEES)

biefstuk steak
eend duck
fricandeau roast pork
gans goose
gehakt minced meat
haasbiefstuk filet steak
ham ham
kalfsvlees veal
kalkoen turkey
kip chicken

konijn rabbit
lamskotelet lamb chops
lamsvlees lamb
lever liver
ragout beef stew
rookvlees smoked meat
rundvlees beef
spek bacon
vleeswaren cold cuts
worst sausage

VEGETABLES (GROENTEN) & SALADS (SLA)

aardappelen potatoes
aardappelpuree mashed potatoes
asperges asparagus
augurken pickles
bieten beets
bloemkool cauliflower
bonen beans
champignons mushrooms
erwten peas
groenten vegetables
knoflook garlic
komkommer cucumber
komkommersla cucumber salad

kool cabbage
patates frites french fries
prei leek
prinsessebonen green beans
radijsjes radishes
rapen turnips
rijst rice
sla lettuce, salad
spinazie spinach
tomaten tomatoes
uien onions
wortelen carrots
zuurkool sauerkraut

DESSERTS (NAGERECHTEN)

appelgebak apple pie
appelmoes applesauce
cake cake
compote stewed fruits
gebak pastry/cake
ijs ice cream
jonge kaas young cheese (mild)

koekjes cookies/biscuits
oliebollen doughnuts
oude kaas mature cheese (strong)
room cream
slagroom whipped cream
smeerkaas cheese spread
speculaas spiced cookies

FRUITS (VRUCHTEN/FRUIT)

aardbei strawberry
ananas pineapple
appel apple
citroen lemon
druiven grapes

framboos raspberry
kersen cherries
peer pear
perzik peach
pruimen plums

BEVERAGES (DRANKEN)

bier (or **pils**) beer
cognac brandy
fles bottle
glas glass
jenever gin
koffie coffee

melk milk
rode wijn red wine
thee tea
water water
witte wijn white wine

COOKING TERMS

gebakken baked, fried
gebraden roast, fried
gegrild grilled
gekookt boiled/cooked
gerookt smoked
geroosterd roasted/toasted/grilled

gestoofd stewed
goed doorbakken well-done
half doorbakken medium
niet doorbakken rare
koud cold
warm hot

Index

See also Accommodations and Restaurant indexes, below.

General Index

A

Aalsmeer, 270
ABC Amsterdam, 178
Absolute Danny, 226
Accommodations, 72–100. *See also* Accommodations Index
  at and near the airport, 99–100
  Amsterdam East, 98–99
  Amsterdam South, 97–98
  avoiding excess charges and hidden costs, 75
  best, 4, 76
  breakfast, 75
  The Canal Belt, 85–90
  complaints, 74
  family-friendly, 80
  frequent-stay programs, 75
  gay and lesbian, 74
  The Jordaan, 92
  landing the best room, 76
  Leidseplein, 90–91
  Museum District & Vondelpark, 92–97
  The Old Center, 76–84
  orientation, 72–73
  rates, 73–74
  Rembrandtplein, 91–92
  reservations, 73
  saving on, 75
  smoking, 73
  standard amenities, 73
  summer stays, 83
  taxes, 74
  Volendam, 263
  The Waterfront, 84–85
Addresses, finding, 41–42
Afsluitdijk Café, 267
Afsluitdijk (Enclosing Dike), 266–267
Agnietenkapel (Church of St. Agnes), 154, 189–190
AH (Albert Heijn) supermarkets, 131
AHV, 175
Airline websites, 294
Air travel, 35–36
Ajax Amsterdam, 178
Akhnaton, 239
Albert Cuypmarkt, 228
Alkmaar, 270–271
All Amsterdam Transport Pass, 39, 43
Allard Pierson Museum, 141, 143
Alliance Gastronomique Néerlandaise, 25
American Book Center, 57, 216–217
Amsteldijk, 204

Amstel FiftyFour, 249
Amstelpark, 204
Amstel River, 186, 204
Amstel Tijgers, 178
Amstelveen, 211
Amsterdam, A Brief Life of the City (Mak), 21
Amsterdam Airport Schiphol, 35
Amsterdam ArenA, 178, 239
Amsterdam Baroque Orchestra, 234
Amsterdam Canal Cruises, 172
Amsterdam Diamond Center, 175, 220
Amsterdam East, 64
  accommodations, 98–99
  restaurants, 132
Amsterdam Electric Tramline Museum (Electrische Museumtramlijn Amsterdam), 166
Amsterdam Gay Pride, 32
Amsterdam (Kers), 22–23
Amsterdam (McEwan), 20–21
Amsterdammertjes, 46
Amsterdam North (Amsterdam-Noord), 61, 64
  restaurant, 134
Amsterdam Pirates, 178
Amsterdam Roots Festival, 31
Amsterdams Brouwhuis Maximiliaan, 190–191
Amsterdamse Bos (Amsterdam Wood), 167–168, 176
  biking, 175
Amsterdam (ship), 165
Amsterdams Historisch Museum (Amsterdam Historical Museum), 143, 189
Amsterdam South, 64
  accommodations, 97–98
  restaurants, 133
Amsterdams Uitburo (AUB) Ticketshop, 231
Amsterdam Tourism & Convention Board, 73
Amsterdam Tulip Museum, 166
Amsterdam West, 64
  restaurant, 134
The Anatomy Lesson (Rembrandt), 154
Andrieshofje, 195
Anne Frankhuis, 138, 183
Anslohofje, 196
Antiek en Curiosamarkt (Antiques and Collectors' Market), 229
Antiquariaat Brinkman, 213
Antiques, 208, 213
Antonia by Yvette, 226
ANWB Disabled Department, 52
ANWB Wegenwacht, 36
Appel, Karel, 77, 144
Arc, 249
Architecture, 18–20
Area codes, 57
The Arms of Riga (Het Wapen van Riga), 192

Arriva buses, 39, 256, 261, 263, 264
The Arsenal, 159
Art, 17–18
  books about, 21–22
Art galleries, 208, 213, 216
Artifex, 55
Artis Zoo, 159–160, 171, 225
Artis Zoo Express, 172
Art Market (Kunstmarkt), 228
Art museums and galleries
  Allard Pierson Museum, 141, 143
  Cobra Museum, 144
  De Appel, 170
  Hermitage Amsterdam, 144–145
  Huis Marseille, 170
  Museum Boijmans Van Beuningen (Rotterdam), 280
  Museum Van Loon, 146, 185
  Museum Willet-Holthuysen, 146, 185
  Rijksmuseum, 139
  SMBA, 170
  Stedelijk Museum, 170
Athenaeum Boekhandel & Nieuwscentrum, 217
Athenaeum Illustre, 154, 189
ATMs (automated-teller machines), 47–48
August Gay Pride Festival, 151
Avercamp, Hendrick, 140
Avis, 36
Avondwinkel (evening store), 223
Azzurro Due, 221

B

Bananenbar, 251–252
A Banquet of the Officers of the St. George Civic Guard (Hals), 17
Bars and cafes, 241–248
  brown cafes, 241–243
  drinking terminology, 244
  drinks at, 245
  English and Irish pubs, 247–248
  gay and lesbian, 249–250
  Jordaan cafes, 248
  modern cafes, 245–247
  tasting houses, 243–245
Bartolottihuis (Bartolotti House), 183
Baseball, 178
Basketball, 178
Beaches, 259, 272, 276, 278
Beatrixpark, 168
Bed & Breakfast Holland, 92
Beer, 12, 245
Beggars, 50
Begijnhof, 152–153, 189
Begijnhofen, 12–13
Begijnhofkapel, 152
Berenstraat, 184
Bethaniënklooster (Bethanien Convent), 190–191

Restaurants